The Practical PC
2nd Edition

Includes an interactive Book-on-CD with videos, animations, pop-up definitions, quizzes, and more!

June Jamrich Parsons

Dan Oja

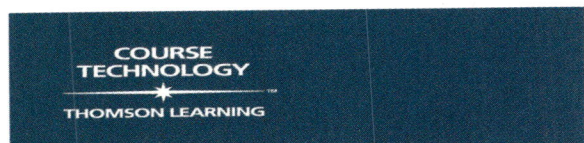

25 Thompson Place, Boston, MA 02210

Australia • Canada • Denmark • Japan • Mexico • New Zealand • Philippines
Puerto Rico • Singapore • South Africa • Spain • United Kingdom • United States

The Practical PC, 2nd Edition; June Jamrich Parsons and Dan Oja

Managing Editor	Greg Donald
Senior Editor	Donna Gridley
Developmental Editor/Project Manager	Catherine Perlich
Production Editor	Debbie Masi
Media Specialist	Fatima Nicholls
Photo and Video Researcher	Abby Reip
Design and Composition	MediaTechnics Corp.
Book-on-CD Development	MediaTechnics Corp.
Prepress Production	GEX, Inc.

© 1999-2001 by Course Technology—ITP®

For more information contact:

Course Technology
One Main Street
Cambridge, MA 02142

ITP Europe
Berkshire House 168-173
High Holborn
London WCIV 7AA
England

Nelson ITP, Australia
102 Dodds Street
South Melbourne, 3205
Victoria, Australia

ITP Nelson Canada
1120 Birchmount Road
Scarborough, Ontario
Canada M1K 5G4

International Thomson Editores
Seneca, 53
Colonia Polanco
11560 Mexico D.F. Mexico

ITP GmbH
Königswinterer Strasse 418
53227 Bonn
Germany

ITP Asia
60 Albert Street, #15-01
Albert Complex
Singapore 189969

ITP Japan
Hirakawacho Kyowa Building, 3F
2-2-1 Hirakawacho
Chiyoda-ku, Tokyo 102
Japan

All rights reserved. This publication is protected by federal copyright law. No part of this publication may be reproduced, stored in a retrieval system, or transmitted in any form or by any means, electronic, mechanical, photocopying, recording, or otherwise, or be used to make a derivative work (such as translation or adaptation), without prior permission in writing from Course Technology.

Trademarks
Course Technology and the Open Book logo are registered trademarks and CourseKits is a trademark of Course Technology. Custom Edition is a registered trademark of International Thomson Publishing.

ITP® The ITP logo is a registered trademark of International Thomson Publishing.

Some of the product names and company names used in this book have been used for identification purposes only and may be trademarks or registered trademarks of their respective manufacturers and sellers.

Disclaimer
Course Technology reserves the right to revise this publication and make changes from time to time in its content without notice.

ISBN 0-619-02074-1

Printed in the United States of America
 1 2 3 4 5 6 7 8 9 10 BM 03 02 01 00

■Preface

▙bout this book

At last, here is a book about the computers that people really use, with practical tips about how to use them. *The Practical PC* provides a state-of-the-art introduction to Windows-based PCs, written in an easy-to-read style. Every book includes an action-packed multimedia Book-on-CD. Each page of the Book-on-CD looks exactly like its corresponding page in the printed book and contains interactive elements such as pop-up definitions, figures that become videos, and end-of-chapter quizzes. The Book-on-CD requires no installation, so it's easy to use at home, at school, or at work.

Each 12-page chapter of *The Practical PC* focuses on a specific topic. The first page introduces the chapter topic, lists the chapter contents, and highlights Book-on-CD media. Each chapter includes the following:

- Five **FAQs**, or "frequently asked questions," address key questions, provide background information, and give specific tips for becoming a more proficient computer user.
- A three-page **Hardware** section in each chapter explains the devices that are typically associated with the chapter topic.
- An **Issues** page highlights an ethical or cultural issue that's relevant to the chapter topic.
- A **Tutorial** section provides step-by-step instructions on developing important computer skills.
- A **QuickCheck** page contains self-test activities.

▙bout the Book-on-CD

Every book includes the innovative Book-on-CD, which is loaded with features to enhance and reinforce learning.

On the CD, the PlayIt! button makes figures come to life as videos and screen animations. You'll see PC hardware in action and tour some of today's most popular software packages.

GrabIt! buttons connect to Internet sites with free or demo versions of software featured in the book.

The Get It? button starts an interactive auto-graded chapter quiz. Take a quiz more than once. Each quiz contains ten randomly selected questions from an extensive test bank. Results can be saved and delivered to an instructor.

What do you think?   Interactive "thought" questions focus on current ethical, social, and cultural computing issues. For the classroom, responses can be consolidated by instructors and displayed as pie charts.

QuickChecks   Interactive end-of-chapter QuickCheck questions provide instant feedback on what you've learned.

Pop-up Definitions & Glossary   Clickable boldface terms display pop-up definitions. A Glossary button provides easy access to all definitions from any page.

Tutorials

Each chapter includes a Tutorial section with step-by-step instructions about an essential computer task.

How to set up your computer	How to install and select printers
How to use Windows controls	How to make slides for an effective presentation
How to download and install software from the Internet	How to make your own CDs
	How to edit a digital photo
How to create and save files	How to work with digitized sound
How to find files	How to change display settings
How to use Windows Backup	How to find the technical specifications for your PC
How to set up your Internet connection	
How to create your own Web pages	How to get technical support
How to use your e-mail address book	How to buy a computer online

Use this book because...

- **You want to learn about computers.** *The Practical PC* will help you understand enough "tech talk" so you can decipher computer ads and hold your own when the conversation turns to computers.
- **You want to learn Windows.** *The Practical PC* will show you how to use Windows controls and manage files so that you can use your computer to do neat stuff without frustration.
- **You want to learn how to use the Internet.** *The Practical PC* will show you how to get connected, use a browser, send e-mail, and launch a search engine.
- **You want to find out what a computer can do for you.** *The Practical PC* will demonstrate all kinds of software—in action—including software for word processing, art, video editing, music composition, and 3-D graphics.
- **You're a beginner or an intermediate computer user.** *The Practical PC* is great for beginners, but there's enough new and useful information to keep you interested even if you have some experience with PCs.

Instructor's supplements

Course Presenter is a lecture presentation tool that provides instructors with a replacement for overhead transparencies. It includes a predesigned presentation for each chapter, including media elements. Instructors can also customize presentations using Microsoft PowerPoint.

Course Test Manager is cutting-edge, Windows-based testing software that helps instructors design and administer printed or online examinations. Course Test Manager automatically grades tests that students take at the computer and will generate statistics on both individual and class performance.

An Electronic Instructor's Manual outlines each chapter, offers valuable teaching tips, and lists answers to QuickCheck questions.

Consolidation Module enables an instructor to consolidate students' chapter quiz scores from student Tracking Disks. This handy module also collects student responses to the "What do you think?" questions on the Issues pages, then converts this data into pie charts that can be displayed to motivate class discussion.

Acknowledgments

The successful launch of this book was possible only because of our extraordinary "ground crews." We would like to extend our profound thanks:

To the students at Northern Michigan University, the University of the Virgin Islands, and countless other universities who have participated in classes and corresponded with us over the 25 (or so) years since we began teaching.

To our development team: Fatima Nicholls for her tireless work pulling together the media for the Book-on-CD, Donna Schuch, Keefe Crowley, Tensi Parsons, Debora Elam, and Sue Oja for Book-on-CD testing and technical reviews, and Abby Reip for her invaluable photo research efforts. We would particularly like to thank our Project Manager/Developmental Editor, Catherine Perlich, for her esprit-de-corps and keen insights about readers, writers, and the world of books.

To our team members' patient and supportive parents, spouses, and significant others.

To the New Perspectives team at Course Technology, who once again provided professional and enthusiastic support, guidance, and advice. Their insights and team spirit were invaluable. Also to Melissa Dezotell, Greg Donald, and Donna Gridley for their editorial support.

To Gary and the crew at GEX, Dean Fossella and Patty Stephan for their valuable input on the book design, and Debbie Masi for her careful and cheerful production proofing.

To the professors and reviewers who expressed their ideas and shared their teaching strategies with us: Dennis Anderson, St. Francis College; Mike Feiler, Merritt College; Shmuel Fink, Touro College; Dennette Foy, Edison Community College; Nancy LaChance, DeVry Institute of Technology; Pauline Pike, Community College of Morris; Tim Stroth, Indian River Community College.

Media credits

Figure 6-1: Video footage courtesy of Western Digital. Figure 8-9: Courtesy of Mitsubishi Wireless Communications, Inc., Personal Mobile Communications Division. Figures 11-6, 7, 8: Courtesy of The University of the Virgin Islands. Figure 12-9: Courtesy of C-Cube Microsystems. Figure 13-1: CAD drawings courtesy of Jessie Aho. Figure 13-9: With permission of Tensi Parsons and Keefe Crowley. Figure 14-1: Musical selections courtesy of Chris Robbert, vocals courtesy of Linette Oliver, narration courtesy of Alvis A. Lockhart. Figure 14-7: Courtesy of Korg USA. Figure 15-5: Courtesy of JPL/NASA/Caltech. Figure 15-6: Courtesy of ViewSonic Corporation. Figure 16-6: Courtesy of Intel Corporation. Figure 16-7: Copyright © 1998 Advanced Micro Devices, Inc. Reprinted with permission of copyright owner. All other rights reserved.

Brief Contents

Introduction
Preface — iii
Before You Begin — x

PART A: PC Basics
Chapter 1: Getting Started — 2
Chapter 2: Looking at Windows — 14
Chapter 3: Installing and Learning Software — 26

PART B: Computer Files
Chapter 4: Naming and Saving Files — 38
Chapter 5: Organizing Files and Folders — 50
Chapter 6: Protecting Your Files — 62

PART C: The Internet, the Web, and E-mail
Chapter 7: Connecting to the Internet — 74
Chapter 8: Browsing and Searching the Web — 86
Chapter 9: Sending E-mail and Attachments — 98

PART D: Application Software
Chapter 10: Writing and Printing Documents — 110
Chapter 11: Making Spreadsheets and Presentations — 122
Chapter 12: Accessing Databases — 134

PART E: Graphics, Sound, and Video
Chapter 13: Working with Graphics — 146
Chapter 14: Recording and Editing Sound — 158
Chapter 15: Creating Desktop Video and Animation — 170

PART F: Upgrades and Expansion
Chapter 16: Looking "Under the Hood" — 182
Chapter 17: Upgrading and Expanding Your PC — 194
Chapter 18: Buying a PC — 206

Index — 218

Contents

PART A: PC Basics

Chapter 1: Getting Started — 2
- Where's the power switch? — 3
- Do I need a disk to start my computer? — 4
- What if my computer asks me for a password? — 5
- Which works better, the mouse or the keyboard? — 6
- How do I turn off my computer? — 7
- Hardware: Desktops, notebooks, and PDAs — 8
- Tutorial: How to set up your computer — 11
- Issue: Computer "haves" and "have-nots" — 12
- QuickChecks — 13

Chapter 2: Looking at Windows — 14
- What's the Windows desktop? — 15
- How do I start an application program? — 16
- What's a window? — 17
- What's a dialog box? — 18
- Which version of Windows do I have? — 19
- Hardware: Alternative input devices — 20
- Tutorial: How to use Windows controls — 23
- Issue: Monopoly is not just a game — 24
- QuickChecks — 25

Chapter 3: Installing and Learning Software — 26
- Where's the instruction manual? — 27
- What's a PDF? — 28
- How do I use online Help? — 29
- What's the purpose of the paperclip cartoon? — 30
- Can I contact the software company for help? — 31
- Hardware: Install and uninstall software on your PC — 32
- Tutorial: How to download and install software from the Internet — 35
- Issue: Is it legal to install this software? — 36
- QuickChecks — 37

PART B: Computer Files

Chapter 4: Naming and Saving Files — 38
- What's a file? — 39
- Can I use any name for a file? — 40
- What's a file extension? — 41
- Can I convert a file from one format to another? — 42
- How do I tell my PC where to store a file? — 43
- Hardware: Floppy disks and floppy disk drives — 44
- Tutorial: How to create and save files — 47
- Issue: Should governments regulate encryption? — 48
- QuickChecks — 49

Chapter 5: Organizing Files and Folders — 50
- How do I get a list of my files? — 51
- How do I change the name of a file? — 52
- What's the best organization for my files? — 53
- How do I copy files to other disks? — 54
- What if I run out of disk space? — 55
- Hardware: Hard disk drives — 56
- Tutorial: How to find files — 59
- Issue: Are deleted files legally garbage? — 60
- QuickChecks — 61

Chapter 6: Protecting Your Files — 62
- Can a computer lose my files? — 63
- Could my PC's hard disk drive just stop working? — 64
- Can a virus wipe out my files? — 65
- How can I protect my files from viruses? — 66
- Do I need a disaster recovery plan? — 67
- Hardware: Tape backup devices — 68
- Tutorial: How to use Windows Backup — 71
- Issue: What about a "good" virus? — 72
- QuickChecks — 73

Contents

PART C: The Internet, the Web, and E-mail

Chapter 7: Connecting to the Internet — 74
What's an Internet connection? — 75
Why would I want to connect to the Internet? — 76
What do I need to get connected? — 77
How do I connect to my ISP? — 78
What's the World Wide Wait? — 79
Hardware: Modems — 80
Tutorial: How to set up your Internet connection — 83
Issue: Do we need anonymous digital cash? — 84
QuickChecks — 85

Chapter 8: Browsing and Searching the Web — 86
What's a Web page? — 87
What's a URL? — 88
How does a browser work? — 89
How do I use a search engine? — 90
Can I save text and graphics that I find on the Web? — 91
Hardware: High-speed and wireless Internet-access equipment — 92
Tutorial: How to create your own Web pages — 95
Issue: The filtering controversy — 96
QuickChecks — 97

Chapter 9: Sending E-mail and Attachments — 98
How does e-mail work? — 99
How do I send and receive e-mail messages? — 100
What's an e-mail attachment? — 101
Is there a size limit for e-mail messages and attachments? — 102
What are smileys, flames wars, and spams? — 103
Hardware: Local area networks — 104
Tutorial: How to use your e-mail address book like a pro — 107
Issue: Just how private is e-mail? — 108
QuickChecks — 109

PART D: Application Software

Chapter 10: Writing and Printing Documents — 110
Can word processing software improve my writing? — 111
How does WP software help me format a document? — 112
Does WP software provide standard document styles? — 113
What's desktop publishing software? — 114
Do I need DTP software in addition to WP software? — 115
Hardware: Printers — 116
Tutorial: How to install and select printers — 119
Issue: What's truth got to do with it? — 120
QuickChecks — 121

Chapter 11: Making Spreadsheets and Presentations — 122
What's a spreadsheet? — 123
How do I create a worksheet? — 124
What if I don't know the right formula? — 125
How do I know if worksheet results are accurate? — 126
How do I create graphs? — 127
Hardware: Computer projection devices — 128
Tutorial: How to make slides for an effective presentation — 131
Issue: Is it the medium or the message? — 132
QuickChecks — 133

Chapter 12: Accessing Databases — 134
What's a database? — 135
Do I need database software? — 136
How would I create my own database? — 137
Can I really create a database with spreadsheet software? — 138
What about databases on the Web and CDs? — 139
Hardware: CDs and DVDs — 140
Tutorial: How to make your own CDs — 143
Issue: Who owns information about me? — 144
QuickChecks — 145

Contents

PART E: Graphics, Sound, and Video

Chapter 13: Working with Graphics — 146
What kinds of graphics can I work with on my PC? — 147
When should I use bitmap graphics? — 148
How do I prepare graphics for Web pages? — 149
When should I use vector graphics? — 150
How do I create 3-D graphics? — 151
Hardware: Digitizing devices — 152
Tutorial: How to edit a digital photo — 155
Issue: Shoes, UFOs, and Forrest Gump — 156
QuickChecks — 157

Chapter 14: Recording and Editing Sound — 158
How does sound capability enhance my PC? — 159
How does my PC record, store, and play digital sound? — 160
How does speech synthesis work? — 161
What should I know about MIDI? — 162
How do I add sound clips to presentations and Web pages? — 163
Hardware: Sound devices — 164
Tutorial: How to digitize sound — 167
Issue: RIAA vs. Rio — 168
QuickChecks — 169

Chapter 15: Creating Desktop Video and Animation — 170
How do I equip my PC to play video? — 171
Can I create my own desktop video? — 172
How do I edit a digital video? — 173
How does compression affect desktop video quality? — 174
How do I create and play an animation? — 175
Hardware: PC display devices — 176
Tutorial: How to change display settings — 179
Issue: Idoru — 180
QuickChecks — 181

PART F: Upgrades and Expansion

Chapter 16: Looking "Under the Hood" — 182
How does a computer work? — 183
What does RAM and processing circuitry look like? — 184
How does data get into chips? — 185
Does a computer use the same code for all types of data? — 186
How does software tie into chips, codes, and circuits? — 187
Hardware: Microprocessors — 188
Tutorial: How to find the technical specifications for your PC — 191
Issue: Who invented the first electronic digital computer? — 192
QuickChecks — 193

Chapter 17: Upgrading and Expanding Your PC — 194
Can I upgrade the processor in my PC? — 195
Will adding RAM improve my PC's performance? — 196
Can I add more hard disk capacity? — 197
How do I add or upgrade other devices? — 198
Can I upgrade my notebook PC? — 199
Hardware: Expansion devices, ports, cards, and slots — 200
Tutorial: How to get technical support — 203
Issue: Upgrade, reuse, recycle, or landfill? — 204
QuickChecks — 205

Chapter 18: Buying a PC — 206
So many options—where do I begin? — 207
Where can I find prices and specifications? — 208
How much computing power do I need? — 209
Where can I find the best deal? — 210
Is it O.K. to "mail order" a PC? — 211
Hardware: Accessories and add-ons — 212
Tutorial: How to buy a computer online — 215
Issue: The ethics of e-shopping — 216
QuickChecks — 217

Index — **218**

x

■Before You Begin

You're going to enjoy using *The Practical PC* and the accompanying Book-on-CD. It's a snap to start the Book-on-CD and use it on your computer. So don't delay—get started right away! The answers to the FAQs (frequently asked questions) in this section will help you begin.

■FAQ   Will the Book-on-CD work on my computer?

The easiest way to find out if the Book-on-CD works on your computer is to try it! Just follow the steps below to start the CD. If it works, you're all set. Otherwise, check with your local technical support person. If you are technically inclined, the system requirements are listed inside the front cover of this book.

■FAQ   How do I start the Book-on-CD?

The Practical PC Book-on-CD is easy to use and requires no installation. Follow these simple steps to get started:

1. Make sure your computer is turned on.
2. Press the button on your computer's CD-ROM drive to open the drawer-like "tray" as shown in the photo below.
3. Place the Book-on-CD into the tray with the label facing up.
4. Press the button on the CD-ROM drive to close the tray, then proceed with Step 5.

To use the Book-on-CD, your computer must have a CD-ROM drive. If you have any questions about its operation, check the manual that was supplied with your computer or check with your local technical support person.

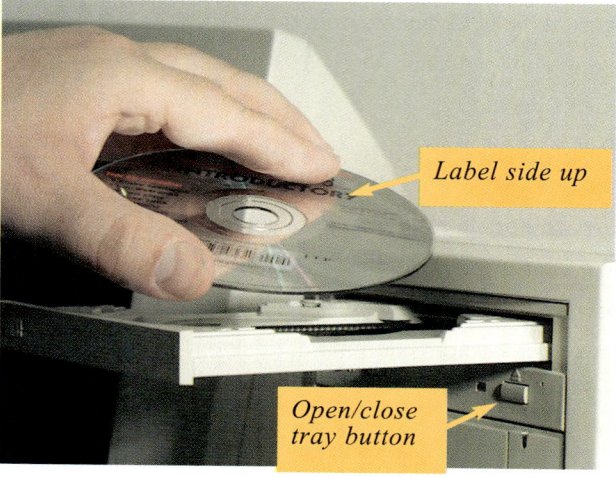

Label side up

Open/close tray button

5. Wait about 15 seconds. During this time, the light on your CD-ROM drive should flicker. Soon you should see the Practical PC Welcome screen.

When you see the Welcome screen, you can take the QuickTour or use the Chapters menu at the top of the screen to begin reading Chapter 1.

If the Welcome screen does not appear, try the instructions in the Manual Start figure below.

Manual Start: Follow the instructions in this figure only if the Welcome screen did **not** appear automatically in Step 5. If you don't see a Start button on your screen, refer to the instructions for Windows 3.1 on page xv.

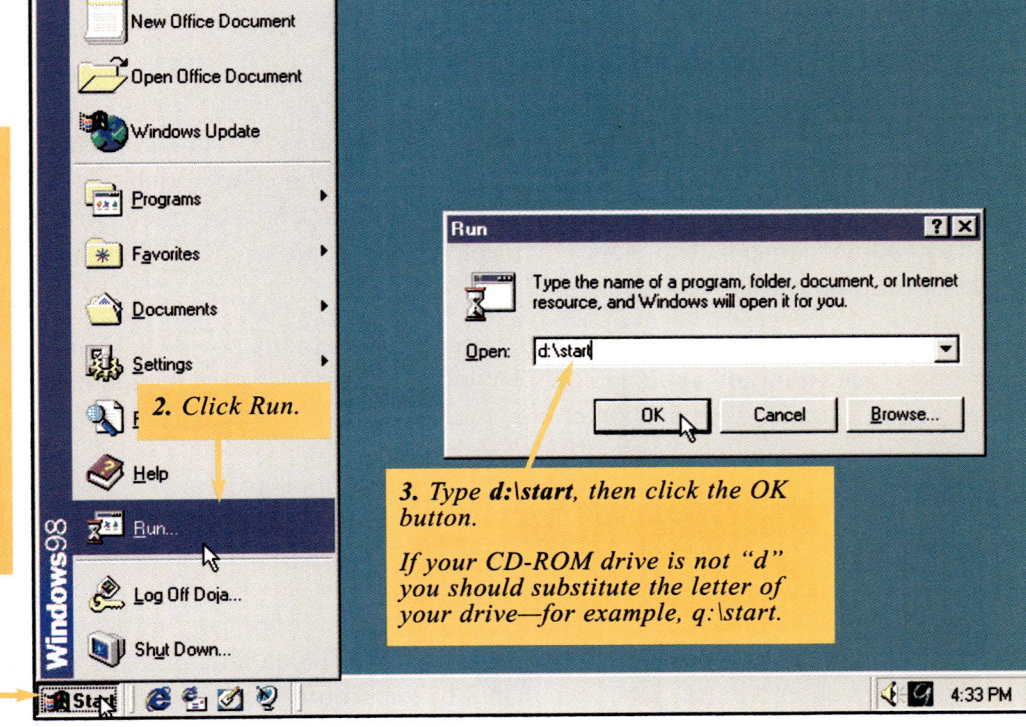

1. Use the mouse to position the arrow-shaped pointer on Start.

2. Click the left button on your mouse to display the Start menu.

2. Click Run.

3. Type **d:\start**, then click the OK button.

If your CD-ROM drive is not "d" you should substitute the letter of your drive—for example, q:\start.

■FAQ How do I end a session?

You'll need to leave the Book-on-CD disk in the CD-ROM drive while you're using it. Before you remove the CD from the drive, exit the program by clicking the File menu at the top of the Welcome screen, then clicking Exit.

■FAQ What's a QuickTour?

On the Welcome screen, you'll see a large button labeled "QuickTour!" Click this button to take a 20-minute tour of *The Practical PC* Book-on-CD. You'll learn how to use its on-screen controls and you'll get an overview of all its features.

■FAQ How do I get the most out of the book and the Book-on-CD?

If you have your own computer, you might want to start the CD and do your reading online. You'll then be able to play the videos as you come to them and click boldface terms to see pop-up definitions. Also, you'll be able to immediately interact with the Issues, Tutorial, and QuickCheck sections at the end of each chapter.

If you do not have a computer, you should read through the chapter in the book. Later, when it is convenient, take your Book-on-CD to a computer at school, home, or work and use the Media menu at the top of the Welcome screen to quickly jump to each video in the chapter. After you view the videos, you can jump to the Issues, Tutorial, or QuickCheck sections and complete those interactive activities.

Take your time. You might want to do each chapter in two sessions by first reading the FAQ (frequently asked question), Hardware, and Issues sections. Then, in a later session, you can complete the Tutorial and QuickCheck sections.

■FAQ What's a Tracking Disk?

A Tracking Disk tracks your progress by saving your responses to the "What do you think?" questions on the Issues pages as well as your scores on the chapter quizzes. You can view or print a summary report of all your scores by using the Tracking Disk menu on the Welcome screen. In an academic setting, your instructor might request your Tracking Disk data to monitor your progress.

If you want to create a Tracking Disk, you'll need a formatted floppy disk. Your Book-on-CD program will tell you when you should insert your Tracking Disk. For more detailed information, check out the Tracking Disk section of the QuickTour.

■FAQ What about sound?

If your computer is equipped for sound, you should hear audio during the videos. If you don't, check the volume control on your computer by clicking the speaker icon in the lower-right corner of your screen. If you're working in a lab or office where sound would be disruptive, consider using earphones. You can also use the Options menu on the Welcome screen to turn sound off. Find out more about this option in the QuickTour.

■FAQ Do I need an Internet connection?

The Internet is a worldwide system of interconnected computers, which you'll learn about in Chapters 7 through 9. The Internet's most popular service is called "the World Wide Web," "the Web," or "WWW." If your PC has Web browser software and a connection to the Internet, you can use the GrabIt! buttons to get free or demo versions of software shown in the figures, tutorials, and videos. This software is not required to use *The Practical PC* book or the Book-on-CD, so don't worry if you lack an Internet connection.

If you have an Internet connection, you can use the GrabIt! buttons to see the list of free and demo software. You can also access our Internet site directly at www.cciw.com/ppc. For those of you who are technically inclined, when you start *The Practical PC* Book-on-CD, it looks for a browser on your computer and will use the first one it finds. If you have another browser installed that you would rather use, you can specify this choice from the Options menu on the Welcome screen.

■FAQ Can I make the type appear larger on my screen?

If the type in the Book-on-CD appears small, your monitor is probably set at a high resolution. The type will appear larger if you reduce the resolution by following the instructions in the figure below. This setting is optional. You can view the Book-on-CD at most standard resolutions, however, your computer should be set to use Windows standard fonts, not large fonts.

If you would like to see larger type on the screen, you can change the Display setting for your monitor by following the numbered steps below. You don't have to change this setting to use the Book-on-CD, however.

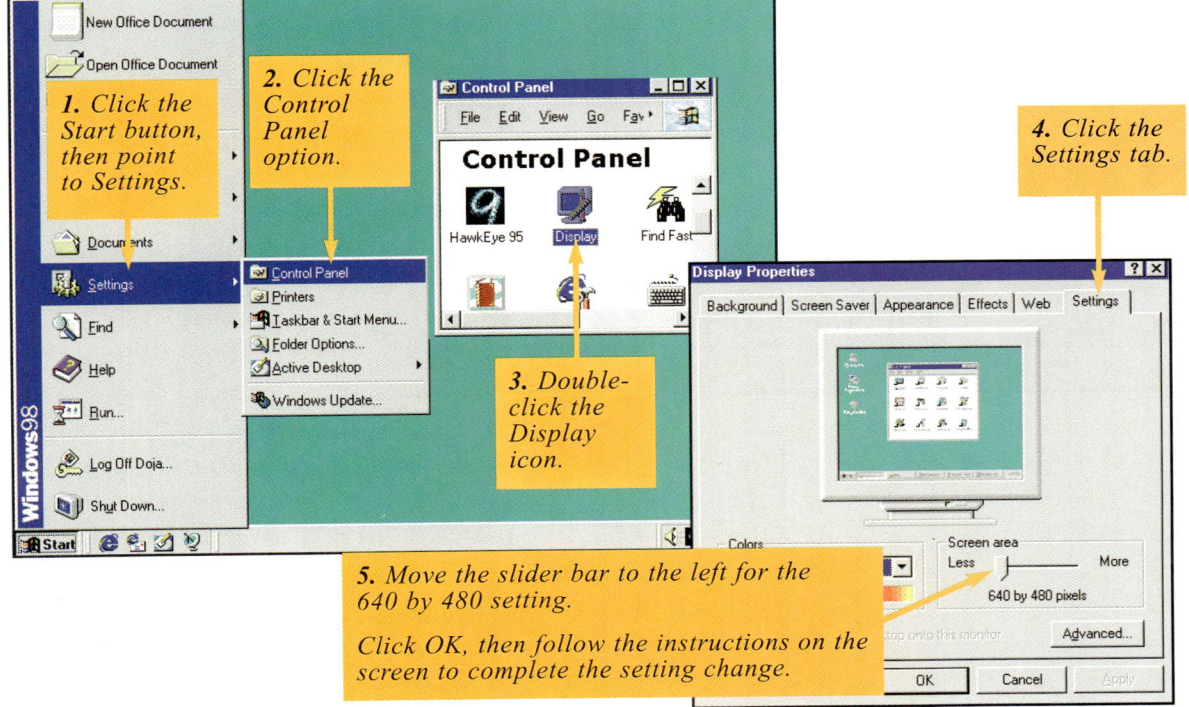

1. Click the Start button, then point to Settings.

2. Click the Control Panel option.

3. Double-click the Display icon.

4. Click the Settings tab.

5. Move the slider bar to the left for the 640 by 480 setting.

Click OK, then follow the instructions on the screen to complete the setting change.

■FAQ Which version of Windows do I need?

Your PC's operating system sets the standard for the way all of your software looks and works. You'll get the details about operating systems in Chapter 2, but for now you should understand that most of today's PCs use a version of the Microsoft Windows operating system—"Windows" for short. The most recent versions of Windows are called Windows 95, Windows 98, Windows Millennium Edition (ME), Windows 2000, and Windows NT. These versions of Windows look very similar and have a common set of features that you can readily learn to use.

All of the figures you see in this book and on the Book-on-CD pertain to Windows 95/98/ME and Windows NT/2000. Therefore, you can expect to learn a lot about these versions of Windows as you read this book.

If you see a screen similar to this one when you start your PC, your operating system is Windows 95/98/ME or Windows NT/2000.

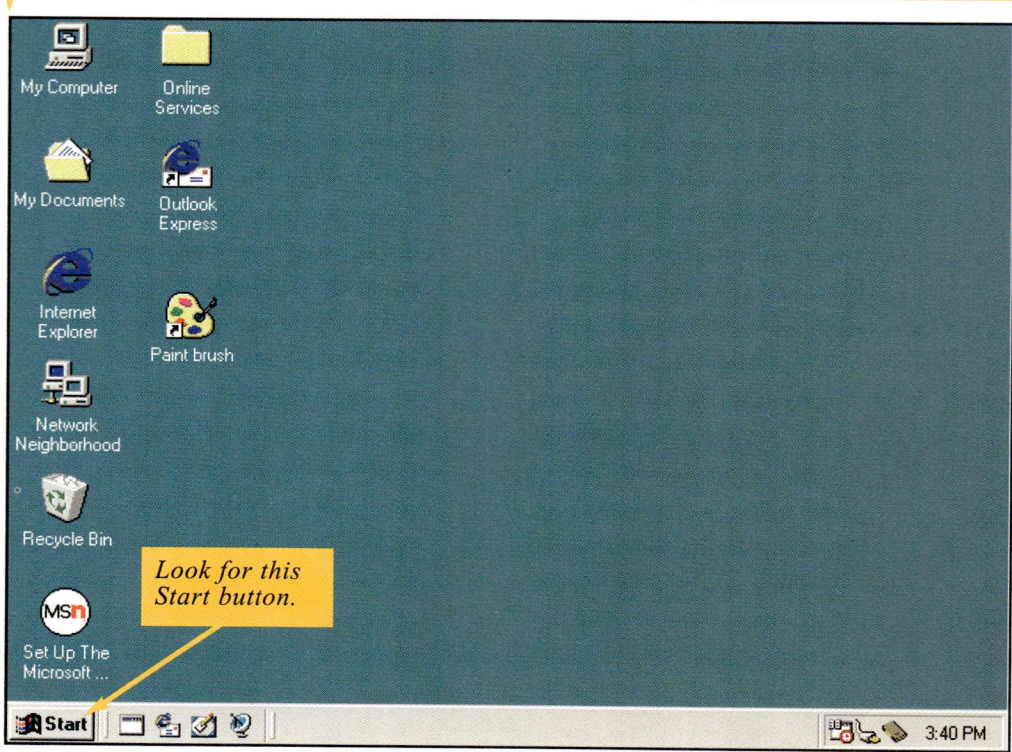

Look for this Start button.

■FAQ What about Windows 3.1?

An earlier version of Windows, called Microsoft Windows 3.1, looks and works differently from more recent version of Windows. Although you can view the Book-on-CD using a computer with Windows 3.1, you should remember that the figures and examples are geared toward Windows 95/98/ME and Windows NT/2000. This feature is handy if your computer uses Windows 3.1, but you are planning to upgrade soon to a more recent version of Windows.

If the screen looks something like the figure below when you first start your PC, your operating system is Windows 3.1.

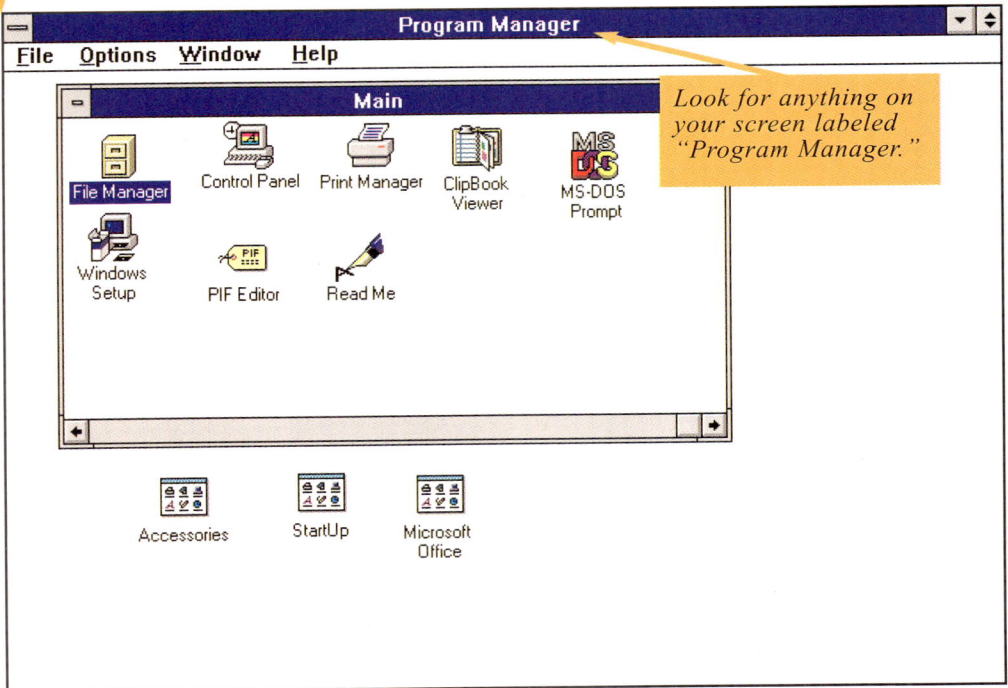

Look for anything on your screen labeled "Program Manager."

If you would like to view *The Practical PC* Book-on-CD using a computer with Windows 3.1, simply go to the next page and follow the numbered steps on the figure.

Windows 3.1 does not have the capability to start a CD automatically, so you'll need to use the manual method. To begin, turn your computer on and make sure that you can see the Program Manager title bar at the top of the screen. If you see a small Program Manager graphic instead, click that graphic, then press the Enter key. Once the Program Manager appears on your screen, you can follow the numbered steps in the figure below.

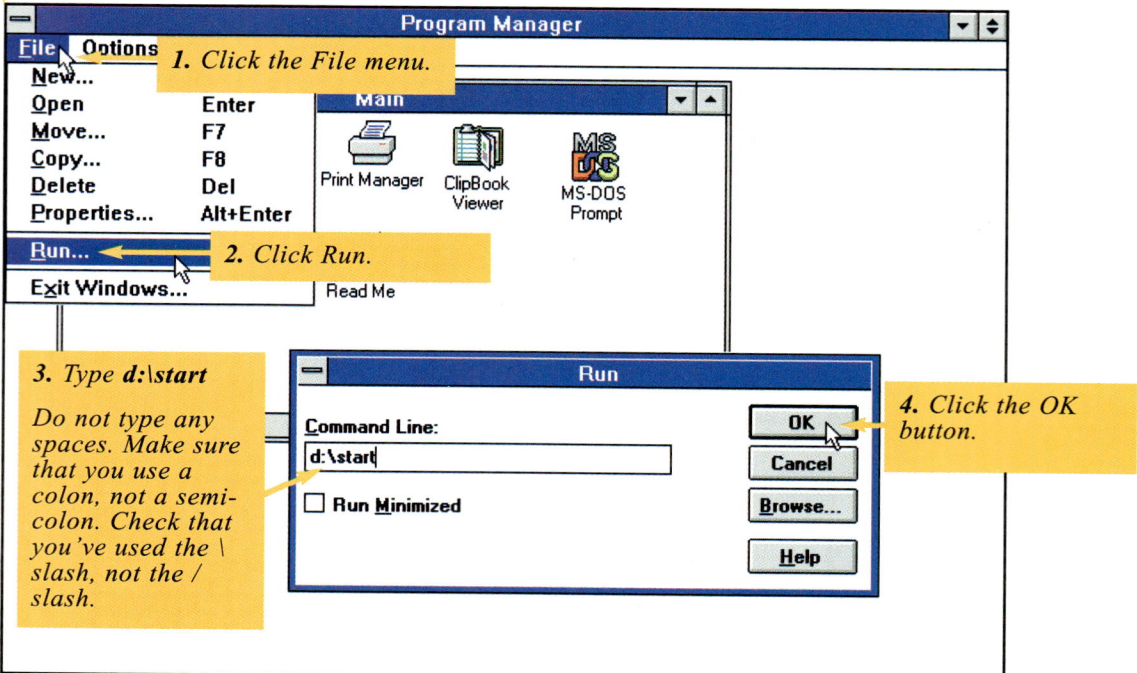

Using Windows 3.1 to view The Practical PC Book-on-CD: After you insert the CD in the CD-ROM drive, follow the numbered steps below.

Computers are easy to customize. Therefore, the method for starting the Book-on-CD might be slightly different for your PC. If you've followed the instructions and still cannot start the CD, ask your technical support person for help.

Note that Windows 3.1 is generally installed on older, slower computers. The speed and performance of the Book-on-CD depends on the speed of your computer—for example, when using Windows 3.1, you might have to wait briefly for videos to begin. You'll learn more about such differences in computer performance as you read *The Practical PC*. Enjoy!

The Practical PC

Chapter 1
Getting Started

What's Inside?

Chapter 1 provides an overview of your computer system, including the terminology and equipment you need to get started. Some of the material might be a review, but don't ignore the explanations that tell you *why* these things work the way they do.

- **FAQs:**

Where's the power switch?	3
Do I need a disk to start my computer?	4
What if my computer asks me for a password?	5
Which works better, the mouse or the keyboard?	6
How do I turn my computer off?	7

- **Hardware: Desktops, notebooks, and PDAs** — 8
- **Tutorial: How to set up your computer** — 11
- **Issue: Computer "haves" and "have-nots"** — 12
- **QuickChecks** — 13

What's on the CD?

Your Book-on-CD contains the entire text of the printed book. But that's not all! On the CD the figures "come to life" through videos and animations. To use the CD, simply insert it into your CD-ROM drive. After a few seconds, you should see the Welcome screen. If the screen doesn't appear, click the Windows Start button, then click Run. In the box type d:\start.exe. If your CD-ROM drive is assigned to a different letter, substitute that letter instead of "d".

- Your first look at the Windows desktop — 5
- Video tips on using the mouse and keyboard — 6
- The right way to turn your computer off — 7
- Step-by-step tutorial on setting up a computer — 11
- Interactive QuickCheck questions — 13

Chapter 1: Getting Started 3

■FAQ where's the power switch?

Your **PC** (personal computer) is a collection of hardware and software components that help you accomplish many different tasks. As you probably know, a computer and any equipment connected to it are called **hardware**. A set of instructions that a computer follows to perform a task is called a program or **software**.

Every computer needs **operating system software** that defines how you interact with the computer and give it commands. When you switch on the computer, it starts the operating system software. You then use the operating system software to start **application software** that helps you produce documents, make calculations, draw pictures, or maintain your to-do list. Most of today's computers use the **Microsoft Windows** operating system ("Windows" for short). For that reason, computers that use Windows are the main focus of this book.

A PC is an electronic device containing a microprocessor. The **microprocessor** is essentially the brain of the computer, carrying out the commands that you issue when you create documents, draw pictures, or manipulate numbers. It works with data representing words, numbers, and pictures held *temporarily* in memory chips called **RAM** (random access memory). Data has a more permanent home on a hard disk, floppy disk, tape, or CD. Devices that are designed to store data *permanently* are referred to as **storage devices**. The microprocessor, memory, and storage devices for a PC are typically housed in a **system unit**. Other components — the monitor, keyboard, mouse, and printer — are connected to the system unit.

The PC's power switch is located on the system unit. A small green light indicates when the power is on. The monitor typically has its own power switch. Because the monitor might take a few seconds to warm up, turn it on before you turn on your PC.

Figure 1-1: A typical desktop computer system consists of a series of components connected to the system unit.

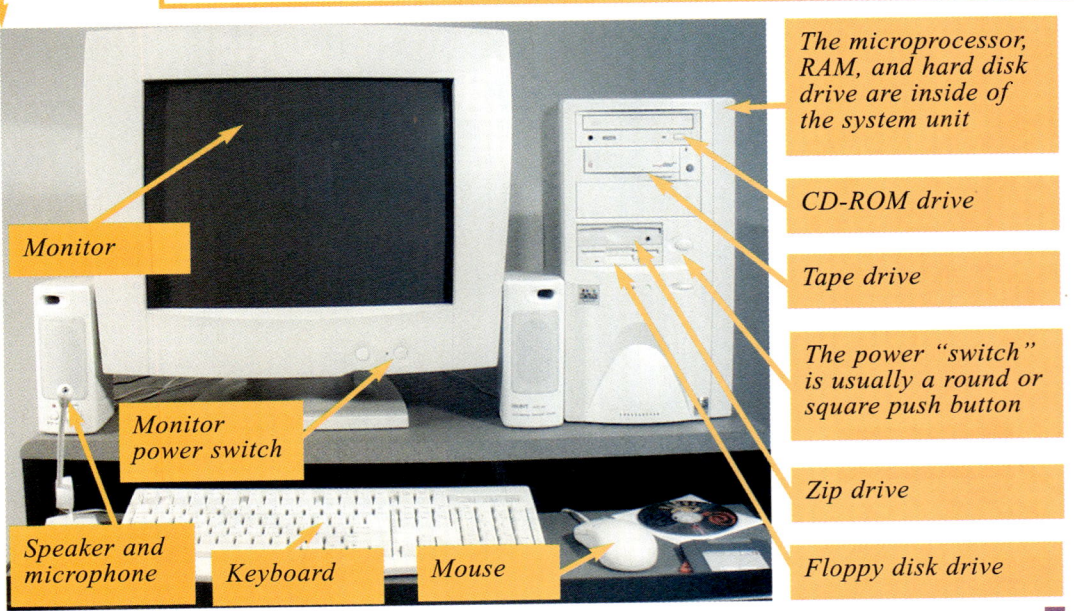

4 Chapter 1: Getting Started

▪FAQ Do I need a disk to start my computer?

You should make it a habit to check that the floppy disk drive is empty before you switch on a computer. The only time you would start the computer with a disk in the floppy disk drive is when the hard disk drive has failed. The reason relates to what happens between the time you flick the power switch and the time your computer is ready to begin the business of computing.

As soon as you switch on the power, your PC starts to "boot up." During the **boot process**, the PC performs diagnostic tests to make sure that the keyboard, storage devices, RAM, and microprocessor are functioning correctly. After testing the hardware, it looks for the operating system programs. Usually, these programs are stored on the computer's **hard disk drive**, a large-capacity storage device located inside the system unit. However, most computers look for them first on the floppy disk drive, just in case the hard disk drive has malfunctioned. You can boot your computer without your hard disk drive by using a special floppy disk called a **system disk**, which contains operating system programs. Most computer manufacturers supply you with such a system disk, or explain how to create one.

What if the hard disk drive is functioning normally and you've inadvertently left a plain data disk in the floppy disk drive? When your computer spots this disk in the drive, it displays a "non-system disk" message. This is your cue to take the disk out of the drive. You can put the disk in later when the boot process ends.

Figure 1-2: When the boot process is complete, you'll see the Windows desktop on your screen. But what happens when your PC doesn't boot correctly? Play this video to find out what to do.

■FAQ What if my computer asks me for a password?

As the boot process proceeds, your computer might display a message asking for your user ID and password. Generally, this message indicates that your computer is a part of a network. A **network** is an interconnected collection of computers, printers, and other devices. You've probably heard of a worldwide network called the Internet, but many small local networks are also maintained by businesses, organizations, and schools. By supplying a valid user ID and password, you can access information stored on other network computers or print on a network printer. Your **user ID** or user name is your network identification and is usually a variation of your name. Your **password** is a series of letters and numbers that provide your security clearance for the network. You can tell anyone your user ID, but you should not disclose your password.

Figure 1-3: When you type your password, it usually appears as a series of asterisks. This security measure hides your password from anyone who might be looking over your shoulder.

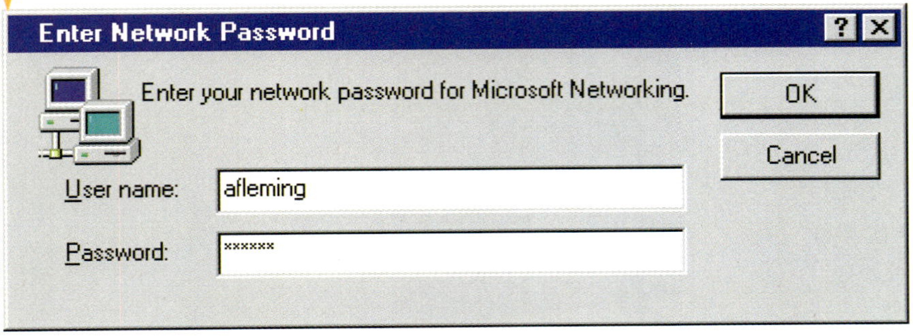

Some networks provide you with a password that you cannot change. Other networks allow you to create your own password and change it as frequently as you like. A secure password is one that is difficult for someone else to guess. When you create a password, don't use your name, the name of a relative, or your birth date. It is also a good idea not to use any word that you might find in the dictionary because a common way of "breaking" or discovering a password is to run through an electronic dictionary, trying all the words it contains. To create a secure password, combine more than one word or combine words and numbers. For example, "U4got" would probably be a secure password.

In today's connected world, you'll typically spend some time "surfing" the Internet to find information, make travel arrangements, purchase gifts, look for career opportunities, and communicate with other computer users. Before you participate in these online activities, you usually have to register. Should you create a different password for every activity? Probably not, because you'll have a difficult time remembering all of them. However, if you use the same password all the time, a person who discovers your password will have access to all of your information. Some experienced computer users have two passwords: one password for financial transactions and an alternative password for less critical transactions.

Chapter 1: Getting Started

 Which works better, the mouse or the keyboard?

Today's computers generally require you to use both a mouse and a keyboard. These **input devices** help you put information into the computer — the documents you write, the artwork you create, the numbers you want to "crunch," and the commands you want the computer to follow.

Beginning computer users generally use the keyboard to enter text, and use the mouse to select the tasks that they want the computer to perform. Experienced users sometimes use the keyboard rather than the mouse to select tasks when they are working with text. Why? Because moving their hands from the keyboard to the mouse interrupts the flow of their work. There is no right or wrong style for using the mouse and keyboard — over time you'll develop your own style and preferences. In the Hardware section of Chapter 2, you'll learn about some new input technologies that might eventually replace your mouse and keyboard.

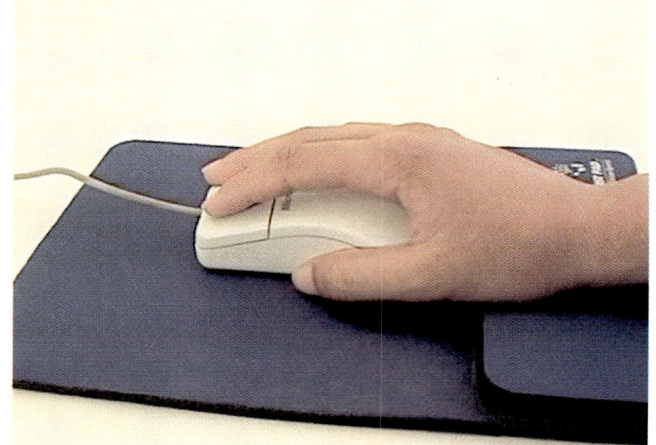

Figure 1-4: The mouse helps you move an arrow-shaped pointer on the screen to select the tasks you want to accomplish. Play this video to see how to drag, click, double-click, and right-click the mouse. You'll also find out how to clean your mouse.

Figure 1-5: It is a good idea to understand all the features of your keyboard. Play this video to find out how to use the Ctrl, Alt, and Windows keys; why you should leave the Num Lock engaged; and how to clean your keyboard.

Chapter 1: Getting Started

■FAQ How do I turn my computer off?

Some computers might look like they're off, when they are only asleep! Many of today's PCs have a power-saver feature called **sleep mode** that turns off the screen after a period of inactivity. You can "wake up" your computer by moving the mouse or pressing a key. Even in sleep mode, your computer consumes a small amount of power and remains susceptible to electrical spikes and surges that can damage electronic equipment. It is a good idea to turn off your PC when you've finished with a computing session. But don't just flick off the power switch. If your PC uses the Windows operating system, you should issue the **Shut Down** command before you turn the power off. The shut down process ensures that your work for this computing session is saved and cleans out any temporary "scratchpad" data that the operating system created but doesn't need to save.

Figure 1-6: You access the Shut Down command from the Windows Start menu. This video explains the recommended way to turn off your computer.

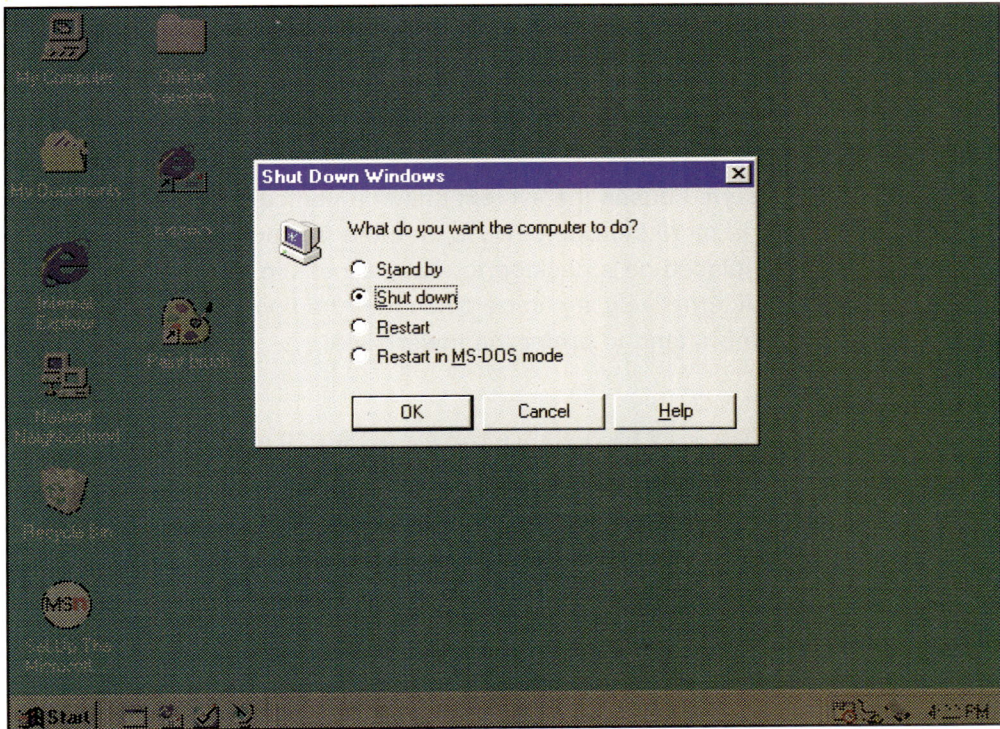

If occasionally you forget to use the Shut Down command before switching off the power, you probably won't damage anything. But you should make it a habit to do things the right way just to avoid potential problems.

Computer software sometimes has "bugs" or errors that cause your computer to "freeze up" or "hang" so it won't respond to your mouse or keyboard commands. If this situation occurs, you won't be able to issue the regular Shut Down command. Before you press the power switch, hold down the Ctrl, Alt, and Del keys at the same time. If only one program has frozen, you'll be able to close that program. You can then try the program again to see if it works correctly.

■Hardware
Desktops, notebooks, and PDAs

Computers come in several configurations that fit on your desk, in your briefcase, or in your pocket. Each has advantages — you might find that you need more than one computer!

A **desktop computer** is designed to be a fairly permanent fixture on your desk. It typically includes hardware components such as a system unit, mouse, keyboard, monitor, speakers, and microphone. You'll tend not to move a desktop computer because it takes some time to disconnect and then reconnect all the components. In addition, the monitor is fairly heavy, so you don't want to tote it around unnecessarily.

A desktop computer provides the most computing power for your dollar. You'll be able to purchase a very serviceable computer with a basic set of software tools for about U.S.$1,000. Desktop computers are available in two basic styles.

The traditional **desktop style** includes a horizontally oriented system unit that generally sits under the monitor. The advantage of traditional desktop styling is its small "footprint," which takes up a minimal amount of desk space but allows easy access to floppy disk and CD-ROM drives.

An alternative **tower style** houses the system unit in a vertically oriented case, which allows you to add more storage devices than the traditional desktop model. The tower unit can be placed on a desktop for easy access to floppy disk drives and CD-ROM drives. Alternatively, it can be placed on the floor to save desk space. Today's consumers tend to prefer the tower style.

Figure 1-7: On the left, an example of traditional desktop styling; on the right, an example of tower styling.

Hardware
continued

Notebook computers, sometimes called laptops, are designed for people on the move. All the essential components — keyboard, screen, disk drives, CD-ROM drive, and pointing device — are housed in a single unit. You can plug a notebook computer into a wall outlet or run it from special batteries that last two to five hours on a single charge.

A notebook and its batteries typically weigh between five and seven pounds. However, when you pack a carrying case with a notebook computer and all the paraphernalia needed for computing, you usually have about 15 pounds to lug around. Adding substantially to the weight is the "power brick" or **AC adapter**, which allows you to plug the notebook into a wall outlet. Most ads for notebook computers omit this important piece of gear from photos and weight specifications.

A notebook computer includes a flat-panel, light-weight **LCD** (liquid crystal display) screen instead of a monitor. LCDs have lower power requirements than monitors, increasing the time that your notebook can run on a battery charge. A notebook's small size limits the number of devices you can add inside the case. To connect devices to your notebook, you can use **PCMCIA cards**, sometimes called PC cards. These cards slide into a small PCMCIA slot. For example, you can purchase PCMCIA cards to connect your computer to phone lines or to a network.

Compared with a desktop computer, a notebook provides less computing power for your dollar because you are paying for portability. You'll spend about U.S.$2,500 to purchase a notebook computer with roughly the same computing power as a U.S.$1,000 desktop computer.

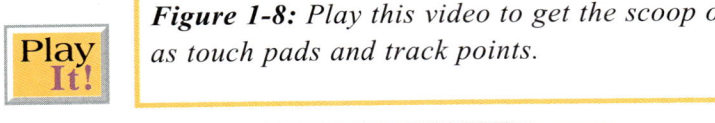

Figure 1-8: Play this video to get the scoop on notebook pointing devices, such as touch pads and track points.

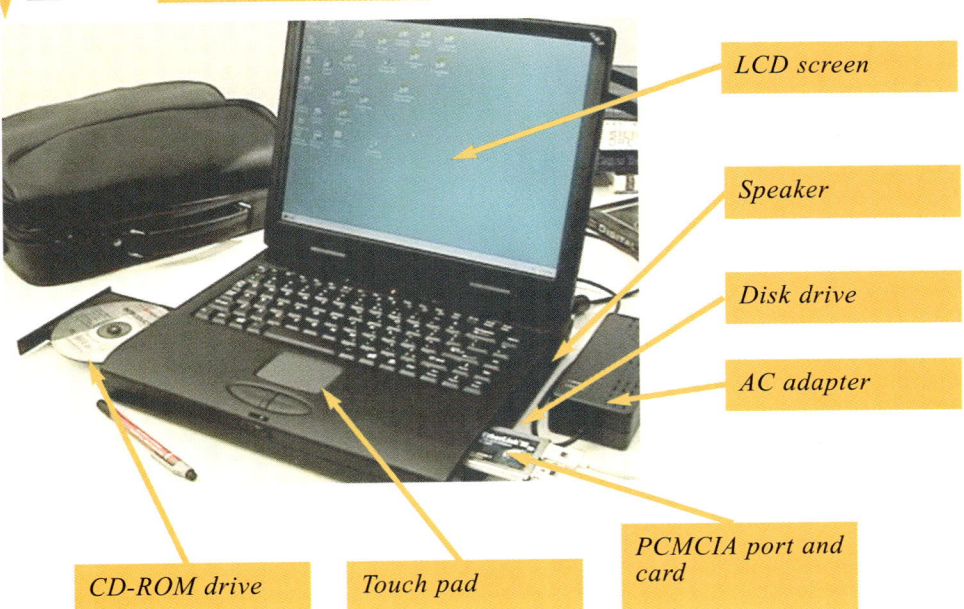

■Hardware
continued

A **PDA** (personal digital assistant) is the solution for people who want a basic level of computer power but who don't want to carry a briefcase full of notebook computer paraphernalia. A PDA, sometimes called a palm top, is a hand-held computer in a one-pound, pocket-sized package, typically priced around U.S.$500.

There are two basic types of PDAs. One type resembles a very small notebook computer and features a tiny screen and keyboard. The other type of PDA has no keyboard, but instead features a touch-sensitive screen that you can write on using a pen-like stylus.

A PDA does not include any type of disk drive. Without a hard disk drive, the operating system and other software programs must be permanently stored in the PDA's circuitry, much like the square root function is hard-wired in a hand-held calculator.

Many PDAs use a scaled-down version of the Windows operating system called **Windows CE**. They also use scaled-down software for scheduling, word processing, spreadsheets, Internet surfing, and e-mail. The documents you create are stored in a special type of **flash memory** that holds data without a constant source of power.

To compensate for a PDA's limited storage capacity, manufacturers provide easy links to connect PDAs to other computers. For example, you can exchange and synchronize your PDA's data with the data on your desktop or notebook computer, so you can keep your schedule up-to-date on both. Also, you can transfer data from your PDA to the storage devices on your desktop computer.

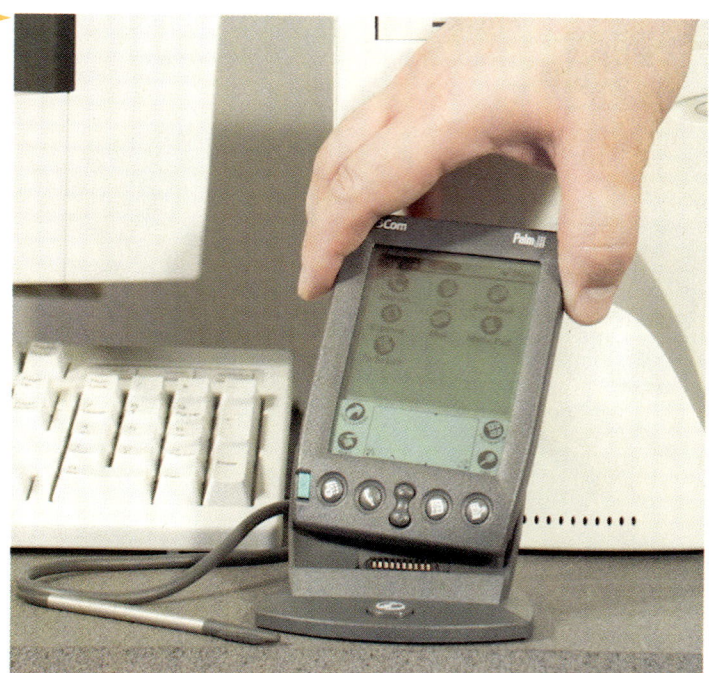

Figure 1-9: When you're away from your full-featured desktop computer, a PDA provides a handy way to maintain your schedule and dash off quick e-mail messages. A special docking bay keeps the data on your desktop computer up-to-date with the data on your PDA.

Chapter 1: Getting Started   11

■Tutorial
How to set up your computer

In addition to its small size, an advantage of a notebook computer is that everything is contained in one unit. The screen, keyboard, pointing device, and disk drives are housed in one easy-to-carry package. Setting up a notebook computer is a breeze. Just swing the screen up into place and plug in the power cable.

Desktop computers present more of a set-up challenge because the system unit, monitor, mouse, keyboard, and speakers are all separate components. When you buy a new computer or move your trusty old computer to a new location, you have to connect each component correctly. As you'll see in the tutorial, the set-up process isn't really difficult. Even if your PC is already set up, the tutorial will help you understand how its components fit together.

When you have completed the tutorial, you should be able to:
- List the hardware components typically shipped in each of the three cartons that contain a computer system.
- Safely unpack your computer's hardware components.
- Connect the keyboard, mouse, monitor, speakers, microphone, and printer to the correct ports on the back of the system unit.
- Describe two benefits of using a surge strip.

 *Figure 1-10:* Suppose you've just purchased a new computer. Click the PlayIt! button to begin the tutorial and find out how to set up your computer. Estimated time: 10-15 minutes. Tracking Disk points: 10.

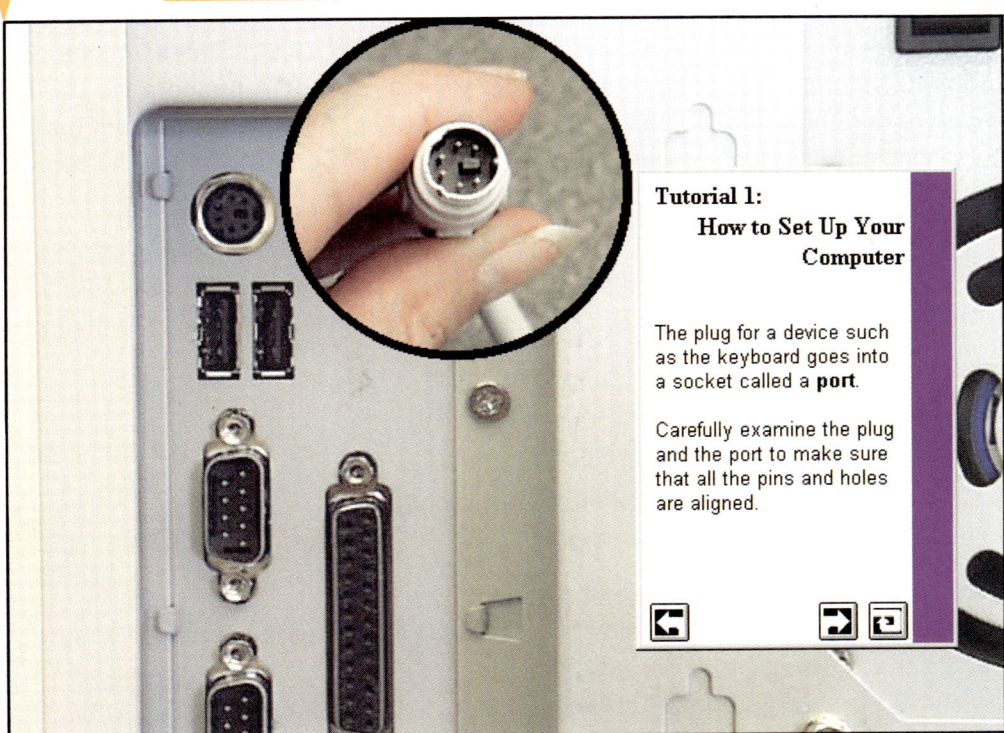

Chapter 1: Getting Started

▪Issue
Computer "haves" and "have-nots"

In 1998, Microsoft's chairman, Bill Gates, announced that he was donating $200 million of his personal fortune and $200 million in matching Microsoft funds to supply computers and Internet access to libraries serving low-income communities. He noted that few low-income families owned computers "and so that's dividing our society and it's moving away from our central belief of equal opportunity."

Is there really a gap between computer "haves" and "have-nots"? Are the economically disadvantaged being denied access to government documents, employment bulletin boards, and other information accessible on the Internet? Are the computer "have-nots" trapped in a low-technology ghetto because they lack the computer skills required to get a well-paying job?

A disturbing report by the U.S. Census Bureau in 1992 indicated that 28% of middle- and high-income families owned a computer, but only 7.4% of poor families and only 4.2% of families receiving Aid to Dependent Children owned one.

Drawing conclusions from this data could be risky. The report is more than six years old. The data doesn't prove whether computer access does, in fact, contribute to economic success. Also, although the data indicates that computers are scarce in low-income homes, it does not indicate if computer access is available through schools or libraries.

Providing information access does not have to involve an expensive government initiative. Computer recycling programs distribute older business computers to schools and libraries worldwide. Many communities have gathered funds and volunteers to create neighborhood computer centers. In the United States, volunteers with the national service organization called Americorps*VISTA promote the use of computers and the Internet in low-income communities. As many volunteers have demonstrated, universal computer and Internet access is a goal that can be tackled one computer at a time.

What do you think?

1. Do you own a computer? ◯ Yes ◯ No ◯ Not sure

2. Do you believe that not having a computer at home is likely to limit a person's chances to improve his or her economic status? ◯ Yes ◯ No ◯ Not sure

3. Do you favor spending tax dollars to make computers available in public libraries? ◯ Yes ◯ No ◯ Not sure

4. Would you favor allowing college students to spend their financial aid money on computers? ◯ Yes ◯ No ◯ Not sure

Save It!

Chapter 1: Getting Started   13

QuickCheck

1. A(n) _____ is the "brain" of your PC, which carries out the commands you issue on data that represents words, numbers, and pictures.

2. Microsoft Windows is _____ software, which the computer starts during the boot process.

3. True or false? The password "one4all" is more secure than "anarchy". _____

4. The Windows _____ command makes sure that your work for a computing session is saved before you turn off the computer.

5. A(n) _____ computer is lighter and more portable than a desktop or laptop computer, but uses scaled-down versions of the operating system and application software.

Check It!

QuickCheck

Enter the name of the computer components in the numbered boxes below.

1. _____
2. _____
3. _____
4. _____
5. _____

Check It!

Get It? While using the Book-on-CD, click the Get It? button to see if you can answer ten randomly selected questions from Chapter 1.

Chapter 2
Looking at Windows

What's Inside?

In Chapter 2, you'll discover why the operating system is the core piece of software on your PC. Plus, you'll find out how to start your software and how to print. Beyond these basics, you'll find up-to-date information on alternative input devices and software, such as touch-sensitive LCDs, force-feedback technology, and voice recognition.

- FAQs:

What's the Windows desktop?	15
How do I start an application program?	16
What's a window?	17
What's a dialog box?	18
Which version of Windows do I have?	19

- Hardware: Alternative input devices — 20
- Tutorial: How to use Windows controls — 23
- Issue: Monopoly is not just a game — 24
- QuickChecks — 25

What's on the CD?

Chapter 2 contains several tours that show you how to use the Windows operating system and some action-packed videos about alternative input devices.

- Find out about all those objects on your screen — 15
- Learn how to start application programs and switch between programs — 16
- Tour a typical application window — 17
- Discover which version of Windows you're using — 19
- See the new force-feedback joystick in action — 21
- Watch a voice-recognition training session — 22
- Take a step-by-step tutorial on using Windows controls — 23

Chapter 2: Looking at Windows   15

■FAQ What's the Windows desktop?

The **Windows desktop** is the gateway to all of the tasks you perform with your PC. It is the screen you see when the boot process is complete, and it remains in the background as you use other software programs.

The Windows desktop is displayed by your PC's operating system. Keep in mind that the main purpose of the operating system is to let you control your computer environment. Graphical objects on the desktop allow you to examine and modify many aspects of this environment, such as the type of printer you'll use, the color scheme for your screen display, or the sensitivity of your mouse.

The desktop contains small graphics called **icons** that represent programs, hardware, and documents. Clicking an icon gives you access to the computer component that it represents. The **taskbar** at the bottom of the screen displays buttons and icons that help you keep track of the status of your computer system, such as the program that you are currently using, the volume setting of your speakers, and the current time.

The **Start button**, which is located on the taskbar, is the main control on the Windows desktop. When you click this button, Windows displays the **Start menu**. You can use this menu to start programs, change your hardware settings, get help, and install software.

Figure 2-1: Click the PlayIt! button for a guided tour of the Windows desktop. The Windows desktop can be customized, so it might look slightly different on your computer. In later chapters, you'll learn how to customize your desktop.

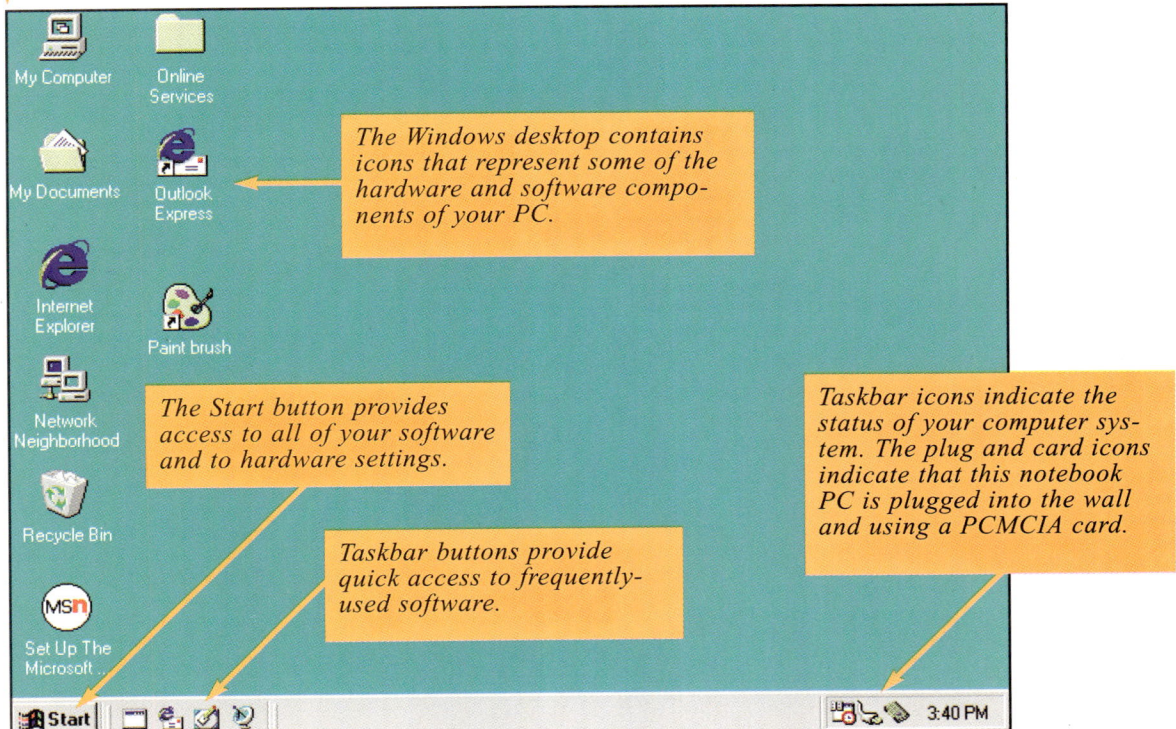

16 Chapter 2: Looking at Windows

■FAQ How do I start an application program?

When the boot process is complete and the Windows desktop appears, your PC is ready for your instructions. Ordinarily, when you turn on your PC, you want to use an application program. An **application program** ("application" or "program" for short) helps you accomplish real-world tasks, such as creating personalized greeting cards, balancing your checkbook, or learning to speak Spanish. As you use your PC, keep in mind that an application and the operating system are both programs, but they have distinctly different purposes. The operating system helps you control your "computer world." An application program helps you accomplish tasks for the real world.

The Windows operating system provides several ways to start an application, but typically you'll use the Start button. When you click this button, the Start menu appears. From the Start menu, select the **Programs option** to display a list of the available application programs. Click any one of the programs and it will start.

In the jargon of computing, starting and using an application is referred to as "running" it. You can run more than one program at the same time. Buttons on the taskbar show you which programs are running. To switch between one program and another, click one of the buttons on the taskbar.

Figure 2-2: Click the PlayIt! button to find out how to start an application program, how to run two programs at the same time, and how to switch between programs.

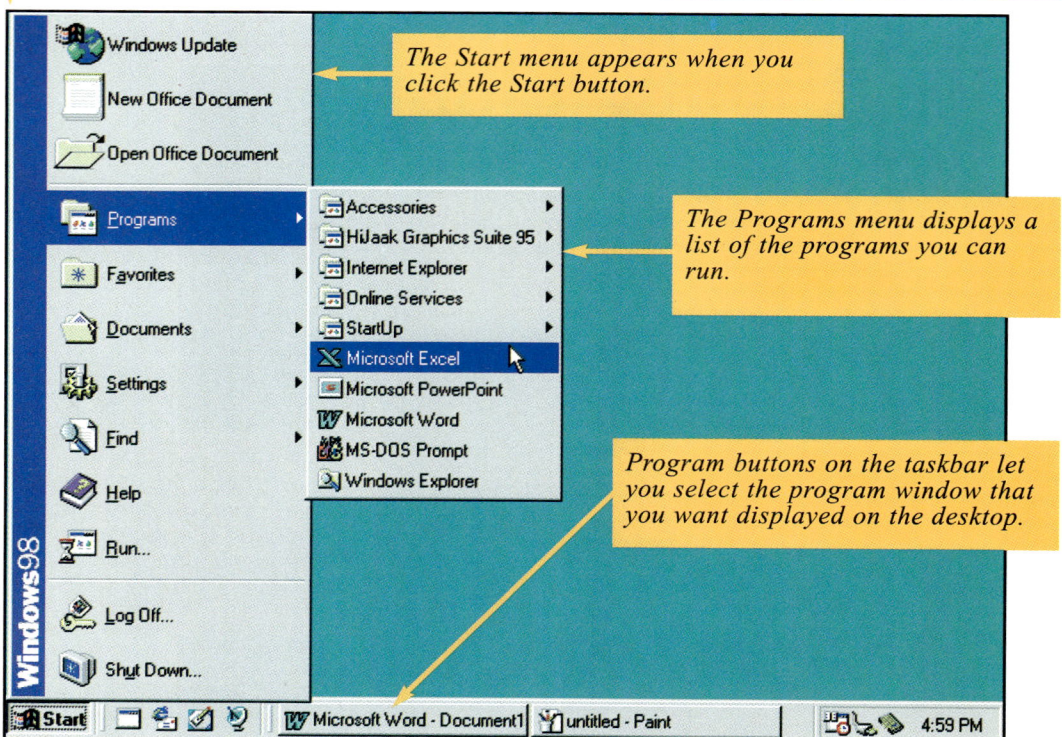

Chapter 2: Looking at Windows   17

■FAQ   What's a window?

The Windows operating system gets its name because everything happens in rectangular viewing areas on the screen called **windows**. Just to clarify, "Windows" with an uppercase "W" refers to the operating system, but "windows" with a lowercase "w" refers to the rectangular areas on the screen. When you start a program, it appears in its own window. The **title bar** of the window indicates the program name and contains three control buttons. The ▭ **Minimize button** shrinks the window to a button on the taskbar. The ☐ **Maximize button** enlarges the window to fill the screen. The ☒ **Close button** closes the window and stops the program.

Typically, the windows in which your application programs appear include a **menu bar** that provides access to the commands that control the application. For example, when you have completed a document, you can store it on a disk by clicking the File menu, then selecting Save from the list of command options.

Below the menu bar, you might see one or more **toolbars** containing small pictures, such as a folder, disk, printer, scissors, and clipboard. Each picture is a **toolbar button** that provides you with a shortcut for accomplishing a task. For example, the toolbar button that looks like a disk is a shortcut for saving a document—you can just click this button instead of clicking the File menu and then selecting the Save command. A **scroll bar** on the side of the window helps you move a document or graphic up and down within the window.

Figure 2-3: Click the PlayIt! button to take a tour of a typical application window and to learn more about using the title bar, control buttons, menu bar, toolbar, and scroll bar.

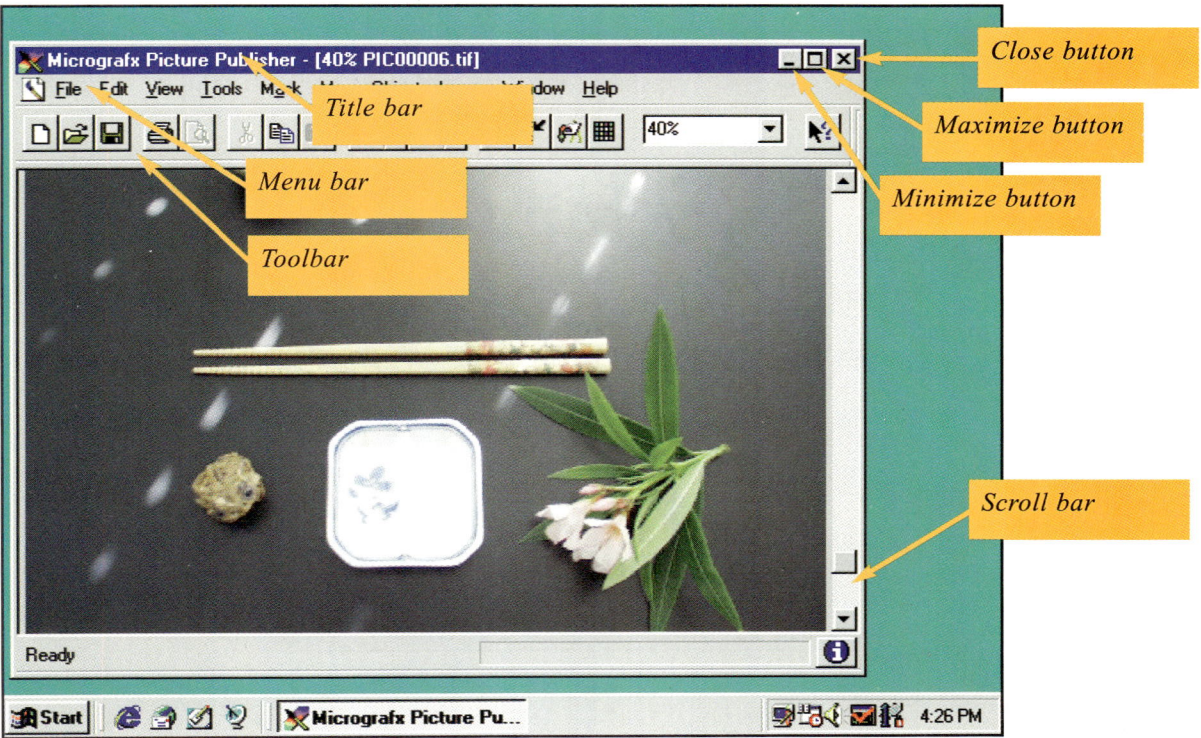

Chapter 2: Looking at Windows

■FAQ What's a dialog box?

A **dialog box** is a small window that appears when you click certain menu options. You can think of it as an order form, like one you might use when ordering a gift from a catalog. Just as you would fill in an order form with the color, size, and price of a gift, you fill in a dialog box with the specifications for accomplishing a task.

Most application programs have hundreds of features. These features have so many variations that it would be inconvenient and nearly impossible to list all of them on menus. For example, when you want to print a document, you can select the Print option from the File menu. But do you want to print the entire document or only selected pages? How many copies do you want? If you're printing multiple copies, do you want the printer to collate the pages? If you're in an office with more than one printer, which one do you want to use? Before the computer can print the document, it needs specific instructions that specify the results you want. A dialog box allows you to provide these instructions.

To fill in the "blanks" in a dialog box, you use a variety of **Windows controls**, such as option buttons, list boxes, spin boxes, check boxes, and dialog box buttons. You'll have an opportunity to try these controls in the tutorial for this chapter.

Figure 2-4: When you want to print, click the File menu, then click Print. The Print dialog box contains examples of the numerous controls you can use to specify the results for a task such as printing.

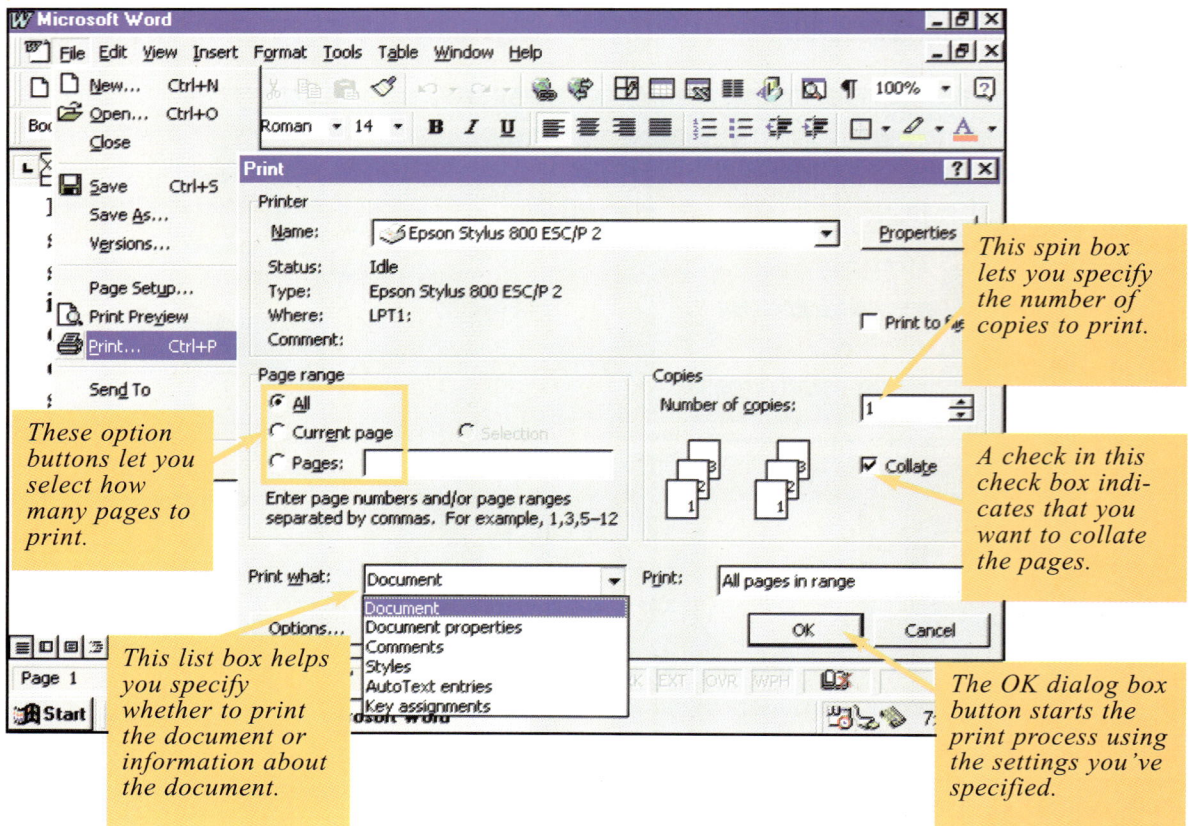

Chapter 2: Looking at Windows

■FAQ Which version of Windows do I have?

The operating system is the core piece of software on your PC. You work with it directly to start programs and organize the documents and other information stored on your disks. The operating system sets the standard for the on-screen controls used for all your application software. In addition, the operating system works behind the scenes to detect equipment failure, maintain security, manage storage space, and communicate with the printer, speakers, and monitor. Microsoft has introduced several versions of the Windows operating system, each one slightly different from the others in terms of features and appearance. It is handy to know which version you are using when you purchase new software, when you call for technical support, and when you shop for tutorials.

Microsoft Windows 3.1 was the first commercially successful version of the Windows operating system. **Microsoft Windows 95** offered significant new features and became the operating system of choice between 1995 and 1998. **Microsoft Windows 98** was released in mid-1998 as an upgrade to Windows 95, and was followed by **Windows ME**(Millennium Edition) in mid-2000. Most individuals and small businesses currently use Windows 98 or Windows ME. Microsoft also offers a line of **Windows NT/2000** operating systems, which were originally designed for networked environments. Windows 95, 98, ME, and NT/2000 look very much the same on the screen and have similar features and controls. Most of the information you will learn in this book applies to these relatively recent versions of Windows.

Figure 2-5: Click the PlayIt! button for a demonstration of two ways to find out which version of Windows you're using.

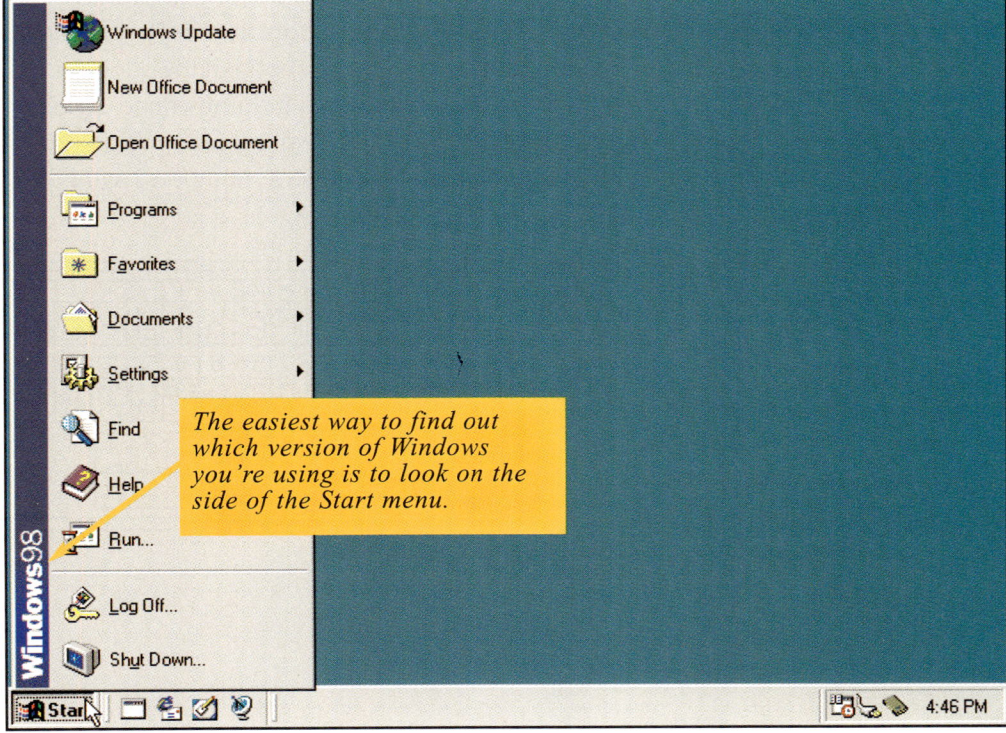

The easiest way to find out which version of Windows you're using is to look on the side of the Start menu.

Hardware
Alternative input devices

What makes a computer easy to use? The answer is a well-designed user interface. A **user interface** is the combination of hardware and software that manages the way humans and computers interact. In a well-designed user interface, accomplishing any task should be easy and learning a new task should be intuitive.

Windows defines the major elements of the user interface for PCs. Virtually every PC software package follows its **graphical user interface** (GUI, pronounced "gooey") model which includes menus, dialog boxes, and toolbars that you manipulate with the keyboard and mouse. The user interface provides two-way communication between you and your PC. It provides an **input** method that allows you to communicate information to the computer. It also provides an **output** method so that the computer can communicate information to you.

The current Windows user interface is the standard for most PCs, but it is not necessarily perfect, nor is it right for every user or every computing device. For example, the keyboard and mouse are great input devices for a standard desktop PC, but they don't work as well for pocket-sized PDAs or for people who don't know how to type.

A **touch-sensitive LCD** provides an alternative input method for small, portable computing devices and for nontypists. It is similar to the flat-panel LCD screens used on notebook computers, but it includes a matrix of sensors that transmit position and pressure information to the computer. A **stylus** is a pen-like device that you use to "write" on the LCD. The shapes of the characters you produce with the stylus are analyzed instantly by **handwriting-recognition software** that attempts to match your squiggles to the letters of the alphabet. Handwriting recognition is a difficult task, given the almost endless variations in handwriting styles. To simplify and speed up the task of analysis, many handwriting-recognition programs require you to print using only a standard set of letters, numbers, symbols, and punctuation marks.

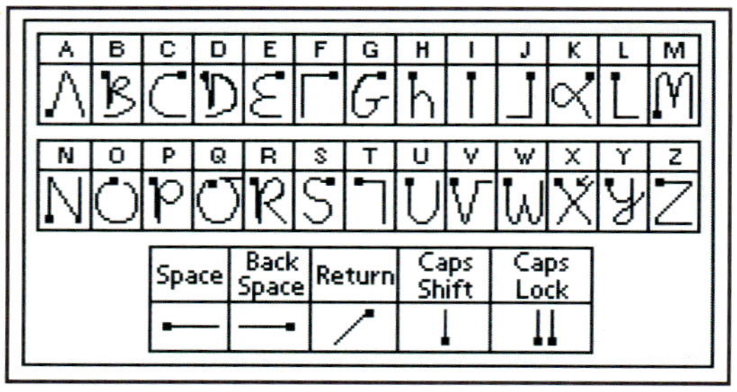

Figure 2-6: The reference card from a pocket-sized PalmPilot PDA shows you how to write the Graffiti alphabet that will be recognized by its handwriting-recognition software. The small squares indicate where to begin each stroke.

■Hardware
continued

As part of the user interface, a touch-sensitive LCD serves a dual purpose—it is both an input and output device. It displays computer output, such as the results of a calculation, but it also collects your written input. A mouse, on the other hand, typically serves only as an input device. This situation is changing, however, as new feedback devices hit the market.

A **feedback device**, as its name implies, supplies you with feedback as you use it. A popular example is the **force-feedback joystick**, an enhanced version of the ordinary joystick you might have used in the past with popular computer games. An ordinary joystick helps you move a screen-based object, such as a pointer, an action figure, or a simulated aircraft. A force-feedback joystick adds another level of interactivity. The computer outputs instructions to this device so that, for example, if your simulated aircraft begins to stall, the joystick starts to vibrate. If you try to take your plane into a steep climb, you feel more and more resistance as your rate of climb increases.

Feedback devices have the potential for more than games. They can become an integral part of the user interface for many home, school, and business applications. For example, imagine the additional control you would gain if your mouse provided feedback about your screen-based desktop. With force-feedback technology, your mouse would seem to bump as you move the pointer over the edges of dialog box buttons. You would sense the ridge at the edge of a window. And, your mouse would stop when the pointer reaches the edge of the screen. Obviously, this feedback technology would be helpful for some people who have vision impairments or physical handicaps that make using a regular mouse difficult. Feedback joysticks are fun, but pricey—about U.S.$150. Feedback mice cost about U.S.$100.

Figure 2-7: A force-feedback joystick works best with software that contains feedback capability. One of the classic feedback games is Sierra Trophy Bass. You use the joystick as a fishing rod to cast out your lure. When a fish grabs the bait, you'll feel a tug. Click PlayIt! to see it.

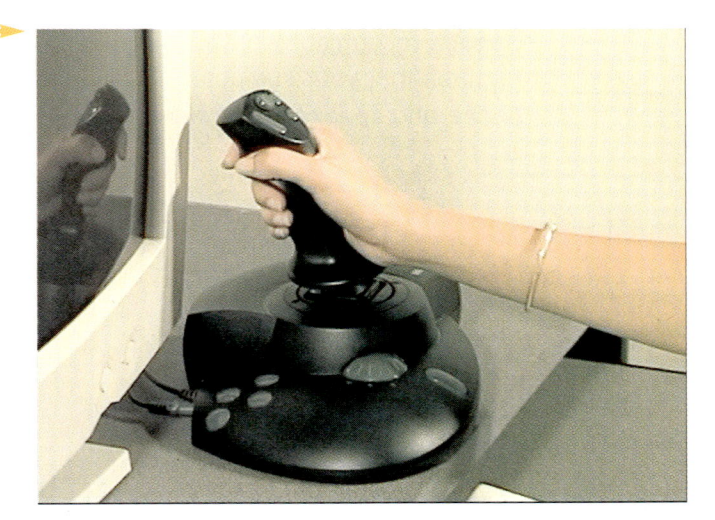

■Hardware
continued

Fans of the original Star Trek will remember Captain Kirk dictating his captain's log to the on-board computer. That was back in 1966. So after all these years, why aren't we talking to our computers? **Speech recognition**, sometimes referred to as voice recognition, is the ability of a computer to identify and interpret human speech. It has not been an easy technology to successfully implement. Even recognizing a single word such as "pen" can be difficult. A Southerner might pronounce the word more like "pin." Coming from a New Englander, it might sound like "payen." A person with a cold might make it sound like "fenmph!" Background noise can also create interference. And how is the computer supposed to know whether you're talking to it or yelling at your dog?

After many years of laboratory research, speech recognition is finally emerging as a viable technology. Many people would prefer to compose a document by dictating, rather than by typing. Is this option possible today? The answer is a qualified "yes." Speech recognition works, but there's a little more to it than just connecting a microphone to your PC and talking into it.

Before you can dictate to your PC, you must install speech-recognition software and train it to understand your speech patterns. This training consists of reading a fairly lengthy section of text provided by the software manufacturer. Today's speech-recognition software has a limited vocabulary—20,000 to 60,000 words, depending on the software you've chosen. You can add new words through a training process in which you type in a new word and repeat it several times. Even after training, however, the software sometimes makes mistakes. For example, you might dictate, "He knew better, but he ate eight steaks." The software interprets this sentence as "He new better, but he 88 stakes." Obviously, it is important to proofread documents that you dictate before printing them.

Speech-recognition software is priced from U.S.$49 to U.S.$700. It typically requires that your computer be equipped for sound input and output using a microphone and speakers or a headset.

Figure 2-8: Using today's speech-recognition software is a learning experience both for you and for the software, but you might find the end result worth the effort. Click the PlayIt! button to see speech-recognition technology in action.

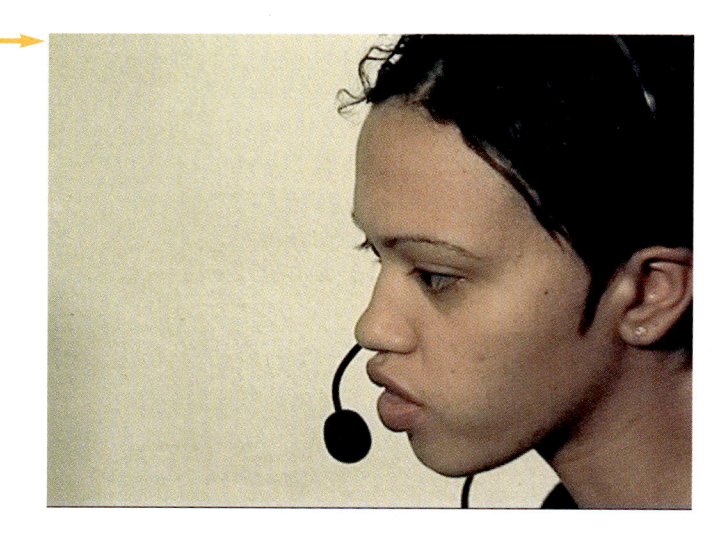

Chapter 2: Looking at Windows   23

■Tutorial
How to use Windows controls

Windows controls are fairly easy to use, but there are certainly many different types: menus, buttons, lists, check boxes, spin boxes, option buttons, and scroll bars. Why such a variety? Different controls allow you to enter different types of specifications. For example, a spin box might be ideal for indicating how many copies of a document you want to print, whereas option buttons might be better for choosing whether to print the whole document or a single page.

Microsoft provides a standard set of Windows controls that you'll find in virtually all application software. Knowing how these controls work makes it easier to learn new software. In this tutorial, you'll have an opportunity to practice using a variety of Windows controls.

When you have completed the tutorial, you should be able to:
- Use the Start button to start a program.
- Identify useful controls on the taskbar.
- Use menus and dialog boxes.
- Use check boxes, option buttons, spin boxes, lists, ToolTips, and scroll bars.

Figure 2-9: *Click the PlayIt! button to begin the tutorial and try out Windows controls such as those described below. Estimated time: 20–25 minutes. Tracking Disk points: 10.*

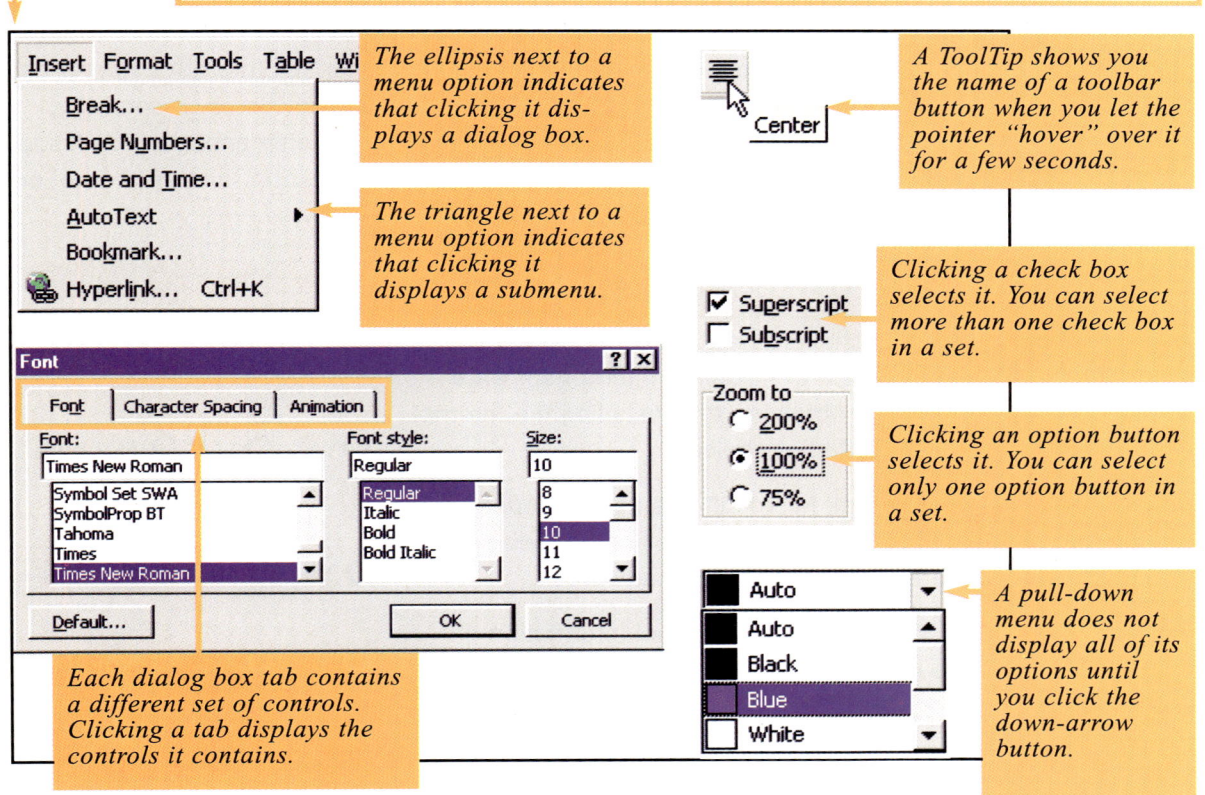

The ellipsis next to a menu option indicates that clicking it displays a dialog box.

The triangle next to a menu option indicates that clicking it displays a submenu.

A ToolTip shows you the name of a toolbar button when you let the pointer "hover" over it for a few seconds.

Clicking a check box selects it. You can select more than one check box in a set.

Clicking an option button selects it. You can select only one option button in a set.

Each dialog box tab contains a different set of controls. Clicking a tab displays the controls it contains.

A pull-down menu does not display all of its options until you click the down-arrow button.

▪Issue
Monopoly is not just a game

In a recent U.S. congressional hearing, a senator asked everyone present to raise their hands if they owned a computer. Almost every hand went up. Next, he asked everyone who had a PC to keep their hands up. A few Macintosh computer owners lowered their hands. Finally, the senator asked those who were using the Microsoft Windows operating system to keep their hands raised. All the hands stayed up. "Now that's a monopoly!" concluded the senator, triumphantly.

A **monopoly** is the exclusive control of a trade, commodity, or service. Does Microsoft have a software monopoly? It is certainly true that more than 80% of the world's computers run Microsoft Windows. However, a monopoly is not necessarily bad—not unless a company uses it to illegally eliminate competition.

Microsoft has been rapidly expanding the features and capabilities of its operating system software. In the past you needed to purchase numerous add-on programs to diagnose hardware problems, add sound capability, display videos, and so on; today this capability is included in Windows. Consumers benefit because they don't have to purchase add-ons. However, an unfavorable result could be that other companies have little hope of publishing and selling similar add-on products.

How many of these add-ons can Microsoft include in its operating system? Some U.S. senators tried to draw a line to prevent Microsoft from including software called Internet Explorer that's designed for surfing the Internet. They maintained that the effect on a competing software product called Netscape Navigator would be devastating. Microsoft was given an ultimatum—either sell Internet Explorer as a separate product or include its competitor's product in the Windows operating system as well. Microsoft refused to comply, and a court battle ensued. This issue has many interesting facets. You might want to explore it further on the Internet or at your local library before you answer the questions below.

What do you think?

1. If you purchase a new computer, would you prefer to use preinstalled Internet software instead of obtaining and installing the Internet software of your choice?   ◯ Yes ◯ No ◯ Not sure

2. Do you think Microsoft has used its operating system monopoly to illegally force people to use its Internet Explorer software?   ◯ Yes ◯ No ◯ Not sure

3. Did you try to find additional information on this issue?   ◯ Yes ◯ No ◯ Not sure

Save It!

Chapter 2: Looking at Windows

QuickCheck A

1. The Windows _____ appears on the screen when the boot process is complete and remains in the background as you use other software programs.

2. If two programs are running at the same time, you can switch between them using the buttons on the _____.

3. A(n) _____ box provides you with controls for entering specifications for a task or command.

4. True or false? Microsoft Windows is classified as application software. _____

5. True or false? Wide variations in pronunciation were one factor that delayed speech-recognition technology from becoming a standard part of the user interface. _____

Check It!

QuickCheck B

Indicate the letter of the desktop element you use to perform each of the following tasks:

1. Close a window ____

2. Display a menu containing the Print option ____

3. Display the Start menu ____

4. Take a shortcut to a menu command ____

5. Shrink a window to a button on the taskbar ____

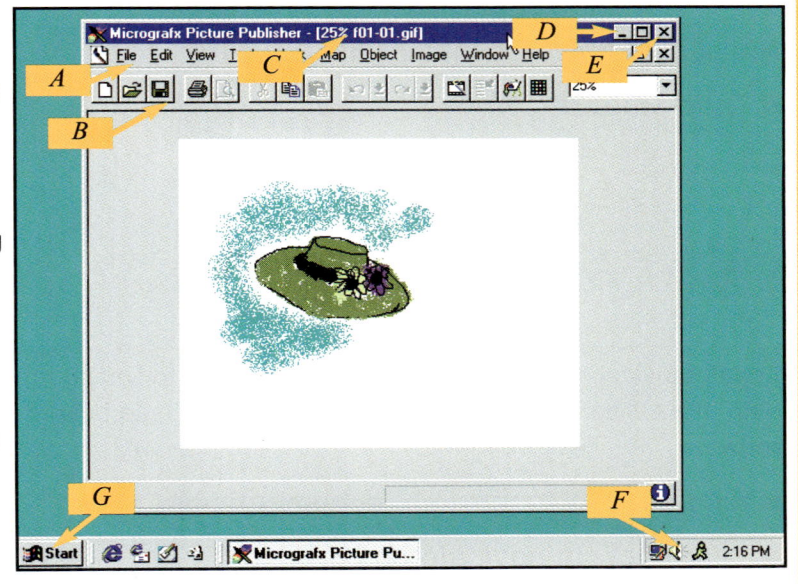

Check It!

Get It?

While using the Book-on-CD, click the Get It? button to see if you can answer ten randomly selected questions from Chapter 2.

Get It?

Chapter 3
Installing and Learning Software

What's Inside?

Chapter 3 provides you with some handy tips for figuring out how to use the software you currently have and for installing new software on your PC.

- FAQs:

Where's the instruction manual?	27
What's a PDF?	28
How do I use online Help?	29
What's the purpose of the paperclip cartoon?	30
Can I contact the software company for help?	31

- Hardware: Install and uninstall software on your PC — 32
- Tutorial: How to download and install software from the Internet — 35
- Issue: Is it legal to install this software? — 36
- QuickChecks — 37

What's on the CD?

Chapter 3 videos and screen tours show you how to find information about your software using Help, the Office Assistant, and PDFs. Plus, you'll see how to install, uninstall, and download software.

- Find out how to use PDF documentation — 28
- Learn how to navigate online Help — 29
- Watch the Office Assistant in action — 30
- Explore the contents of a software box — 32
- Learn how to install software from floppy disks or CDs — 33
- Learn the recommended way to uninstall software — 34
- Find out how to use the GrabIt! button to get software from the Internet — 35

Chapter 3: Installing and Learning Software 27

■FAQ where's the instruction manual?

When you're installing software or learning how to use it, you might need to refer to **software documentation**. Software publishers typically provide several types of documentation, and each type serves a specific purpose.

A **reference manual**, sometimes called a user manual or user reference, contains detailed descriptions of the software's features. Don't try to read this manual from cover to cover! Like a dictionary or encyclopedia, you should use it to look up information when you run into a problem or when you want to find out how a particular software feature works.

An **installation guide** provides information about installing the software on your PC. Sometimes it is separate from the reference manual—you typically find this guide in the CD case.

A **Readme file** is an online document that contains installation notes and information about last-minute changes to the software and its features.

A **software tutorial** provides step-by-step lessons on how to use the features of a software product. Tutorials come in several formats, including those you view on the screen, those you read in a book, those you watch on video tape, and those you listen to on audio cassette.

The documentation that's included with a software package is not always sufficient for everyone, so you might want to purchase supplemental reference manuals and tutorials from a bookstore or computer store. When selecting a manual or tutorial, make sure that it is written for the same version of the software that you're using.

Figure 3-1: A Readme file is sometimes installed along with the software and then can be accessed from the Programs menu. If the Readme file is not installed, you can locate it manually. You'll read about locating files in Chapter 4 and Chapter 5.

Typically, a Readme file contains technical information about specialized problems. If you can't find a solution in the reference manual, the Readme file is the next place to look.

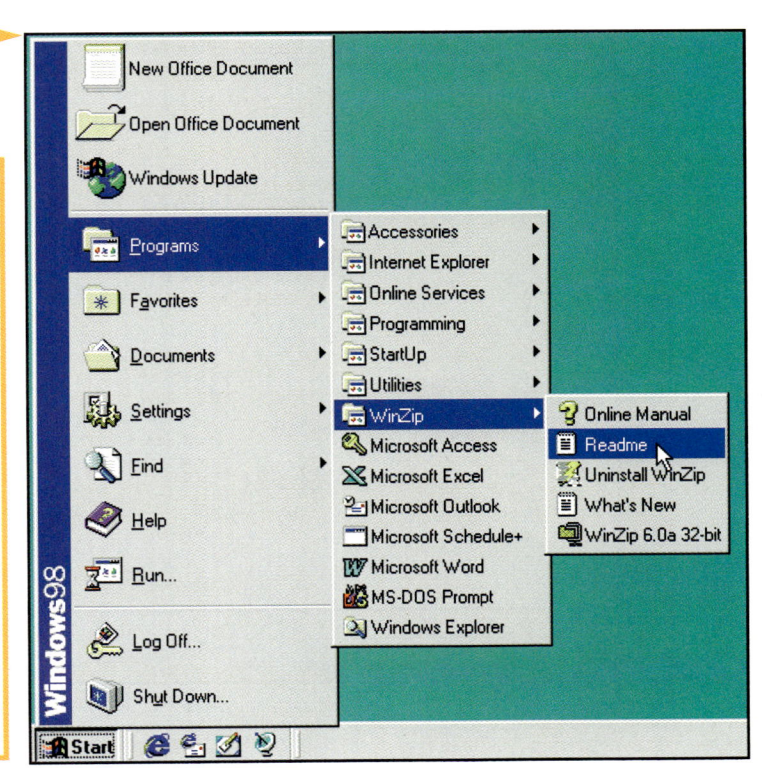

■FAQ What's a PDF?

In the past, software reference manuals were typically distributed in printed format. As publishers added more features to their software, however, printed manuals became huge and costly. For example, one popular software tool for computer programmers included printed documentation weighing 26 pounds! The trend today is to convert reference manuals into electronic documents that can be viewed on a computer screen, stored on a CD, or distributed on the Internet.

A **PDF** (portable document format file) is a special type of electronic document that can be displayed on virtually any PC. Many software publishers use PDFs for software documentation because the text and diagrams they contain appear on the screen just about the same way they would look in a printed book. PDFs are also used for many other types of documents. Examples include back issues of magazines, NCAA sports statistics, and U.S. Census Bureau tables and graphs.

To display a PDF on your PC's screen, you need a software program called **Adobe Acrobat Reader**. Luckily, this program is available for free—it comes preinstalled on many computer systems, it is supplied on most CDs that contain PDFs, or you can transfer it to your computer from the Internet.

Figure 3-2: Click the PlayIt! button to discover how to use Adobe Acrobat Reader to look through a PDF file that contains documentation for a software product.

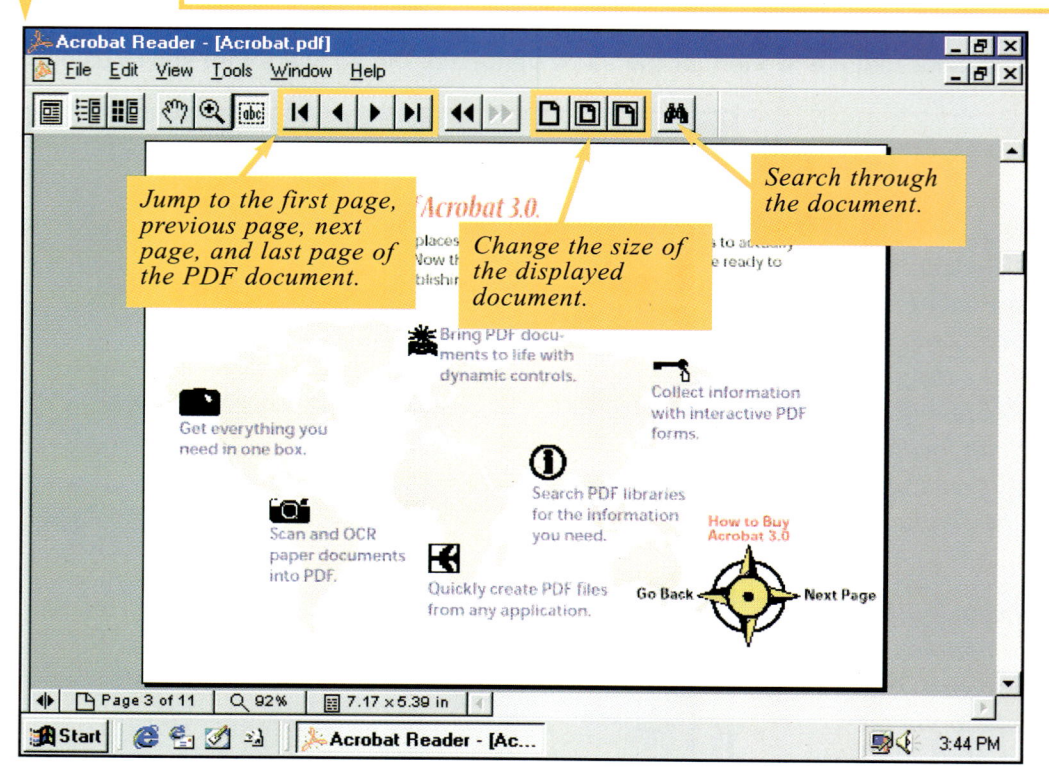

Chapter 3: Installing and Learning Software 35

■Tutorial
How to download and install software from the Internet

Grab It!
Adobe Acrobat Reader

Many companies and organizations maintain Internet computer "sites," containing software, documentation, and other information that is available to the public. The Internet is a great source for free software and trial versions of commercial software. For example, if you need the Adobe Acrobat Reader software, you can find it on the Internet. The GrabIt! buttons featured in the margins of this book will help you locate software on the Internet.

Before you can install and use software from the Internet, you have to transfer it to your PC. This process is called **downloading**. If you're using a PC at work or at school, check with a supervisor to make sure that it's OK to download software. Some software is very large and takes a long time to download, so be prepared to wait. After you download software, you should follow the rules given for its use.

When you have completed the tutorial, you should be able to:
- Use a GrabIt! button to download software from the Internet.
- Print the installation instructions.
- Understand how installing software from the Internet differs from installing software from a CD.

Play It!

Figure 3-9: Click the PlayIt! button to learn how to download and install software from the Internet. You can use this tutorial even if you don't currently have Internet access. Estimated time: 15–20 minutes. Tracking Disk points: 10.

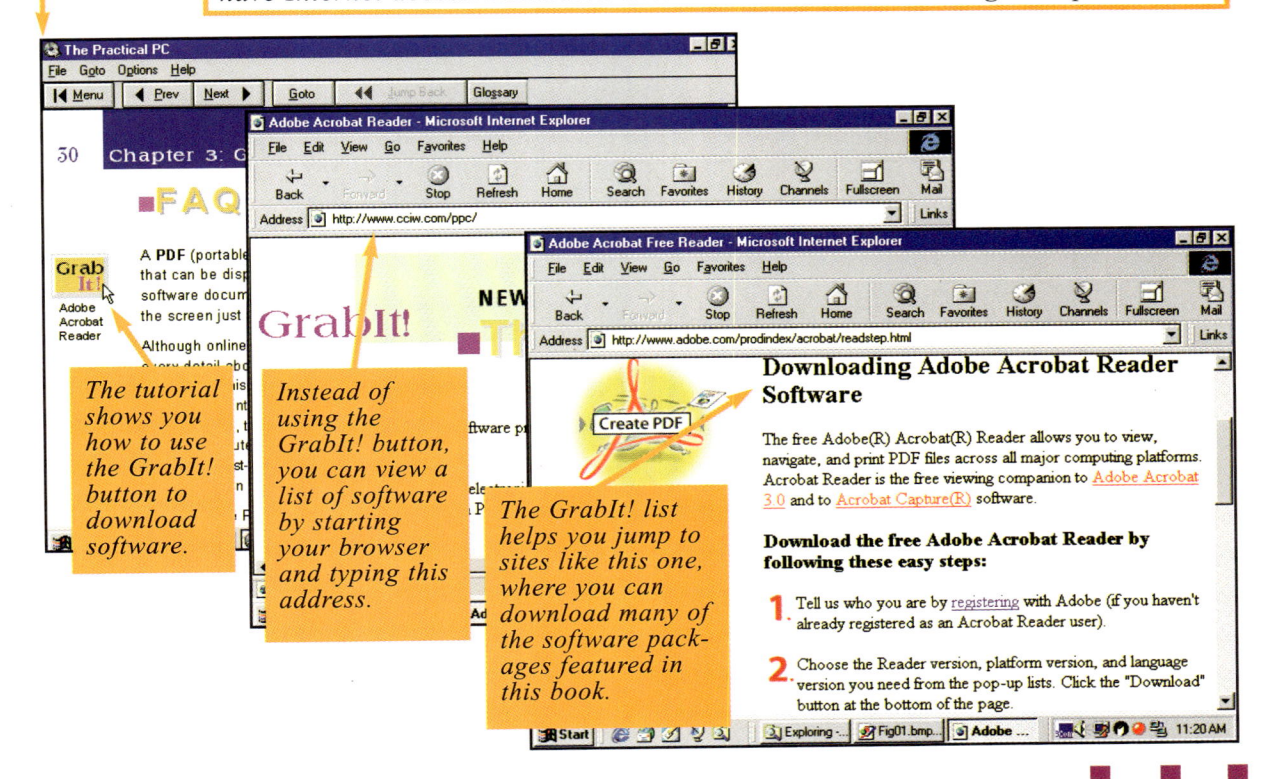

The tutorial shows you how to use the GrabIt! button to download software.

Instead of using the GrabIt! button, you can view a list of software by starting your browser and typing this address.

The GrabIt! list helps you jump to sites like this one, where you can download many of the software packages featured in this book.

■Issue
Is it legal to install this software?

To answer the question "Is it legal to install this software?" you'll have to read the package or documentation to find out whether it is commercial, freeware, shareware, or demo software. Like books, movies, and music, software is protected by copyright law in most countries. Under copyright law it is illegal to copy software except to install it and to make a backup copy in case the original version stops working correctly.

Commercial software is marketed for a profit by a software publisher that requires strict adherence to copyright rules. This software often comes with a **license agreement** that further restricts the way you can use it. Look for the terms of the license on the box, CD case, or disk packaging.

Although copyright law protects all software, a software developer can ease the restrictions on copying by creating freeware, shareware, or demo software. **Freeware** is usually provided free of charge. The software developer retains the copyright, but gives blanket permission to download the software from the Internet, install it, copy it multiple times, and give copies to friends. **Shareware** is also copyrighted, but the developer lets you install the software and share it with friends on a trial basis for a short period of time. You and your friends are on your honor to register and pay for the software if you use it beyond the trial period. A **demo** is a special version of commercial software that is often scaled down for demonstration purposes. You can install the demo software to see how it works before you purchase the full commercial version.

If you don't follow regulations for the use of commercial, shareware, freeware, and demo software you might not be using it legally. Software that is illegally copied, installed, sold, and used is called **pirated software**. The Software Publishers Association collects piracy statistics and offers a toll-free hotline for anonymously reporting software piracy. It estimates that U.S.$12 billion of software is used illegally, often in places you would least expect it, such as schools and businesses.

What do you think?

1. Have you ever used pirated software? ○ Yes ○ No ○ Not sure

2. Before reading about this issue, did you understand the difference between freeware, shareware, commercial, and demo software? ○ Yes ○ No ○ Not sure

3. If you discovered pirated software in use at your school or office, would you report it? ○ Yes ○ No ○ Not sure

Save It!

Chapter 3: Installing and Learning Software 37

QuickCheck A

1. True or false? You must install all of the program modules from the distribution CD every time you want to use the software it contains. _____

2. True or false? The easiest way to access a PDF is to click Help on the menu bar at the top of the screen. _____

3. The operating system maintains a(n) _____ to keep track of the hardware and software installed on your PC.

4. You have to _____ software from the Internet before you can install it.

5. You can freely copy and install _____, but if you use it beyond the trial period you are supposed to register it and pay the developer a fee for its use.

Check It!

QuickCheck B

Type the letter of the object that helps you accomplish each of the tasks listed below.

1. Access Windows Help _____

2. Get help by entering a question _____

3. Look at a list of Help topics _____

4. Look through the entire text of online Help to find a specific word or term _____

5. Activate the Help pointer _____

A — pointer with ?
B — ? icon
C — paperclip with lightbulb
D — Index
E — Contents
F — Search
G — Options
H — Start

Check It!

Get It?

While using the Book-on-CD, click the Get It? button to see if you can answer ten randomly selected questions from Chapter 3.

Get It?

Chapter 4

Naming and Saving Files

What's Inside?

All of the documents, pictures, and music that you create with your PC are stored as files. Chapter 4 helps you understand how to best name your files, where to store them, and how to use them. It emphasizes how to open and save files from within your application software.

- **FAQs:**

What's a file?	39
Can I use any name for a file?	40
What's a file extension?	41
Can I convert a file from one format to another?	42
How do I tell my PC where to store a file?	43

- Hardware: Floppy disks and floppy disk drives   44
- Tutorial: How to create and save files   47
- Issue: Should governments regulate encryption?   48
- QuickChecks   49

What's on the CD?

Don't miss the Chapter 4 videos and screen tours that provide all the basics about files and floppy disk storage. You'll pick up information on hard disk storage in Chapter 5.

- Learn two ways to open a file   39
- Discover how to convert a file from one format to another   42
- Learn how to select a storage device, create a folder, and follow a path   43
- Dissect a floppy disk   44
- Find out how to format a floppy disk   46
- Take a step-by-step tutorial to create, save, open, and modify files   47

Chapter 4: Naming and Saving Files

■FAQ What's a file?

A **file** is a collection of data that has a name and is stored on a computer disk, tape, or CD. Virtually all of the information that you can access from your PC is stored as files. For example, each document, graph, or picture that you create with application software is stored as a file. The Web pages that you view from the Internet are also stored as files, as are the program modules shipped on the distribution CD of a software package. Files can be divided into two categories: executable files and data files. Understanding the difference between these two categories is important because you use executable files in a different way than you use data files.

An **executable file** is a program module containing instructions that tell your PC how to perform specific tasks. Your PC "executes" these instructions to complete tasks such as sorting lists, searching for information, printing, or making calculations. For example, the word processing program that tells your PC how to display and print text is an executable file. The main executable files on your computer are listed on the Windows Programs menu, and you typically use this menu to select the one that you want your PC to execute.

A **data file** contains words, numbers, and pictures that you can manipulate. For example, a document that you create using word processing software is a data file. You have several ways to access a data file, including the Start menu's Documents option and the Open option on your application software's File menu.

Figure 4-1: You can open recently used files from the Documents menu. Click the PlayIt! button to learn another handy method for opening files.

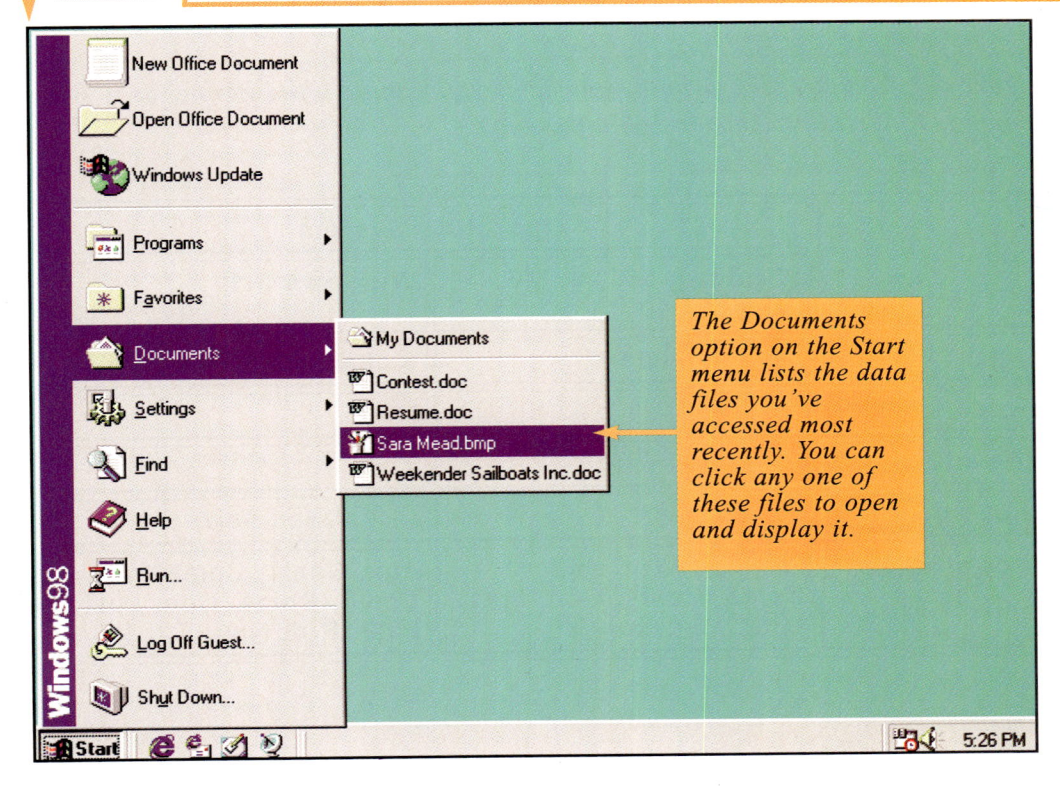

The Documents option on the Start menu lists the data files you've accessed most recently. You can click any one of these files to open and display it.

Chapter 4: Naming and Saving Files

■FAQ Can I use any name for a file?

You'll create many files as you use application software. You'll create documents with word processing software, graphs with spreadsheet software, and pictures with graphics software. As you're creating documents, graphs, and pictures, your PC holds your data in memory. When you're ready for your PC to **save a file** by transferring it to more permanent disk storage, you must give it a unique name.

PC operating systems originally limited the length of a file name to eight characters or less. Also, a file name could not contain any spaces. These limitations made it difficult to create descriptive file names. A file name such as "Letmjord" might indicate a letter written to Michael Jordan. "Orgch599" might be the name of a file containing an organizational chart updated in May 1999. If you use a PC with Windows 3.1, you will be limited to eight-character file names. Even when using more recent versions of Windows, you might encounter older software that has not been updated to allow longer file names. If you're not sure about file name limitations for an application, check Help or refer to the reference manual.

Beginning with Windows 95, file names containing as many as 255 characters became permissable. With Windows 95, 98, and NT you can use file names such as "Letter to Michael Jordan" and "Organizational Chart-Updated May 1999". This capability, which came to be known as **long file names**, makes it much easier to find a specific file based on its name.

Long file names also allow you to control capitalization. Most people tend to use the same capitalization for file names as they would use for a title, using uppercase for the first letter of every word except articles and prepositions. Windows is not **case sensitive**, however. Even though you can use uppercase and lowercase, the file name "Report" is the same as "report" or "REPORT".

Figure 4-2: You can give virtually any name you want to a file as long as it conforms to the rules summarized in this table.

| | Operating System ||
	Windows 95, 98, ME, NT, 2000	**Windows 3.1**
Maximum length	255 characters	8 characters
Spaces allowed?	Yes	No
Numbers allowed?	Yes	Yes
Characters not allowed	\ ? : " < >		/ [ ] ; " \ : ,	* ?
File names not allowed	Aux, Com1, Com2, Com3, Com4, Con, Lpt1, Lpt2, Prn, Nul	Aux, Com1, Com2, Com3, Com4, Con, Lpt1, Lpt2, Prn, Nul

Chapter 4: Naming and Saving Files

▪FAQ What's a file extension?

A **file extension** is a set of characters added to a file name that indicates the file's type or origin. For example, the file extension .doc indicates a file that was created with Microsoft Word word processing software. A file extension is separated from the main file name with a period, but no spaces. File extensions have a maximum length of three characters. The full name of your letter to Michael Jordan, including the file extension, would be "Letter to Michael Jordan.doc".

Each software application that you use typically has a default file extension. In "tech speak," a **default** is a standard setting that always goes into effect unless you manually change it. A default file extension is the extension that an application uses unless you specify otherwise. For Microsoft Word the default file extension is .doc, for Microsoft Excel it is .xls, for Adobe Acrobat Reader it is .pdf, and for Microsoft Paint it is .bmp.

Hundreds of file extensions exist, and the situation would be pretty grim if you had to remember the extension for each program you use. Happily, you don't generally have to memorize file extensions—instead, your software automatically adds the correct one when you save a file.

A file extension indicates the **file format** in which it is stored. File extensions are sometimes abbreviated versions of the file format names. For example, the three-character .htm file extension indicates that the file is stored in HTML file format.

Files are stored in different formats because they contain different types of data. A document, for example, is typically stored in a different format than a video is. Some file formats, however, allow you to include multiple types of data in a single file, such as a document and a picture. Within a category such as documents, different file formats allow different features. Both DOC and TXT file formats store documents. The TXT file format stores only plain text, whereas the DOC file format allows you to store boldface, italic, and underlined text.

Figure 4-3: A file's format indicates what type of data it contains. This table shows you some of the many file formats that exist for each type of file.

File Contents	File Format
Document	DOC TXT WPS WPD WRI RTF SAM ASCII
Database	MDB DBF
Spreadsheet	XLS WK4
Graphic	BMP TIFF GIF JPEG EPSF PCX WMF
Sound	WAV MIDI
Video	AVI MPEG MOV
Web page	HTML
Programs	EXE COM SYS DLL VBX OCX

Chapter 4: Naming and Saving Files

■FAQ Can I convert a file from one format to another?

A software application typically works with the one file format indicated by the default file extension. Microsoft Works, for example, uses WPS as its document file format. This application is designed to display the contents of WPS files and provide you with tools to manipulate what you see displayed. But suppose that you receive a disk containing a document in TXT format. Can Microsoft Works display this document? Most software includes **import routines** that open different file formats and convert them to the default format. Although Microsoft Works cannot work directly with the TXT file format, its import routine can open documents in TXT format and then convert them to WPS format. An **export routine** allows you to save files in a format other than your software's default format.

Sometimes you must be creative to take advantage of your software's import and export routines. Suppose that you have a customer who uses word processing software that produces documents in SAM format. Your software does not have an import routine for this format, and your customer does not have an export routine for your WPS format. Can you exchange files? The answer is yes, if you can find a common format on your lists of import and export routines. You might discover that your customer can export RTF (rich text format) files and you can import them. Your customer can then convert the SAM file into RTF format. When you receive the RTF file, your software can import it and convert it to a WPS file.

Figure 4-4: Most software displays a list of import formats in the Open dialog box and a list of export formats in the Save dialog box. Click the PlayIt! button to see how to import and export document files with Microsoft Word.

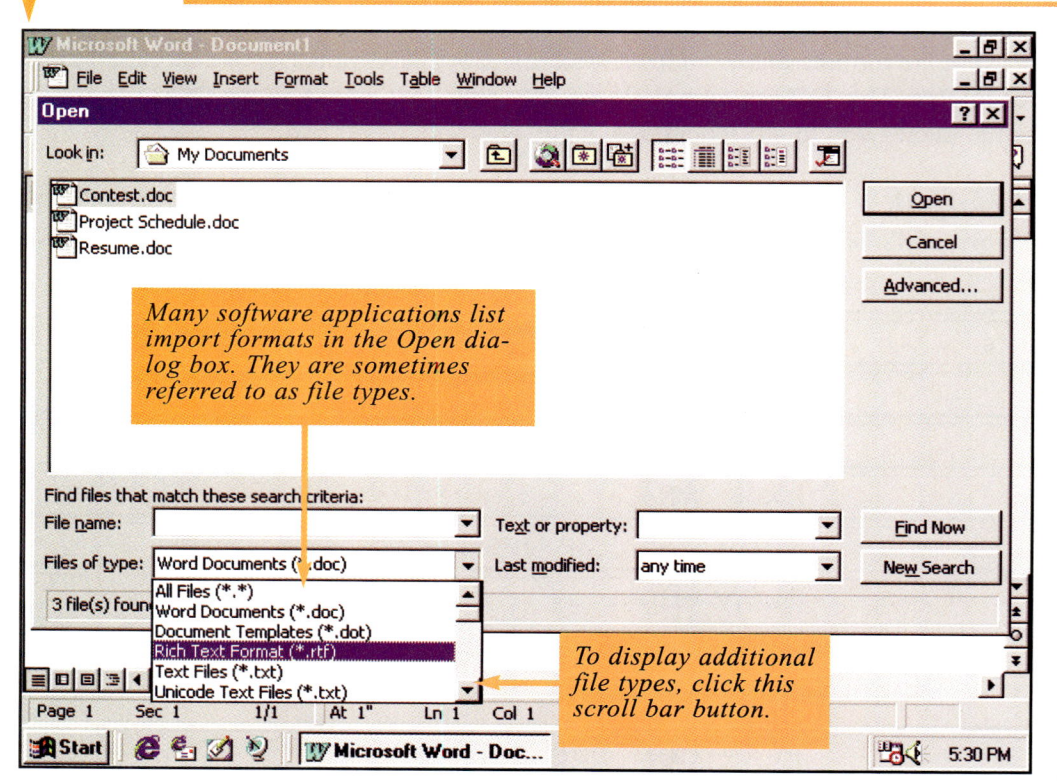

Many software applications list import formats in the Open dialog box. They are sometimes referred to as file types.

To display additional file types, click this scroll bar button.

Chapter 4: Naming and Saving Files 43

■FAQ How do I tell my PC where to store a file?

You'll usually store files on your PC's hard disk—of all your storage devices, it has the highest storage capacity and the quickest retrieval time. If you want to transport a file, however, you might choose to store it on a floppy disk. If you want to share the file with others, you could store it on a network hard disk. Each storage device on your PC is identified by a unique **device letter**. Typically, the device letter for the floppy disk drive is A and for the hard disk drive it is C. If your PC is part of a network, the main network drive is usually identified by the letter F. Your PC's hard disk drive is called "drive C," the floppy disk drive is "drive A," and so on.

When you save a file, your software asks where to store it. You can select a storage device from the list provided or enter the device letter with the file name. For example, if you enter C:Journey Home.doc, the file will be stored on your PC's hard disk. Notice that a colon separates the device letter from the file name.

Folders allow you to group and organize files for easy retrieval. You might create a folder called Genealogy to hold all your files on family history. The device letter, folder, file name, and extension provide the information necessary to store a file in a certain place, then locate it again. This information is sometimes referred to as a **path**, because like a woodland path it leads you to a destination. The path C:\Genealogy\Journey Home.doc provides you and your PC with the information necessary to save and locate the Journey Home file.

Figure 4-5: Click the PlayIt! button to see how to select a storage device, create a folder, and follow a path to a file.

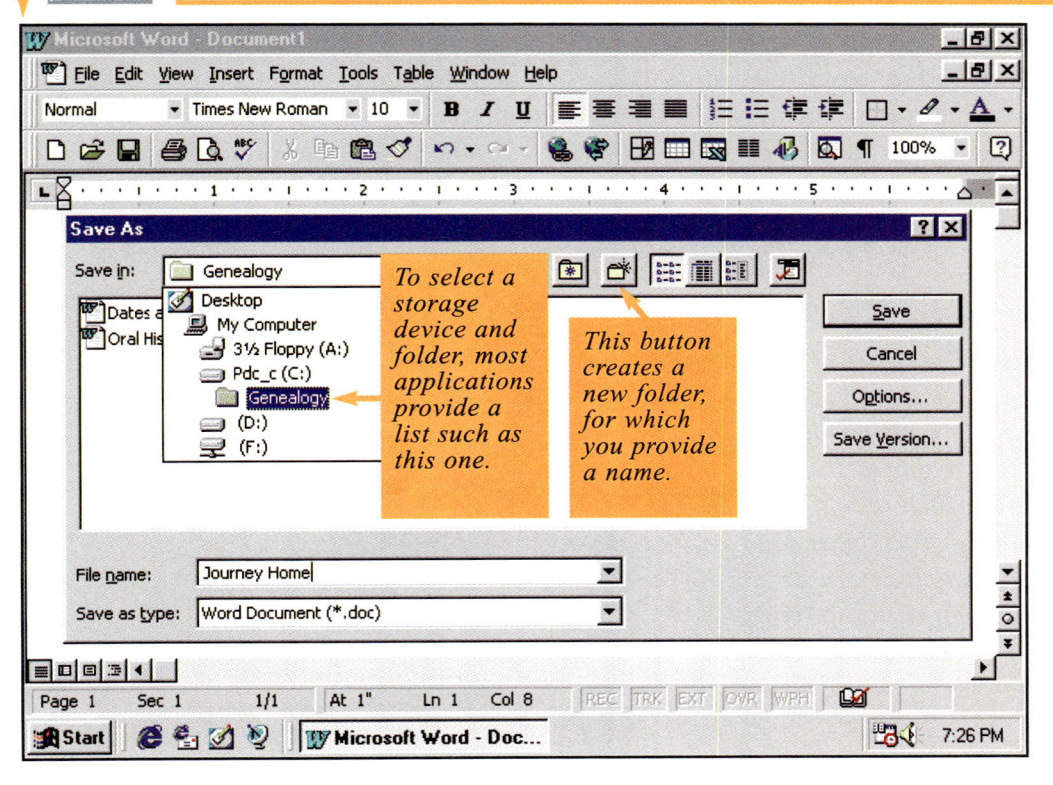

To select a storage device and folder, most applications provide a list such as this one.

This button creates a new folder, for which you provide a name.

■Hardware
Floppy disks and floppy disk drives

A **floppy disk** is a removable storage medium typically housed in a 3.5-inch square case. It is useful when you want to store one or more files on a disk that you can remove and transfer to a different PC. Once you've stored a file on a floppy disk, you can transport it between a school lab and your home PC, or between PCs at work and home. You can also send a floppy disk through the mail to share files with friends or clients. You can save a copy of an important file on a floppy disk and stash it in a secure location such as a bank safe-deposit box.

The disk surface that holds data is protected by a rigid plastic case. A spring-loaded **access hatch cover** on the disk case opens to expose the disk surface when the disk is inserted into a disk drive. You should always insert the metal access hatch first, making sure that the disk label faces up. The disk case also contains a small **write-protect window**. If you open this window, your PC cannot change the data on the disk. This feature is handy when your disk contains an important file that should not be erased or modified.

A floppy disk offers durable and dependable storage if cared for properly. Avoid exposing the disk to high temperatures. Be careful not to leave it on the dashboard of your car in the summer sun, because it might warp or melt. A disk that has been left in freezing temperatures should be allowed to warm to room temperature before you use it. The data on a disk is stored as magnetized particles, so keep disks away from refrigerator magnets and other magnetic fields.

For long-term storage, a clean and dry environment is best. Moisture encourages the growth of mold and mildew that can make a disk unusable. In humid climates, store disks in a sealed plastic bag along with some moisture-reducing desiccant packets. Dust and smoke can also interfere with the ability of the disk drive to retrieve data from a disk. Storing your disks in a covered plastic box can prevent dust and smoke buildup.

Figure 4-6: *Click PlayIt! for an in-depth look at a floppy disk. A floppy disk gets its name from the thin, flexible disk that's sealed inside its square plastic case. Despite the hard plastic case, you should not call it a "hard disk." Chapter 5 explains more about the difference between floppy disks and hard disks.*

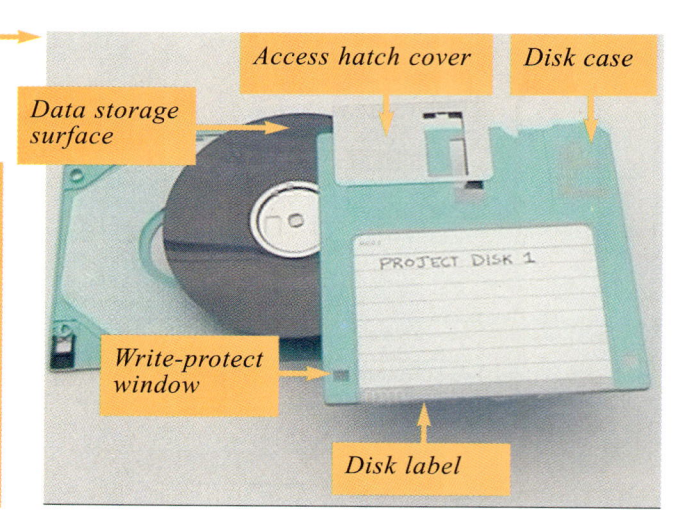

Chapter 4: Naming and Saving Files 45

■Hardware
continued

A **floppy disk drive** is the device that stores data on a floppy disk and later retrieves that data so you can see it on the screen. Virtually every computer has a floppy disk drive. If you need to share a file with other PC users, it is safe to assume that they'll have storage devices that work with a floppy disk.

Unfortunately, many of today's files—especially graphics and sound recordings—are much too large to fit on a floppy disk. New high-capacity disks store more data than a standard floppy disk but still feature the same durability. Storage capacity is measured in bytes, kilobytes (one thousand bytes, abbreviated KB), megabytes (one million bytes, abbreviated as MB), or gigabytes (one billion bytes, abbreviated as GB). A **byte** stores the equivalent of a single character, such as a letter, number, or punctuation mark. A standard floppy disk has the capacity to store approximately 1.44 MB. A larger-capacity disk called a **Zip disk** stores 100 or 250 MB. Another popular high-capacity disk, called a **SuperDisk**, stores 120 MB.

The type of disk that you can use depends on the disk drives installed in your PC. A standard floppy disk drive accepts only 1.44 MB floppy disks and older low-capacity 720 KB disks. To use Zip disks, your PC requires a special Zip drive. Typically, a Zip drive would not replace a standard floppy disk drive because it does not work with standard floppy disks. SuperDisks also require a special type of disk drive called an LS-120 drive. An LS-120 drive works with both SuperDisks and standard floppy disks. For this reason, it has become a popular replacement for the standard floppy disk drive. To discover whether your PC has a Zip or LS-120 drive, look for a Zip or SuperDisk logo on the front of the drive or refer to the user manual for your PC.

Figure 4-7: Pictured from top to bottom: Zip, SuperDisk, and standard floppy disks and drives.

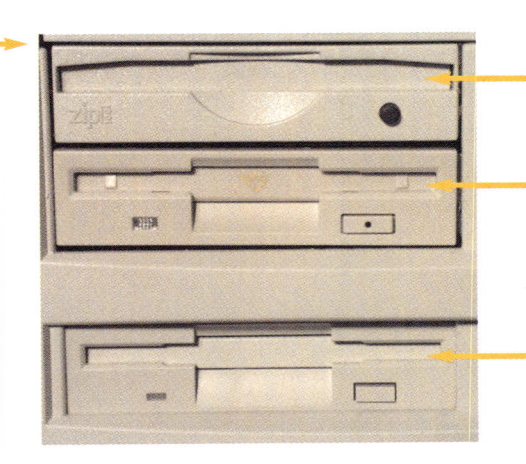

■Hardware continued

What actually happens when a disk drive stores data on a disk? The answer to this question explains why some disks can store more data than others and why a disk must be formatted before it can be used for data storage.

Internally, a PC represents data using 0s and 1s. For text, a special coding system called **ASCII** (American Standard Code for Information Interchange) uses series of 1s and 0s to represent letters, numbers, or punctuation marks. In some ways the ASCII code is similar to Morse code, but instead of using dots and dashes, ASCII uses 0s and 1s. For example, the ASCII code 01000001 represents an uppercase "A". To store this character on a disk, the disk drive uses a **read/write head** to magnetize tiny metallic particles on the disk surface. The magnetic polarization of each particle indicates whether it is a 1 or a 0. A group of eight polarized particles represents one character and requires one byte of storage space.

The size and density of the metallic particles determine the amount of data that can be packed into any given area on the disk surface. The smaller the particles and the more densely they are packed, the more data a disk can hold. It is just like packing fruit: you can get lots more lemons than watermelons into a box. This principle explains why a Zip disk can store more information than a standard floppy disk, even though both have approximately the same physical dimensions.

To simplify the process of storing and locating data, a disk is divided into concentric circles called **tracks**. These tracks are then divided into **sectors**. Each sector is numbered. Your PC's operating system records the sector numbers that hold the data for each of your files. The process of dividing a disk into sectors is called **formatting**. A disk must be formatted before you store data on it. Today, when you purchase disks, they're generally preformatted. You just need to read the label to make sure it indicates "IBM PC format," not "Mac format."

Figure 4-8: Click the PlayIt! button to walk through each step in the process of formatting a disk. If you purchase unformatted disks, you'll need to format them before you use them. Formatting erases all data on a disk. Before you reuse old disks, you might want to format them to erase unneeded data.

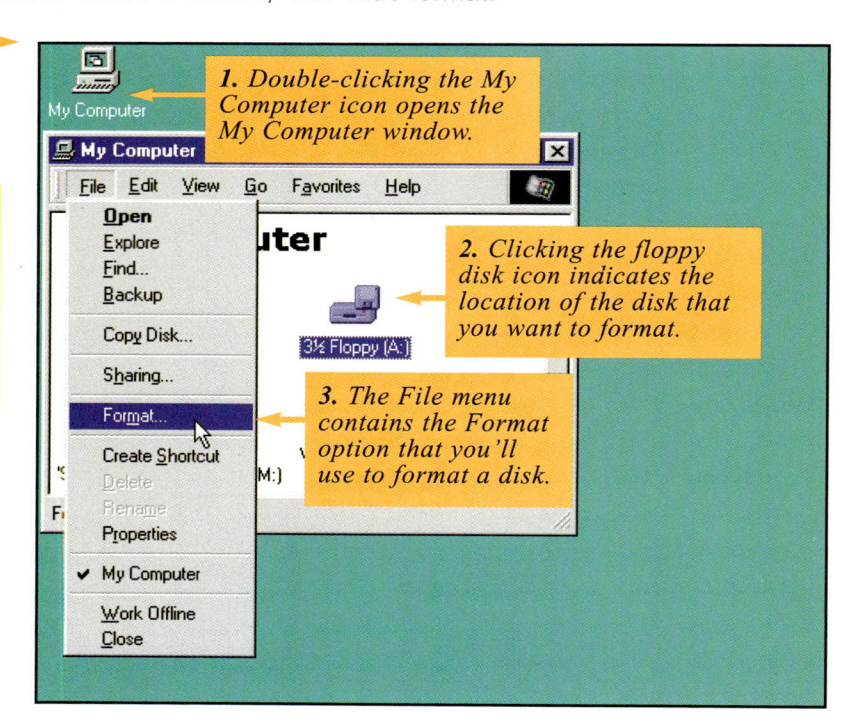

1. Double-clicking the My Computer icon opens the My Computer window.

2. Clicking the floppy disk icon indicates the location of the disk that you want to format.

3. The File menu contains the Format option that you'll use to format a disk.

Chapter 4: Naming and Saving Files

■Tutorial
How to create and save files

You can create files using several different techniques, but the process typically begins by opening the application that you'll use to enter your data. Depending on the application, you might have to use the New command before entering the text, graphics, or sounds for the new file. When you are ready to store the file, use the Save option on the File menu. To complete the save process, you will specify the device letter and folder for the file location, then give the file a name.

When you have completed the tutorial, you should be able to:
- Use the New option on the File menu to create a new document.
- Use the Save option on the File menu to save a document on disk.
- Specify the disk and folder in which a file will be located.
- Open a file, modify it, then use the Save As command to save the file under a different name.

Figure 4-9: Click the PlayIt! button to begin the tutorial and learn how to use File menu options to create, save, open, and modify a file. Estimated time: 15–20 minutes. Tracking Disk points: 10.

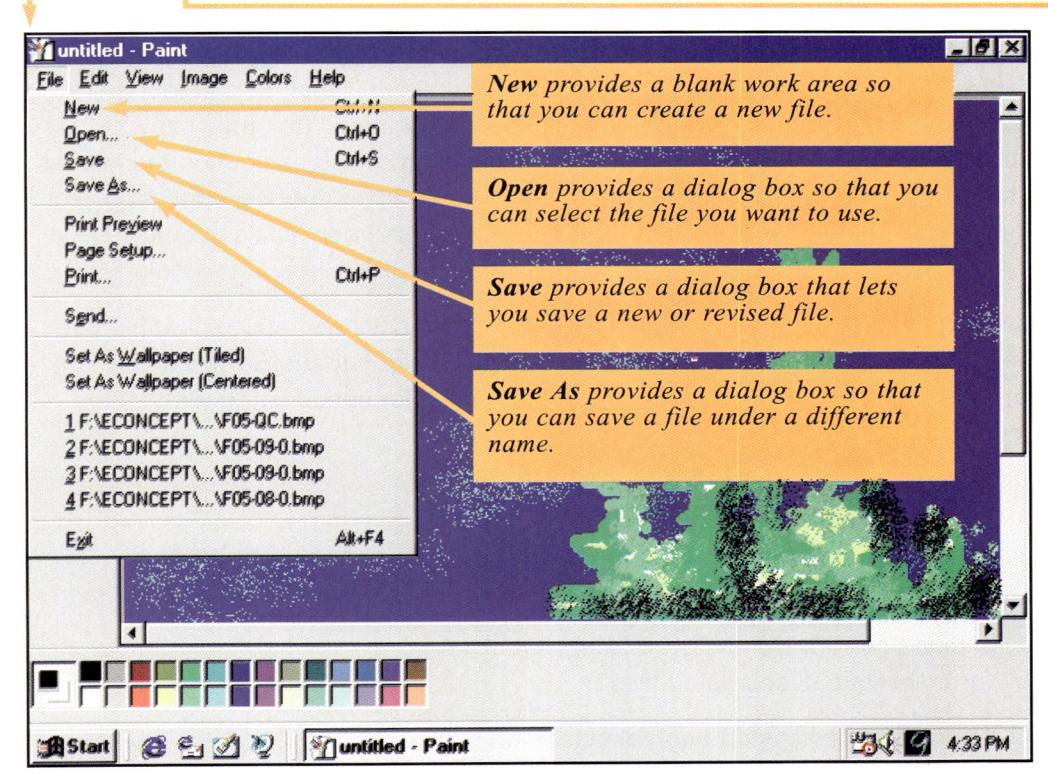

New provides a blank work area so that you can create a new file.

Open provides a dialog box so that you can select the file you want to use.

Save provides a dialog box that lets you save a new or revised file.

Save As provides a dialog box so that you can save a file under a different name.

■Issue
Should governments regulate encryption?

Grab It!
Encryption Software

Government agencies, banks, corporations, and individuals sometimes want to keep the contents of their computer files safe from prying eyes. **Encryption software** uses a secret code or "key" to scramble file content. In the course of normal transactions, decoding requires the use of the same type of encryption software and the "key" for unscrambling the file. Although cryptographers can use computer technology to break into encrypted files without the key, this task becomes more difficult as encryption techniques become more complex. Certain encryption techniques, called **strong encryption**, are almost impossible to break.

The increasing use of encrypted files is making some governments uneasy. Information about drug deals, international terrorism, and racketeering might be stored in encrypted format or transmitted on the Internet. What if law enforcement cryptographers can't break the code to access these documents?

Some governments would like to limit civilian use of encryption methods to those for which law enforcement agencies have the master decoding key. Civil rights advocates oppose this scheme because it seems to violate basic privacy rights—analogous to your local police demanding a copy of your house keys.

Some governments regulate strong encryption technology by classifying it as a military weapon. U.S. regulations, for example, make it illegal for a researcher to send strong encryption software to a colleague in China so that they can exchange encrypted research data. Even discussing strong encryption techniques in the presence of non-U.S. citizens could be illegal. Civil rights advocates object to such regulations as a violation of the right to speak freely in classrooms, academic conferences, and other public forums about encryption technologies.

The issues surrounding government control of encryption technologies have been debated during court cases such as *Junger* v. *Christopher* and *Bernstein* v. *Department of State*. A good source of additional information is the Electronic Frontier Foundation, on the Internet at www.eff.org.

What do you think?

1. Would you ever want to encrypt the files you have stored on your PC?   ◯ Yes ◯ No ◯ Not sure

2. Should your government have a universal key for unlocking all encrypted files?   ◯ Yes ◯ No ◯ Not sure

3. If someone devises an unbreakable encryption scheme, do you think that your government should attempt to keep it a secret?   ◯ Yes ◯ No ◯ Not sure

Save It!

Chapter 4: Naming and Saving Files   49

QuickCheck A

1. A(n) _____ file contains the documents and pictures that you create, whereas a(n) _____ file contains instructions that tell your PC how to perform specific tasks.

2. True or false? If your PC has Windows 98, you can name a file ACME Annual Report First Draft. _____

3. True or false? If your PC has Windows 98, you can have a file named Resume and a file named RESUME in the same folder. _____

4. The process of _____ a disk divides it into tracks and sectors.

5. C:\JobSearch\Resume.doc would be referred to as the file _____.

Check It!

QuickCheck B

Based on the settings shown in the Save As dialog box, fill in the boxes below to indicate where and how the file will be saved.

1. The file name will be _____.

2. The device letter is ____.

3. The folder name is _____.

4. The file extension is ____.

5. The file will be stored on a(n) _____ disk drive.

Check It!

Get It?

While using the Book-on-CD, click the Get It? button to see if you can answer ten randomly selected questions from Chapter 4.

Get It?

Chapter 5
Organizing Files and Folders

What's Inside?

Chapter 5 provides tips on organizing files and folders so that you can easily locate them. The Hardware section focuses on your PC's hard disk, with information on how it works and how to keep it performing at peak efficiency.

- **FAQs:**

How do I get a list of my files?	51
How do I change the name of a file?	52
What's the best organization for my files?	53
How do I copy files to other disks?	54
What if I run out of disk space?	55

- Hardware: Hard disk drives — 56
- Tutorial: How to find files — 59
- Issue: Are deleted files legally garbage? — 60
- QuickChecks — 61

What's on the CD?

In Chapter 5, you'll take an in-depth look at how to use Windows Explorer. You'll also go behind the scenes to explore the mysteries of your hard disk drive.

- Tour Windows Explorer — 51
- Learn two ways to rename a file — 52
- Discover how the experts move and copy files — 53
- Learn how to copy an entire floppy disk — 54
- Watch the Recycle Bin in action — 55
- Take a video tour inside a hard disk drive — 56
- Discover how to use defragmentation and other disk utilities — 58
- Take a step-by-step tutorial on finding files — 59

Chapter 5: Organizing Files and Folders 51

■FAQ   How do I get a list of my files?

Your application software's Open dialog box and Save dialog box provide a list of files, but their space limitations make it difficult to see the big picture—all of your PC's storage devices, folders, and files. For a complete list of files and a full set of tools for organizing those files, most PC experts turn to Windows Explorer.

Windows Explorer is a part of the Windows operating system that's designed to help you find and organize the files on your PC. It lists files in alphabetical order by title, in order by size, by type, or by date created so that you can search for a specific file. If locating a file is difficult because you've stored files in the wrong folder or you've jammed hundreds of files into the same folder, you might find it useful to periodically use Windows Explorer to streamline your file system. You can change file or folder names, move files to different folders, move folders to different disks, delete individual files, or delete entire folders and the files they contain.

To start Windows Explorer, select it from the Programs menu. Windows Explorer provides several methods for accomplishing file management tasks. Experts tend to prefer the right-click method that you'll learn in this book because it works for all the desktops available with Windows 95/98/ME and Windows NT/2000. **Right-clicking** means to press the right, not the left, mouse button. When you right-click a file name or folder, Windows Explorer displays a shortcut menu that lists the options for that file, including Copy, Delete, Open, and Rename.

Figure 5-1: Click PlayIt! for a guided tour of Windows Explorer. Learn how to select a storage device, folder, or file, and how to sort files. You'll even find out how to start programs and display documents without using the Start button.

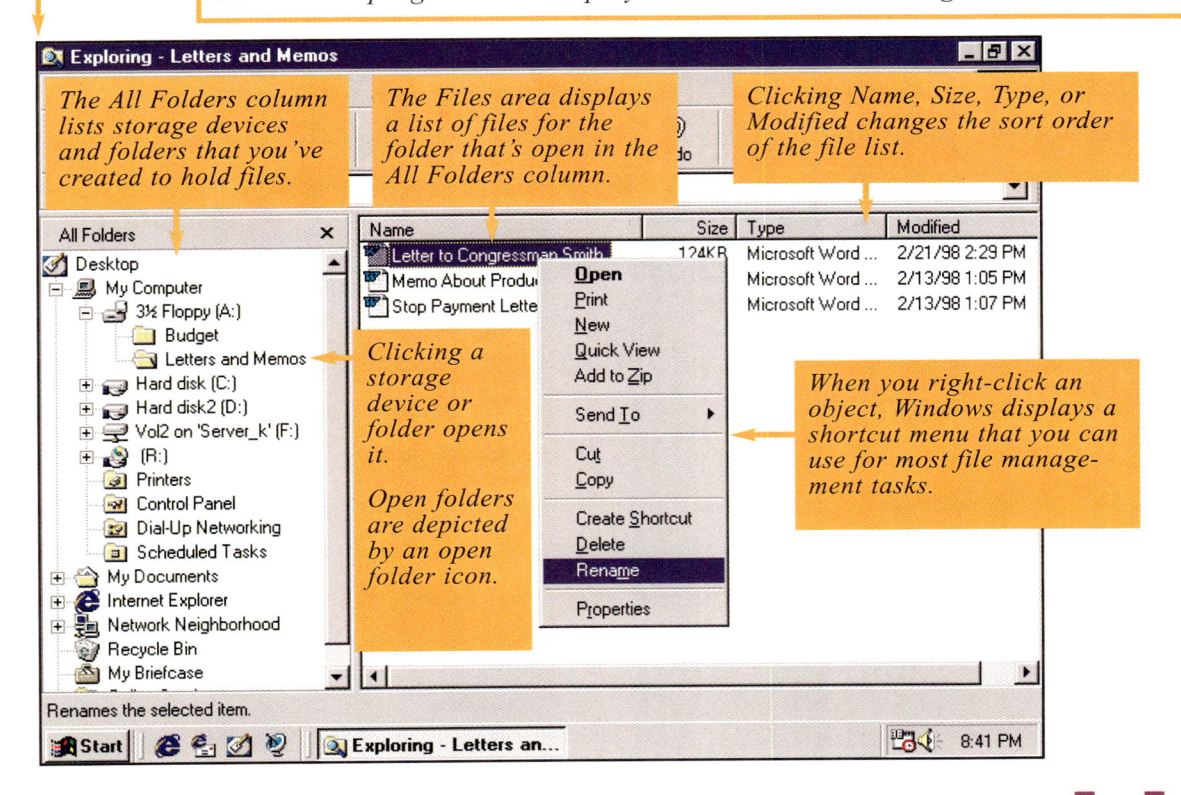

The All Folders column lists storage devices and folders that you've created to hold files.

The Files area displays a list of files for the folder that's open in the All Folders column.

Clicking Name, Size, Type, or Modified changes the sort order of the file list.

Clicking a storage device or folder opens it.

Open folders are depicted by an open folder icon.

When you right-click an object, Windows displays a shortcut menu that you can use for most file management tasks.

52 Chapter 5: Organizing Files and Folders

■FAQ How do I change the name of a file?

Once you have located a file with Windows Explorer, it's easy to change its name. This process is called **renaming**. To rename a file, you select it, then type a new name. You might want to rename a file so its name better describes its contents. You might also want to standardize the names of similar files—Playoff 1998, Playoff 1999, Playoff 2000—so that they appear in sequence.

Renaming files is fairly straightforward, except for a little twist involving file extensions. Windows allows you to hide file extensions. When this option is in effect, file extensions are not displayed, but they still exist. Windows has simply hidden them from your view. If you would like to change this option on your PC, select Options (or Folder Options) from the Windows Explorer View menu, then adjust the "Hide file extensions" option on the View tab.

Before you rename a file, look at the file name to see if it includes an extension. If you see .doc or another extension, then Windows is set to display file extensions. In this case, when you rename a file you must type the file extension along with the new name. As a rule, you should use the same file extension as in the original name. If you forget to type the file extension, Windows displays a reminder. If Windows is hiding file extensions, it is not necessary to type the file extension. In this case, when you rename a file your PC automatically retains the old file extension for the new file name.

Figure 5-2: To rename a file, you can type the new file name right over the old name, or you can right-click the file name, then select the Rename option on the shortcut menu. Click PlayIt! to find out how these two options work.

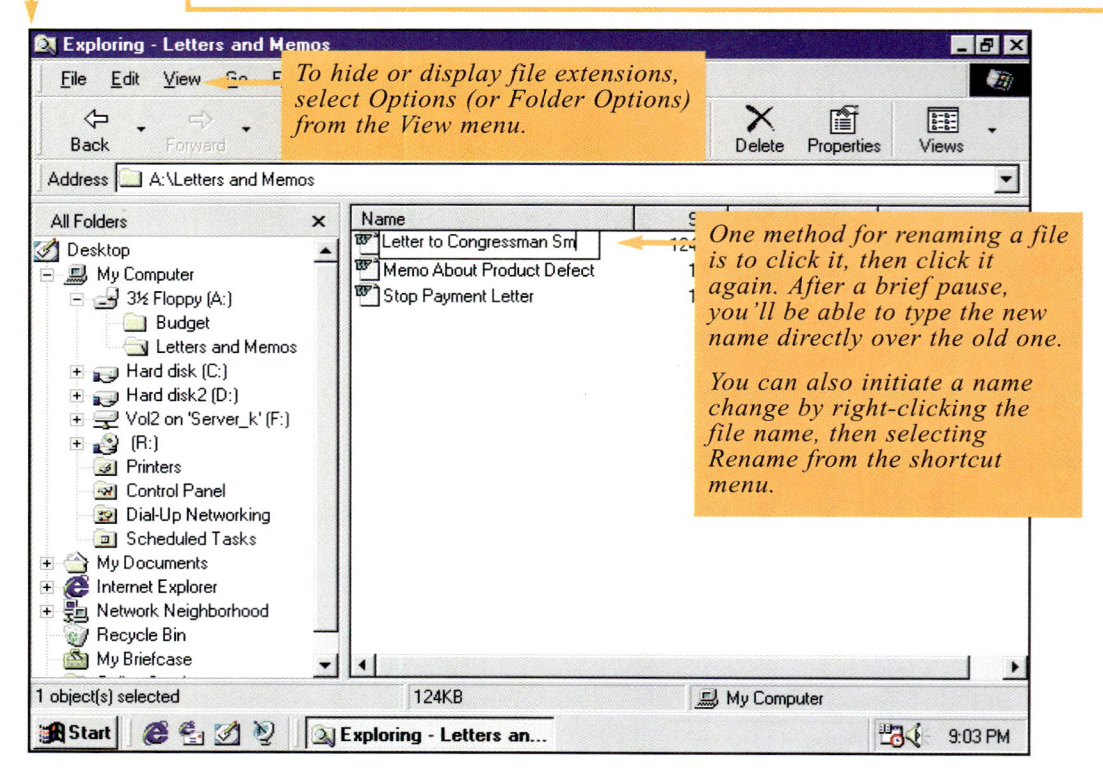

To hide or display file extensions, select Options (or Folder Options) from the View menu.

One method for renaming a file is to click it, then click it again. After a brief pause, you'll be able to type the new name directly over the old one.

You can also initiate a name change by right-clicking the file name, then selecting Rename from the shortcut menu.

Chapter 5: Organizing Files and Folders

■FAQ What's the best organization for my files?

Folders help you organize files. The key to organizing your files is to create a clearly structured set of folders. If the number of files in a folder exceeds what you find to be a manageable size, don't hesitate to create additional folders and move files into them. To create new folders while in Windows Explorer, click the File menu, then select New. You can also create folders within folders, called **subfolders**, to further compartmentalize or group files.

When you **move** a file, Windows removes or "cuts" the file from its current location and places it on the **Windows Clipboard**—a temporary holding area in your PC's memory. After you select a new location for the file, Windows "pastes" it from the Clipboard to that location. Associating the process of moving files with "cut and paste" will help you remember the sequence of commands needed to move a file.

Here are a few hints to help you improve the organization of your files:

- Always store your data files in a folder.
- Create subfolders of the hard disk folder called My Documents to hold your data files. Use descriptive names for all your folders.
- Group your data files into folders by project or by type.
- Try not to store your data files in the folders that contain program modules for your application software.
- The first level under a device should contain only folders, not files.

Figure 5-3: Click the PlayIt! button to learn how to use Windows Explorer to move single files, groups of files, and folders.

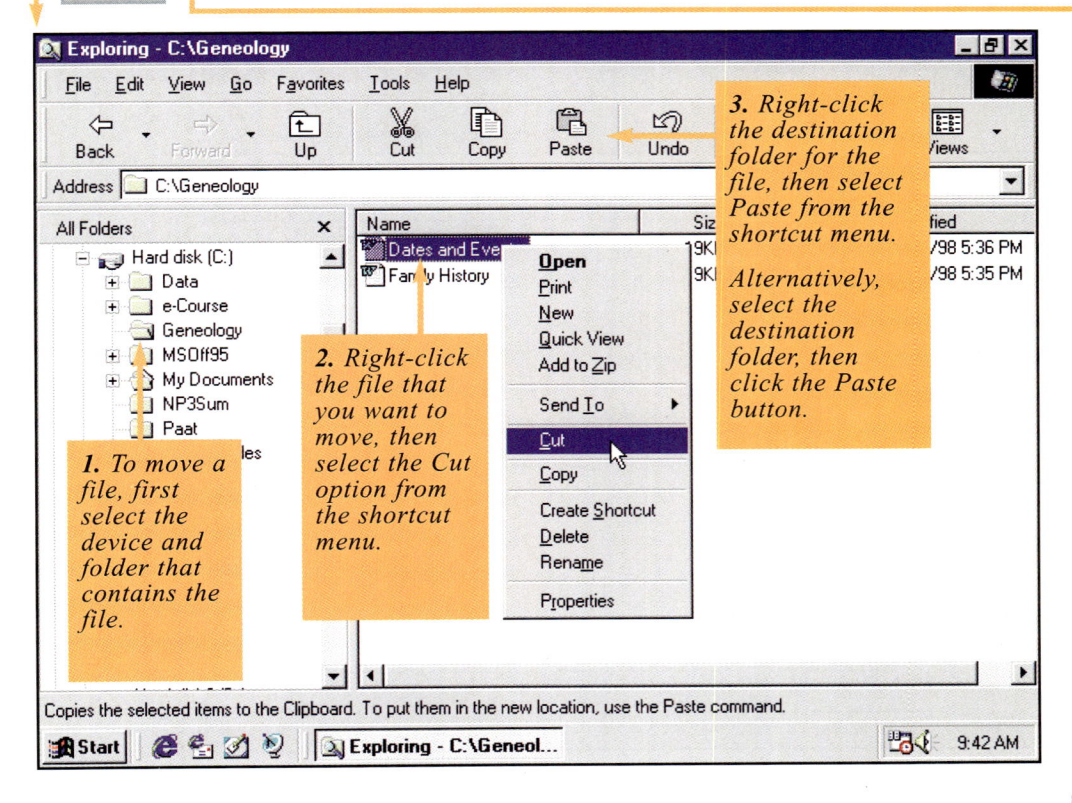

1. To move a file, first select the device and folder that contains the file.

2. Right-click the file that you want to move, then select the Cut option from the shortcut menu.

3. Right-click the destination folder for the file, then select Paste from the shortcut menu.

Alternatively, select the destination folder, then click the Paste button.

53

Chapter 5: Organizing Files and Folders

▪FAQ How do I copy files to other disks?

Typically, you copy a file when you want to create a duplicate. You could copy a file onto a floppy disk to send to a friend or coworker. You might copy a group of important files to a Zip disk, which you could store in a secure location. To **copy** a file, Windows places a duplicate of the file on the Clipboard. The original file remains in its present location. After you select a location for the copy, your PC pastes the file from the Clipboard to the new location. Think of copying files as "copy and paste" to help remember this sequence of commands.

Because most PC owners store their files on their PCs' hard disks, floppy disks are seldom used except for transporting files from one computer to another. In some circumstances, however, a floppy disk—not the hard disk—becomes your primary storage medium. For example, you might be a student using a university computer lab. You never know which lab computer you'll use, so you must keep your files on a floppy disk.

Windows has a **Copy Disk** feature that quickly and easily makes a copy of your floppy disk, even if you only have one floppy disk drive! Copy Disk copies the entire contents of the floppy disk into the memory of your PC, then asks you take the disk out of the drive and replace it with a blank disk. The contents of memory are then transferred to the blank disk, and you end up with an exact duplicate of your original floppy disk.

Figure 5-4: Click the PlayIt! button to learn how to copy an entire floppy disk. If you're using a Tracking Disk, apply what you learn to make a copy of it.

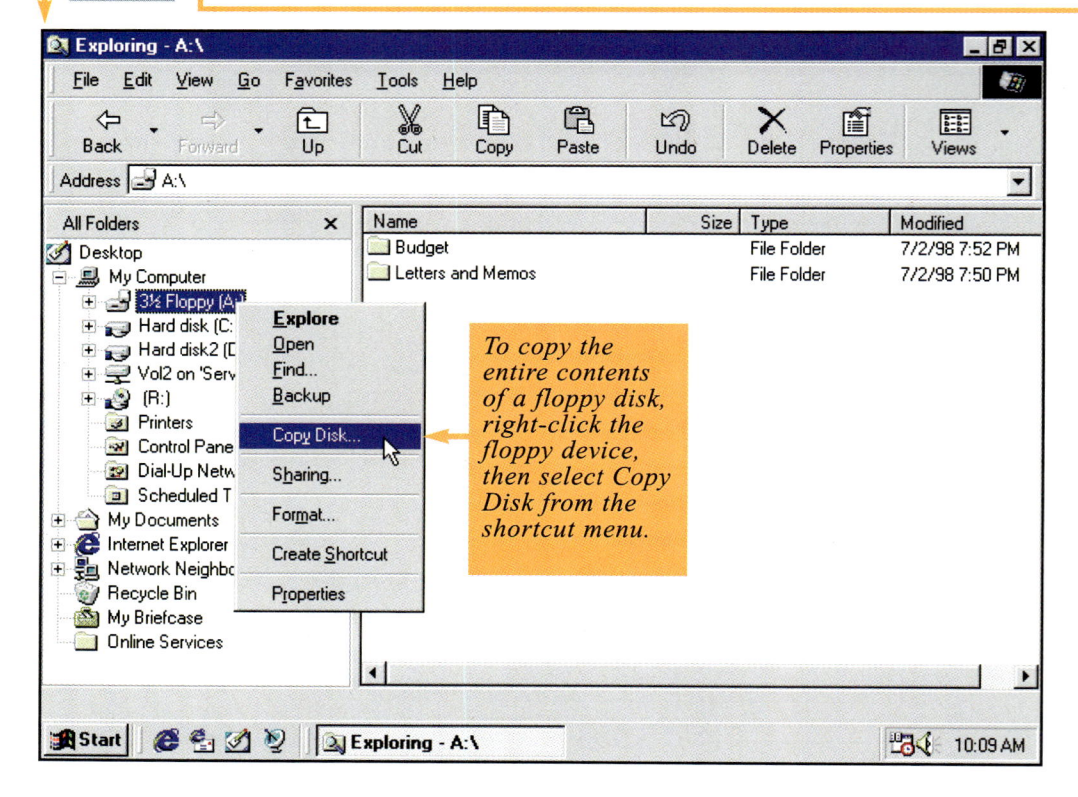

To copy the entire contents of a floppy disk, right-click the floppy device, then select Copy Disk from the shortcut menu.

Chapter 5: Organizing Files and Folders

■FAQ What if I run out of disk space?

If you run out of disk space, Windows displays a "Disk Full" message. This message usually means that it's time for some PC housecleaning. If your hard disk is full, don't immediately begin to uninstall programs and delete files. Instead, you can usually clear lots of hard disk space by emptying your PC's Recycle Bin.

The **Recycle Bin** is a holding area for the files you've deleted from your PC's hard disk. When you delete a file from the hard disk, its name is removed from the Windows Explorer file list, but the file itself remains on the disk and continues to occupy disk space. This space is not released until you empty the Recycle Bin. It's nice to know that a deleted file is not gone forever until you empty the Recycle Bin, but you should remember that it holds only hard disk files. The Recycle Bin doesn't keep files that you've deleted from floppy disks, Zip disks, and SuperDisks.

If emptying the Recycle Bin does not free up enough hard disk space for you to continue working, your next step would be to uninstall any software that you no longer use. Deleting a single software application might provide room for hundreds of data files. When you uninstall software, remember to use the Control Panel's Add/Remove Programs icon—don't delete it using Windows Explorer.

You delete data files not so much because you've run out of disk space, but because you no longer need the files. Using Windows Explorer you can easily delete a file by right-clicking it, then selecting the Delete option.

Figure 5-5: Click the PlayIt! button to find out how to delete a file and how to use the Recycle Bin.

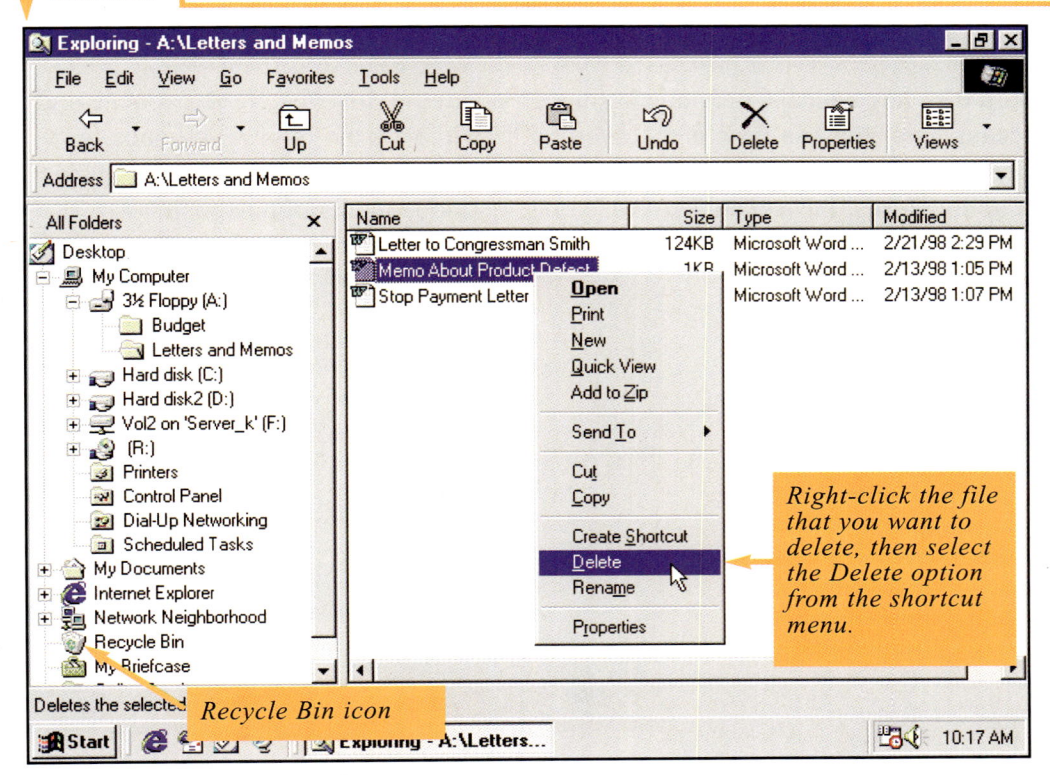

Right-click the file that you want to delete, then select the Delete option from the shortcut menu.

Recycle Bin icon

Hardware
Hard disk drives

In this chapter, you've learned about managing files with Windows Explorer. Where are most of those files stored? The answer—on your PC's hard disk. A **hard disk** is a circular, rigid storage medium that is made of aluminum or glass and coated with metallic particles. One or more of these disks and their corresponding read/write heads are sealed inside a **hard disk drive**, which is then usually mounted inside the system unit of your PC. The hard disks inside the drive are called **platters**. A typical PC hard drive usually contains two platters.

Because hard disk platters are sealed inside the drive, they cannot be removed. This constraint would seem to be a disadvantage. In a sense, a floppy disk drive has unlimited storage capacity because you can insert and remove floppy disks. With a hard disk drive, the storage capacity is limited to the hard disk that's sealed inside the case. Sealing the disk inside the case can also be an advantage. It isolates the disk from airborne contaminants such as dust and smoke particles. With these particles safely locked out, the data on a hard disk can be packed in very tightly and recognized without error by the read/write heads. If the disk was not sealed inside a case, the data could not be so tightly packed and disk capacity would drop to that of a Zip disk or SuperDisk.

Snug inside their isolated environment, hard disks operate very efficiently and store huge amounts of data. A typical hard disk could hold as much as 6.4 or 8.4 GB of data. By comparison, a standard floppy disk drive stores only 1.44 MB. A Zip disk stores 100 to 250 MB. Remember that a gigabyte (GB) is 1 billion bytes and a megabyte (MB) is only 1 million bytes.

Hard disk ads typically provide information about the drive's storage capacity and access time. **Access time** is the average time it takes the read/write heads to locate and collect data from the disk. Today's hard disk drives have access times of about 10 ms (milliseconds). That's only ten thousandths of a second!

Figure 5-6: A typical PC hard disk drive contains two platters and their corresponding read/write heads. The platters spin continuously to provide fast access time. The drive pictured has had its case removed. Don't try this at home or you'll damage the disk drive.

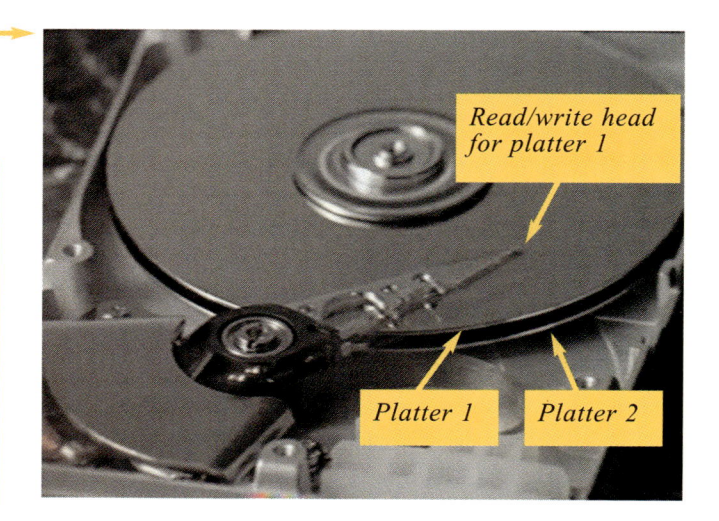

■Hardware
continued

The hard disk that your PC uses in its main storage device is typically a **fixed disk**—a nonremovable disk that's sealed inside the disk drive. If you need the storage capacity of a hard disk but the transportability of a floppy disk, a removable hard disk might be the solution. A **removable hard disk**, sometimes called a disk cartridge, is a plastic case that contains a hard disk platter and read/write heads. It requires a special disk drive that costs from U.S.$100 to U.S.$300. The popular Jaz disks require an Iomega Jaz drive; the Orb cartridges require an Orb drive. Jaz disks have either a 1 or 2 GB capacity and cost between U.S.$100 and $125. Orb 2.2 GB cartridges cost approximately U.S.$40.

How do removable hard disks fit into the overall storage picture for your PC? They are a somewhat specialized storage solution, typically employed when you need to transport projects that are too large to fit on a Zip disk or SuperDisk, or when you are working with too many large projects to fit on your fixed hard disk. A removable hard disk offers an additional measure of security for important projects, such as accounting systems. At the end of the day, a removable disk can be placed in a secure location, keeping the data safer from unauthorized access than if it were left on your PC's hard disk.

The disadvantages of removable hard disks include cost and reliability. Both Orb cartridges and Jaz disks cost more than a Zip disk or SuperDisk. Removable hard disks tend to have more reliability problems than fixed hard disks and they tend to fail much more frequently than floppy disks. Many of these problems are related to wear and tear during transport, or mishandling. If a hard disk cartridge is inserted out of alignment, damage is likely to occur and the disk might become unusable.

Figure 5-7: A removable Jaz disk requires a Jaz drive. Though typically mounted inside the system unit, the drive mechanism for either a removable or fixed disk drive can be external to the computer, like the one pictured here. A parallel or SCSI cable connects an external drive to the PC.

■Hardware
continued

In the course of adding, modifying, and deleting files, the efficiency of your PC's hard disk begins to decrease so that it takes longer to store, find, and retrieve files. Why does this happen and what can you do about it?

Like a floppy disk, a hard disk is divided into sectors. Each sector is a fixed size and can hold a certain amount of data. Although a file does not have to fill a sector, your PC must use more than one sector for a large file. For most efficient hard disk operation, your PC should place the data for a large file in adjacent sectors so that the read/write head can quickly move from one part of the file to the next. Your files are not always stored so efficiently. In the course of revising your files, the sectors in which they are stored can become scattered all over the disk.

In "tech speak" a file that is stored in nonadjacent sectors is referred to as a **fragmented file**. A disk containing many fragmented files is called a **fragmented disk** and is not operating at peak efficiency. Windows provides a **defragmentation utility** that you can use periodically to put the data for each file in adjacent sectors. Defragmentation does not affect the way your files and folders appear to be arranged in Windows Explorer. Instead, this operation takes place behind the scenes. The only difference you might notice after defragmenting your disk is that it seems to retrieve and store your files more quickly. Most experts recommend that you defragment your hard disk at least two or three times a year.

Figure 5-8: You can access defragmentation and other handy disk utilities from the Properties dialog box. Click the PlayIt! button to see how to defragment a disk and to find out how much space is available on your PC's hard disk.

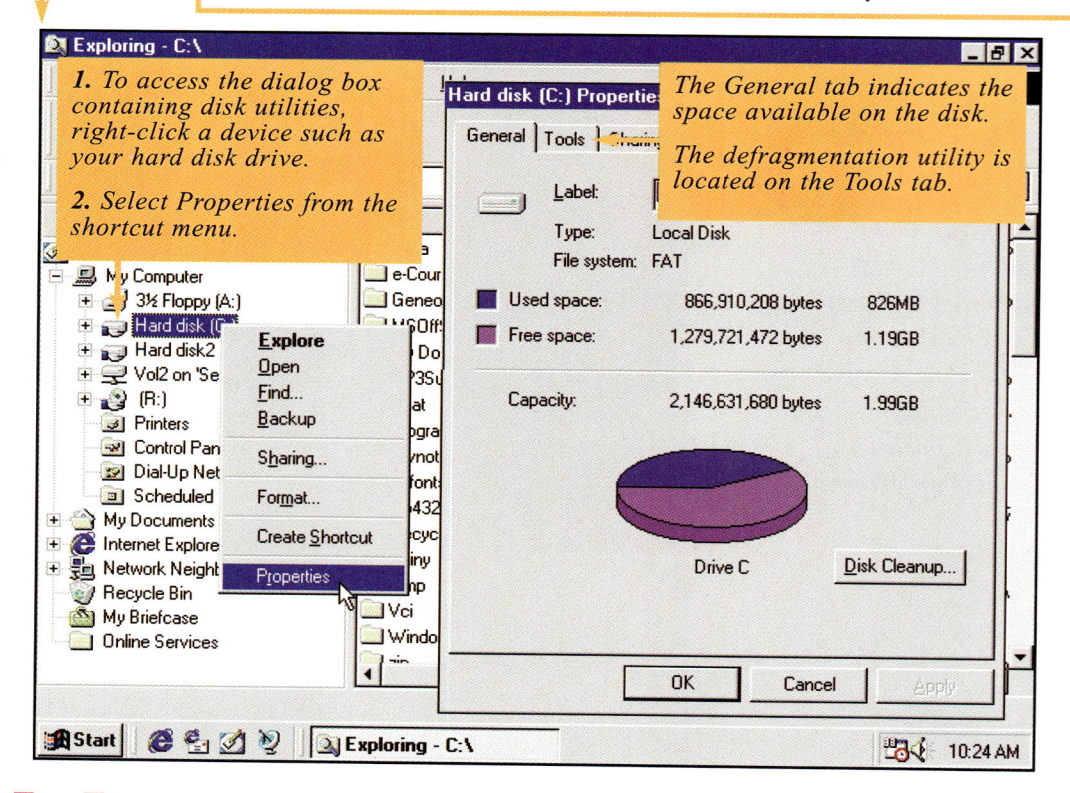

1. To access the dialog box containing disk utilities, right-click a device such as your hard disk drive.

2. Select Properties from the shortcut menu.

The General tab indicates the space available on the disk.

The defragmentation utility is located on the Tools tab.

Chapter 5: Organizing Files and Folders

■Tutorial
How to find files

You can use Windows Explorer to search for a file by manually checking the list of files in each folder. If you have many folders and don't remember which one holds a particular file, this search process could take quite a long time. Windows provides a way to automate the search process by using the Find program.

The **Find program** accepts information describing the file that you want to find—its title, the date it was created, or its size. If the file contains a document, you can even provide a phrase or two from within its text. In this tutorial, you'll learn how to use the Find program.

When you have completed the tutorial, you should be able to:
- Start the Find program.
- Use the Name & Location, Date, and Advanced tabs to enter a file description.
- Select and open the file you want from the list of files that the Find program produces as a result of its search.

Figure 5-9: Click the PlayIt! button to begin the tutorial and discover how to use the Find program. Estimated time: 10–20 minutes. Tracking Disk points: 10.

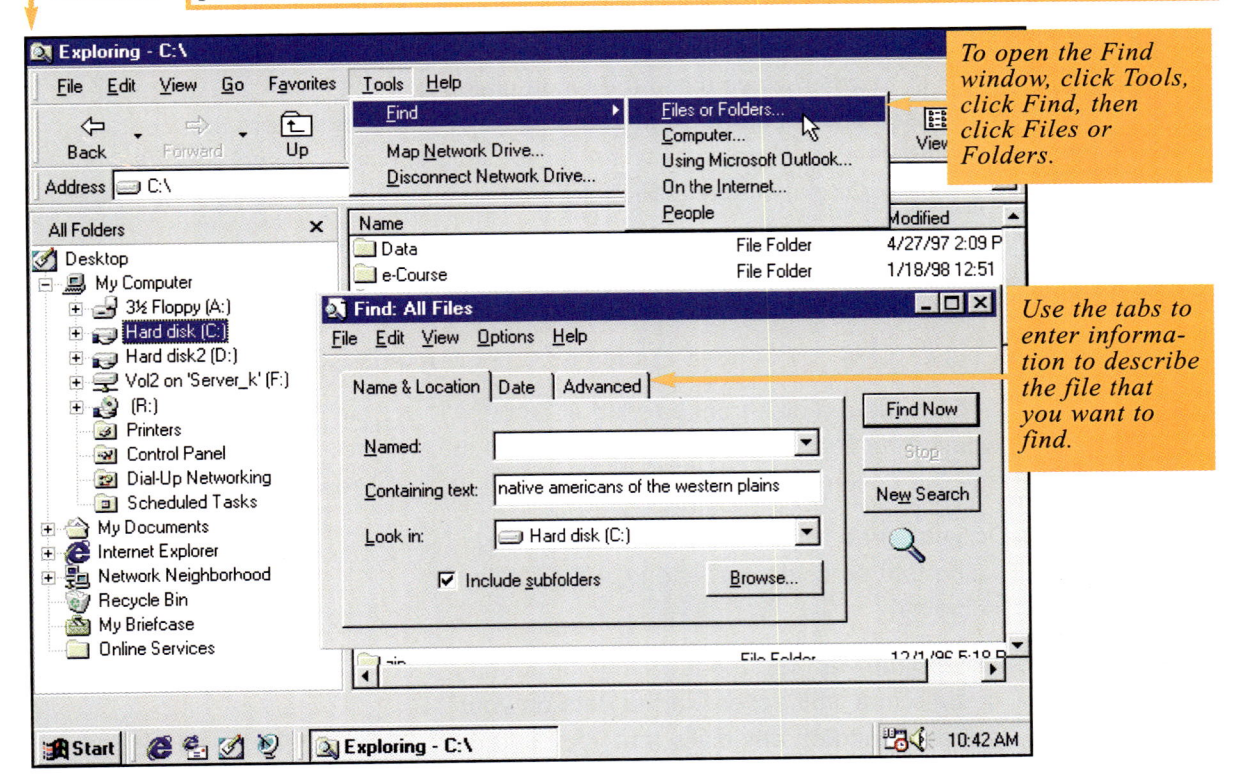

To open the Find window, click Tools, click Find, then click Files or Folders.

Use the tabs to enter information to describe the file that you want to find.

■Issue

Are deleted files legally garbage?

In a highly publicized drug case, police searched through trash bags left on the curb by a suspected cocaine dealer. The evidence they collected led to a conviction, which was appealed because the police had not obtained a search warrant. The conviction was upheld by the U.S. Supreme Court, which ruled that garbage left on the curb is in the public domain and police can search it without a warrant.

What does this case have to do with computers? You already know that the files you delete from your PC's hard disk are not really gone—they're just marked for deletion and sent to the Recycle Bin. This "garbage" remains on your computer and can be accessed by anyone. What might surprise you is that even emptying the Recycle Bin does not actually erase your files from the disk. Instead, the file data remains on the disk until the operating system needs those sectors for new data. Deleted data might remain on a disk—a floppy disk, hard disk, or removable hard disk—for years. Anyone who is sophisticated in the use of computers can rummage through this file garbage, but is it legal and ethical to do so?

Your computer is not on the curb, so it is not in the public domain. The files it contains are probably protected by laws that make it illegal for high-tech thieves to gain unauthorized access and that prevent law enforcement agents from search and seizure without a search warrant. But what about files that you send out on disk? When you send a disk containing files, you expect those files to be accessed in "normal" ways using the Open dialog box or Windows Explorer. If someone uses special software to search for and view the sectors that contain deleted files, is it an illegal activity similar to using special lock picks to enter a locked house? Or is it simply "snooping"—a legal, but not very ethical, activity?

On a closing note, if you want to make sure that you're not sending odd bits of files on your disks, perform a full format on the disk before you copy files to it.

What do you think?

1. If you receive a disk from a friend or client, would it be ethical to use special software to see the contents of deleted sectors?   ⓞYes ⓞ No ⓞ Not sure

2. Do you agree with the U.S. Supreme Court ruling that curbside garbage is in the public domain?   ⓞ Yes ⓞ No ⓞ Not sure

3. Are you familiar with the laws in your country or state that limit access to the data on your computer and on any disks that you send out?   ⓞ Yes ⓞ No ⓞ Not sure

Save It!

Chapter 5: Organizing Files and Folders   61

QuickCheck A

1. "[_____] and paste" describes the process of *moving* a file; "[_____] and paste" describes the process of *copying* a file.

2. Without a set of well-structured [_____], it might be difficult to locate files.

3. True or false? When you see the "Disk Full" message, you should immediately delete some of your data files from the hard disk. [____]

4. True or false? The Recycle Bin allows you to recover files that you mistakenly deleted from a hard disk or a floppy disk. [____]

5. A hard disk becomes [_____] when the sectors that contain a file are scattered in different areas of the disk.

Check It!

QuickCheck B

For each description below, enter the letter of the corresponding Windows Explorer object:

1. The storage device that contains the product defect memo [____]

2. The first file in the Letters and Memos folder [____]

3. The file that's being deleted [____]

4. The control that alphabetizes the files by name [____]

5. The shortcut menu [____]

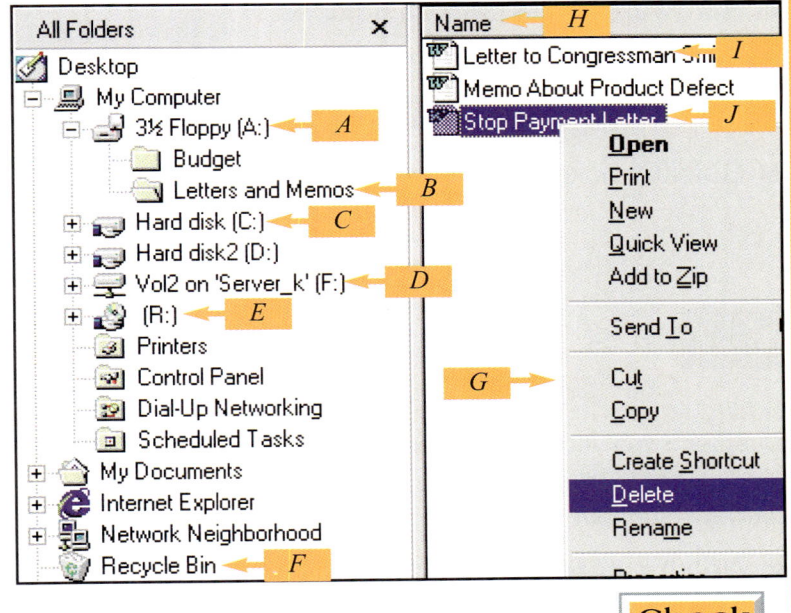

Labels on screenshot:
- A: 3½ Floppy (A:)
- B: Letters and Memos
- C: Hard disk (C:)
- D: Vol2 on 'Server_k' (F:)
- E: (R:)
- F: Recycle Bin
- G: (shortcut menu)
- H: Name
- I: Letter to Congressman Smith
- J: Stop Payment Letter

Check It!

Get It?

While using the Book-on-CD, click the Get It? button to see if you can answer ten randomly selected questions from Chapter 5.

Get It?

Chapter 6

Protecting Your Files

What's Inside?

Chapter 6 has the gruesome details on the disasters that might befall your important data files—fires, floods, hurricanes, tornados, viruses, head crashes, and hard drive failures. It includes tips for avoiding some disasters and devising a recovery plan for those disasters that you can't prevent.

- FAQs:

Can a computer lose my files?	63
Could my PC's hard disk drive just stop working?	64
Can a virus wipe out my files?	65
How can I protect my files from viruses?	66
Do I need a disaster recovery plan?	67

- Hardware: Tape backup devices   68
- Tutorial: How to use Windows Backup   71
- Issue: What about a "good" virus?   72
- QuickChecks   73

What's on the CD?

Chapter 6 is a veritable film festival that includes a disaster movie (hard disk crash), a mystery (finding bad sectors), a medical drama (the virus hunt), and a documentary (the tape backup tour). It's fun, but also serious business. Losing files can cost you time and money.

- Watch a hard disk head crash!   63
- Learn how to scan your hard disk to find bad sectors   64
- Go on a virus hunt   66
- Take a video tour of tape backup devices   68
- Take a step-by-step tutorial on using Windows Backup   71

Chapter 6: Protecting Your Files 63

■FAQ Can a computer lose my files?

Yes, files on your PC can become inaccessible or "lost" as a result of an alarming variety of events, including power outages, fires, floods, storms, breakage, and even normal wear and tear. You've probably heard someone complain, "I was almost finished with that project when I lost the whole thing!" The source of the problem might have been a power loss caused by an outage at your community's power plant, a blown house fuse, or simply someone tripping over the PC's power cord and pulling it out from the socket. When you work on files, they are temporarily held in RAM, but this circuitry requires power to hold data. When the power goes out, any open files will disappear immediately from memory.

You can take steps to avoid losing files because of power problems. While you're creating or revising a file, make sure that you save it every five or ten minutes. Once the file is saved on a disk, a power outage is unlikely to affect it. Some software automatically saves your files at set intervals. Make sure that this feature is activated. If you live in an area with frequent power outages, you might want to purchase a battery-powered backup device called a **UPS** (uninterruptible power supply), which will feed your computer enough power so that you can close your files and shut down normally when the power goes out. An inexpensive UPS is available for less than U.S.$100.

A power outage usually affects only the files you have open at the time. Natural disasters, such as fires, floods, hurricanes, and tornadoes, can wipe out your entire computer and all of your files. Even in the course of normal use, your PC's hard disk can become damaged by a **head crash**. During normal operation, the read/write head hovers just above the disk surface, but does not touch it. However, as a result of mechanical problems, stray dust particles, or jarring the drive, a read/write head might literally crash into the disk surface and damage the particles in the sectors that hold your data. Even one damaged sector might make it impossible for your PC to open an entire file. Many head crashes are not preventable, because they are caused by mechanical problems, but you can avoid some head crashes if you take care not to move your computer while it is on.

Play It!

Figure 6-1: A head crash can be disastrous. In the worst case, damaged sectors are part of the Registry or other files that keep track of file locations on your hard disk. If your PC is unable to access this information, you might not be able to access any of your data or program files.

Chapter 6: Protecting Your Files

■FAQ Could my PC's hard disk drive just stop working?

A head crash might make it impossible to access some or all of the files on your PC's hard disk. A hard drive can also stop working or "fail" because of abnormalities on the disk surface, mechanical problems, or circuit malfunctions. When a hard disk drive stops working, it is called a **disk crash**. A hard drive often crashes without warning, but if you begin to have difficulty accessing some of your files, it might be a signal that the drive is about to fail. You should immediately check for bad sectors on your hard disk. A **bad sector** is an area of the disk surface that cannot reliably store data because of manufacturing defects, head-crash damage, or deterioration. If a part of a file is stored in a bad sector, you will not be able to access the file at all.

Most hard disks have some bad sectors, but these are cordoned off when the hard disk is initially formatted. Your PC's operating system keeps track of the bad sectors, ensuring that no data is stored there. Sectors can also go bad in the normal course of operation. Until the operating system adds these sectors to the bad sectors list, your PC might try to store data there. You can use a Windows program called **ScanDisk** to update the operating system's list of bad sectors. If new sectors seem to go bad every few weeks, you should consider replacing your hard disk drive before it fails entirely and all of your files become inaccessible.

Figure 6-2: Windows includes a program called ScanDisk that checks for bad sectors on a disk's surface. Click the PlayIt! button to find out how to use the Windows ScanDisk program.

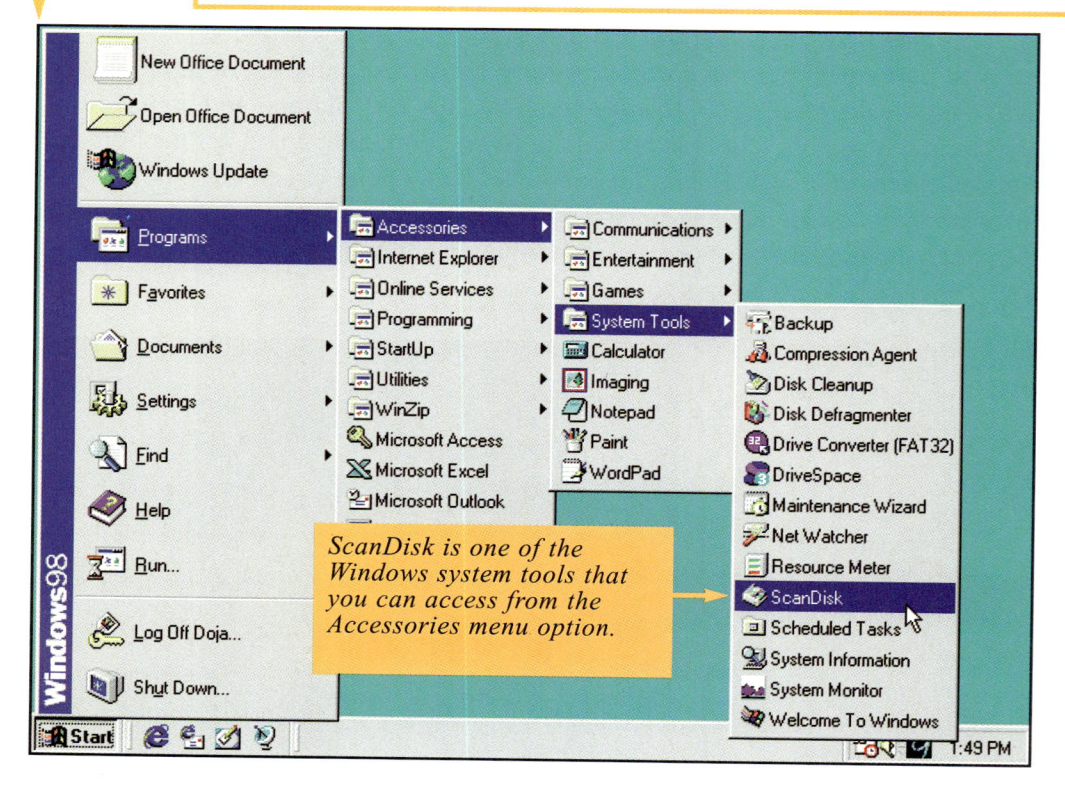

ScanDisk is one of the Windows system tools that you can access from the Accessories menu option.

FAQ Can a virus wipe out my files?

A **virus** is a small computer program that's hidden within a legitimate software application or file. It can reproduce and spread from one file to another. For example, when you run a program where a virus lurks, you also run the virus program. Undetected, the virus creates a replica of itself, which attaches to another program. Now, running either of the infected programs will replicate and spread the virus. If you send one of these infected files to another person, the process of replication will begin in his or her PC.

The success of a virus depends on its ability to remain undetected on your PC long enough to spread to other files and to other PCs. By infecting other files, such as those on floppy disks, a virus increases its chances of survival even after being discovered.

In addition to replicating itself, a virus can take action by delivering its payload. A **payload** might simply be an annoying message, or might be something more serious—it might prevent access to the files on your hard disk, erase files, or randomly change data in your files. The events that can trigger the payload include dates (March 6 for the famous Michelangelo virus), a file reaching a specific size, or a certain combination of keystrokes.

Be alert for these symptoms of a virus infection on your PC:
■ Your PC displays unusual messages, such as "Your computer is stoned."
■ The hard disk suddenly fills up with oddly named files.
■ Your PC seems to operate significantly slower than previously.
■ You cannot access your hard disk or your PC reboots unexpectedly.
■ Some of your files are missing or difficult to access.
■ Files that you have not opened recently have become significantly larger.

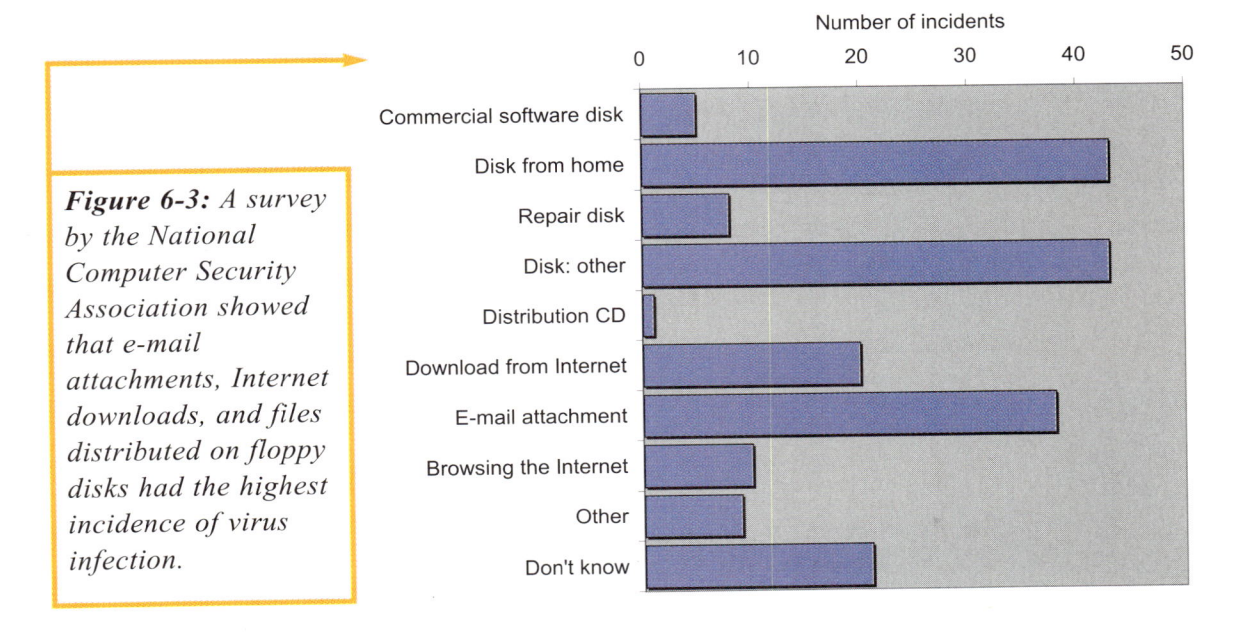

Figure 6-3: A survey by the National Computer Security Association showed that e-mail attachments, Internet downloads, and files distributed on floppy disks had the highest incidence of virus infection.

Source	Number of incidents
Commercial software disk	
Disk from home	
Repair disk	
Disk: other	
Distribution CD	
Download from Internet	
E-mail attachment	
Browsing the Internet	
Other	
Don't know	

Chapter 6: Protecting Your Files

■FAQ How can I protect my files from viruses?

Grab It!
Antivirus Software

Experts recommend that you practice "safe computing" by scanning for viruses before you open files that originate from other PCs or the Internet. You can use **antivirus software** to scan for and remove viruses from infected files. Look for antivirus software at your local computer store or on the Internet.

When you fire up your antivirus software, it scans through your PC's memory and the files on any disks that you select, looking for the tell-tale signature of a virus. A **virus signature** is a selection of unique bytes that, like fingerprints, uniquely identify a virus and distinguish it from the legitimate files on your PC. Because new viruses appear every week, you should update your virus software regularly. Companies that publish antivirus software typically provide these updates as free downloads from the Internet.

The following tips will help you protect your files against viruses:
- Regularly use antivirus software to scan your files.
- Update your antivirus software every few months so it recognizes new viruses.
- When you download files from the Internet, scan them before you use them.
- Whenever you receive a disk, scan the files it contains before you copy them to your hard disk, run them, or open them.
- If your application software includes an option to protect against macro viruses that infect document and spreadsheet files, make sure it is activated.

Play It!

Figure 6-4: Click the PlayIt! button to find out how to scan for viruses using antivirus software.

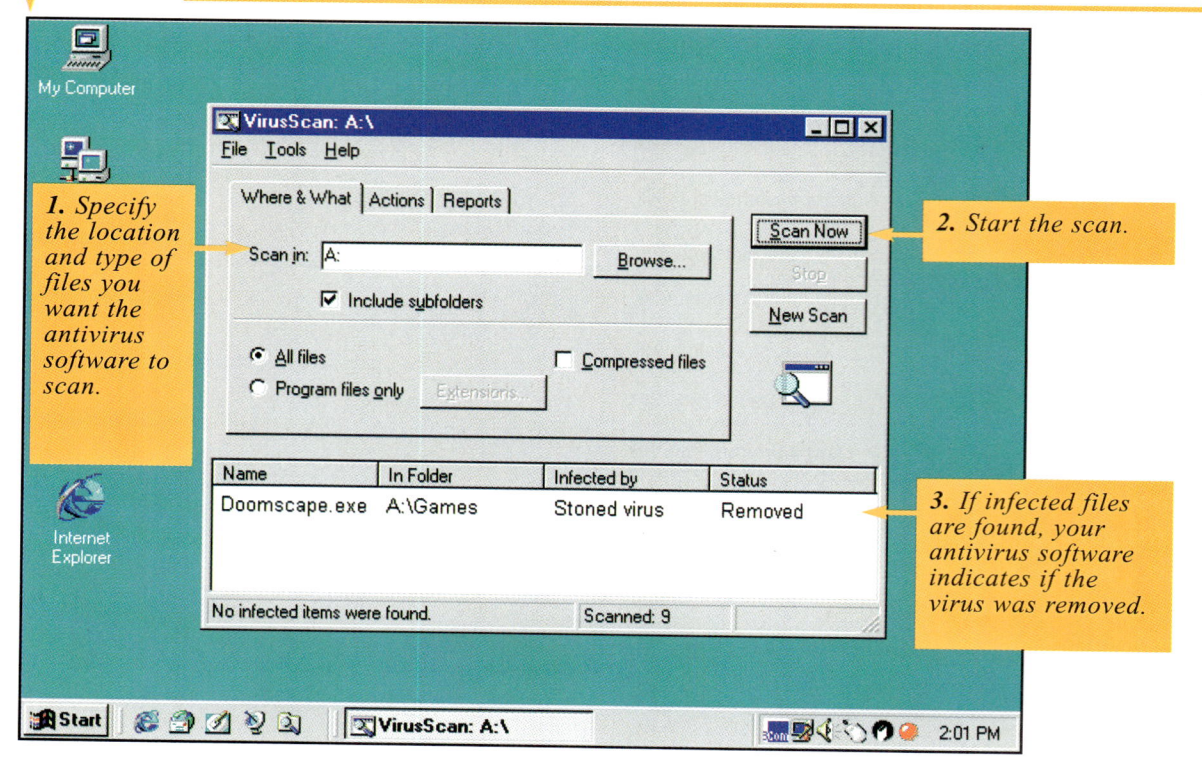

1. Specify the location and type of files you want the antivirus software to scan.

2. Start the scan.

3. If infected files are found, your antivirus software indicates if the virus was removed.

■FAQ Do I need a disaster recovery plan?

You can't predict the disasters that might damage your computer system. You can't prevent hard disk failure. You might not detect a virus until it has deleted your files. Consequently, you need a plan for recovering your data if it gets wiped out. Your plan might not be as comprehensive as the disaster plan for a business, but it should be designed to recover your essential data with minimum hassle.

The best insurance you have against losing all your files is to make a backup. A **backup** is a duplicate copy of one or more files. It provides a set of files that you can **restore** to the hard disk of a functioning PC in the aftermath of a PC disaster, such as a hard disk failure or serious virus attack. Although some businesses have **mirror systems** that allow them to replace a malfunctioning PC with a functioning duplicate, that is not the purpose of a backup. A backup is meant to be restored to a functioning hard disk. A backup is not an archive. An **archive** contains historical data that you might need to access only occasionally. Instead of occupying space on your primary storage device, an archive is usually stored on a CD that you insert only when you need the data that it contains.

Experts recommend that you back up periodically, but how frequently depends on the amount of work that you can afford to lose. If you can't afford to redo a week's work, then you should back up your data more frequently than once per week. You should also keep several sets of backups in case one set becomes damaged. It is a good idea to scan for viruses before you make a back up your data—you certainly don't want viruses lurking on your backups. Make sure that you clearly label your backups and keep them in a safe place, preferably away from your computer. You can store your backups on floppy disks, Zip disks, SuperDisks, removable disks, or tape.

Figure 6-5: The medium that you select for your backups depends on your budget, the size of your hard disk, the size of the files that you want to back up, and the value of your data.

Backup Medium	Advantages	Disadvantages
Floppy disks	Inexpensive and satisfactory for making a backup copy of a limited number of data files.	Requires too many disks for a complete system backup.
Zip or SuperDisks	Reliable, and especially useful for larger data files.	Cost of drive and disks.
Removable hard disks	Enough storage capacity for a full-system backup.	Disks are fairly expensive and somewhat less reliable than other media.
Tapes	Inexpensive, reliable technology with capacity for a full-system backup.	Cannot use backup files directly from tape—they must be transferred to a hard disk.

Hardware
Tape backup devices

Although you can use almost any storage medium for backup, one of the most cost-effective solutions is magnetic tape. The **magnetic tape** that's used for computers is a long strip of thin plastic, coated with metallic particles that can be magnetized like the particles on a floppy or hard disk. Unlike a disk, however, a tape is a sequential medium. The data on a **sequential-access storage medium** is stored in a series or sequence. To access the data midway through a tape, your PC starts at the beginning of the tape and advances through the reel to the location of the data—a process analogous to locating and playing a particular song on an audio cassette tape. In contrast, a disk is considered a **random-access storage medium** because the read/write head can jump directly to any area of the disk to retrieve data—a process analogous to skipping directly to your favorite track on an audio CD.

Before disk drives became available, tape was cutting-edge storage technology. Today, tape is too slow for use as a primary storage medium. It has an average access time of 5 seconds—much slower than a hard drive's 10-millisecond access time. For backups, however, access time is not a major concern because the goal is to sequentially stream all your files from the hard disk to the tape. If the hard drive fails, the files on tape are sequentially streamed back onto a working hard disk so that they can be accessed from a random-access medium.

Tapes and tape drives are inexpensive. You can purchase a tape drive for less than U.S.$200. A 7 GB tape large enough to hold the entire contents of your PC's hard disk costs from U.S.$15 to U.S.$35. Like most storage devices, tape drives are available in external and internal models. Most people prefer the internal model unless their PC's system unit is filled with other devices. If you have more than one computer, an external tape drive that connects to the PC's parallel port can be transported between the computers to back up the files on both.

Play It!

Figure 6-6: The speed with which a tape drive transfers data to and from the hard disk is measured in megabytes (MB) per minute. External tape drives that connect to your PC's parallel port tend to have relatively slow transfer rates, about 20 MB/minute. Tape drives that use an EIDE or SCSI port transfer data at rates up to 120 MB/minute.

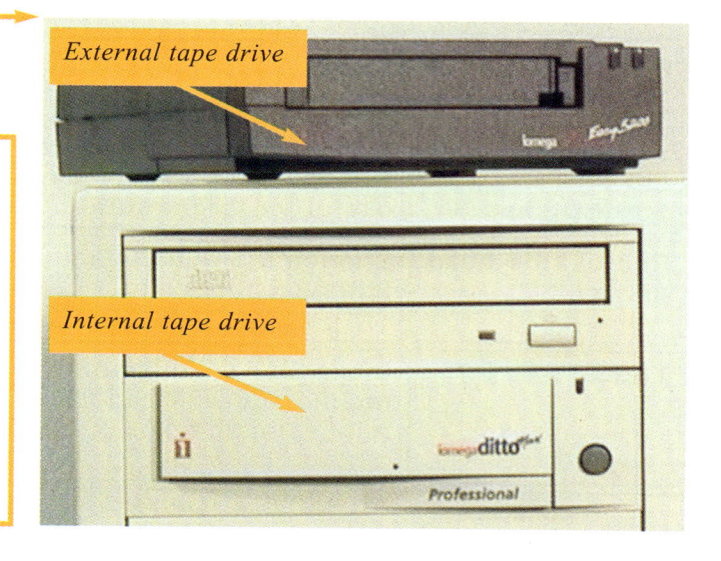

External tape drive

Internal tape drive

■Hardware
continued

Computer tapes are housed in **tape cartridges**, also referred to as data cartridges and data cassettes. A typical tape cartridge costs from U.S.$15 to U.S.$50, depending on its storage capacity. Buying tapes is a little like buying windshield wiper blades. Just as each make and model of car requires a different set of blades, different models of tape drives require different tapes. You can bring your old tape into the store and look for an exact match, but many companies produce data tapes—Sony, Maxell, Fuji, 3M, Verbatim, TDK, and others—so you might not be able to get exactly the same brand. How do you find the correct tape?

When purchasing a tape, you need to look for a part number and storage capacity that are compatible with your PC's tape drive. The documentation for your tape drive will list the compatible tapes. As an example, your documentation might specify a QIC-3020 or Travan TR-3 cartridge with 3.2 GB capacity. The part number indicates whether the tape is a QIC, DAT, DC, DLT, Travan, 4mm data tape, or 8mm data tape. Tape capacity is expressed in gigabytes (GB), as is hard disk capacity. For a full backup, it's handy to have a tape with enough capacity to accommodate all the data stored on your hard disk.

Read your documentation carefully. Some tape drives can read data that has been recorded on different types of tapes, but cannot record or "write" to all of them. For example, your tape drive might read QIC-80, QIC-80W, and QIC3010 cartridges, but read and write only QIC-3020 and TR-3 cartridges. Because you want to record data (write it) and "play" it back to your hard drive (read it), for this example you would purchase a QIC-3020 or TR-3 tape.

Figure 6-7: Tape cartridges are available in many models and from many different manufacturers. Before you purchase tapes for your tape backup device, make sure you carefully read the documentation supplied with the tape drive.

■Hardware
continued

What's the most effective strategy for tape backup? The answer to this question depends on the value of your data and the number of files you create and revise. As a rule of thumb, you should back up your files once a week. If you're producing a lot of work or working on a very important project, you might want to back up more frequently. Most tape backup manufacturers provide **tape backup software** that allows you to set up an automated backup schedule and specify which files to back up.

A **full backup**, as its name suggests, backs up all the files you've selected—usually all of the files on your hard disk. You should make a full backup at least once after you have installed all of your software and hardware. After this initial full backup, it is not necessary to take the time or tape space to make a full backup every week, because many of the files on your computer never change. Your PC's hard disk contains hundreds of megabytes of application program modules that will remain just as they were when you copied them from the distribution CD.

In between full backups, you can save time by making incremental backups. An **incremental backup** stores only those files that have been created or modified since the last backup. Every time you make an incremental backup, only new and revised files are added to your backup tapes. The number of incremental backups that you make between full backups depends on how many files you create and modify each day. As a rule of thumb, you should make a full backup of your home computer once a month to minimize the complexity of the restoration process in the event of a hard disk crash.

Restoring the data from a full backup simply means streaming the data from your backup tape onto a functioning hard disk. If you have incremental backups, you would first restore your most recent full backup, then restore each of the incremental backups. The restoration process is controlled by your backup software. You simply follow the directions on the screen and insert the appropriate backup tapes.

Make sure that you clearly label each backup tape to indicate the date it was created and whether it was a full or incremental backup. Store your tapes in a safe place away from your computer. For maximum security, store your backup tapes "off site" at your office, at a neighbor's house, or in a bank safe-deposit box.

Figure 6-8: *Don't forget to regularly back up your files! Put a reminder on your calendar or in your to-do list.*

Chapter 6: Protecting Your Files   71

▪Tutorial
How to use Windows Backup

The Windows operating system includes a program called **Backup** that you can use to create a full system backup, a backup of selected files, or an incremental backup. Although many backup programs refuse to copy any files that you have open at the time of a backup, the Windows Backup program backs up the Registry file, even though it is open, because it is crucial for restoring your computer system to its original state. If the software supplied with your tape drive does not back up the Registry, you might want to use the Windows Backup program instead.

How can you tell if your backup actually contains files that you can restore to your hard disk? You should test your backup procedure by backing up a few files and then restoring them to your hard disk.

When you have completed the tutorial, you should be able to:
- Start the Windows Backup program.
- Perform a complete system backup.
- Select files for a backup set.
- Restore files from a backup set.

> **Play It!**
>
> **Figure 6-9:** Click the PlayIt! button to learn how to use the Windows Backup program to back up and restore your important files. Estimated time: 20–25 minutes. Tracking Disk points: 10.

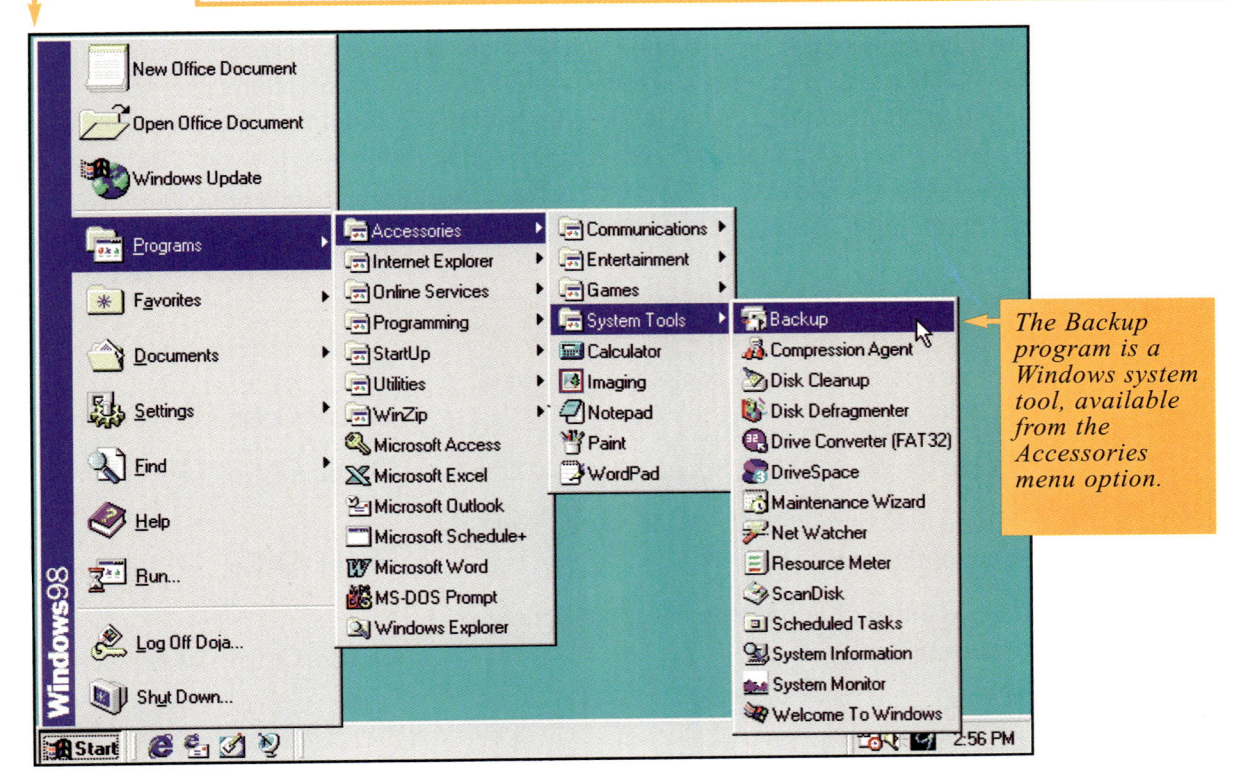

The Backup program is a Windows system tool, available from the Accessories menu option.

■Issue
What about a "good" virus?

Like "tagging" subway cars with spray-painted graffiti, creating a virus has some element of artistry and risk. The artistry lies in the satisfaction of creating a really brilliant virus that can elude detection from antivirus software and cause just the right amount of mischief on the infected PC. Some twisted person apparently took much delight in creating a virus that bellows in an Arnold Schwarzenegger-like voice, "Your files have just been TERMINATED!", as the file names disappear one-by-one from Windows Explorer.

Creating a virus can be a risky business. Most states have laws that punish deliberate attacks on computer systems. Also, a surprisingly effective ad hoc group of virus watchdogs in the computer community seems to be able to track most viruses to their source. The authors of several viruses have been caught. Some have apologized that their creations somehow "escaped" into the wild of public computing and infected PCs in businesses, schools, and homes. Other virus authors claim that they created viruses as a public service to point out security holes and flaws in antivirus software.

Computer viruses have a bad reputation because they are not just a minor nuisance—they cost businesses millions of dollars each year in lost productivity. They cost individuals countless frustrating hours to reconstruct the data in infected files. Could there be a "good" virus? Suppose someone designs a virus that spreads from one computer to another to hunt down the Terminator virus. Would it be O.K. to release this virus-hunting virus? It could prevent millions of Terminator virus infections. Unfortunately, it could also introduce new problems into some computing environments. What if the virus hunter entered a hospital computer system, and for some unintended reason caused major processing errors? Because it is impossible to anticipate interactions between all possible software programs, it is difficult to determine if the benefits of "good" viruses might outweigh their risks.

What do you think?

1. Have you ever used a computer that had a virus? ◯ Yes ◯ No ◯ Not sure

2. Have you ever lost a file because of a virus? ◯ Yes ◯ No ◯ Not sure

3. Does the computer you use most regularly have antivirus software? ◯ Yes ◯ No ◯ Not sure

4. Do you think the benefits of "good" viruses outweigh their risks? ◯ Yes ◯ No ◯ Not sure

Save It!

Chapter 6: Protecting Your Files

QuickCheck A

1. A power outage is most likely to affect the data (a) in RAM, (b) on the hard disk, or (c) on a floppy disk. The letter of the correct answer is _____.

2. The Windows _____ program looks for bad sectors; the Windows _____ program copies files to a tape or disk for safe-keeping.

3. Antivirus software looks for a unique _____ that identifies the virus and distinguishes it from the legitimate files on your PC.

4. True or false? A tape drive is the ideal device to use for creating a backup, an archive, or a mirror system in case your PC has a hard drive failure. _____

5. A hard disk is a(n) _____-access medium, whereas computer tape is a(n) _____-access medium.

Check It!

QuickCheck B

Based on the specifications for the Ditto tape drive and what you've learned about tape backup devices, indicate whether each of the following is true or false:

1. Will back up an entire 2 GB hard disk in about one minute. ☐

2. Stores data on a random-access medium. ☐

3. The tape drive is an external model. ☐

4. Can back up data on QIC-80 tapes. ☐

5. Maximum capacity 3.2 GB. ☐

Specifications:
- **1600MB capacity (up to 3200 MB compressed)**
- **Average backup time up to 19MB/minute**
- **Reads and writes QIC-3020 and Travan TR-3 cartridges**
- **Reads QIC-80, QIC-80W, QIC-80XL, QIC-3010, QIC-3010W and Travan cartridges**
- **Up to 2000Kbits/sec transfer rate**
- **Supports standard and enhanced parallel ports**
- **Second connector for your printer**
- **200,000 hours MTBF (25% duty cycle)**
- **2-year warranty**

Check It!

Get It?

While using the Book-on-CD, click the Get It? button to see if you can answer ten randomly selected questions from Chapter 6.

Get It?

Chapter 7
Connecting to the Internet

What's Inside?

The Internet is in the news and on everyone's mind. Chapter 7 provides the information you need to get connected. In Chapter 8 you'll learn about the Web, and in Chapter 9 you'll learn about e-mail.

- FAQs:
  - What's an Internet connection? — 75
  - Why would I want to connect to the Internet? — 76
  - What do I need to get connected? — 77
  - How do I connect to my ISP? — 78
  - What's the World Wide Wait? — 79
- Hardware: Modems — 80
- Tutorial: How to set up your Internet connection — 83
- Issue: Do we need anonymous digital cash? — 84
- QuickChecks — 85

What's on the CD?

The Internet has so much to offer that the twelve pages in Chapter 7 can merely get you started on an exploration of the fascinating Internet world called "cyberspace." On the CD, you'll get a taste of Internet action by taking a shopping trip to the popular Amazon.com book and music store. Then, you'll find out how to set up and troubleshoot your Internet connection.

- Take an Internet shopping trip — 76
- Find out how to use Dial-Up Networking to connect to the Internet — 78
- Discover how to install a modem — 81
- Troubleshoot your modem using the Control Panel — 82
- Take a step-by-step tutorial on setting up an ISP connection — 83

Chapter 7: Connecting to the Internet

■FAQ What's an Internet connection?

The **Internet** is a global communications network that carries a variety of computer-generated data, such as documents, e-mail, pictures, videos, and music. It provides numerous services, such as the tremendously popular World Wide Web. Sometimes called a "network of networks," the Internet is composed of computers and other communications devices that are connected by communications lines. An **Internet connection** is simply the way that your computer gains access to this data communications network.

The computer that you use to access the Internet is called a **client computer**. Like a customer who orders food in a restaurant, your client computer orders information and then waits for it to arrive. A client computer does not have to remain permanently connected to the Internet. Instead, you need to establish a connection only when you choose to access information. If you use a computer in a school or corporate network, the network would generally provide an Internet connection. From your home computer, you typically connect to the Internet using phone lines—a type of connection called a **dial-up connection**.

When you establish a dial-up connection, your client computer connects to an ISP, such as AOL (America Online) or AT&T Worldnet. An **ISP** (Internet service provider) is a company that sells access to the Internet, just as a telephone company sells access to phones lines or a cable company sells access to television broadcasts. Your ISP connects to an **NSP** (network service provider), such as IBM, MCI, PSINet, or UUnet. The NSP, in turn, connects to other NSPs, to ISPs, and to Internet servers.

An **Internet server**, sometimes called a host, is a computer that stores information and "serves" it out to customers, researchers, employees, and other interested parties. Internet servers generally remain connected to the Internet at all times and provide the majority of information that you will access on the Internet.

Figure 7-1: To connect to the Internet, your home PC establishes a dial-up connection to one of the ISP's modems. The ISP is connected to an NSP over a high-speed communications link. Interconnections between ISPs, NSPs, and Internet servers provide you with access to information from any of these sources.

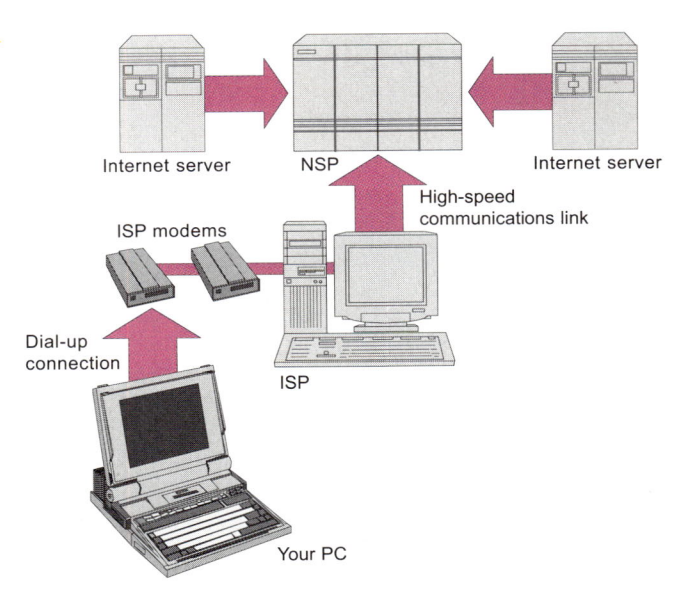

Chapter 7: Connecting to the Internet

■FAQ Why would I want to connect to the Internet?

The Internet has plenty to offer. Just imagine.... After you wake up in the morning, you take a hot cup of java over to your computer, connect to the Internet, and check the latest news. You browse through an online newspaper that's customized to provide your local weather and news topics of interest to you. While you're online, you play a video report of today's financial news. It is not necessary to wait for a scheduled broadcast to find out how your stocks are doing. Then you just have time to check the NBA playoff scores before racing off to work.

At the office, you settle into your cubicle and fire up your computer to check your e-mail. Courtesy of the Internet, you can send and receive mail just about anywhere on the planet—and your message often arrives in less than an hour. An e-mail from your supervisor reminds you to make plans for an upcoming trade show in Cincinnati. You connect to an online travel service, review flight schedules, compare prices, and book a ticket. How about a hotel? You can quickly find lots of information about Cincinnati hotels, restaurants, and entertainment. Before logging off, you check today's Dilbert cartoon. You can relate to it.

During lunch, you munch on a sandwich at your desk and check out your favorite online music store. You listen to a few new tunes and take advantage of a 3-for-$20 CD sale. An afternoon meeting with the sales team from Los Angeles takes place in the videoconference room, with your images and voices transmitted over the Internet. It's almost like being there.

Back home after work, you connect to the Internet to check your bank balance and make sure your latest paycheck was automatically deposited. Then you work on the MBA course that you're taking online. You "hand in" your assignment using the Internet, so that your instructor can grade it tomorrow. You wind up your evening in an online chat group discussing the movie you saw last weekend—two thumbs up. You can do all this and more once you're connected to the Internet.

Figure 7-2: Click the PlayIt! button to take a shopping tour of an Internet bookstore.

■FAQ What do I need to get connected?

A modern Elizabeth Barrett Browning might have written, "How do I access the Internet, let me count the ways...." Her list might have included cell phones, computers, televisions, fax machines, and an ever-expanding array of Internet-ready gadgets. A typical Internet connection, however, consists of a computer, a modem, a phone line, an ISP, and communications software.

You can use a desktop computer, a notebook computer, or palm-sized PDA to access the Internet, but the computer must have a device such as a modem to make a connection. A **modem** is an electronic device that converts the data from your computer into signals that can travel over a normal phone line to your ISP. A standard phone cable connects the modem in your computer to the wall jack for your telephone.

Once your modem is connected to your phone line, you must select an ISP. Most ISPs charge about U.S.$20 per month for Internet access. The ISP supplies you with a phone number that your computer can call to make an Internet connection. When your computer modem dials this phone number, one of your ISP's modems answers and establishes a connection to the Internet. The ISP also supplies you with an e-mail account, a user ID for billing, and a password for security purposes.

When selecting an ISP, you should ask the following questions:
■ Does the ISP provide a local phone number for your Internet connection?
■ Can it offer a connection speed that is compatible with your modem?
■ Will you receive all the software necessary to connect to the ISP, surf the Internet, and manage your e-mail?
■ Can you add e-mail accounts for other members of your family?
■ Does the monthly subscription rate include unlimited access time?
■ Does the ISP offer additional services, such as hosting personal Web pages?
■ Can you access the ISP from other cities without paying for a long-distance call?
■ Can you get technical support during the hours that you're likely to be online?

Grab It!
ISP Sign-up Kits

The final piece of the Internet-connection puzzle is the **communications software** that helps your computer control your modem, dial your ISP, and send and receive data. Most of the communications software that you need is included with Windows. Your ISP might provide additional software as part of the sign-up kit that you use to subscribe.

Figure 7-3: Large ISPs, such as AOL, AT&T Worldnet, and MSN (Microsoft Network), typically provide you with free software that automatically sets up your Internet access and e-mail account.

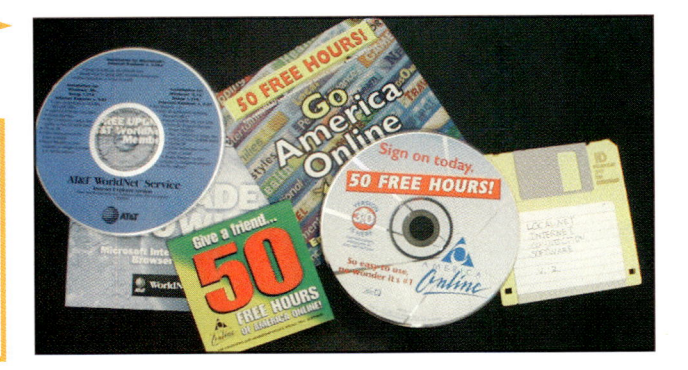

Chapter 7: Connecting to the Internet

■FAQ How do I connect to my ISP?

Once your modem and communications software have been installed, connecting to the Internet is very simple. Your computer dials the preprogrammed phone number for your ISP, connects to one of your ISP's modems, and sends your account ID and password for verification. After your ISP has verified your account, you can surf the Internet for information and collect your e-mail.

You can manually initiate the connection procedure or a software application can initiate the connection automatically. Many software applications are "Internet-smart," meaning that they automatically dial and connect to the Internet when it's necessary to send or receive data. Most word processing software is Internet-smart, as is e-mail software. When it is time for an Internet-smart application to send or receive data, it typically displays a message asking if you want to go online. Responding "yes" initiates the dialing sequence.

When data transfers are complete, you should disconnect from the Internet so that your phone line isn't tied up. Use the Disconnect button or menu option in your software to end your connection. Many software applications have a "Hang up when finished" setting that tells the application to automatically disconnect when data transfer is complete. If you spend lots of hours online, you might request that your phone company supply you with a second telephone line.

Play It!

Figure 7-4: If you want to manually initiate an Internet connection, you can easily use Windows Dial-Up Networking by selecting it from the Accessories menu (Windows 95) or the Communications menu (Windows 98).

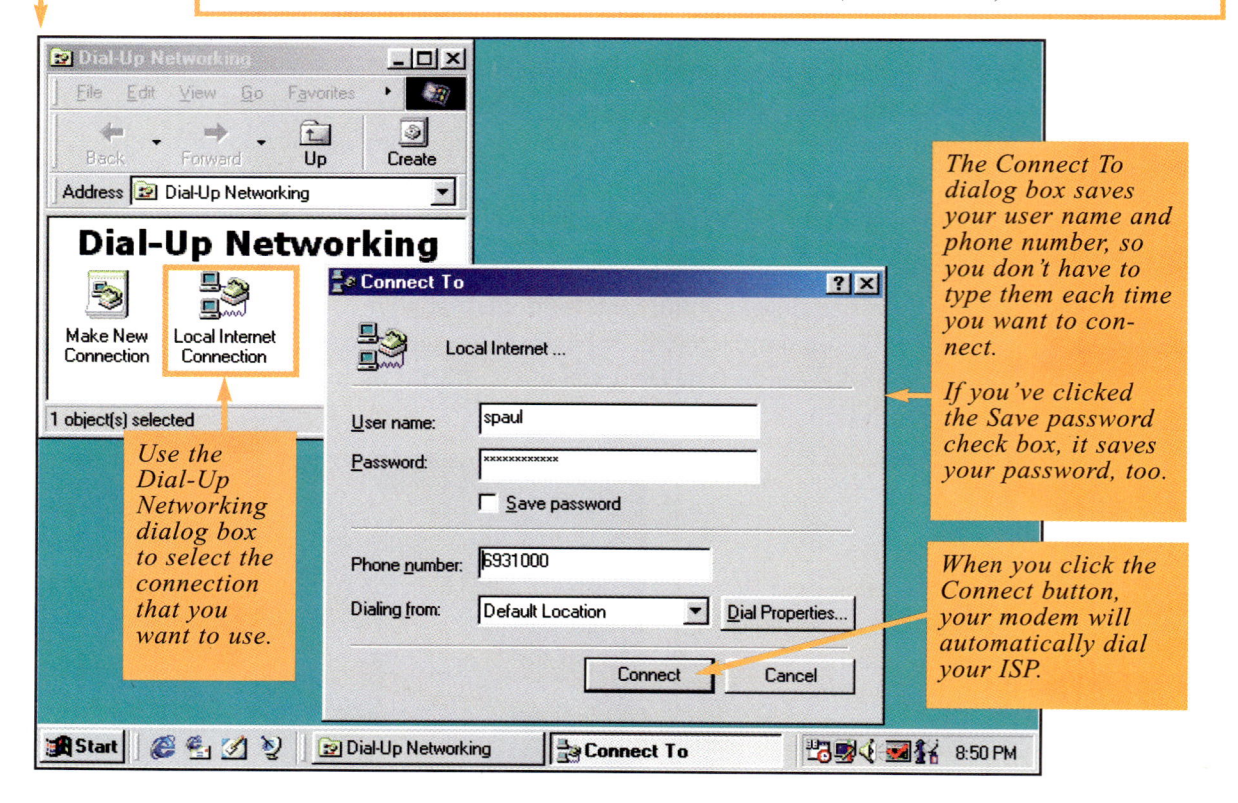

Use the Dial-Up Networking dialog box to select the connection that you want to use.

The Connect To dialog box saves your user name and phone number, so you don't have to type them each time you want to connect.

If you've clicked the Save password check box, it saves your password, too.

When you click the Connect button, your modem will automatically dial your ISP.

Chapter 7: Connecting to the Internet

■FAQ What's the World Wide Wait?

Internet use is growing at a phenomenal rate. Every week, the Internet carries about the same amount of information as is contained in all the books in the U.S. Library of Congress. Usually, this data moves along at a pretty good clip. Sometimes, however, high data volumes and technical difficulties cause data traffic jams dubbed the "World Wide Wait." This expression is humorously derived from "World Wide Web," the name of an extremely popular Internet service.

When you use the Internet today, you have to expect some slowdowns. You might get a busy signal when you try to connect to your ISP. A download can take hours. Information from an Internet server sometimes seems to travel at a snail's pace. Many Internet traffic jams are caused by insufficient bandwidth. **Bandwidth** is a measure of the transmission capacity of a communications link. Just as a multi-lane freeway can carry lots of traffic, a communications link with a high bandwidth can carry a large volume of data. When sufficient Internet bandwidth is not available, your data waits for its turn in the transmission queue—and you wait, too.

You can take steps to avoid the World Wide Wait. First, to provide maximum bandwidth at your point of connection to the Internet, make sure that your PC has the fastest modem that you can afford. Avoid connecting to the Internet at peak times, such as 8:00 a.m., when every office worker in your time zone collects e-mail. If your ISP's modems are frequently busy, consider switching to a different ISP. And make sure you disconnect when data transfers are complete, so that others can connect to your ISP.

Figure 7-5: Use this table to discover why you might be waiting for Internet data, and what to do about it.

Symptom	Probable Cause and Potential Solution
Busy signal—cannot connect.	All of your ISP's modems are currently in use. Try again later.
Overall response time seems much slower than usual.	Usually results from insufficient bandwidth between your ISP and the NSP. Consider a different ISP.
Slow response from a particular server.	The server might be trying to service too many customers at that time. Try again later.
Disconnected without warning.	Possibly a bad connection or a bad phone line. Make sure that your phone line is free of static when you make voice calls. Also, make sure that you've disabled call waiting on your telephone.
Downloads take too long.	You might be using a slow modem—refer to the Hardware section of this chapter for a discussion of modem speeds. Your ISP might have lots of traffic or the Internet server supplying the download might be trying to service too many customers. Try again later.

Chapter 7: Connecting to the Internet

■Hardware
Modems

The word "modem" is derived from the terms "*mod*ulate" and "*dem*odulate" because a modem has the ability to convert (modulate and demodulate) signals. This ability is especially handy for converting the digital signals from your computer into analog signals that can travel over telephone lines. Internally, your PC moves and stores data as **digital signals** using a series of 1s and 0s. The Internet, which was designed for computer communication, also works with digital signals. However, the telephone system that you use to connect to your ISP was originally designed to carry sounds and voices using wave-shaped **analog signals**, similar to those you'd see on an oscilloscope. Your modem can convert your PC's data into sounds for its journey over the phone lines to your ISP. When your ISP receives these analog signals, it converts them back into digital signals that can speed along the Internet's communications links.

Modems are available in three configurations: internal, external, and PCMCIA. An **internal modem** plugs directly into the main circuit board inside your PC's system unit. An opening in the back of the system unit allows you to connect the phone cable. Internal modems are popular because they do not require desk space. At U.S.$50 or less, they are the least expensive type of modem.

An **external modem** is housed in a separate case outside of the PC's system unit. It is connected to the computer using a serial cable, and to the phone jack using a standard phone cable. The advantages of an external modem include its portability and its visible status lights, which flicker on and off to show you when the modem connects and transfers data. External modems typically require external power, so you have to plug them into a wall outlet. An external modem costs about U.S.$20 more than an equivalent internal modem.

A **PCMCIA modem** is housed on a credit-card-sized PCMCIA card. Handy for notebook computer users, a PCMCIA modem is compact and easily transportable, but can cost twice as much as an internal modem.

Figure 7-6: The external modem pictured at the left of the photo requires an external power source. The internal modem (top right) is designed to plug directly into the main circuit board of your PC. The PCMCIA card in the foreground provides both modem and network connections.

Chapter 7: Connecting to the Internet

■Hardware
continued

The speed at which a modem transmits and receives data is measured in **Kbps**—thousands of bits per second. A **bit** is a single 0 or 1 in the string of bytes that represents data. By today's standards, modem speeds of 14.4 Kbps or 28.8 Kbps are relatively slow. A speed of 33.6 Kbps is presently the fastest speed at which a modem can send data from your PC to your ISP. However, data that originates from the Internet can travel "downstream" to your PC at a faster rate—up to 56 Kbps if the phone lines in your community are in good shape.

This boost in downstream transmission speed requires that both you and your ISP have a **v.90 modem**, which allows your ISP to send data as digital signals directly from the Internet to your PC without first changing it into analog signals. This ability to bypass the analog-to-digital conversion is one of the many benefits of the new digital equipment now used by most local phone companies for voice and computer data. Keep in mind, however, that actual data transmission speeds can be quite a bit slower than 56 Kbps, depending on the condition of your phone line and the level of Internet traffic.

Modems include a variety of bells and whistles, most notably fax and voice-mail capability. A **data/fax modem** can communicate with fax machines to send and receive faxes. Your modem cannot actually scan or print a paper document, however, so you can send only documents that you have stored as files on your computer. The faxes that your modem receives are stored on your PC's hard disk until you print them on your computer printer. Note, too, that these documents are stored as pictures of a page, not as a file containing text that you can edit.

A **data/voice modem** gives your PC the ability to function as a fancy answering machine. It can answer voice calls, play a selection of pre-recorded messages, and store messages in mailboxes assigned to different members of your family or different employees in a business. Both outgoing and incoming messages are stored on your PC's hard disk and can be played using your computer's sound system and speakers.

Figure 7-7: When installing a modem, always follow the manufacturer's instructions. The installation process might require software, either provided on the original Windows distribution CD or by the modem manufacturer. Click PlayIt! for some tips on installing a modem.

Does your PC have an internal modem? Look for phone jacks like these on the back of the system unit.

Hardware continued

A modem is a fairly durable piece of technology, but it is connected to a telephone line that can occasionally carry damaging electrical spikes. To protect your modem, you might consider routing the cable from the phone jack through a surge strip that's equipped with modem jacks. Like any other circuit-based component in your PC, a modem can sometimes misbehave. The cause could be as simple as a loose cable, or as serious as a malfunction in the modem circuitry.

If your modem doesn't seem to work, try these troubleshooting tips:

- Make sure that the plastic ends of the phone cable are firmly plugged into your modem and into the telephone wall jack.
- Double-check that the phone cable is plugged into the correct jack at the back of your computer. Your computer documentation will indicate which of the two jacks to use for the modem.
- If you're using an external modem, make sure it is plugged in and turned on.
- Make sure the phone line is working. If in doubt, plug a phone into the wall jack and make sure that you have a dial tone.
- Dial your ISP using a regular phone to ensure that its line is not busy and that your computer is dialing the correct number. You should hear a series of tones when the ISP's modem answers.
- Use the Control Panel to diagnose installation and connection problems.

Figure 7-8: What if your modem stops working or you install a new modem and it doesn't seem to work? Click PlayIt! to learn how to troubleshoot modem problems using the Control Panel.

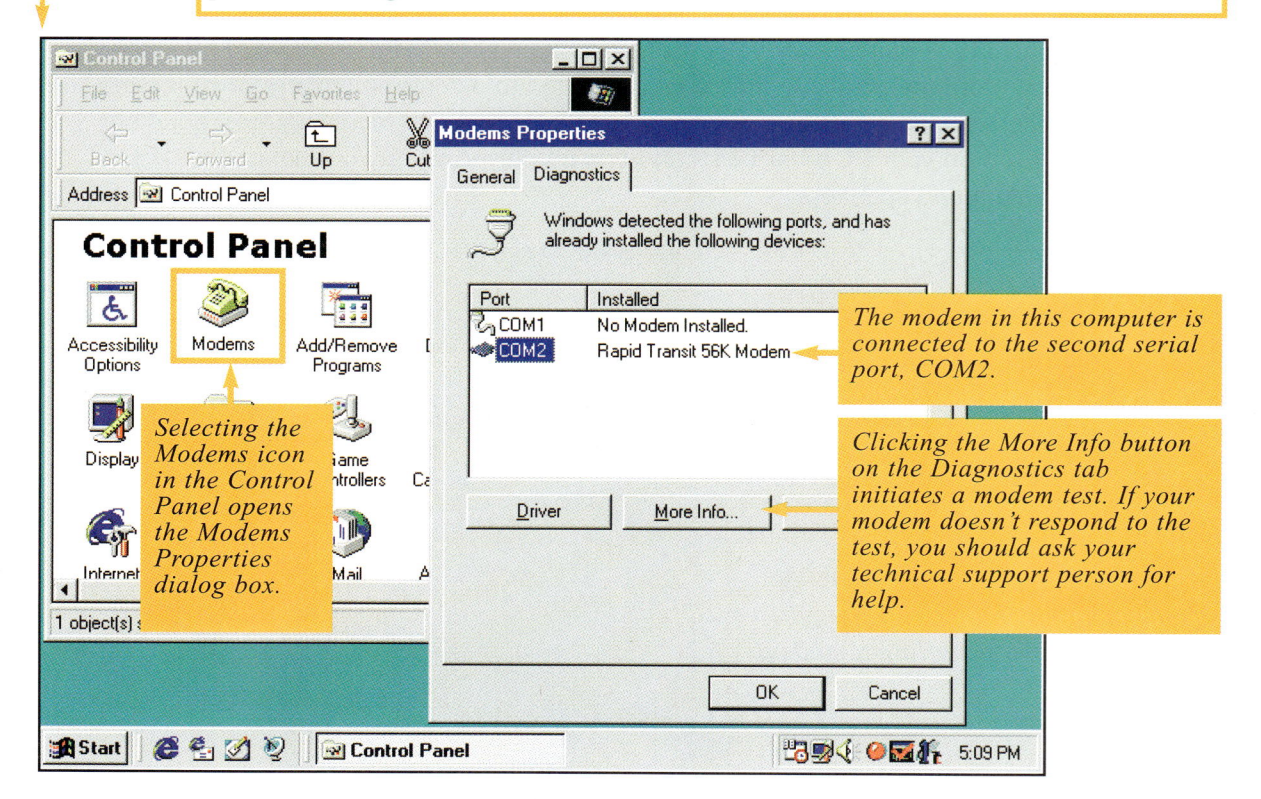

Selecting the Modems icon in the Control Panel opens the Modems Properties dialog box.

The modem in this computer is connected to the second serial port, COM2.

Clicking the More Info button on the Diagnostics tab initiates a modem test. If your modem doesn't respond to the test, you should ask your technical support person for help.

Chapter 7: Connecting to the Internet

■Tutorial
How to set up your Internet connection

To connect to the Internet, you can choose a national ISP or a local ISP. A **national ISP** operates in a wide geographical area and offers local dial-up connections for many cities and larger towns. If you travel frequently, you might find this coverage handy because you can connect to your ISP from any city that it services. A **local ISP** is typically owned and operated by a business in your local community. It offers local dial-up connections even in small towns and rural areas. Service can be just as good as, or better than that of a national ISP.

Your ISP generally supplies you with the software that you'll need to set up your Internet connection. Even without such software, you can use **Windows Internet Connection Wizard** to establish an account with one of the larger national ISPs. This tutorial shows you how to use this wizard.

When you have completed the tutorial, you should be able to:
- ■ Outline the steps required to set up an Internet connection.
- ■ Use Windows Internet Connection Wizard to sign up with a national ISP.
- ■ Cancel Internet service from an ISP.

Figure 7-9: Click the PlayIt! button to begin the tutorial that simulates the process of signing up with a national ISP. Estimated time: 15–20 minutes. Tracking Disk points: 10.

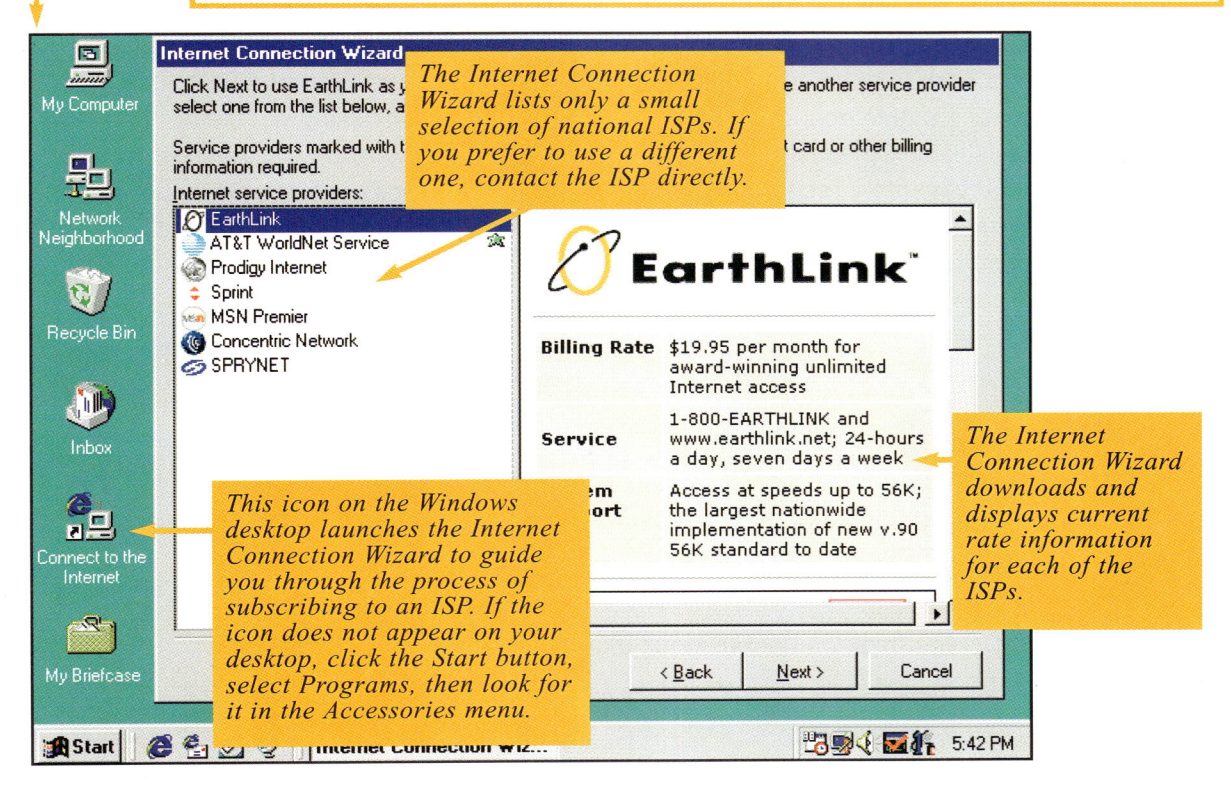

The Internet Connection Wizard lists only a small selection of national ISPs. If you prefer to use a different one, contact the ISP directly.

This icon on the Windows desktop launches the Internet Connection Wizard to guide you through the process of subscribing to an ISP. If the icon does not appear on your desktop, click the Start button, select Programs, then look for it in the Accessories menu.

The Internet Connection Wizard downloads and displays current rate information for each of the ISPs.

83

■Issue
Do we need anonymous digital cash?

The Internet is increasingly used for **e-commerce** activities, such as shopping online, paying utility bills, and subscribing to various online services. E-commerce typically requires e-payment. Today's consumer usually pays for online transactions using a credit card. But many people wonder if it is safe to transmit their credit card information over the Internet. Could their credit card numbers be intercepted, and then used by crooks?

Although it is possible to intercept data flowing over the Internet, it is not so easy to filter out credit card numbers from the rest of the data. Your credit card number is more likely to be stolen by someone who finds a receipt in your trash or by a dishonest restaurant employee who jots down your card number while processing your dinner payment. Online security at most e-commerce sites further protects your credit card transactions by providing a special connection that encrypts your card number as it travels over the Internet. Although it is fairly safe to use your credit card on the Internet, the process has what many people view as a major disadvantage—it leaves a trail of what you buy and who you pay. Many consumers would prefer to use an anonymous form of payment.

Digital cash is an electronic replacement for cash that can be stored by your PC and spent on the Internet—without leaving a trail to its source. Several companies have unveiled prototypes for digital cash, but none has gained widespread use because some critical issues remain unresolved. For example, can private firms issue digital cash, and can they profit from its use? Currently, only governments issue cash because controlling the money supply plays an important role in maintaining a stable economy. Is it possible to create digital cash that cannot be stolen or falsified? Obviously consumers and merchants alike want assurances that the digital cash they receive is authentic. Is it really a good idea to have anonymous transactions? Many honest consumers think so, but so do many criminals. Consumers would enjoy much more privacy with regard to their purchases, but governments would not be able to keep close tabs on taxable income.

What do you think?

1. Have you ever made a purchase from the Internet using a credit card? ○ Yes ○ No ○ Not sure

2. Do you think that most people believe that using a credit card in a restaurant is safer than using a credit card on the Internet? ○ Yes ○ No ○ Not sure

3. Do you think that anonymous digital cash is a good idea? ○ Yes ○ No ○ Not sure

Save It!

Chapter 7: Connecting to the Internet   85

QuickCheck A

1. A typical Internet connection requires a computer, a modem, a phone line, an Internet service provider, and _____.

2. When you connect to the Internet, the modem on your PC dials the phone number for a(n) _____.

3. The cause of many Internet traffic jams is insufficient _____.

4. True or false? If you dial your ISP, but get no response, all of the ISP's modems could be busy. _____

5. True or false? A v.90 modem sends and receives data at 56 Kbps. _____

Check It!

QuickCheck B

Fill in the letter from the diagram that correctly matches each description:

1. An ISP modem _____
2. An Internet server _____
3. An NSP _____
4. A digital connection _____
5. An analog connection _____

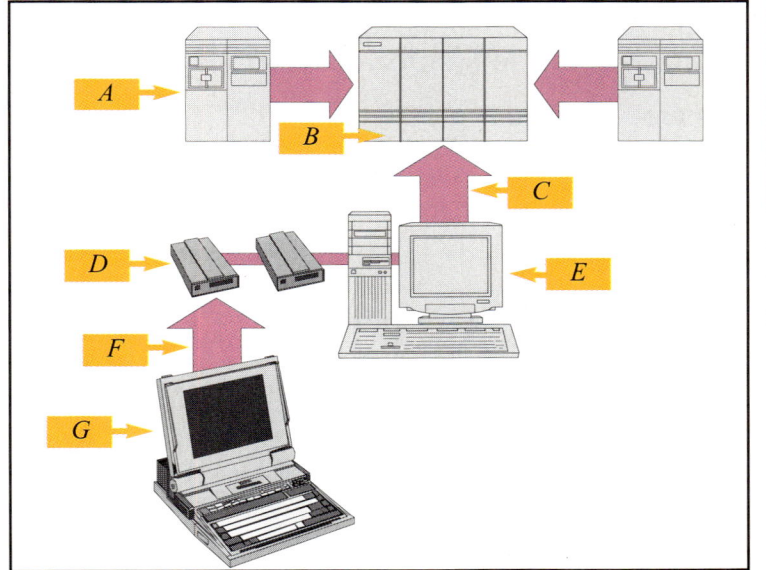

Check It!

Get It?

While using the Book-on-CD, click the Get It? button to see if you can answer ten randomly selected questions from Chapter 7.

Get It?

Chapter 8
Browsing and Searching the Web

What's Inside?

The Web is the real jewel in the crown of the Internet. You've seen references to it in magazines and on TV. Web addresses, such as www.nationalgeographic.com, direct you to Web sites where you can find information, order products, interact with other people, and more! Chapter 8 highlights the Web's key features and provides tips for surfing the Web like a pro.

- FAQs:

What's a Web page?	87
What's a URL?	88
How does a browser work?	89
How do I use a search engine?	90
Can I save text and graphics that I find on the Web?	91

- Hardware: High-speed and wireless Internet-access equipment — 92
- Tutorial: How to create your own Web pages — 95
- Issue: The filtering controversy — 96
- QuickChecks — 97

What's on the CD?

In Chapter 8, you'll find out how to use a Web browser and a search engine, the two required software tools in the Web surfer's toolkit. Also, you'll learn how to incorporate the information that you find on the Web in your own documents and Web pages.

- Discover the story behind Web page text, graphics, and video links — 87
- Find out how to use a Web browser — 89
- Learn how to search the Web using Yahoo! — 90
- See how easily you can save a copy of a Web page — 91
- Take a step-by-step tutorial on creating Web pages — 95

Chapter 8: Browsing and Searching the Web

■FAQ What's a Web page?

A **Web page** is a specially coded document that can contain text, graphics, videos, and sound clips. Millions of these pages are interlinked and available on the **Web** (a nickname for the World Wide Web), an Internet service second in popularity only to e-mail. The links between pages, sometimes called **hypertext links**, allow you to follow a thread of information from one Web page to another.

The computers that store Web pages are known as **Web servers**. Each Web server hosts one or more **Web sites** that contain information about a specific topic, company, organization, person, event, or place. The person who creates, updates, and maintains a Web site is called a **Webmaster**.

The main page for a Web site is sometimes referred to as a **home page**. Any page on a Web site can be linked to the home page, to other pages at the same Web site, or to pages at other Web sites anywhere in the world. **Text links** usually appear as blue or green underlined words. Some Web pages also have **graphics links** that appear as pictures, rather than as underlined text. When you point to a text or graphics link, the arrow-shaped pointer changes to a hand-shaped **link pointer**. By clicking a link, you are requesting the Web page indicated by the link. To fulfill your request, a Web server sends a copy of of the linked Web page to your PC's memory. Your PC can then display the Web page on the screen.

Figure 8-1: Click the PlayIt! button to take a guided tour of a typical Web page. You'll learn how to use text and graphics links to "surf" from one page to another, plus you'll see how Web pages play videos and sound clips.

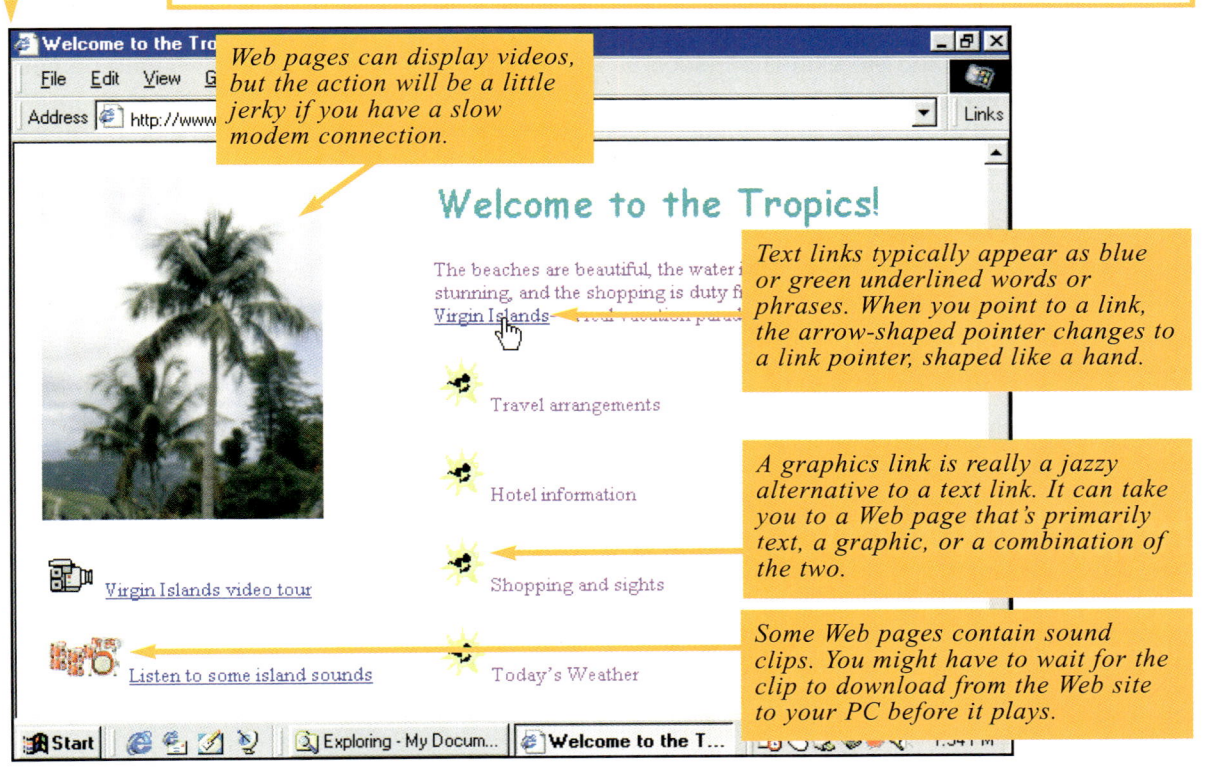

Web pages can display videos, but the action will be a little jerky if you have a slow modem connection.

Text links typically appear as blue or green underlined words or phrases. When you point to a link, the arrow-shaped pointer changes to a link pointer, shaped like a hand.

A graphics link is really a jazzy alternative to a text link. It can take you to a Web page that's primarily text, a graphic, or a combination of the two.

Some Web pages contain sound clips. You might have to wait for the clip to download from the Web site to your PC before it plays.

Chapter 8: Browsing and Searching the Web

■FAQ What's a URL?

A **URL** (uniform resource locator) is essentially a Web page address—it specifies the Web server that stores the page, the folder (or folders) that hold the page, and the name of the page. If you are not using a link to jump to a Web page, you will need to enter its URL manually. As a hypothetical example, suppose that you want to find out about a new promotion sponsored by the Coca-Cola Company. You could look for the URL in one of the many Internet directories on the shelves of a library or bookstore, but you can often guess the URL of a Web site's home page once you understand how URLs are constructed.

Most URLs begin with http://. The acronym **HTTP** stands for Hypertext Transfer Protocol, a standard used by Web servers for transmitting Web pages over the Internet. Some financial Web sites encrypt transmissions by using Secure HTTP or Secure Sockets Layer. The URL for a secure site would begin with https://.

The next part of the URL is the Web server's name, which usually begins with www and includes the name of a company, organization, or person. Periods separate the parts of a server name, as in http://www.cocacola.com. The last part of the server name indicates a Web server category or **top-level domain**, such as .com for commercial businesses, .org for professional and nonprofit organizations, .gov for the U.S. government, or .edu for educational institutions. A top-level domain might also indicate a country, such as .ca for Canada or .uk for the United Kingdom. You can generally connect to a Web server by entering the server name. Entering http://www.cocacola.com should connect you to Coca-Cola's home page.

In addition to the home page, a Web server typically stores hundreds or thousands of other Web pages identified in the last part of the URL by a folder name, file name, and file extension, such as /contest/rules.htm. Unlike Windows path names which use backslashes, URLs use forward slashes to separate the folder name from other parts of the path. Most Web pages have an .html or .htm extension because they are stored in HTML format. **HTML** (Hypertext Markup Language) is a file format that contains embedded instructions called "tags" that produce specific effects, such as bold text, colored backgrounds, or underlined links.

Figure 8-2: When you enter a URL, make sure you type it exactly as written. If you are guessing the URL of a Web server, use all lowercase letters. URLs don't contain any spaces, so never add a space before or after a period or a slash.

http://www.cocacola.com/contest/rules.htm

Web protocol

Server name, including top-level domain

Web page folder, name, and extension

Chapter 8: Browsing and Searching the Web 89

■FAQ How does a browser work?

Grab It!
Browsers

A **Web browser** (or "browser" for short) is the software that displays Web pages on your computer screen by interpreting **HTML tags** that are embedded in each Web page. Your browser understands, for example, that when it encounters the HTML tag <U> in the text of a file, it should underline text until it reaches a </U> tag. A browser also handles links between Web pages. When you click an underlined link, your browser sends the link's URL to the Web server, which in turn sends the linked page to your PC. Two of today's most popular browsers are Microsoft Internet Explorer and Netscape Navigator.

Special computer programs called **plug-ins** extend the variety of files and media that your browser can display on a Web page. Certain types of video and sound files, for example, might require plug-ins. If a Web page requires a plug-in that your browser doesn't have, you will typically see a message indicating which plug-in is needed and the site from which it can be downloaded.

Sometimes, your browser interacts with a Web server to create a cookie. A **cookie** is a message that contains information to help a Web server identify you and, perhaps, customize the information that it presents. When you access a Web site that uses cookies, you typically fill out a form with information such as your name, e-mail address, and interests. This information is encapsulated as a cookie and sent to your browser, which stores the cookie on your PC. Whenever you access this Web site, your browser sends the cookie back to the Web server for its use.

Play It!

Figure 8-3: Click PlayIt! to tour a browser and find out how it interprets HTML tags behind the scenes to display a beautifully formatted Web page.

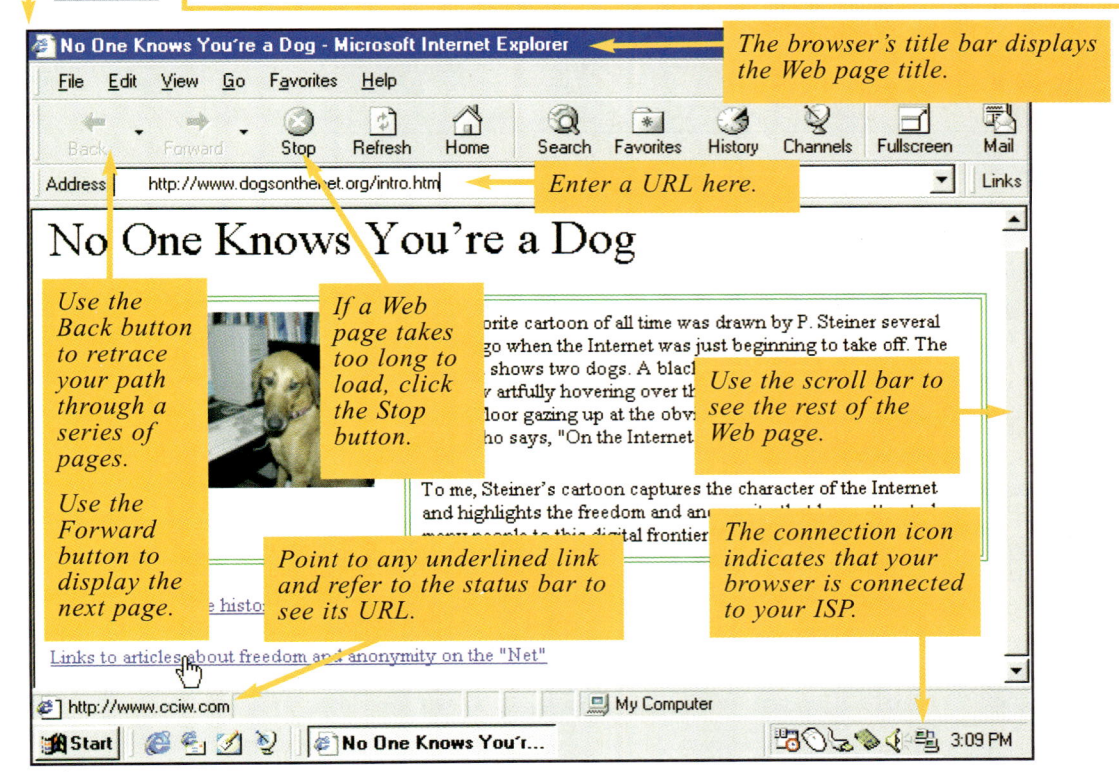

The browser's title bar displays the Web page title.

Enter a URL here.

Use the Back button to retrace your path through a series of pages.

Use the Forward button to display the next page.

If a Web page takes too long to load, click the Stop button.

Point to any underlined link and refer to the status bar to see its URL.

Use the scroll bar to see the rest of the Web page.

The connection icon indicates that your browser is connected to your ISP.

Chapter 8: Browsing and Searching the Web

■FAQ How do I use a search engine?

Just as a librarian catalogs books, a **search engine** catalogs Web pages to make it easier to find information. Popular search engines such as Yahoo!, Alta Vista, Lycos, and Excite help you sift through the millions of Web pages on the Internet. Like any other Web site, a search engine has a URL. To search with Yahoo!, for example, you would use your browser to connect to www.yahoo.com. Once you've connected to a search engine, you can search by selecting topics from an indexed list, or you can enter words and phrases that describe the kind of information you want to find.

Most search engines can handle both simple and complex searches. For a simple search, you just enter a topic and, perhaps, a few synonyms. To find information about losing weight, for example, you might enter "weight loss diet calories." A search engine will respond by showing you a list of results or "hits" for Web pages that contain information on one or all of these topics. The list will include a short summary of each page and an underlined link that you can use to jump directly to it. With a simple search, a search engine often returns a huge list that might contain more than 10,000 hits. To get a smaller, more targeted list, you must use more sophisticated search techniques. Because each search engine provides a slightly different set of advanced search tools, you should consult your search engine's online Help for details on composing advanced searches.

Figure 8-4: Yahoo! lets you browse through an indexed list of topics, enter simple searches, or compose advanced searches. Click the PlayIt! button to find out more about using search engines.

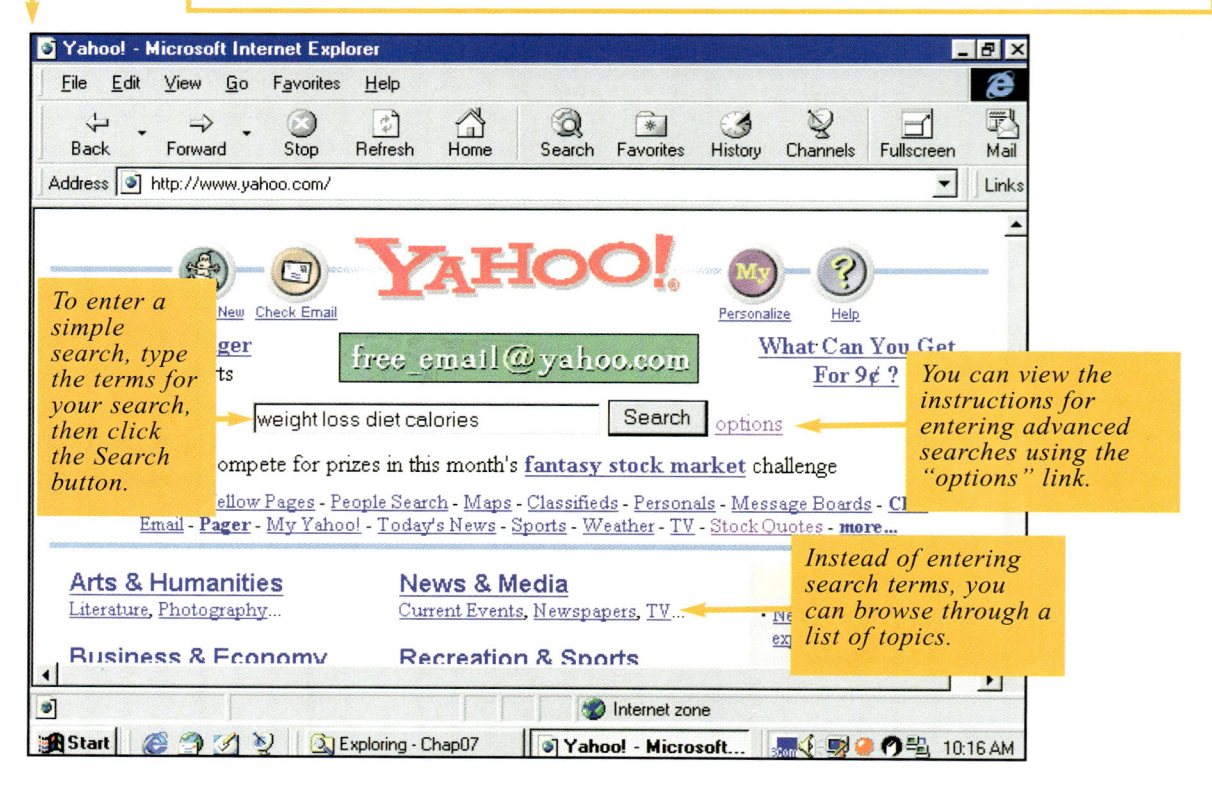

To enter a simple search, type the terms for your search, then click the Search button.

You can view the instructions for entering advanced searches using the "options" link.

Instead of entering search terms, you can browse through a list of topics.

Chapter 8: Browsing and Searching the Web

■FAQ Can I save text and graphics that I find on the Web?

If you come across an interesting article or graphic on the Web, you might want to print it or save it on your PC. To print a Web page, use your browser's Print button or the Print option on the File menu. Before printing, you might want to use the Page Setup option on the File menu to ensure that the Web page URL will appear on each sheet of the printout. Instead of printing, you can save a copy of an entire Web page, or just save selected paragraphs. You can also save copies of Web page graphics, including photos and borders.

When using material from the Web, make sure that you respect the author's intellectual property rights. Assume that everything you see on the Web is copyrighted. If you would like to use a graphic that you've downloaded, you should obtain permission first by e-mailing the copyright holder. Look for an e-mail address at the bottom of the Web page that contains the graphic or on the main page for the site. When you incorporate Web page text excerpts into your documents, you must include a citation that follows a standard style such as MLA or APA. The citation must contain the author's name, the title of the Web page, the title of the site, the date of publication, the date when you accessed the page, and the URL for the page. Note the following example of a citation using the MLA style:

Canine, Claire. "No One Knows You're a Dog." <u>Dogs on the Net</u>. 1998. 11 Nov. 1999 <http://www.dogsonthenet.org/intro.htm>.

Figure 8-5: *Click the PlayIt! button to find out how to save a copy of the text and graphics that you find on Web pages.*

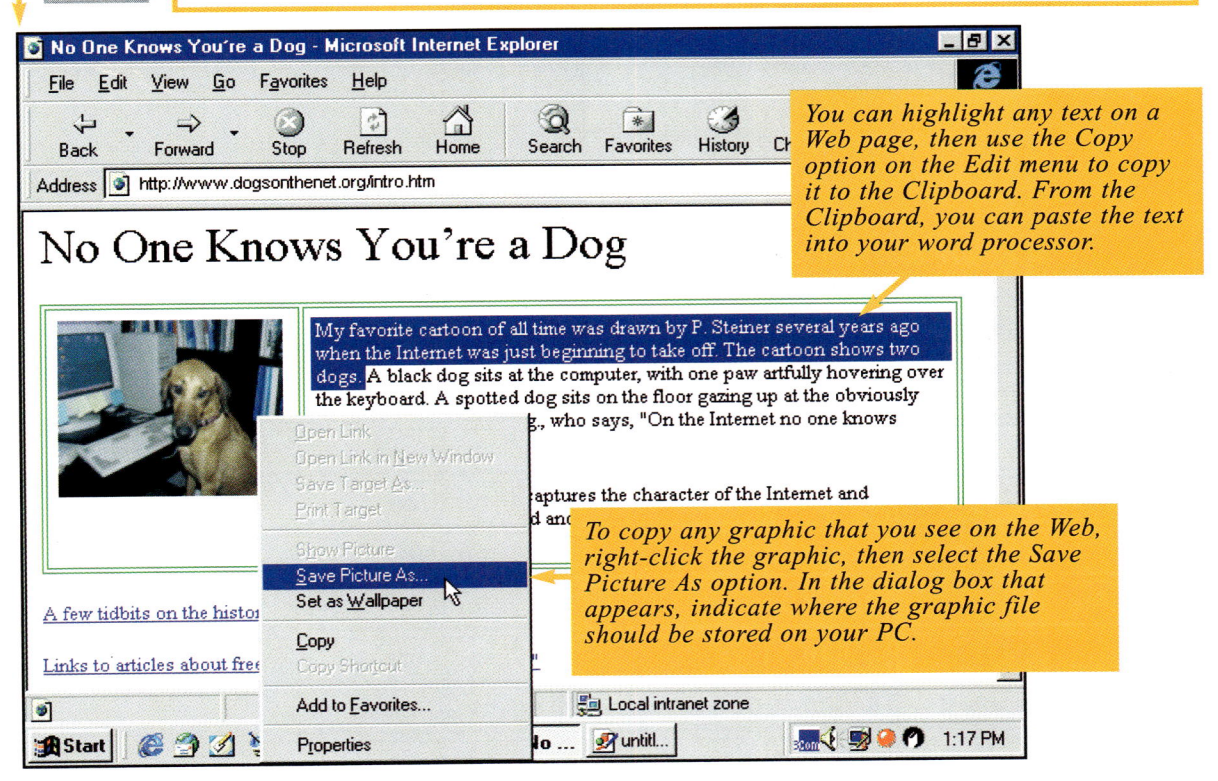

You can highlight any text on a Web page, then use the Copy option on the Edit menu to copy it to the Clipboard. From the Clipboard, you can paste the text into your word processor.

To copy any graphic that you see on the Web, right-click the graphic, then select the Save Picture As option. In the dialog box that appears, indicate where the graphic file should be stored on your PC.

Hardware
High-speed and wireless Internet-access equipment

The Hardware section of Chapter 7 described how you can use a modem and a regular household phone line to access the Internet and Internet services such as the Web. But a phone line and modem have limitations. Response time can be slow even with a 56 Kbps modem. You might experience frustrating busy signals when trying to connect to your ISP. Your PC is also anchored to the phone line, which is not optimal for traveling and other mobile applications.

Telephone, cable TV, satellite TV, and cellular phone companies want to provide alternative communications links for the rapidly growing horde of Web surfers. High-speed alternatives include ISDN and DSL, direct satellite service, and cable modems; mobile wireless alternatives include voice/data cellular phones and cellular modems. As Figure 8-6 indicates, high-speed connections tend to get data to you faster—sometimes much faster—than 33.6 or v.90 modem connections. However, traffic can jam up on any Internet service if too many subscribers try to connect at the same time and access large data files.

ISDN service is a medium-speed service which uses a pair of standard telephone lines and a special modem to provide data transfer speeds up to 128 Kbps for a monthly charge of up to U.S.$100. ISDN is available in many areas.

DSL (Digital Subscriber Line Service) and its variations, ADSL or SDSL, offer Internet connections of between 1 Mbps and 4 Mbps over a special telephone line for a monthly fee ranging from U.S.$50 to $200. Unfortunately, DSL is only available in limited locations.

Phone companies also offer **T-1 service**, which provides your own high-speed communications link to the Internet. This service is currently too expensive for most individuals and small businesses.

Figure 8-6: You can experience a remarkable reduction in download time by using a high-speed Internet connection.

Connection Type	Connection Speed	Download Time for a 10 MB File
Telephone	33.6 Kbps	40 minutes
Telephone	56 Kbps	24 minutes
ISDN	128 Kbps	10 minutes
Satellite	400 Kbps	4 minutes
T-1	1,540 Kbps	52 seconds
DSL, ADSL, xDSL	1,000-4,000 Kbps	80 to 20 seconds
Cable TV	4,000 Kbps	20 seconds

Chapter 8: Browsing and Searching the Web

■Hardware
continued

Small satellite dishes are popping up like mushrooms in metropolitan and rural areas. **Direct satellite service** (DSS) provides access to transmissions beamed directly from a satellite to your own satellite dish. Some DSS companies now offer data services as well as television shows, so that for a monthly fee you can use your dish to receive Web pages and other information from the Internet. With current technology, your satellite dish can receive data, but cannot send it. Therefore, you must use a regular telephone modem to send data to the Internet. This limitation is not a major disadvantage, however, because the data that you send—a URL, for example—is only a few characters, compared to the potentially huge text, graphics, sound, and video files that you might receive as Web pages.

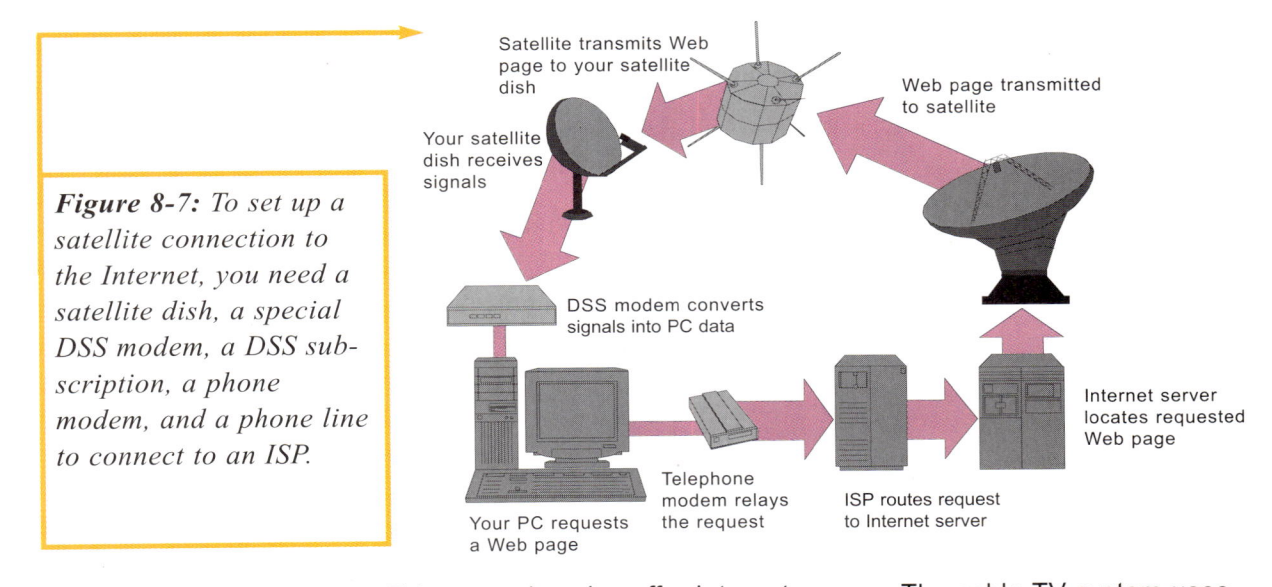

Figure 8-7: To set up a satellite connection to the Internet, you need a satellite dish, a special DSS modem, a DSS subscription, a phone modem, and a phone line to connect to an ISP.

Some cable TV companies also offer Internet access. The cable TV system uses coaxial cables—those now-familiar thick cables with tube-like gold or silver connectors. These cables have a very high bandwidth, making them ideal for carrying large data files as well as television broadcasts. Cable TV companies currently offer the fastest Internet connection option that individual PC owners can afford.

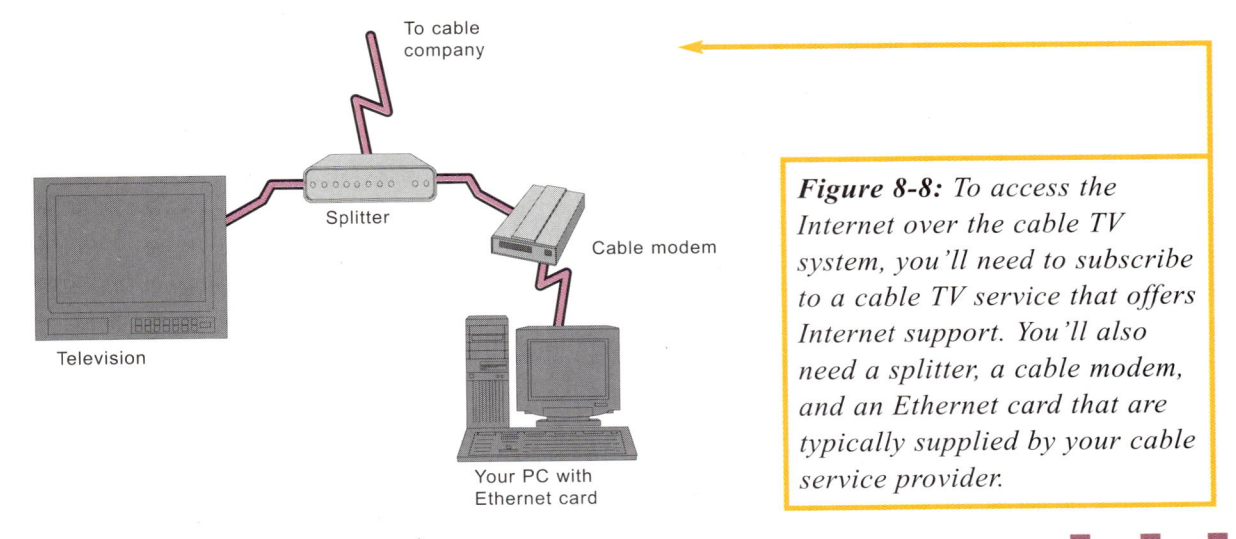

Figure 8-8: To access the Internet over the cable TV system, you'll need to subscribe to a cable TV service that offers Internet support. You'll also need a splitter, a cable modem, and an Ethernet card that are typically supplied by your cable service provider.

■Hardware
continued

If you cherish the mobility and convenience of your cellular phone, you might wonder whether mobile Internet access is possible. Cellular phone companies currently provide two options for mobile Internet access: hand-held voice/data phones and cellular phone modems. To use either option, you must sign up for cellular phone service and purchase the necessary hardware devices.

Figure 8-9: With an enlarged LCD display, communications software, and a built-in modem, a souped-up cellular phone provides wireless access to e-mail and other Internet data. Before you invest in one of these phones, make sure that you don't find the tiny screen and keyboard too limiting.

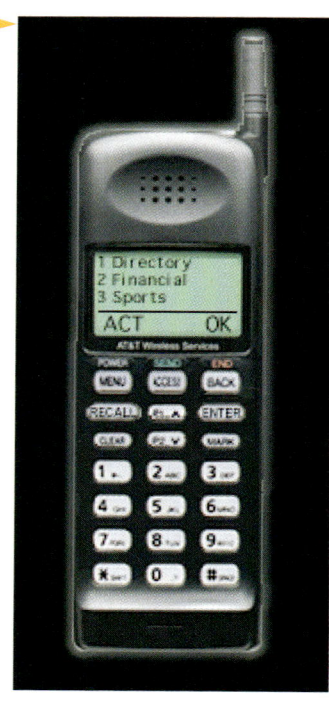

Think about holding the Internet in your hand. That's the idea behind a new generation of voice/data cellular phones that provide access to e-mail, the Web, and other Internet services. These devices are truly portable. As you can imagine, however, a display screen that shows only a fraction of what you would see on a PC monitor can be quite limiting.

Voice/data cellular phones are available from several manufacturers, including Nokia, Motorola, and Qualcomm. Typically, Internet access services put additional charges on your monthly cellular phone bill, and you might be limited to Web sites that are specially formatted for display on a small screen.

What if you can't get by with a miniscule display and keyboard, but still want the mobility offered by cellular service? You can connect any desktop or notebook PC to a cellular modem. This solution is particularly handy if you're using a notebook computer away from your home. For example, you can use your cellular modem to connect to the Internet from your local library, your car, or your client's office.

Figure 8-10: You can connect your PC to a cellular phone with a special cellular modem. Once all of your equipment is connected, you can dial your ISP and access Internet data over your cellular phone, instead of using your conventional phone.

Chapter 8: Browsing and Searching the Web

■Tutorial
How to create your own Web pages

Grab It!
Web Page Authoring Software

You can create your own set of Web pages for the world to access. All you need is software that generates HTML documents and an ISP that will host your Web pages. Most word processing software today has the capability to produce HTML documents. For example, Microsoft Word can be quite suitable for creating your personal Web pages. Software specifically designed for creating Web pages includes Netscape Composer and Microsoft FrontPage. You can find this software at a computer store or on the Internet. Your ISP might allow you to post your personal Web pages, and educational institutions sometimes provide this service to students and faculty. In this tutorial you'll learn how to use Microsoft Word to create and revise Web pages.

When you have completed the tutorial, you should be able to:
- Create a Web page and save it in HTML format.
- Add links and graphics to a Web page.
- View and test the page using a browser.
- Examine the HTML tags embedded in a Web page.

Play It!

Figure 8-11: Click the PlayIt! button to begin the tutorial and learn how to create your own Web page. Estimated time: 20–30 minutes. Tracking Disk points: 10.

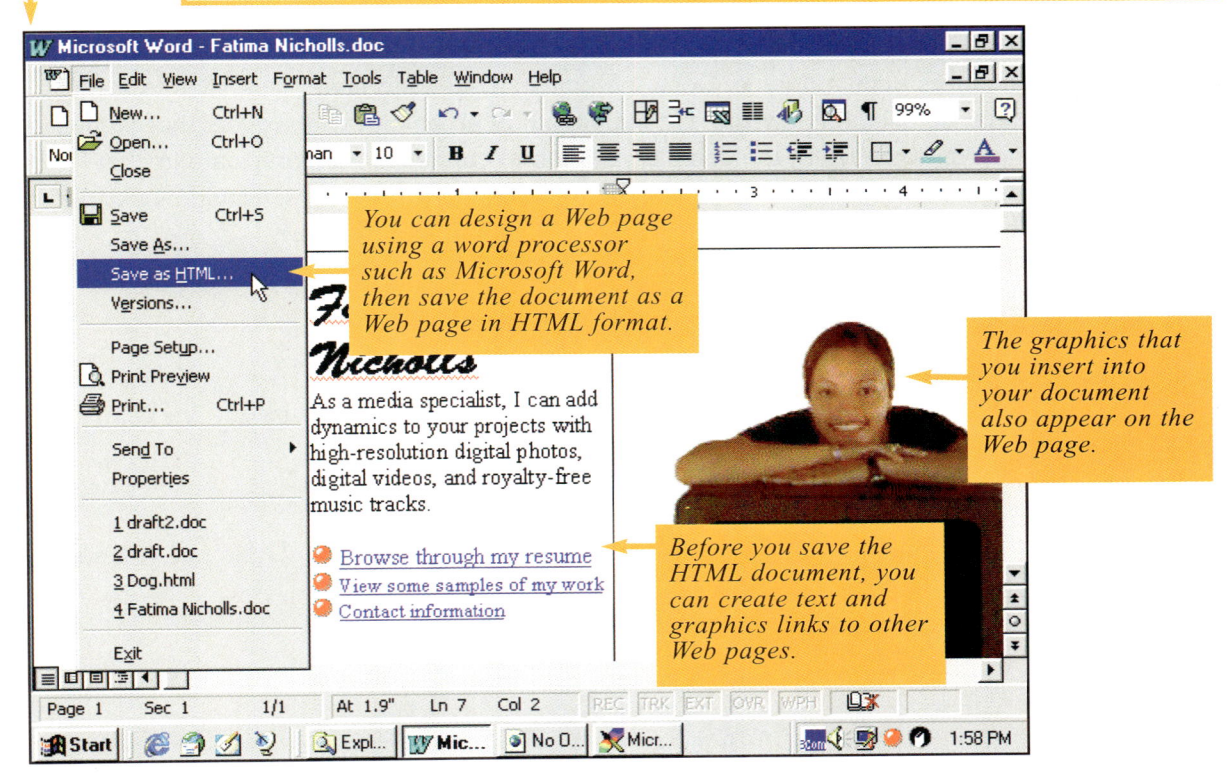

You can design a Web page using a word processor such as Microsoft Word, then save the document as a Web page in HTML format.

The graphics that you insert into your document also appear on the Web page.

Before you save the HTML document, you can create text and graphics links to other Web pages.

▪Issue
The filtering controversy

Democracies have a rich tradition of free speech and a free press that stands watch against censorship. Developments on the Internet have brought new attention to the tug of war between free speech and public decency. Without too much effort, anyone surfing the Internet can find some very unsavory material, including child pornography, hate group rhetoric, terrorist handbooks, graphic violence, and sexually explicit Web pages that go way beyond kinky sex.

Grab It!
Filtering Software

Many parents are concerned about what their children might encounter while surfing the Web. Even an innocent search for "Valentine" might lead to Web sites where sex is on sale. **Filtering software** makes it possible to block access to certain Web sites. Parents can install this software on their home PCs, select the sites that they want to block, and use a password to prevent anyone else from removing the blocks. In many communities, children also have access to the Internet from computers at school and the public library. Although filtering software makes it possible to block access to sites on these PCs, some librarians are reluctant to use it. They fear that it would be impossible to reach a consensus on the sites that should be filtered.

Without agreement on the advisability of using filtering software on computers accessed by children, it would seem improbable that schools and libraries would filter Internet access on PCs that are typically used only by adults. This idea really smacks of censorship. But suppose that some students in a university computer lab regularly download sexually explicit material that makes students at nearby computers uncomfortable. Does the university need to filter these sites to avoid a sexual harassment lawsuit? Or, suppose that an employer discovers that many employees are using the company's Internet connection to participate in chat groups and browse online help-wanted ads during work hours. Would blocking sites in this situation be reasonable or would it be censorship?

What do you think?

1. If you had children, would you use filtering software on your home PC to block access to certain Web sites?   ○ Yes ○ No ○ Not sure

2. Do you think schools and public libraries that provide Internet access to children should use filtering software?   ○ Yes ○ No ○ Not sure

3. Do you believe that in some situations it is appropriate to use filtering software on computers accessed only by adults?   ○ Yes ○ No ○ Not sure

Save It!

Chapter 8: Browsing and Searching the Web

QuickCheck A

1. Now that you understand how URLs are constructed, you could guess that the URL for Microsoft's home page is http://[_____].

2. Your PC is able to display a Web page correctly because your browser can interpret [_____] tags.

3. If you enter your name and e-mail address on a Web page form, the Web server will probably create a(n) [_____] containing this information and store it on your PC.

4. True or false? When in doubt, enter a URL using all lowercase letters. [_____]

5. True or false? ISDN service provides the fastest Internet connection that's affordable to an individual PC owner. [_____]

QuickCheck B

Fill in the letter from the diagram that correctly matches each description below:

1. A text link [_____]
2. A URL [_____]
3. The link pointer [_____]
4. Connection icon [_____]
5. Browser toolbar [_____]

Get It?

While using the Book-on-CD, click the Get It? button to see if you can answer ten randomly selected questions from Chapter 8.

Chapter 9

Sending E-mail and Attachments

What's Inside?

Chapter 9 takes you from e-mail basics to more advanced topics such as attachments and file compression. You'll get some tips on "netiquette" and in the hardware section you'll learn how networks provide an alternative to dial-up connections for accessing the Internet and e-mail.

- FAQs:

How does e-mail work?	99
How do I send and receive e-mail messages?	100
What's an e-mail attachment?	101
Is there a size limit for e-mail messages and attachments?	102
What are smileys, flame wars, and spams?	103

- Hardware: Local area networks — 104
- Tutorial: How to use your e-mail address book like a pro — 107
- Issue: Just how private is e-mail? — 108
- QuickChecks — 109

What's on the CD?

In addition to the basics of creating, reading, replying to, and forwarding e-mail, you'll learn how to send attachments, how to compress those attachments for more efficient transmission, and how to use your e-mail address book.

- Brush up on sending, reading, replying to, and forwarding e-mail — 100
- Learn how to attach graphics, sound, and video files to your e-mail — 101
- Find out how to zip and unzip e-mail attachments — 102
- Tour the Network Neighborhood — 106
- Take a tutorial to learn how to use an e-mail address book — 107

Chapter 9: Sending E-mail and Attachments

■FAQ How does e-mail work?

E-mail is an electronic version of the postal system. An **e-mail message** is an electronic document that can be transmitted from one computer to another, usually over the Internet. E-mail has become enormously popular because it is easy to use, delivers mail in a matter of hours, and lets you broadcast the same message simultaneously to more than one person. The computers and software that provide e-mail services form an **e-mail system**. At the heart of a typical e-mail system is an **e-mail server**—a computer that essentially acts as a central post office serving a group of people. It runs special **e-mail server software** that provides an electronic mailbox for each person, sorts incoming messages into these mailboxes, and routes outgoing mail over the Internet to other e-mail servers. Many ISPs maintain an e-mail server to handle e-mail for their subscribers.

Grab It! E-mail Client Software

To access an e-mail system, you must have an account on its e-mail server and your PC must have **e-mail client software** that helps you read, compose, and send messages. Most e-mail client software is inexpensive or free. For example, Microsoft Outlook Express is shipped with Windows, Netscape Mail is shipped with Netscape Navigator, and Eudora is available on the Web as shareware. Before using your e-mail client, you must provide it with configuration information. Your ISP will typically supply this information when you subscribe.

E-mail is a **store-and-forward technology**, which means that the e-mail server *stores* incoming messages until your client computer connects and requests them. The server then *forwards* this mail to your computer when you're ready to read it. Using store-and-forward technology, you don't miss any messages that arrive when you're not connected—they're stored on the server. This approach also allows you to minimize your connect time because you can read and compose messages offline, then connect only when you want to download your new mail from the server or upload mail that you've composed.

Figure 9-1: Your e-mail server receives your mail and stores it until you request that it be downloaded to your computer.

When you compose new messages, they are typically stored on your PC until you are ready to transmit them to the e-mail server, which then sends them on to the recipients.

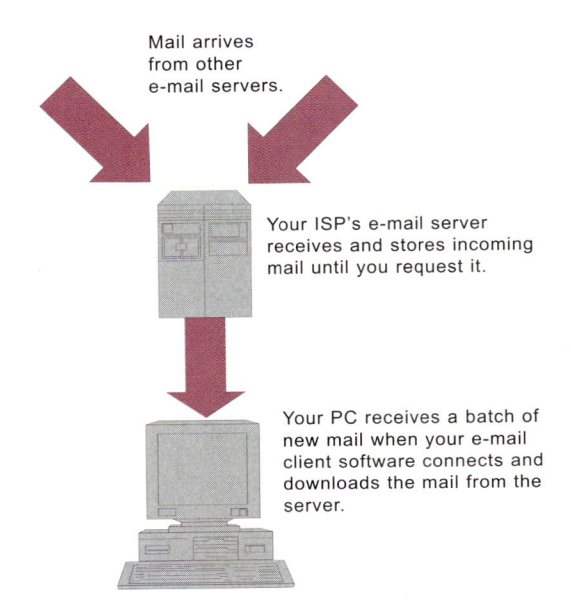

Mail arrives from other e-mail servers.

Your ISP's e-mail server receives and stores incoming mail until you request it.

Your PC receives a batch of new mail when your e-mail client software connects and downloads the mail from the server.

Chapter 9: Sending E-mail and Attachments

■FAQ How do I send and receive e-mail messages?

Basic e-mail skills include composing new messages, reading messages that you receive, replying to those messages, and forwarding messages. To compose a new message, simply fill in the e-mail header and then type the text of your message. When you use a dial-up connection, you'll typically compose your messages offline and queue them in your Outbox. The **Outbox** is a folder on your PC's hard disk that temporarily stores your newly created e-mail messages. When you're ready to send the messages, you connect to the mail server. Your e-mail client software will then transmit the message files from your Outbox to the mail server.

To read your mail, you must first connect to the mail server and download new messages to your **Inbox**, a folder on your PC's hard disk that holds incoming e-mail. Your e-mail software displays a list of messages in your Inbox. Unread messages are indicated by an icon, boldface, or colored type.

To reply to a message, simply click the Reply button. Your software will automatically open a new message, address it, and fill in the subject line. Typically, it will also display the text of the original message, with each line being preceded by a ">" symbol. By incorporating the original text with your reply, both you and the message recipient can have a complete record of the correspondence. It is customary to type your reply above the original message, or intersperse your reply within the lines of the original message. You can also forward the entire text of a message to a third party if you would like to share its contents.

Figure 9-2: Click the PlayIt! button for an overview of sending, reading, replying to, and forwarding e-mail.

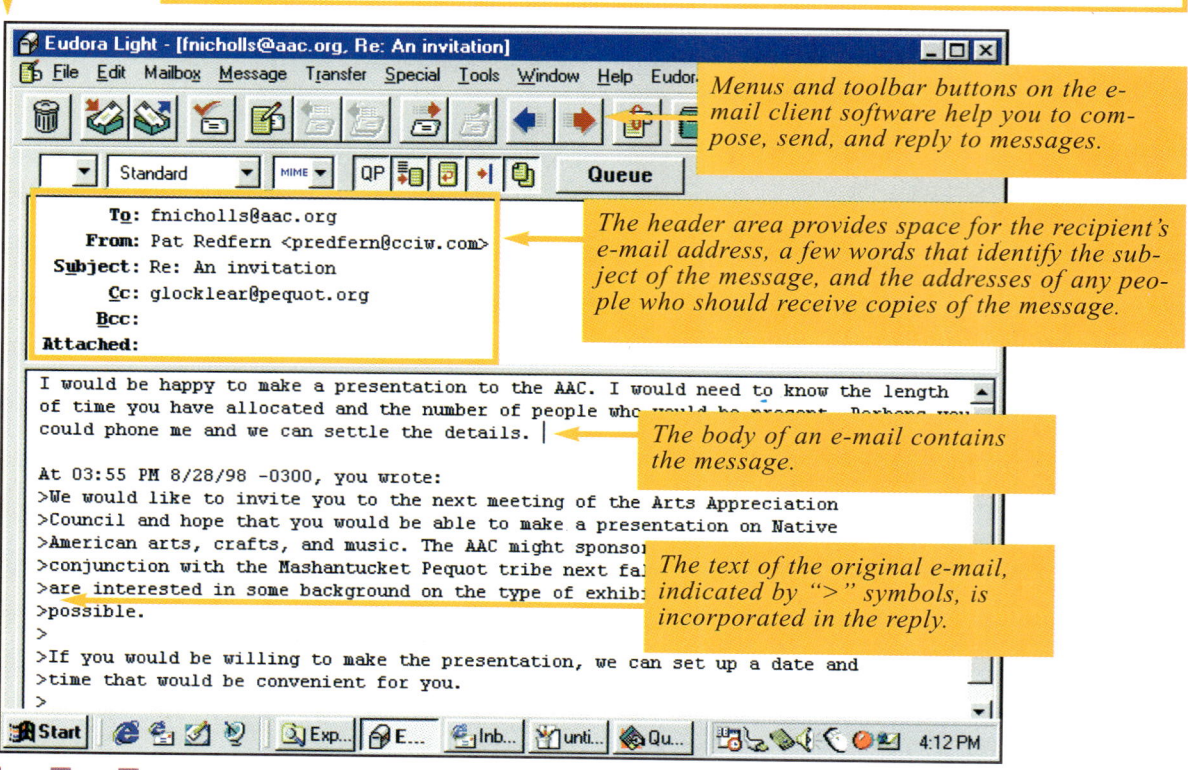

Menus and toolbar buttons on the e-mail client software help you to compose, send, and reply to messages.

The header area provides space for the recipient's e-mail address, a few words that identify the subject of the message, and the addresses of any people who should receive copies of the message.

The body of an e-mail contains the message.

The text of the original e-mail, indicated by ">" symbols, is incorporated in the reply.

Chapter 9: Sending E-mail and Attachments

■FAQ What's an e-mail attachment?

You don't have to know what kind of computer or software the recipient of your e-mail uses because the e-mail system makes any necessary translations. However, the system is set up to handle only plain, unformatted text files. To send formatted text, graphics, video, or sound files, you can use e-mail attachments. An **e-mail attachment** is a file that travels along with an e-mail message. You can attach a file with virtually any format, including DOC, BMP, WAV, and EXE.

Most e-mail software indicates the existence of an attachment with an icon, such as a paper clip. Typically, the person who receives an attachment can double-click the icon to open the attachment. However, it will open only if the recipient's PC has software that can work with files stored in the format of the attachment. For example, if you receive an e-mail message with a DOC attachment, your PC must have Microsoft Word software to open and display the attachment. To help the recipient open your attachment, in the body of the regular e-mail message you should indicate which software you used to create it. You might say, for example, "This e-mail includes a DOC attachment that I created with Microsoft Word 97."

Some attachments harbor viruses, so you should exercise caution when opening them—especially those with an .exe extension. You might want to use antivirus software to scan attachments before you open them. Refer to the Help facility of your antivirus software for recommendations on how to use it for attachments.

Figure 9-3: Click the PlayIt! button to learn how to attach files, open attachments, and scan attachments for viruses.

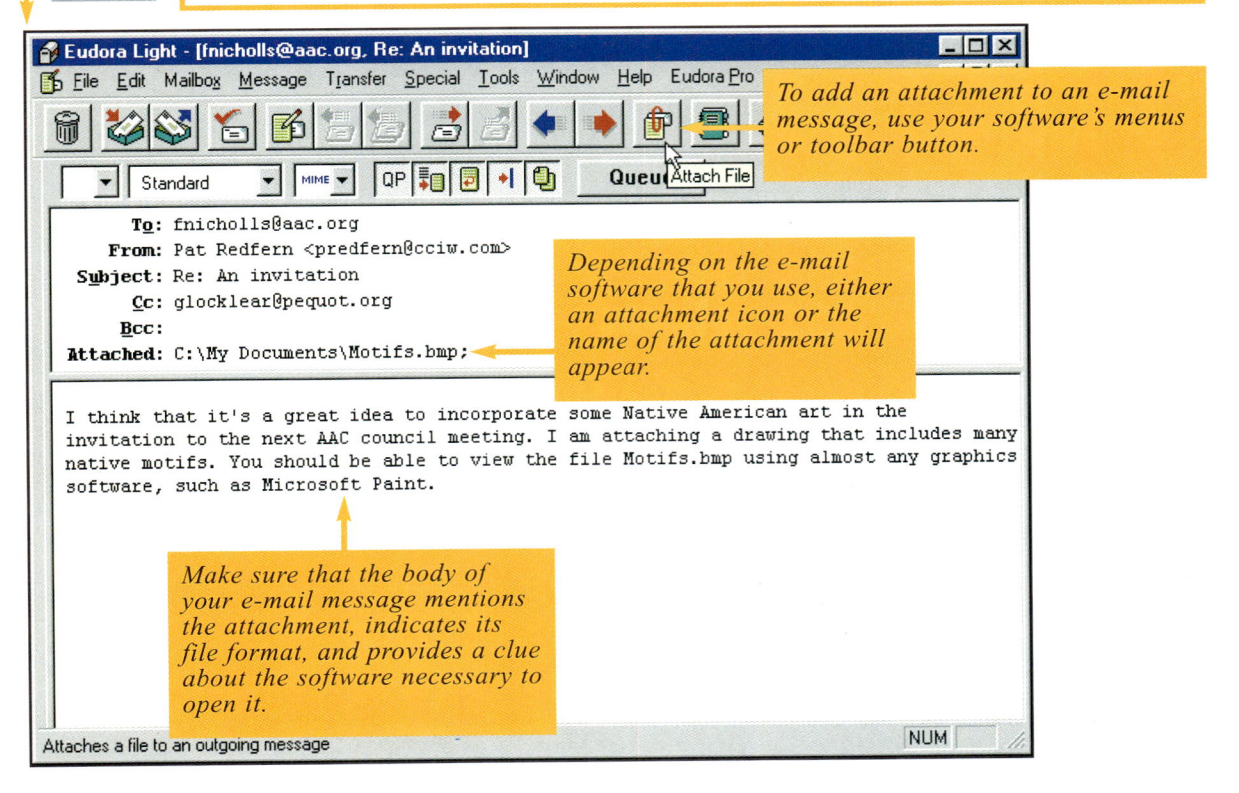

To add an attachment to an e-mail message, use your software's menus or toolbar button.

Depending on the e-mail software that you use, either an attachment icon or the name of the attachment will appear.

Make sure that the body of your e-mail message mentions the attachment, indicates its file format, and provides a clue about the software necessary to open it.

Chapter 9: Sending E-mail and Attachments

■FAQ Is there a size limit for e-mail messages and attachments?

Some e-mail systems limit the size of the e-mail messages and attachments that they will accept and forward. Typically, this limit is 1 MB, so you should try to keep the size of your attachments below this limit. Sound, graphics, and video files can easily exceed this limit, but you might still be able to send such a file if you "zip" it to make it smaller before you attach it.

Grab It!
Compression Software

Compression software "zips" or reduces the size of a file using techniques such as scanning for patterns of words in a text file or patterns of colors in a graphics file and recoding those patterns using fewer bytes. The compressed version of the original file is then stored in a new, smaller file that requires less storage space and transmission time. Compressed files typically have a .zip file extension. Before they can be viewed, they must be "unzipped" to their original size.

Some file formats can be shrunk to less than half their original size, whereas other file formats don't seem to compress at all. Many video and sound formats shrink to about half their original size. Most text formats, such as DOC and TXT, shrink quite dramatically, as do some graphics formats, such as BMP and TIFF. Other graphics formats, such as JPEG and GIF, are already compressed, so using compression software does not affect the size of these files. If you're not sure whether compression software will shrink a file, first try to compress the file, then compare the original and compressed file sizes shown by your compression software.

Play It!

Figure 9-4: If you receive e-mail with a compressed file attachment, you'll typically need to unzip the file before you can use it. Click the PlayIt! button to find out how to use compression software to zip and unzip attachments.

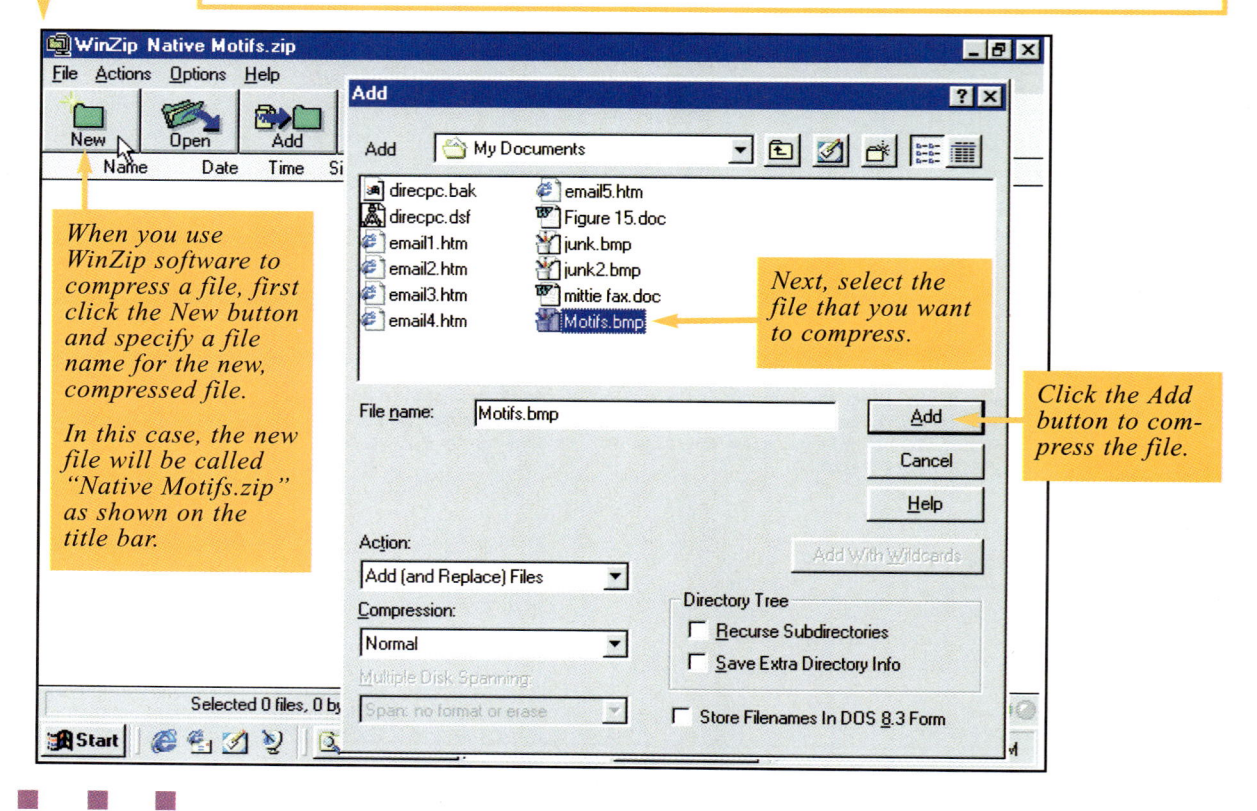

When you use WinZip software to compress a file, first click the New button and specify a file name for the new, compressed file.

In this case, the new file will be called "Native Motifs.zip" as shown on the title bar.

Next, select the file that you want to compress.

Click the Add button to compress the file.

■FAQ What are smileys, flame wars, and spams?

It doesn't take long to get initiated into the e-mail club. Within days of sending your first e-mail, you're likely to receive replies containing odd little symbols called **smileys** or emoticons. E-mail communication lacks the body language and vocal intonations that give us clues to meaning and intent in face-to-face conversations, but e-mailers have devised a visual way to add some of these clues. The original smiley :-) is formed using a colon, a hyphen, and a right parenthesis. Tip your head to the left to see the smiling face. This smiley usually means that the preceding statement is intended to be friendly, not inflammatory.

To add emphasis or emotion to e-mails, some people resort to TYPING IN ALL CAPS—the Internet equivalent of shouting. Use this technique sparingly, because you probably don't want your message to start a flame war. A **flame war** is an exchange of controversial or insulting messages that become increasingly nasty as one person tries to get the other's goat, so to speak.

The Internet might seem like an "anything goes" sort of place, but there exists an unwritten code of behavior or etiquette, sometimes referred to as **netiquette**. Flame wars are considered bad netiquette because they are rude and use Internet bandwidth unproductively. **Spams**—sending unsolicited junk e-mail to huge numbers of people—are another dubious use of Internet bandwidth.

When you send e-mail, follow these tips to ensure that you use correct netiquette:
■ Read your mail regularly. E-mail travels rapidly and your correspondents expect a quick response.
■ Maintain a professional image by using standard grammar and capitalization. If your e-mail software includes a spelling checker, use it.
■ Think before you send potentially controversial or inflammatory mail. You don't want to start a flame war. Use smileys to help clarify your intentions.
■ Don't reply to a group if your reply is meant for only one member of a group.
■ Don't waste bandwidth with unnecessary mail. For example, it is rarely necessary to send a message saying "I received your e-mail."
■ When possible, zip e-mail attachments to reduce their size and transmission time.

Figure 9-5: *Smileys, sometimes called emoticons, can help your e-mail messages convey the correct tone.*

;-)
The winking emoticon means "don't take this seriously."

:-(
The frowning emoticon indicates unhappiness or displeasure.

:-o
The "o-shaped" mouth on this emoticon indicates surprise.

Hardware
Local area networks

When using e-mail from your PC at home, you typically use a dial-up connection to access your local ISP. In contrast, the computers in many school labs and businesses are connected to a LAN, which provides a continuous Internet connection. A **LAN** (local area network) is a collection of computers and other devices connected within a limited geographical area. Sometimes simply called a "network," a LAN differs from the Internet in that it is smaller, privately owned, and does not necessarily use the same communications technology. A LAN can provide many services, such as shared access to software, files, printers, and the Internet. For an organization or business, these shared resources generate considerable savings. As an example, instead of attaching a printer to each computer, a single printer can be shared by a group of computers connected to a LAN.

Using a computer on a network does not differ much from using a stand-alone PC. Software supplied by the network appears on the Start menu, files can be accessed using Windows Explorer, and your printouts are automatically routed to a nearby network printer. If your LAN provides Internet access, you can compose and read messages as usual, but you don't have to establish a dial-up connection to send and receive mail.

The key devices connected to a LAN are workstations, network servers, and hubs. A **workstation** is a standard PC that's connected to a LAN to take advantage of network resources. A **network server** is a computer that provides some service to the workstations. For example, a **file server** provides access to data files and software; a **print server** controls the activities of one or more shared printers; and an **e-mail server** provides e-mail service. A **hub** is a device that provides a centralized point of connection for all other devices on the LAN.

Figure 9-6: Network devices can be connected in a variety of configurations, depending on the underlying LAN technology, such as Ethernet, FDDI, Token Ring, and ATM. The most popular LAN technology today is Ethernet, which uses a hub as the centralized point of connection for all workstations and servers on the network.

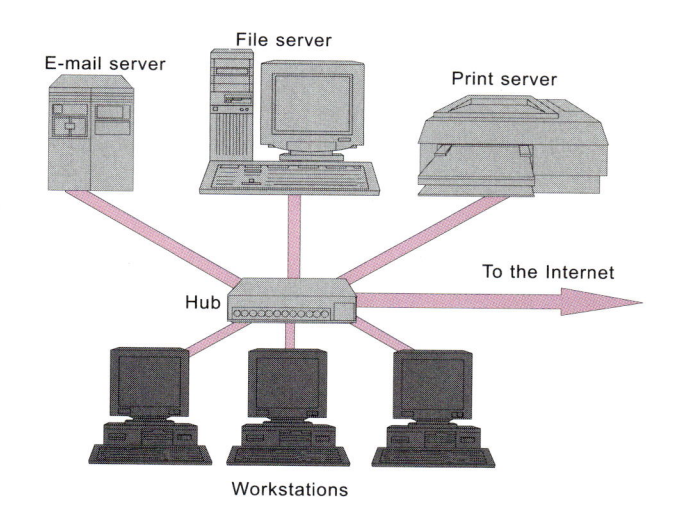

■Hardware continued

LANs are typically installed and supported by computer professionals called **network specialists**. As a person who uses a network workstation, you probably will not have to install a network. You might have to perform rudimentary troubleshooting, however, so it is valuable to know something about the hardware that connects your computer to the network.

A **NIC** (network interface card) is a small circuit board that connects a PC to a local area network. In a desktop PC, the NIC plugs directly into the main board inside the system unit. An opening in the back of the unit allows you to connect the network cable to the NIC. In a notebook computer, the NIC is usually a credit-card-sized PCMCIA card that can easily be removed to disconnect the computer from the network when you travel.

Workstations are typically connected to a network using 10Base-T or coaxial cables. A **10Base-T cable**, has square plastic connectors that look much like those on a standard telephone cable. A **coaxial cable**, recognizable by its round silver connectors, is the same as that used to hook up cable TV.

Figure 9-7: *If your workstation is a desktop PC, you'll see the network interface card connections at the rear of the system unit. Your network connection will use either 10Base-T (pictured) or coaxial cable. For basic troubleshooting, make sure that the cable is securely connected to the NIC.*

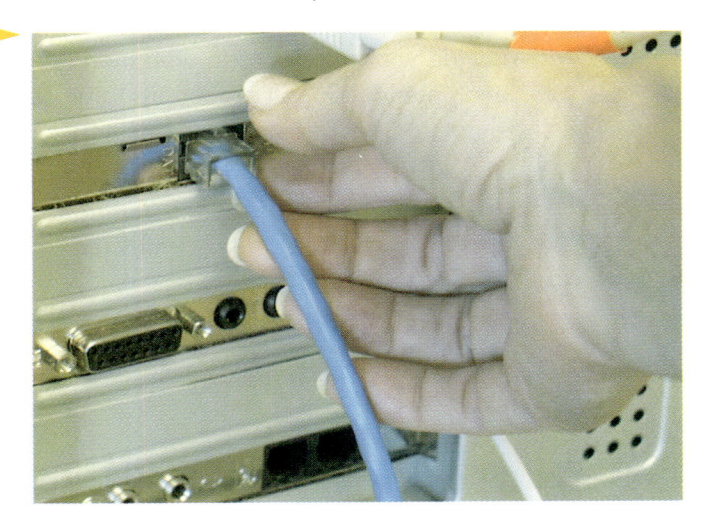

Figure 9-8: *If your workstation is a notebook computer, the network interface card slides into a PCMCIA slot. For basic troubleshooting, make sure that the card is fully inserted and that all cables are securely connected.*

■Hardware
continued

When you boot your PC, the Windows operating system automatically checks the Registry to find out whether a network interface card has been installed. As the boot process continues, you will be asked to enter a password supplied by your network specialist. Typically, Windows will then execute a special set of instructions called a **login script** that automatically connects your workstation to one or more servers and printers. Your login script is generally created and installed by your network specialist.

From your workstation, you can get an overview of the entire network by using the **Network Neighborhood icon** on the Windows desktop. Clicking this icon displays a window that lists the servers and printers connected to the network. Your workstation's ability to access the network devices displayed in the Network Neighborhood window depends on which access rights you've been assigned by your network specialist. Your login script gives you automatic access to one or more servers. In addition, your network specialist might provide you with login passwords to access other servers or even other workstations on the network.

When using a network, you should do your part to maintain its security. Do not provide your password to unauthorized users. Also, make sure that you follow the recommended logoff procedure to disconnect from the network when you have completed your computing session.

Figure 9-9: Click the PlayIt! button to find out how the Network Neighborhood window lists the devices connected to a LAN.

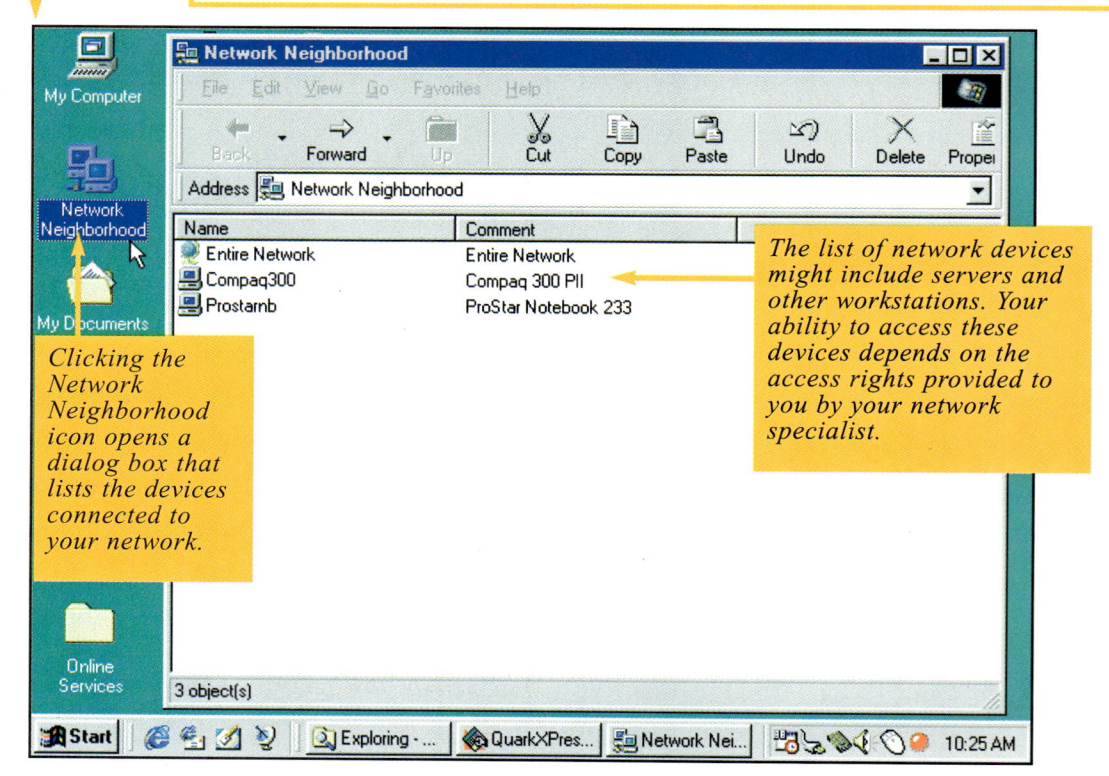

Clicking the Network Neighborhood icon opens a dialog box that lists the devices connected to your network.

The list of network devices might include servers and other workstations. Your ability to access these devices depends on the access rights provided to you by your network specialist.

Chapter 9: Sending E-mail and Attachments

■Tutorial
How to use your e-mail address book like a pro

Although you can manually type the address of each e-mail recipient in the message header, you might forget someone's address. It is also easy to make a typing error that will bounce the e-mail back to you, branded "address unknown." Most e-mail software includes an address book that keeps a list of frequently used addresses. Instead of manually typing the address for each message, you can select an address from the address book.

The address book also allows you to create mail groups, composed of multiple e-mail addresses. By selecting the group from your address book, you can conveniently send an e-mail message to everyone in the group.

When you have completed the tutorial, you should be able to:
■ Open an e-mail address book.
■ Enter individual e-mail addresses in the address book.
■ Send a message to an individual listed in the address book.
■ Create a group in the address book and send mail to everyone in the group.

Figure 9-10: Click the PlayIt! button to begin the tutorial. You'll learn how to use an e-mail address book and discover how to simplify e-mail addressing tasks. Estimated time: 10–15 minutes. Tracking Disk points: 10.

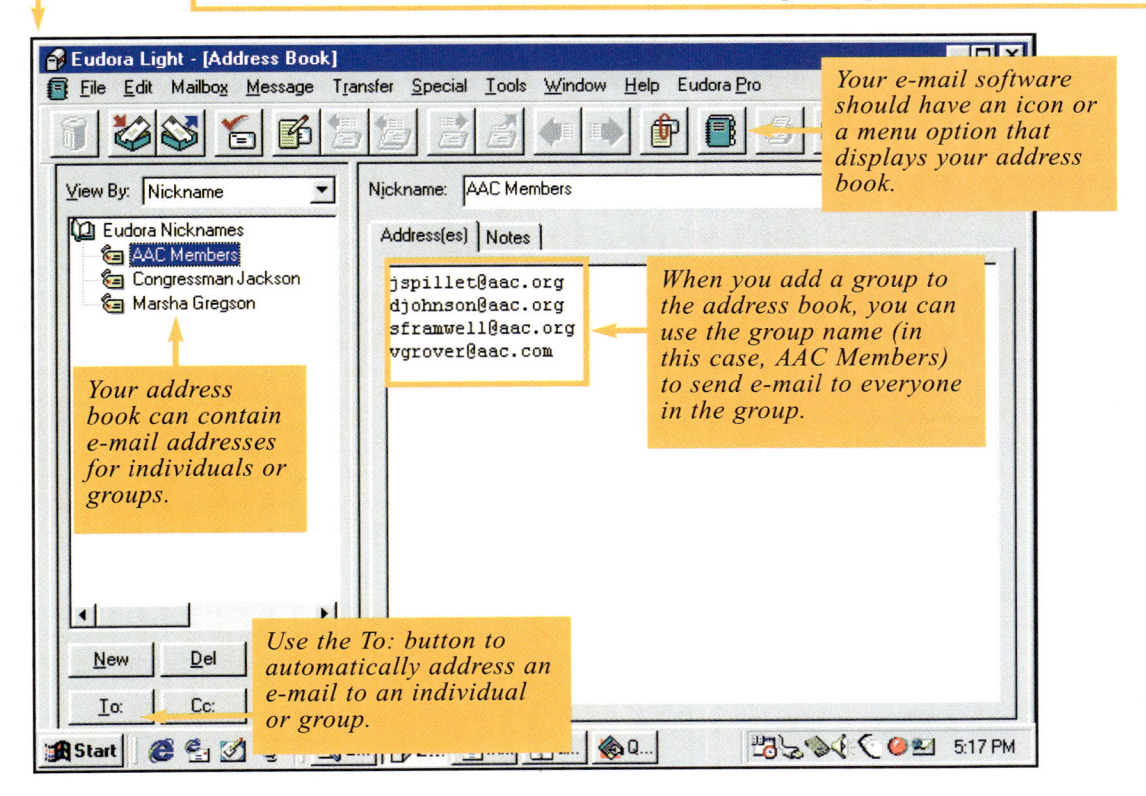

Your e-mail software should have an icon or a menu option that displays your address book.

When you add a group to the address book, you can use the group name (in this case, AAC Members) to send e-mail to everyone in the group.

Your address book can contain e-mail addresses for individuals or groups.

Use the To: button to automatically address an e-mail to an individual or group.

Issue
Just how private is e-mail?

Most people assume that e-mail has similar privacy protections as telephone conversations and as letters that are carried by the postal service. That is not necessarily the case, however. The electronic technology that makes e-mail so popular also tends to make it less private than a phone call or a letter. It is easy for the recipient of an e-mail message to forward copies of it to other people. The contents of an e-mail message might appear on a technician's screen in the course of system maintenance or repairs. Also, your e-mail messages—including those that you have deleted from your own PC—might be stored on backups and archives of an e-mail server where you cannot control access to them.

When a CalTech student was accused of sexually harassing a female student by sending lewd e-mail to her and to her boyfriend, investigators retrieved all of the student's e-mail from archives of the e-mail server. The student was expelled from the university even though he claimed that the e-mail had been "spoofed" to make it look as though he had sent it, when it had actually been sent by someone else.

In 1996, a Pillsbury employee was fired from his job for making unprofessional comments in an e-mail to his supervisor. The employee sued the company, but lost. Although the company had repeatedly assured its employees that e-mail was private, the court ruled that the employee's right to privacy did not outweigh the interests of the company that owned the e-mail system. Courts have been reluctant to grant unlimited privacy rights because e-mail could be used to distribute trade secrets, disrupt business, plan criminal activities, or harass other employees.

Until the legal system resolves the many issues surrounding e-mail, you should think of e-mail as a postcard, rather than as a letter. Assume that your e-mail might be read by people other than the person to whom it was sent, and save your controversial comments for face-to-face conversations.

What do you think?

1. Do you think most people believe that their e-mail is private?   ⭘ Yes ⭘ No ⭘ Not sure

2. Do you agree with CalTech's decision to expel the student who was accused of sending harassing e-mail to another student?   ⭘ Yes ⭘ No ⭘ Not sure

3. Do you think that e-mail should have the same privacy protections as telephone conversations and mail under U.S. laws?   ⭘ Yes ⭘ No ⭘ Not sure

Save It!

Chapter 9: Sending E-mail and Attachments

QuickCheck A

1. True or false? Store-and-forward technology allows you to minimize dial-up connect time because you can read and compose messages offline. ☐

2. An e-mail attachment might harbor a virus, and you should be particularly suspicious of attachments with a(n) ☐ extension.

3. Because some e-mail systems impose a size limit on the mail they accept, as a rule of thumb attachments should be smaller than ☐ megabyte(s).

4. Compressed files typically have a(n) ☐ file extension.

5. True or false? You must use the Network Neighborhood as your e-mail client software if your computer is connected to a LAN. ☐

Check It!

QuickCheck B

Fill in each blank, based on the e-mail shown at right.

1. The name of the person who wrote this e-mail: ☐

2. The recipient's e-mail address: ☐

3. Does this e-mail include an attachment? ☐

4. The name of this e-mail software: ☐

5. The symbol that indicates the lines of the original message: ☐

Check It!

Get It?

While using the Book-on-CD, click the Get It? button to see if you can answer ten randomly selected questions from Chapter 9.

Get It?

Chapter 10

Writing and Printing Documents

What's Inside?

A computer with preinstalled software typically includes a software suite or an integrated software package that provides a set of basic tools for producing documents, making calculations, creating presentations, and getting organized. Chapter 10 focuses on the software you use to produce documents.

- FAQs:

Can word processing software improve my writing?	111
How does WP software help me format a document?	112
Does WP software provide standard document styles?	113
What's desktop publishing software?	114
Do I need DTP software in addition to WP software?	115

- Hardware: Printers — 116
- Tutorial: How to install and select printers — 119
- Issue: What's truth got to do with it? — 120
- QuickChecks — 121

What's on the CD?

Chapter 10 screen tours show you how to improve your writing with word processing software and how to create professional publications with desktop publishing software. This chapter's video feature looks at laser printers.

- See a thesaurus, grammar checker, and spelling checker in action — 111
- Learn how formatting improves the "look" of a document — 112
- Find out how to use document templates — 113
- Take a tour of desktop publishing software — 114
- Get the scoop on laser printers — 118
- Take a step-by-step tutorial on how to install and select printers — 119

Chapter 10: Writing and Printing Documents 111

■FAQ Can word processing software improve my writing?

Word processing (WP) software provides a set of tools for entering and revising text, adding graphical elements, then formatting and printing documents. Although many people regard WP software as a tool for improving the appearance of documents, it also provides resources for improving the quality of your writing. Popular WP software includes Microsoft Word, WordPerfect, and Lotus Word Pro.

Good writing requires a coherent progression of ideas expressed in grammatically correct sentences using carefully selected descriptive words. Before you focus on how your document looks, pay attention to how it reads by using your WP software to organize your ideas and clarify your wording. Entering text on screen gives you the flexibility to first sketch in your main points, then move them around to improve the progression of your ideas.

Once you're satisfied with the flow of ideas, use your WP software to improve wording and sentence structure. A built-in **grammar checker** can help you spot awkward sentences and other grammatical faux pas. It reviews your document sentence-by-sentence and offers suggestions for improvement. To make your writing really sparkle, boost your vocabulary by using the built-in **thesaurus**, which displays synonyms for any word that you select. Your WP software can also help you find and fix spelling errors. A **spelling checker** compares each word in your document to an electronic dictionary. If you've used a word that is not in the dictionary, the spelling checker displays a list of possible alternatives.

Figure 10-1: Click the PlayIt! button to see how your writing can improve when you use a thesaurus, grammar checker, and spelling checker.

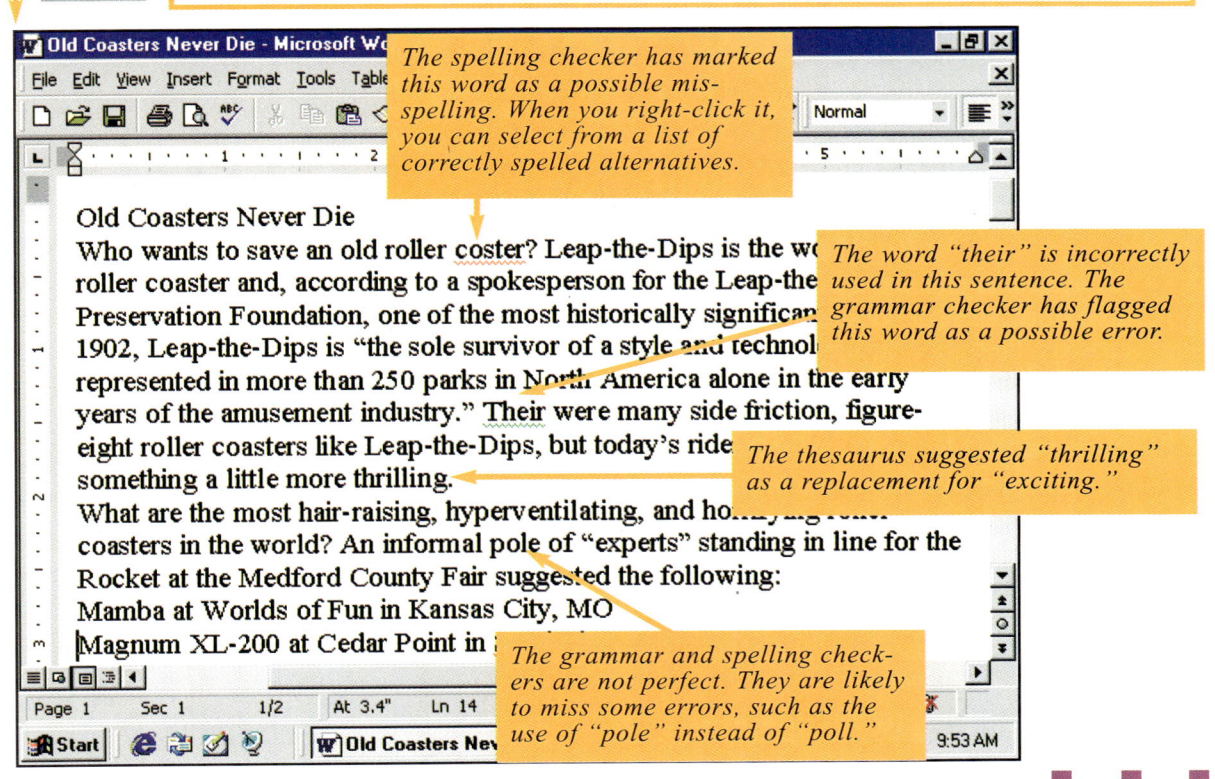

The spelling checker has marked this word as a possible misspelling. When you right-click it, you can select from a list of correctly spelled alternatives.

The word "their" is incorrectly used in this sentence. The grammar checker has flagged this word as a possible error.

The thesaurus suggested "thrilling" as a replacement for "exciting."

The grammar and spelling checkers are not perfect. They are likely to miss some errors, such as the use of "pole" instead of "poll."

■FAQ How does WP software help me format a document?

You can use your WP software to **format** a document and change its appearance to create a professional, high-impact, or casual look. When you first type the "raw" text for a document, don't press the Enter key at the end of each line—just keep typing. Your WP software will automatically **word wrap** to the next line. You should, however, press the Enter key at the end of a title or paragraph. Think of this "raw" text as strings of characters that form paragraphs, that exist on a page. You will later be able to apply formats at the character, paragraph, or page level.

Grab It! Fonts

You can format one or more characters in a document to change the font, color, and size. The term **font** refers to the design or typeface of each text character. You can also add effects such as bold, italics, and underlining. To apply character formats, you'll typically use the mouse to select the text to be formatted, then use a toolbar button or menu option to indicate the format that you want.

Paragraph format options include margin settings, line spacing, bulleted and numbered lists, columns, centering, left and right alignment, and "justification" that creates even right and left margins. To apply paragraph formats, make sure that you're working within the paragraph, then use a menu option to select a format.

Page format options apply to an entire document and include adding header text at the top of each page, adding footer text at the bottom of each page, changing the page size, and automatically numbering pages.

Play It!

Figure 10-2: *Click the PlayIt! button for a quick tour of character, paragraph, and page formatting.*

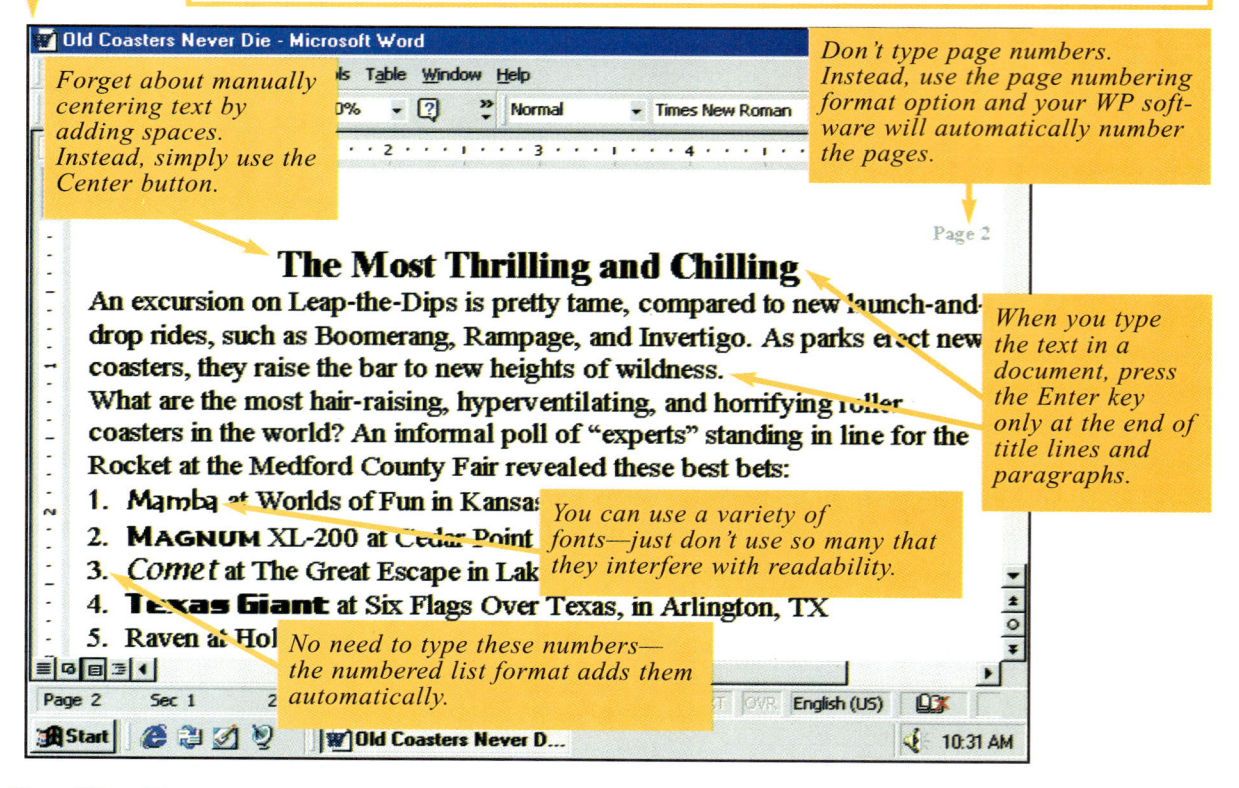

Forget about manually centering text by adding spaces. Instead, simply use the Center button.

Don't type page numbers. Instead, use the page numbering format option and your WP software will automatically number the pages.

When you type the text in a document, press the Enter key only at the end of title lines and paragraphs.

You can use a variety of fonts—just don't use so many that they interfere with readability.

No need to type these numbers—the numbered list format adds them automatically.

The Most Thrilling and Chilling

An excursion on Leap-the-Dips is pretty tame, compared to new launch-and-drop rides, such as Boomerang, Rampage, and Invertigo. As parks erect new coasters, they raise the bar to new heights of wildness.

What are the most hair-raising, hyperventilating, and horrifying roller coasters in the world? An informal poll of "experts" standing in line for the Rocket at the Medford County Fair revealed these best bets:

1. **Mamba** at Worlds of Fun in Kansas
2. **MAGNUM** XL-200 at Cedar Point
3. *Comet* at The Great Escape in Lak
4. **Texas Giant** at Six Flags Over Texas, in Arlington, TX
5. Raven at Hol

Chapter 10: Writing and Printing Documents   113

■FAQ   Does WP software provide standard document styles?

A **style** is a set of character and paragraph attributes that you can name and define. For example, you might name a style "body text" and define it as a small-size Arial font, single-spaced, and left-aligned. Your word processor typically keeps track of the styles you define in a **style list**. Once you have defined a style, you can apply all of its attributes in one operation by making a selection from the style list.

Grab It!
Word Templates

The "look" of a document depends on the style settings that you use for each element, such as titles, body text, tables, and footnotes. A collection of such settings is referred to as a **style sheet**. You can save style sheet settings as a **template** so that you can produce documents with a similar "look." If you are unsure about the proper style to use for a document such as a business memo, your WP software might provide a predesigned template with appropriate headings, margin settings, and so on. Using a template is easy. Simply open the template, type the text for your document, and apply styles as needed.

In addition, your WP software might provide **template wizards** that further simplify the process of creating a document. A template wizard asks you a series of questions about the document that you want to create, then essentially creates the document for you based on your answers. Wizards are commonly supplied for letters, memos, resumes, and faxes.

Play It!

Figure 10-3: Click the PlayIt! button to find out how to create styles, use templates, and activate a template wizard.

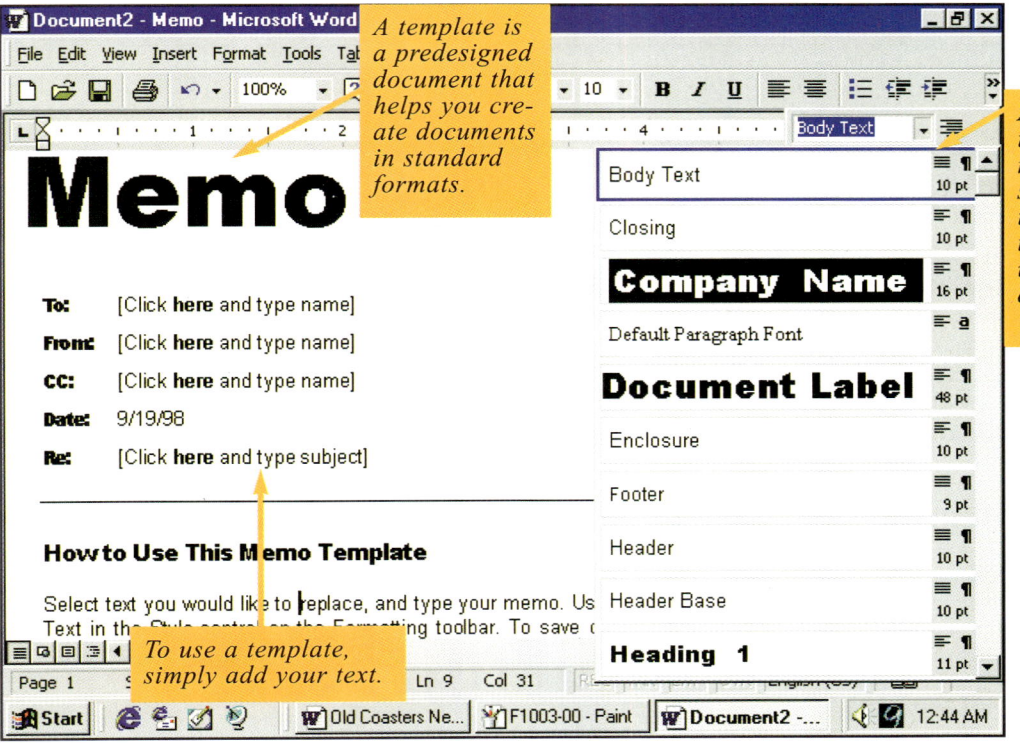

A template is a predesigned document that helps you create documents in standard formats.

A style list includes names and samples of the styles that you can use with this document.

To use a template, simply add your text.

Chapter 10: Writing and Printing Documents

■FAQ What's desktop publishing software?

Grab It!
DTP Software Demos

Desktop publishing (DTP) software provides a set of tools to design and print typeset-quality documents using your PC. It is the software of choice for documents that will be widely distributed, such as newsletters, brochures, corporate reports, and books. Popular DTP software includes Adobe PageMaker, Microsoft Publisher, and QuarkXPress.

Typically, DTP software is not the tool that you use to author and edit a document. Instead, you use it to collect and incorporate all the elements for a publication. For example, you would write, edit, and check the spelling of a document using WP software, then import that text into your DTP software. You would also prepare photos and diagrams using graphics software, and then import them as well.

DTP software's major advantage is the flexibility and precision it provides for positioning text and graphical elements on a page. You can designate rectangular areas on the page called **frames** and fill each one with either text or graphics. To achieve a pleasing layout, you can move, resize, and overlap these frames.

The appearance of your printed document is affected by the quality of your printer. If your printer cannot produce high-quality output, you might be able to use it to print only drafts of your document. For the final printout, you can deliver your files to a professional printing press. You'll learn more about printers in the Hardware section.

Play It!

Figure 10-4: DTP software has essentially replaced typesetting, even for glossy magazines, newspapers, and books. Click the PlayIt! button to take a tour of DTP software.

Your work area is frame-based—you position text and graphics in rectangular boxes that you can then move, resize, and overlap.

A floating toolbar provides easy access to frequently used DTP tools.

You can link text from one frame to another, so it is easy to continue an article on a different page.

Chapter 10: Writing and Printing Documents   115

▪FAQ Do I need DTP software in addition to WP software?

As a rule of thumb, you can probably create most of your documents using word processing software. You might consider adding desktop publishing software to your PC if you frequently produce graphics-intensive brochures, magazines, newsletters, or professionally printed books.

Today's WP software has evolved far beyond typewriter emulation and now incorporates many DTP features. Therefore, the capabilities of WP and DTP software overlap to some extent. The difference between these two types of software is often one of degree. For example, although WP software can work with color graphics, DTP software provides more flexibility for positioning, modifying, labeling, and color-adjusting those graphics. You can send documents produced with WP software to a professional print shop, but you might find that more print shops can accommodate files created with DTP software.

After you have worked with both WP and DTP software, you will be better able to judge which one is appropriate for a particular project. In the meantime, don't hesitate to start by using WP software for any project. If layout and formatting become too complex for your WP software, you can easily import the document into DTP software, then lay it out and format it.

Figure 10-5: *Use this chart to compare the strengths and weaknesses of WP and DTP software to see if you need both.*

Document Production Feature	WP	DTP
Create outlines and autonumbered paragraphs	strong	weak
Check grammar	strong	weak
Track revisions made by authors and editors	strong	weak
Generate footnotes	strong	weak
Generate an index or table of contents	strong	adequate
Check spelling	strong	strong
Generate tables	strong	adequate
Work with columns of text	adequate	adequate
Control spacing between letters and lines for typeset look	adequate	strong
Incorporate and manipulate graphics	adequate	strong
Add callouts or text labels to graphics	weak	strong
Incorporate elaborate page headers	weak	strong
Generate full-color "plates" for a professional printer	weak	strong

☺ strong   😐 adequate   ☹ weak

Chapter 10: Writing and Printing Documents

■Hardware
Printers

A **printer** is a device that converts computer output into images on sheets of paper or other media, such as labels, envelopes, transparencies, or iron-on transfers. Today's printers tend to use one of three technologies: dot matrix, ink jet, or laser. Despite their differences, all three technologies produce characters and graphics as a series of small dots.

The quality or sharpness of an image depends on its **resolution**—the density of the gridwork of dots that create it. Printer resolution is measured by the number of dots it can print per linear inch, abbreviated as **dpi**. At normal reading distance, a resolution of about 900 dots per inch appears solid to the human eye, but a close examination of color sections on a page will reveal the dot pattern. Although 900 dpi might be considered sufficient for magazines, expensive "coffee-table books" are typically produced on printers with 2,400 dpi or higher resolution.

When PCs first began to appear in the late 1970s, dot matrix printers were the technology of choice. Still in use today, **dot matrix printers** produce characters and graphics by using a matrix of fine wires. As the print head noisily clatters across the paper, the wires strike the ribbon and paper in a pattern prescribed by your PC. With a resolution of 140 dpi, a dot matrix printer produces low-quality output with clearly discernible dots forming letters and graphics. Dot matrix speed is typically measured in characters per second (cps). A fast dot matrix device can print at speeds up to 455 cps—about five pages per minute.

Today, dot matrix printers, which are sometimes referred to as "impact printers," are used primarily for "back-office" applications that demand low operating cost and dependability, but not high print quality. A U.S.$4 ribbon can print more than 3 million characters before it needs to be replaced. Unlike many newer printer technologies, a dot matrix printer actually strikes the paper and therefore can print multipart carbon forms.

Play It!

Figure 10-6: The print head in a dot matrix printer contains a row of fine wires that strike the ribbon and paper to produce a matrix of dots that form characters or graphics. Click the PlayIt! button for a quick demonstration.

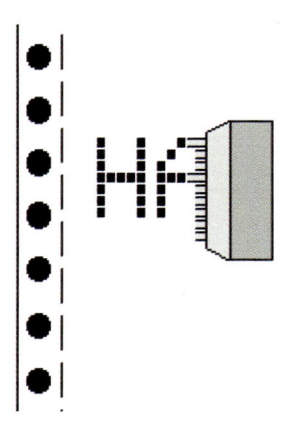

Hardware continued

An **ink jet printer** has a nozzle-like print head that sprays ink onto the paper to form characters and graphics. Today's most popular printer technology, ink jets produce low-cost black-and-white or color printouts. The print head in a color ink jet printer consists of a series of nozzles, each with its own ink cartridge. Most ink jet printers use **CMYK color**, which requires only cyan (blue), magenta (pink), yellow, and black inks to create a printout that appears to have thousands of colors. Alternatively, some printers use six ink colors to print additional midtone shades that create slightly more realistic photographic images.

Operating costs for an ink jet printer are reasonable. You'll need to periodically replace the black ink cartridge and a second cartridge that carries the colored inks. Each replacement ink cartridge costs between U.S.$25 and U.S.$35. Under realistic use, your costs for color printing will be between 5 and 15 cents per page. A potential hidden cost of operating an ink jet printer is special paper. Although you can satisfactorily print documents with small graphics and line art on the same type of inexpensive paper that you might use in a photocopier, high-quality photo printouts require special paper that can cost between U.S.$0.08 and U.S.$1.50 per sheet. Typically, this special paper has a super smooth finish that prevents the ink from bleeding and creating dull colors.

Today's ink jet printers have excellent resolution; depending on the model, it can range from 600 dpi to 1,440 dpi. You can expect to pay more for a printer with a higher resolution to get better quality when printing photographic images. Some ink jet printers achieve their ultra-high resolution by making multiple passes over the paper. Although it might seem logical that this technique would slow down the printing process, even multiple-pass ink jet printers produce a respectable five pages per minute. You can purchase a good-quality ink jet printer for about U.S.$300. Manufacturers include Hewlett-Packard, Epson, Lexmark, Okidata, Canon, and NEC.

Figure 10-7: An ink jet printer sprays colored inks from its nozzle-like print heads. A color ink jet printer typically uses one black ink cartridge and another cartridge that contains the rest of the ink colors.

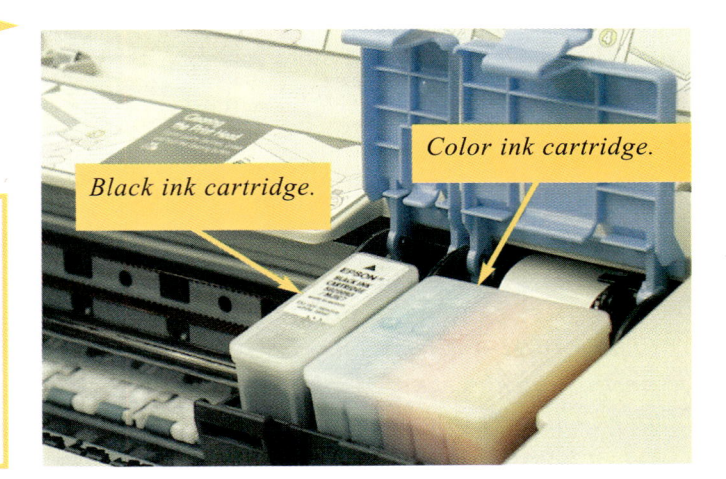

Black ink cartridge.

Color ink cartridge.

■Hardware continued

A **laser printer** uses the same technology as a photocopier to "paint" dots of light on a light-sensitive drum. Electrostatically charged ink is applied to the drum, then transferred to paper. You can purchase laser printers at two price points. Inexpensive "desktop" or "personal" models, priced under U.S.$400, are quite suitable for black-and-white printing of a limited number of copies. More expensive "professional" laser printers with color or extended-run capacity begin at U.S.$1,000 and quickly exceed the U.S.$3,000 mark.

As with other printer technologies, print speed and resolution will be key factors in your purchase decision. Personal laser printers produce six to eight pages per minute at a resolution of 600 dpi. Professional models pump out 15 to 25 pages per minute at 1,200 dpi. The **duty cycle** of a printer is specified in pages per month (ppm) and indicates how much work you can expect your printer to produce without breaking down. A personal laser printer has a duty cycle of about 3,000 ppm—that means about 100 pages a day. You won't want to use it to produce 5,000 campaign brochures for next Monday, but would find it quite suitable for printing ten copies of a five-page outline for a meeting tomorrow.

Some people are surprised to discover that laser printers are less expensive to operate than ink jet printers. On average, you can expect to pay about 2 cents per page for black-and-white laser printing. This per-page cost includes periodically replacing the toner cartridge and drum. A toner cartridge and a drum unit each cost about U.S.$70, though prices vary by manufacturer and model.

Laser printers accept print commands from a PC, but use their own printer language to construct a page before printing it. **Printer Control Language** (PCL) is the most widely used printer language, but some printers also use the **PostScript** language, which is preferred by many publishing professionals. Printer languages require memory, and most lasers have between 2 and 8 MB. A large memory capacity is required to print color images and graphics-intensive documents. A laser printer comes equipped with enough memory for typical print jobs. If you find that you need more memory, check the printer documentation for information.

Figure 10-8: A laser printer uses electrostatically charged ink called toner. Click the PlayIt! button to take a tour of a laser printer and see how it works.

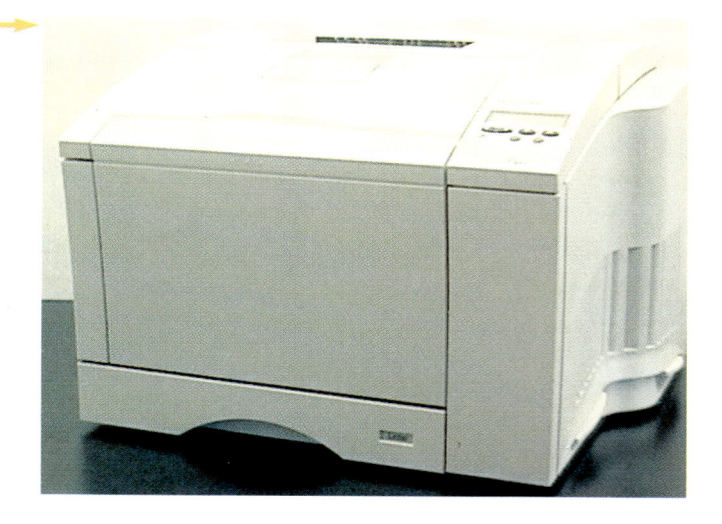

Chapter 10: Writing and Printing Documents

■Tutorial
How to install and select printers

In the tutorial for Chapter 1, you learned how to set up a printer and connect it to your PC. Windows will spot this new equipment and display the Add Printer wizard to help you install the necessary printer driver. A **printer driver** is a software program that sets up communications between the printer and your PC. Windows includes a set of printer drivers, but if you have just connected a new-model printer, Windows might require a driver from the floppy disk or CD supplied by the printer manufacturer. After installing the printer driver, you can use the printer.

Windows allows you to connect multiple printers to your PC. You must designate one as the **default printer** that Windows will use for all your printouts unless you specify otherwise. In this tutorial, you'll learn how to install printer drivers, choose a default printer, and select a printer when you print a document.

When you have completed the tutorial, you should be able to:
- Use the Add Printer wizard to install a printer driver.
- Designate a default printer.
- Select the printer that you want to use for a printout.
- Check the status of a print job.

Figure 10-9: Click the PlayIt! button to learn how to use the Add Printer wizard and select the printer for your printout. Estimated time: 10–15 minutes. Tracking Disk points: 10.

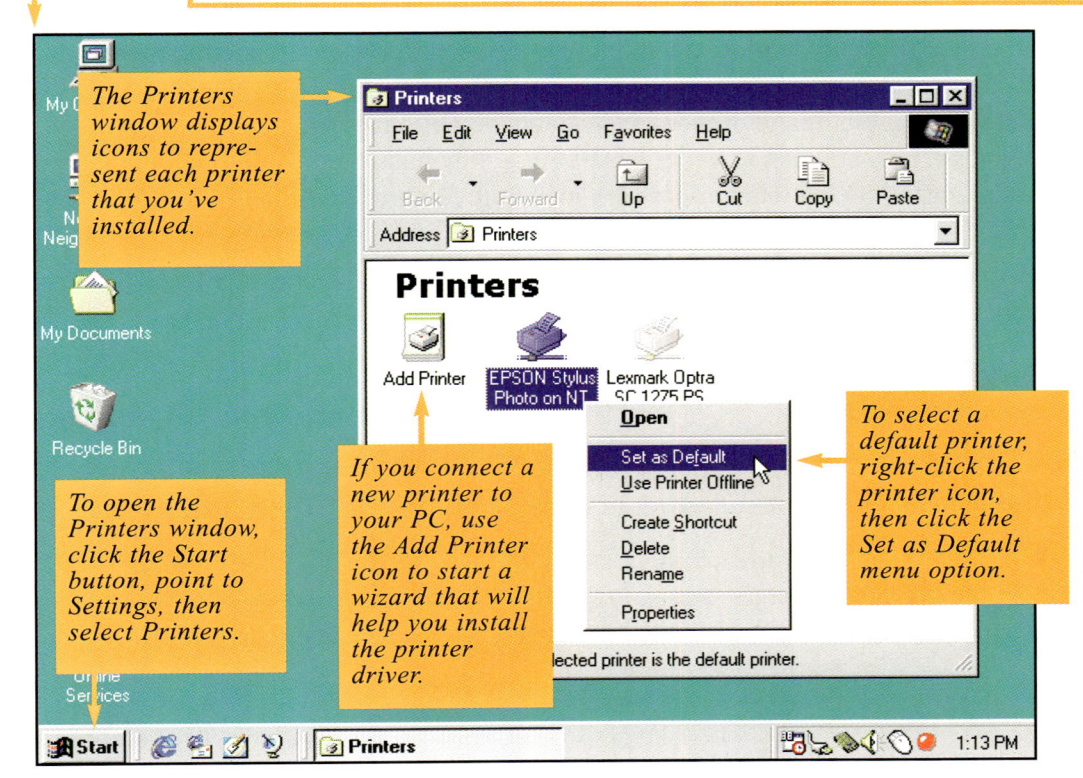

The Printers window displays icons to represent each printer that you've installed.

To open the Printers window, click the Start button, point to Settings, then select Printers.

If you connect a new printer to your PC, use the Add Printer icon to start a wizard that will help you install the printer driver.

To select a default printer, right-click the printer icon, then click the Set as Default menu option.

■Issue
What's truth got to do with it?

You live in the Information Age. Ironically, much of the information that you read and hear is just not true. False and misleading information predates the Information Age, but now it propagates more rapidly, fed by new technologies and nurtured by "spin doctors." As one commentator has suggested, "The danger is that we are reaching a moment when nothing can be said to be objectively true, when consensus about reality disappears. The Information Age could leave us with no information at all, only assertions."

In a more innocent era, the source of information provided a clue about its reliability. Television network news was usually dependable. You could generally rely on newspaper reports and information in books. Now, however, the yardstick once used to measure the reliability of information is being challenged by technology and by changes in the relationship between mass media and their audience. Using DTP software, virtually anyone can produce brochures, pamphlets, and books that look professional and official. Using Web authoring software, it is easy to design a professional Web site and stock it with misinformation. In an Internet chat group, anyone can start a rumor that propagates via the Net and eventually achieves the status of an "urban legend." Editorializing has softened "hard" news, and news stories are often selected for their sensationalism, rather than for their importance.

Who should be responsible for ensuring the accuracy of information? Holding writers accountable for their "facts" does not seem to be working. Governments, already overburdened with other problems, have scant resources available to sift through mountains of information and set the record straight. It seems, then, that the burden of verifying facts is ultimately left to the reader—or watcher, as the case may be. But many of these individuals do not have the time, motivation, expertise, or resources to verify facts before they pass them on through the information mill. This information problem might prove particularly difficult to solve.

What do you think?

1. In your opinion, can people typically recognize false information in print, on the Web, or on TV?   ◯ Yes ◯ No ◯ Not sure

2. Have you believed information from a reliable source that you later discovered was false?   ◯ Yes ◯ No ◯ Not sure

3. Do you think that governments should penalize people who knowingly disseminate false information?   ◯ Yes ◯ No ◯ Not sure

Save It!

Chapter 10: Writing and Printing Documents   121

QuickCheck A

1. True or false? In the phrase "Goldilocks and the tree bears," a spelling or grammar checker will flag the word "tree" because it is missing the letter "h." ☐

2. When you initially type the "raw" text for a document, you should press the Enter key only at the end of a title or ☐.

3. A(n) ☐ includes the style settings necessary to duplicate the look of a previously designed document.

4. True or false? WP software was designed to produce documents that look professionally typeset. ☐

5. DTP software uses rectangular ☐ to hold text and graphics.

Check It!

QuickCheck B

In the right-hand column of the table, indicate which type of printer would **best** fit the job. Abbreviate your answers using **D** for dot matrix, **J** for ink jet, and **L** for laser.

1. An individual wants to print color photographic images of family and friends	
2. A school secretary wants to print 75 copies of the black-and-white program for tomorrow's school play	
3. A salesperson needs to print out a multipart carbon invoice form	
4. A professional publisher specializes in full-color brochures	
5. A student wants a dependable low-cost color printer	

Check It!

Get It? While using the Book-on-CD, click the Get It? button to see if you can answer ten randomly selected questions from Chapter 10.

Get It?

Chapter 11

Making Spreadsheets and Presentations

What's Inside?

Chapter 11 begins with a whirlwind tour of spreadsheet software. If you want to make a presentation based on the results you produce with spreadsheet or any other software, you'll be interested in the overview of computer projection devices in the Hardware section. The tutorial focuses on a related topic—how to use presentation software.

- FAQs:

What's a spreadsheet?	123
How do I create a worksheet?	124
What if I don't know the right formula?	125
How do I know if worksheet results are accurate?	126
How do I create graphs?	127

- Hardware: Computer projection devices — 128
- Tutorial: How to make slides for an effective presentation — 131
- Issue: Is it the medium or the message? — 132
- QuickChecks — 133

What's on the CD?

Chapter 11 animates spreadsheet software to show you how to create worksheets and graphs. In addition, a video shows you how to set up presentation equipment.

- Tour a spreadsheet gallery for some ideas you can use — 123
- Hear some helpful hints from spreadsheet veterans — 124
- Learn how to incorporate functions in your worksheets — 125
- Find out what can happen if you don't test your worksheets — 126
- See the Chart wizard in action — 127
- Assemble the hardware you'll need for a group presentation — 129
- Take a tutorial on how to use presentation software — 131

Chapter 11: Making Spreadsheets and Presentations

■FAQ What's a spreadsheet?

A **spreadsheet** is a tool for working with numbers. It is arranged in a grid of columns and rows forming **cells** that hold labels, numbers, and formulas. You can use spreadsheets for simple or complex calculations, such as computing loan payments, figuring out your taxes, or dividing expenses with your roommates.

Spreadsheet software, such as Microsoft Excel, Quattro Pro, and Lotus 1-2-3, allows you to create electronic spreadsheets that you can easily edit, print, save, post on the Web, or transmit via e-mail. An electronic spreadsheet is often referred to as a **worksheet**. A worksheet functions much like a visual calculator. You place each number needed for a calculation in a cell of the grid. You can then enter formulas to add, subtract, or otherwise manipulate these numbers. Your spreadsheet software automatically calculates the formulas and displays the results. As an added bonus, it can create graphs based on the data in a worksheet.

Using spreadsheet software helps ensure the accuracy of your calculations by displaying all of your data and formulas on screen. It can also help you to create numeric models of real-world entities. As an example, you could create a numeric model of a new business, then examine projected income and expenses to determine whether the business will make you rich beyond your wildest dreams. You can even use your model to examine several alternative **"what-if" scenarios**, such as "What if sales are double what I projected?" or "What if sales are only half of what I projected?"

Figure 11-1: Click the PlayIt! button to take a tour of some handy and innovative spreadsheets.

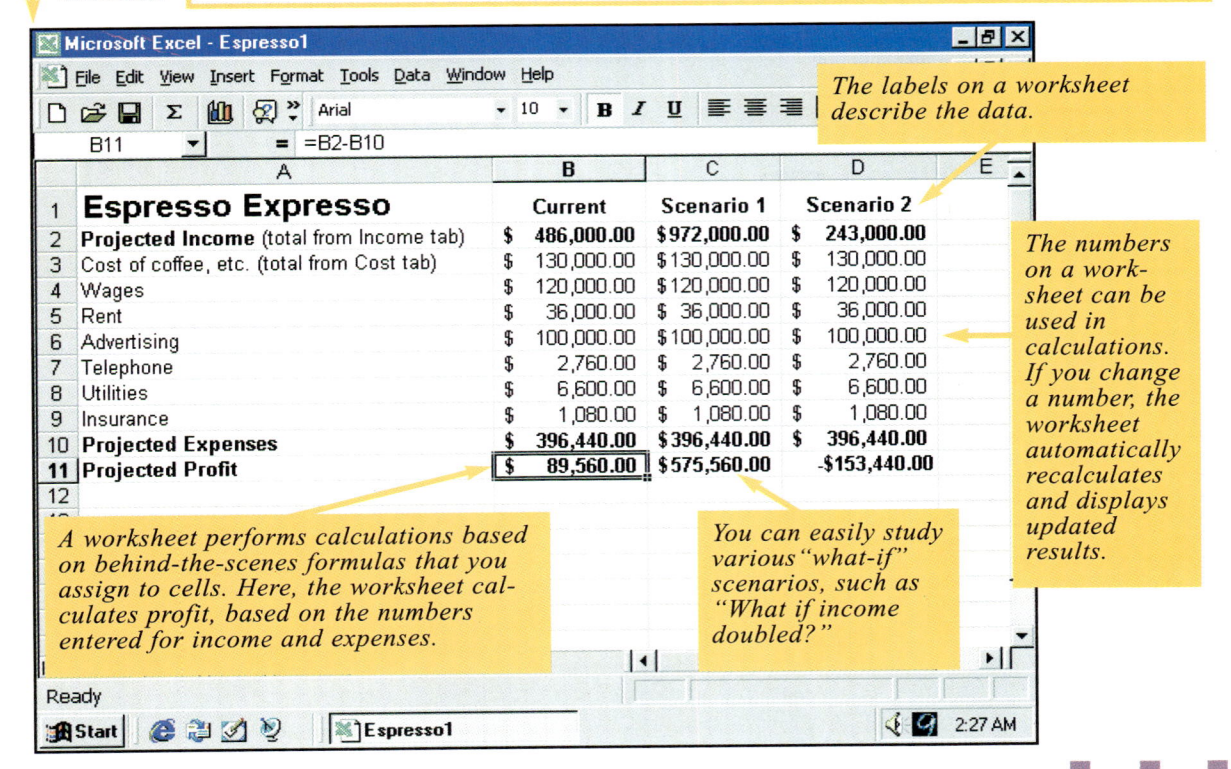

	A	B	C	D
1	Espresso Expresso	Current	Scenario 1	Scenario 2
2	Projected Income (total from Income tab)	$ 486,000.00	$972,000.00	$ 243,000.00
3	Cost of coffee, etc. (total from Cost tab)	$ 130,000.00	$130,000.00	$ 130,000.00
4	Wages	$ 120,000.00	$120,000.00	$ 120,000.00
5	Rent	$ 36,000.00	$ 36,000.00	$ 36,000.00
6	Advertising	$ 100,000.00	$100,000.00	$ 100,000.00
7	Telephone	$ 2,760.00	$ 2,760.00	$ 2,760.00
8	Utilities	$ 6,600.00	$ 6,600.00	$ 6,600.00
9	Insurance	$ 1,080.00	$ 1,080.00	$ 1,080.00
10	Projected Expenses	$ 396,440.00	$396,440.00	$ 396,440.00
11	Projected Profit	$ 89,560.00	$575,560.00	-$153,440.00

The labels on a worksheet describe the data.

The numbers on a worksheet can be used in calculations. If you change a number, the worksheet automatically recalculates and displays updated results.

A worksheet performs calculations based on behind-the-scenes formulas that you assign to cells. Here, the worksheet calculates profit, based on the numbers entered for income and expenses.

You can easily study various "what-if" scenarios, such as "What if income doubled?"

■FAQ How do I create a worksheet?

After you have a clear idea of the purpose of your worksheet, you can begin by entering the title and the labels that will identify your data. Next, you enter the numbers or "values" that will be incorporated in calculations. Finally, you enter formulas in any cells where you want the result of a calculation to appear.

A **formula** specifies how to add, subtract, multiply, or divide the numbers in worksheet cells. Typically, a formula begins with an equal sign (=) and contains cell references instead of the "raw" numbers for a calculation. A **cell reference** is the column and row location of a cell. In Figure 11-2, the projected income of $486,000.00 is in column B and row 2, so its cell reference is B2. To create the formula that calculates profit (=B2-B10), you should use this cell reference instead of the actual number. Then, if the projected income changes, you can simply enter the new number in cell B2, but you won't have to change the formula. The worksheet will recalculate the profit based on the new number you've entered.

After you've entered labels, numbers, and formulas, you can format your worksheet to make it more attractive and easier to understand. Formatting options include font treatments, cell colors, and data alignment within the cells. An additional set of formatting options helps you control the way your numbers are displayed, such as whether to include $ signs, decimal places, and commas.

Figure 11-2: Seasoned worksheet veterans have developed tips and tricks for making effective worksheets. They'll share some of these with you when you click the PlayIt! button.

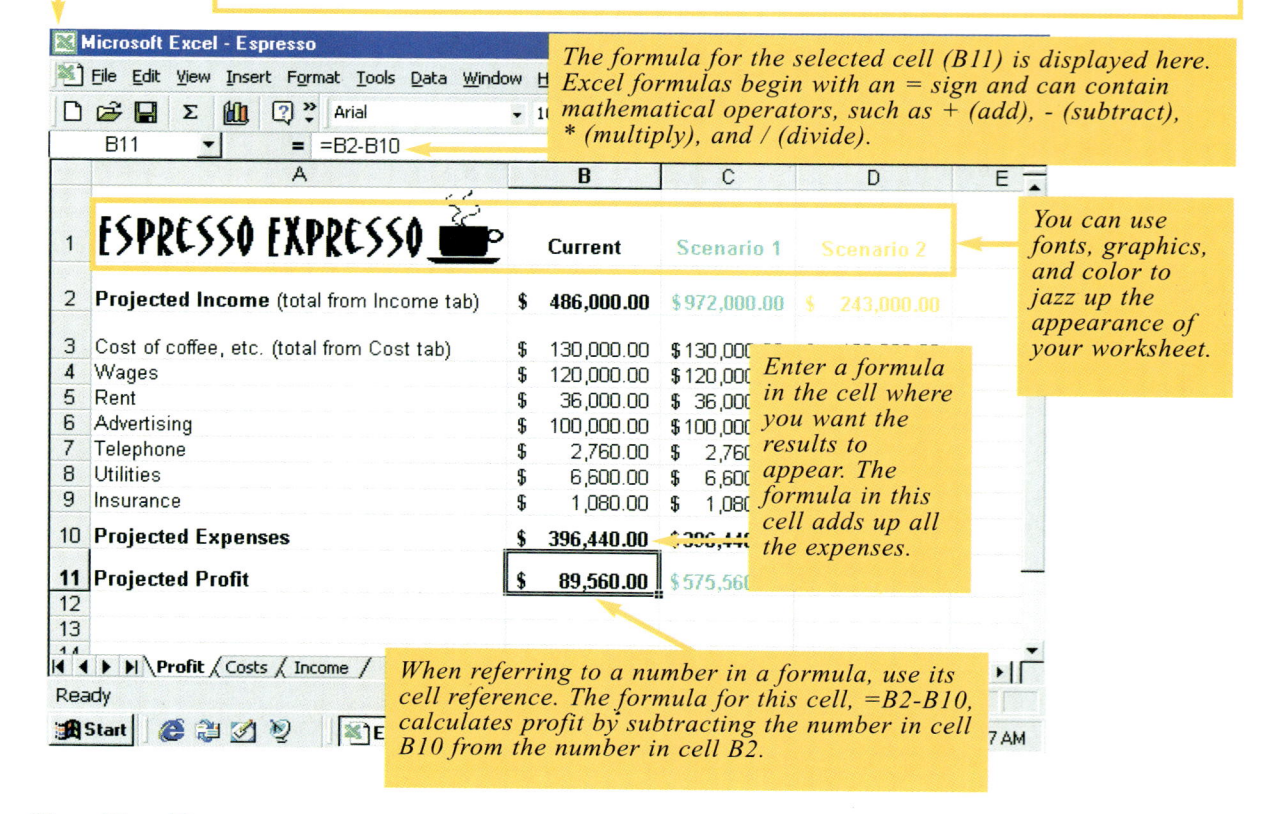

The formula for the selected cell (B11) is displayed here. Excel formulas begin with an = sign and can contain mathematical operators, such as + (add), - (subtract), * (multiply), and / (divide).

You can use fonts, graphics, and color to jazz up the appearance of your worksheet.

Enter a formula in the cell where you want the results to appear. The formula in this cell adds up all the expenses.

When referring to a number in a formula, use its cell reference. The formula for this cell, =B2-B10, calculates profit by subtracting the number in cell B10 from the number in cell B2.

Chapter 11: Making Spreadsheets and Presentations

■FAQ What if I don't know the right formula?

Some formulas are easy to figure out. If you follow baseball, you know that a player's batting average is the number of hits divided by the number of times at bat. Easy. But suppose that you're looking at new cars and you want to calculate your monthly payments for a spiffy red Toyota. You'll need to factor in interest rates, the number of payments, and the cost of the car. What's the formula?

Spreadsheet software includes built-in **functions**, which are predefined formulas that perform simple or complex calculations. Handy functions include AVERAGE, SUM, PMT (calculate monthly payments), STDEV (calculate a standard deviation), and ROUND (round off a decimal number). To use a function, simply select it from the function list, then follow the on-screen instructions to select the cells that contain arguments for the calculation. An **argument**, sometimes called a "parameter," is a value or cell reference that a function uses as the basis for a calculation. When you use the PMT function to calculate monthly car payments, the arguments include the interest rate, number of payments, and cost of the car. The arguments for a function are generally separated by commas and enclosed in parentheses.

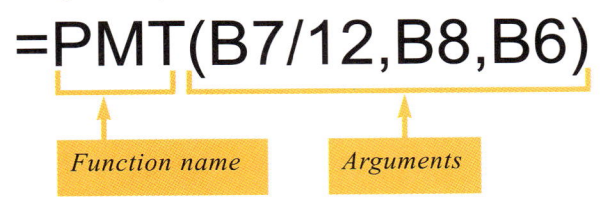

$$=PMT(B7/12, B8, B6)$$

Function name | Arguments

Figure 11-3: Click the PlayIt! button to explore worksheet functions and learn how to incorporate them in your worksheets.

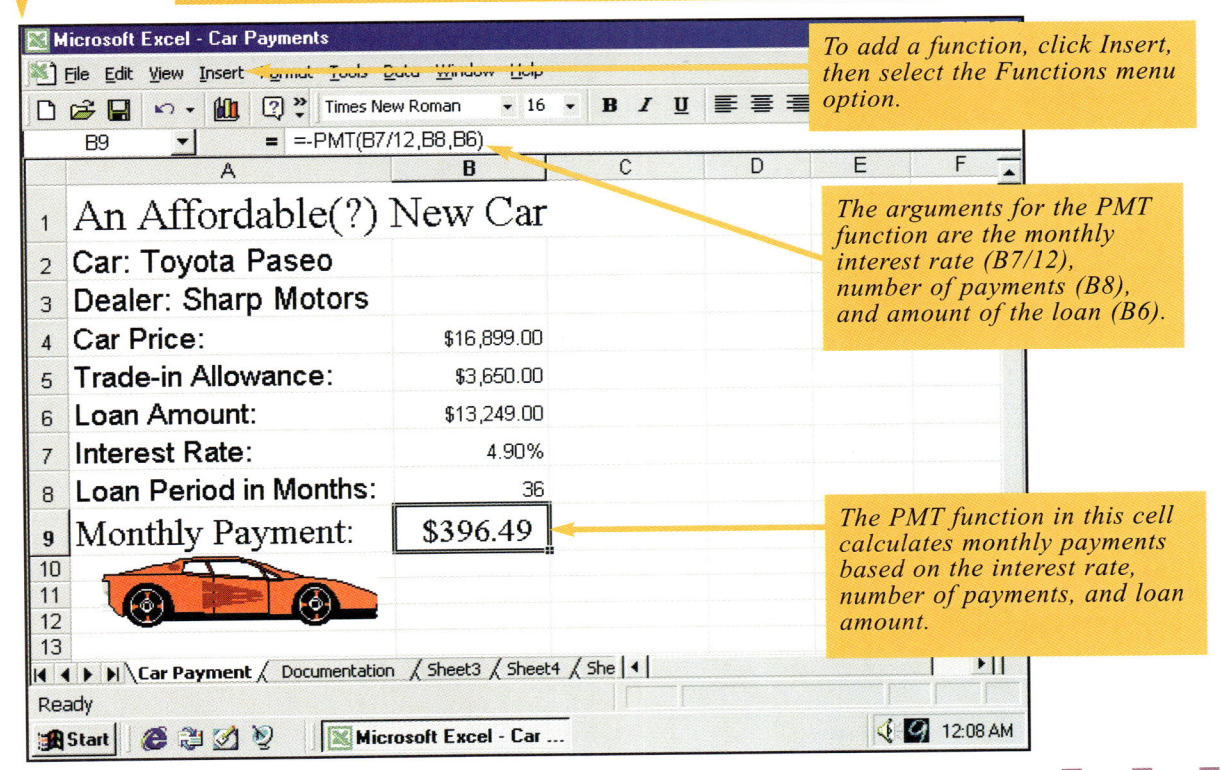

To add a function, click Insert, then select the Functions menu option.

The arguments for the PMT function are the monthly interest rate (B7/12), number of payments (B8), and amount of the loan (B6).

	A	B
1	An Affordable(?) New Car	
2	Car: Toyota Paseo	
3	Dealer: Sharp Motors	
4	Car Price:	$16,899.00
5	Trade-in Allowance:	$3,650.00
6	Loan Amount:	$13,249.00
7	Interest Rate:	4.90%
8	Loan Period in Months:	36
9	Monthly Payment:	$396.49

The PMT function in this cell calculates monthly payments based on the interest rate, number of payments, and loan amount.

Chapter 11: Making Spreadsheets and Presentations

■FAQ How do I know if worksheet results are accurate?

The person who creates a worksheet is responsible for its accuracy. Therefore, before you use or distribute a worksheet, you should test it to verify that it produces the correct results. Most spreadsheet software includes sophisticated tools for testing worksheets. If possible, however, you should first simply check the results using a hand calculator or data that is known to be correct. Worksheet errors typically result from one of the following factors:

- A value that you entered in a cell is incorrect due to a typographical error.
- A formula contains a mathematical operator that is not correct, includes an incorrect cell reference, or is simply the wrong formula.
- A formula produces the wrong results because the order for the calculations is not correct. Spreadsheet software first performs any operations in parentheses, then performs multiplication and division, and finally performs addition and subtraction. For example, the result of the formula =2+10/5 is 4, whereas the result of =(2+10)/5 is 2.4.
- A specified series of cells does not encompass all the values needed for a calculation. For example, you may have intended to sum the values in cells C5 through H5, but specified cells C5 through G5.
- The worksheet was created using a built-in function, but the wrong cells were selected as the arguments. For example, in the PMT function, the first argument is supposed to be the interest rate, but if it has been assigned to the cell that contains the loan amount, the PMT function will produce the wrong result.

Figure 11-4: Click the PlayIt! button for tips on how to check the accuracy of your worksheets.

Oops! An "A" would be nice, but this student's spreadsheet is inaccurate. The percentage should be 89% and the grade should be "B." Can you spot the errors?

Chapter 11: Making Spreadsheets and Presentations

■FAQ How do I create graphs?

Most spreadsheet software includes features that create graphs, sometimes called "charts" in spreadsheet terminology. A graph is based on the data in a worksheet. When you alter the data in your worksheet, the graph will automatically reflect the change. Typically, you'll want to graph the data contained in one or more ranges. A **range** is a series of cells. For example, the range B3:B6 includes cells B3, B4, B5, and B6. The range for a graph is also referred to as a "data set" or "data series." To create a graph comparing apple and grape production, one range of data would be apple production and the other would be grape production.

Your spreadsheet software allows you create many types of graphs, such as bar, line, pie, column, scatter, area, doughnut, and high-low-close graphs. You can even add graphics to bar and column charts. For example, instead of a plain bar depicting fruit yield, you can stack up a series of apples on one set of bars and a series of grapes on the other set.

Creating a graph requires a few easy steps:
- Plan your chart by deciding which worksheet data you want to chart and the type of chart you want to use.
- Activate the Chart wizard for step-by-step instructions on creating the chart.
- Use the Chart and formatting menu options to change the appearance of the chart labels, data markers, and dimensions.

Figure 11-5: Excel's Chart wizard escorts you through the process of creating a graph from the data in a worksheet. Click PlayIt! to see how it works.

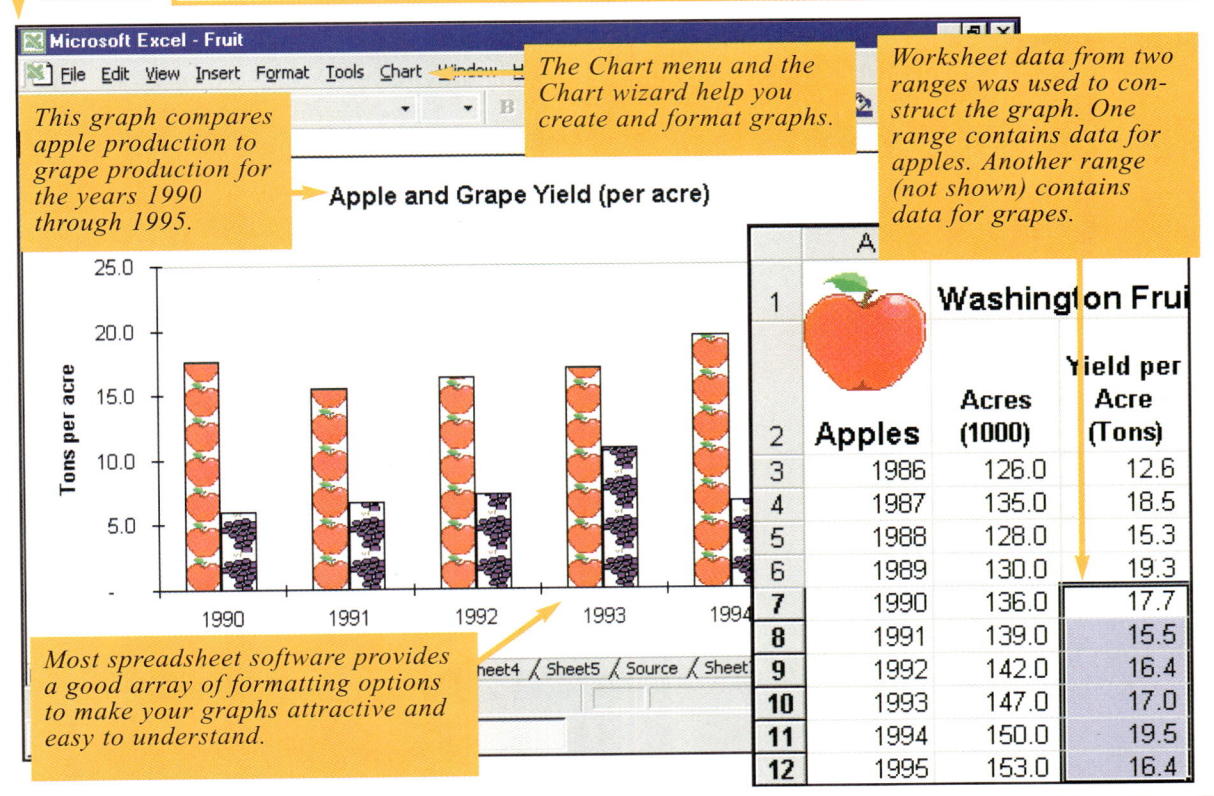

This graph compares apple production to grape production for the years 1990 through 1995.

The Chart menu and the Chart wizard help you create and format graphs.

Worksheet data from two ranges was used to construct the graph. One range contains data for apples. Another range (not shown) contains data for grapes.

Most spreadsheet software provides a good array of formatting options to make your graphs attractive and easy to understand.

	Apples	Acres (1000)	Yield per Acre (Tons)
3	1986	126.0	12.6
4	1987	135.0	18.5
5	1988	128.0	15.3
6	1989	130.0	19.3
7	1990	136.0	17.7
8	1991	139.0	15.5
9	1992	142.0	16.4
10	1993	147.0	17.0
11	1994	150.0	19.5
12	1995	153.0	16.4

Hardware
Computer projection devices

One of the components of a typical office suite, **presentation software**, helps you create a series of graphics called **slides** to use as a backdrop for a speech, lecture, or sales presentation. It provides all the tools you need to combine text, diagrams, worksheets, graphs, animations, and sound effects into a series of electronic slides. You can display these slides on a PC monitor for a one-on-one presentation. For group presentations, a **computer projection device** can project your slides on a wall screen in a conference room or theater.

A computer projection device is not the type of equipment that you should be tempted to purchase for your home computer. Its high price is more typically affordable by a school, library, or business. However, computer projection devices are becoming so commonplace that you are likely to have an opportunity to use one—for example, when you pitch a new publicity campaign to your company's best client, when you give that oral report in your anthropology class, when you brief volunteers for the United Way campaign, or even when you're trying to convince the city council to put some effort into urban renewal. Two types of projection devices are popular today; LCD projection panels and LCD projectors.

LCD projection panels are the least expensive type of projection device. Envision a semi-transparent LCD panel, which you place on an overhead projector like a giant slide. The light from the overhead projector shines through the image shown on the LCD panel and projects it on a wall screen.

Priced at U.S.$1,000 to U.S.$2,500, LCD projection panels are a relatively low-cost solution for schools and libraries that already have overhead projectors. The low cost of this technology reflects it weaknesses, however. Images projected by LCD panels tend to lack brightness and do not work well unless the room is fairly dark.

Figure 11-6: An LCD projection panel uses an overhead projector as its light source. The panel connects to a PC from which it receives the images that it displays.

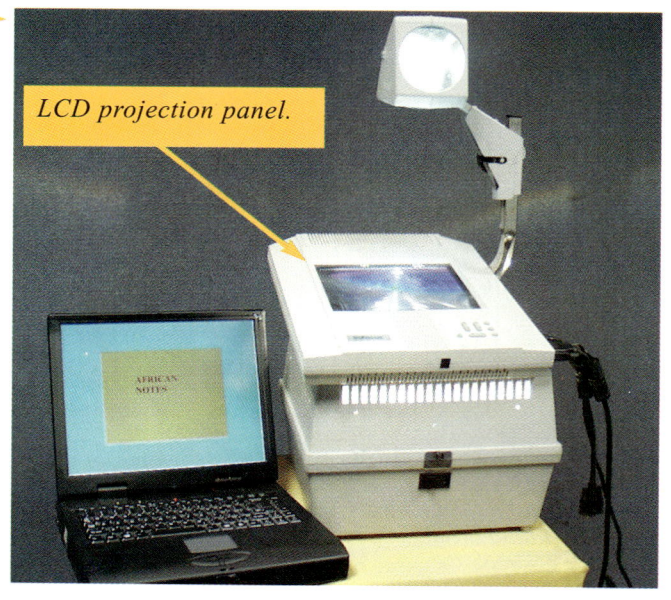

Chapter 11: Making Spreadsheets and Presentations

■Hardware
continued

A second computer projection technology, usually referred to as an **LCD projector**, encases an LCD panel and light source in an 11 to 20 pound box about the size of a case of Pepsi. Because it does not require an overhead projector, an LCD projector is the obvious choice when portability is important. Its other advantage is the amount of light it projects. Brightness is measured in ANSI lumens. Many LCD projectors produce 650 ANSI lumens or more, suitable for displaying presentations in a well-lighted room. The price of an LCD projector reflects its ANSI lumens rating. A projector with a 700 ANSI lumens rating costs about U.S.$3,000, whereas a projector with a 1000 ANSI lumens rating costs about U.S.$5,000.

LCD projectors typically include "bells and whistles" to enhance presentations. A built-in loudspeaker is handy for playing any sound effects that you've added to your presentation slides. A remote control lets you adjust the focus and turn the projector on and off from across the room. Some projectors feature computerless operation—you copy slides from your PC to a PCMCIA memory card, which you then insert into the projector's PCMCIA slot.

Keystone control is available on several LCD projector models. **Keystoning**, the bane of professional speakers and audio-visual specialists, is the tendency of projected images to appear more like trapezoids than true rectangles. It occurs when the projector is not positioned directly in line with the middle of the screen. Because it is often practical to mount the projector on a table that's lower than the screen or on the ceiling above the screen, keystoning is a common artifact of presentations. Keystone control compensates for the position of the projector to produce a professional-looking rectangular image.

[Play It!]

Figure 11-7: LCD projectors are hot items for business and education. Manufacturers include Proxima, ViewSonic, Philips, Toshiba, Sony, and InFocus. Click PlayIt! to find out how to connect an LCD projector to a notebook PC.

Hardware continued

Technology is great—when it works. But it doesn't always work. Occasional problems with your PC will typically affect only your personal productivity, but when you must depend on presentation equipment, technology glitches can become very public. It's awfully nerve-wracking to stand in front of a group of 100 people while someone tries to track down a replacement bulb for the LCD projector. You can avoid many of the curveballs that technology throws your way if you get serious about planning and preparing for your presentation.

- Determine whether presentation equipment will be available. If you plan to use your own notebook computer, make sure it is compatible with the projection device and that the correct connecting cables will be supplied. If you will use a computer other than your own, make sure the necessary software has been installed.
- Check out the equipment ahead of time. If possible, schedule a trial run the day before your presentation. Connect your computer and display a few slides so you are certain that everything works.
- Make sure that your audience will be able to see and hear your presentation. During your trial run, sit in the back of the room and make certain that the text on your slides is large enough to be easily read.
- Arrive early. Allow at least 30 minutes to set up your equipment and connect it to the presentation device.
- Know how to get technical support. If you are unfamiliar with any of the equipment, you might request the presence of a technical support person during your trial run or while you set up. Find out how you can contact a technician if you run into problems during the presentation.
- Be prepared for problems. Find out what to do if the projector bulb burns out. If you're using a notebook PC with batteries, keep your power cord handy. If this presentation can make or break your career, you might consider printing copies of your most important slides, so that you can distribute them to your audience in case of a power failure.

Figure 11-8: You can make an effective presentation using a PC, presentation software, and an LCD projector, but it requires advance planning and preparation.

Chapter 11: Making Spreadsheets and Presentations 131

■Tutorial
How to make slides for an effective presentation

Presentation software is optimized to create slides containing text, sound effects, and graphics. You can design your slides from scratch, but you'll also find a good selection of ready-made **slide templates** that contain professionally designed background graphics and fonts in sizes that are easy to read when projected on a wall screen.

Grab It! — PowerPoint Templates

Most office suites include a collection of clip art images that provide eye-catching additions to documents, spreadsheets, and slides. For a truly multimedia presentation, you can add sound effects to your slides. You can incorporate even more visual interest by selecting active **transition effects** between slides, such as fades, wipes, and dissolves.

When you have completed the tutorial, you should be able to:
- Select a slide template to use as the theme for your presentation.
- Create a slide with a bulleted list.
- Add clip art and sound effects to a slide.
- Select a transition effect.
- Add lecture notes for your script.

Play It!

Figure 11-9: Click the PlayIt! button to begin the tutorial and learn how to assemble slides for a presentation. Estimated time: 10–15 minutes. Tracking Disk points: 10.

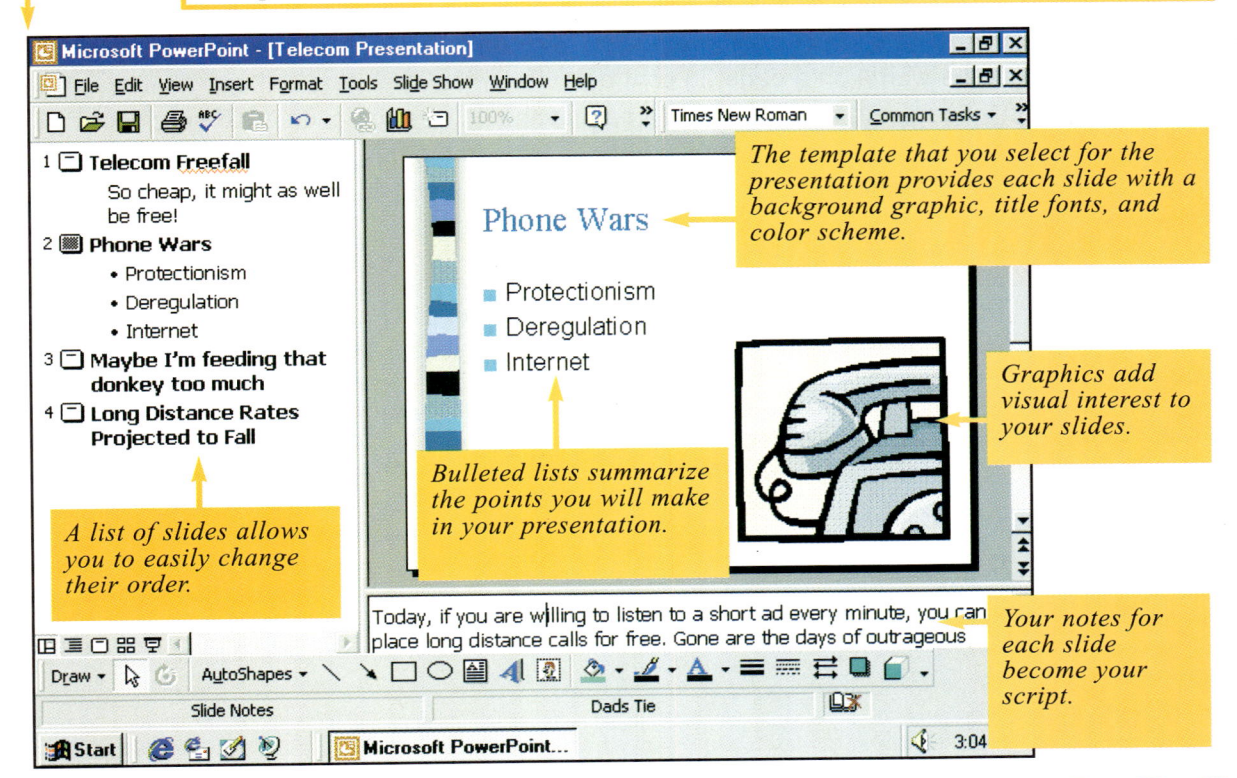

A list of slides allows you to easily change their order.

The template that you select for the presentation provides each slide with a background graphic, title fonts, and color scheme.

Bulleted lists summarize the points you will make in your presentation.

Graphics add visual interest to your slides.

Your notes for each slide become your script.

■Issue
Is it the medium or the message?

A Canadian professor named Marshall McLuhan coined the phrase "the medium is the message" to express the idea that media, such as films, books, and television, have an impact far greater than that of the material they communicate. Suppose that you're surfing the Web and encounter a site with light pink text. This site might as well carry no message as far as you're concerned. You might skip it because the text is too difficult to read. A clear case of the medium (that awful light pink text) becoming the message (nothing).

"The medium is the message" is not, however, the last word of advice for people who create documents, spreadsheets, and presentations. It would be a miscalculation to believe that your content doesn't matter as long as it is wrapped up in a flashy package. Today's media-savvy audience might be entertained by flash, but easily penetrate its thin veil to critically examine your ideas.

But "the medium is the message" might have a deeper meaning to convey, too. According to commentator John Mackenzie, it "implies that the physical and architectural characteristics of media exert greater evolutionary control over our ideas and institutions than the content we superimpose on them." In other words, the media, not the messages, shape our cultures, our ideas, and even our personalities. By the time a student reaches college, he or she will have spent over 17,000 hours watching television and playing video games. The parents and grandparents of this student, having divided their attention between print and electronic media, might quite literally be on a different psychological wavelength. Print is a leisurely medium that allows time for reflection and constructing mental images to supplement the words on a page. In contrast, the rapidly changing collage of television and video game images requires participants to develop quite a different set of mental skills. And now we must add the Web to the mix of media, and wonder how that, too, might affect the evolution of individuals and cultural groups.

What do you think?

1. Do you believe that McLuhan was correct in saying that "the medium is the message"? ○ Yes ○ No ○ Not sure

2. Do you agree that, as a rule of thumb, the time you devote to preparing for a presentation should be divided as 50% research and writing, 50% designing electronic slides? ○ Yes ○ No ○ Not sure

3. Do you believe that new media such as the Web can fundamentally change the personality and thought patterns of an entire generation? ○ Yes ○ No ○ Not sure

Save It!

Chapter 11: Making Spreadsheets and Presentations   133

QuickCheck A

1. You can design a worksheet to be a numeric _____ that you can use to examine "what-if" scenarios.

2. D9, A6, and Q8 are examples of cell _____.

3. SUM, PMT, and AVERAGE are spreadsheet _____.

4. True or false? If you create a graph showing baseball players' homeruns, you can change the number of runs for a player on the worksheet and the graph will automatically reflect the change. ____

5. True or false? Most computer projection devices use LCD technology. ____

Check It!

QuickCheck B

Indicate the letter that correctly matches each description.

1. A cell containing a label ____

2. A cell containing a number ____

3. A cell containing a formula ____

4. The formula for cell B11 ____

5. A "what-if" analysis ____

Check It!

Get It?

While using the Book-on-CD, click the Get It? button to see if you can answer ten randomly selected questions from Chapter 11.

Chapter 12
Accessing Databases

What's Inside?

In Chapter 12, you'll find out how to decide if you need database software, learn how to create your own databases, and think about some of the privacy issues associated with databases that contain information about you. The Hardware section examines CD and DVD storage—key technologies for storing and distributing large files and databases.

- **FAQs:**
  - What's a database? — 135
  - Do I need database software? — 136
  - How would I create my own database? — 137
  - Can I really create databases with spreadsheet software? — 138
  - What about databases on the Web and CDs? — 139
- Hardware: CDs and DVDs — 140
- Tutorial: How to make your own CDs — 143
- Issue: Who owns information about me? — 144
- QuickChecks — 145

What's on the CD?

Chapter 12 screen tours and videos show you the inner workings of databases and DVD technology.

- Take a tour of database software — 136
- Discover how to create your own database — 137
- Explore the data-handling features of spreadsheet software — 138
- Look at some cool CD and Web databases — 139
- Take a video tour of the new DVD technology — 141
- Take a step-by-step tutorial on making CDs — 143

Chapter 12: Accessing Databases 135

■FAQ What's a database?

In popular usage, the term "database" simply means a collection of data, such as a phone book, flight schedules, or a store's inventory list. You've probably encountered both freeform and structured databases. A **freeform database** is a loosely structured collection of information, usually stored as documents. You could consider the documents stored on your computer to be a freeform database. A CD containing back issues of *Time* magazine would be another example. You could even regard the Web, with its millions of documents, as a freeform database.

A **structured database** contains information that is organized as fields, records, and files. A **field** contains a single piece of information, such as a name, birth date, or ZIP code. A **record** contains fields of information about a single "entity" in the database—a person, place, event, or thing. A group of similarly structured records form a **file**, also referred to as a "table."

When two or more related files are treated as a single unit, you have a **relational database**. For example, a video store database might include a file of movies and a file of customers. Suppose that a customer checks out the new *Star Wars* movie. The clerk simply enters the customer number on the Star Wars record. If the movie is never returned, the customer number acts as a link to the customer file that displays the customer's address, phone number, and credit card billing information.

Figure 12-1: *In a relational database, two or more files can be linked or "joined" to display related data.*

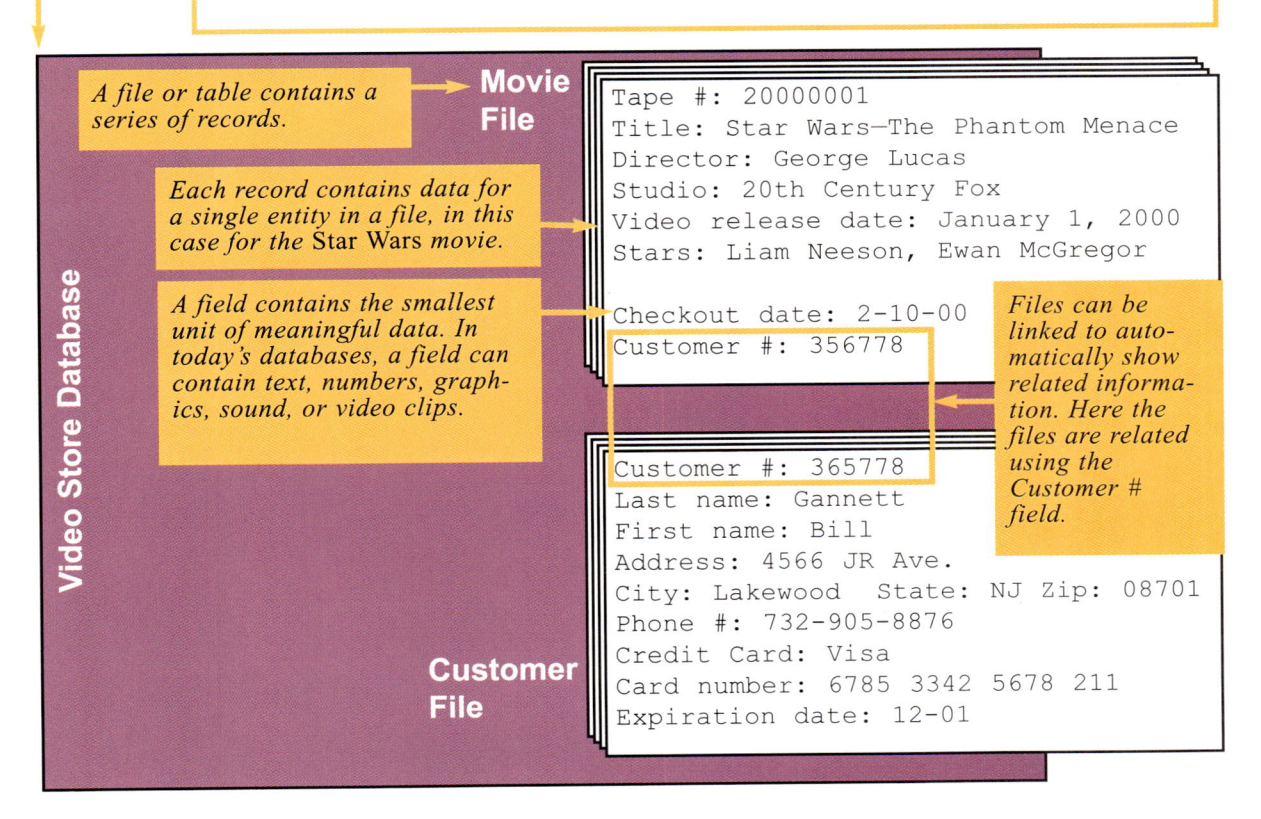

Video Store Database

A file or table contains a series of records. → **Movie File**

Each record contains data for a single entity in a file, in this case for the *Star Wars* movie.

A field contains the smallest unit of meaningful data. In today's databases, a field can contain text, numbers, graphics, sound, or video clips.

```
Tape #: 20000001
Title: Star Wars—The Phantom Menace
Director: George Lucas
Studio: 20th Century Fox
Video release date: January 1, 2000
Stars: Liam Neeson, Ewan McGregor

Checkout date: 2-10-00
Customer #: 356778
```

Files can be linked to automatically show related information. Here the files are related using the Customer # field.

```
Customer #: 365778
Last name: Gannett
First name: Bill
Address: 4566 JR Ave.
City: Lakewood   State: NJ Zip: 08701
Phone #: 732-905-8876
Credit Card: Visa
Card number: 6785 3342 5678 211
Expiration date: 12-01
```

Customer File

Chapter 12: Accessing Databases

■FAQ Do I need database software?

Grab It!
Simple File and Database Software

Database software, sometimes referred to as database management software (DBMS), provides a set of tools to enter and update information in fields, delete records, sort records, search for records that meet specified criteria, and create reports. Most people use databases with surprising frequency, but might not need database software. Why? Consider the databases that you typically access. You might access a database to register online for a class at a college or university. You might search a product database at a Web site such as Amazon.com. You might access your bank's database at an ATM to check your account balance. To access such databases, you use database software that runs on a computer at the host site—not on your own PC. Therefore, you do not need database software to interact with the databases at school, on the Web, or at your bank. Having database software is useful only to create and maintain your own databases.

If you have a use for database software, a variety of options are available. For example, Microsoft Access provides a wealth of data management capabilities, but using it to create production-quality databases requires a substantial learning commitment. Corel Paradox, Lotus Approach, and FileMaker Pro might be easier to learn and include the basic features needed to manage typical files and databases. For dealing with simple files, you might use the database modules of Microsoft Works or Claris Works. You can also use spreadsheet software for simple databases. You'll learn more about this option in a later FAQ.

Play It!

Figure 12-2: Click the PlayIt! button for a tour of database software. You'll learn how you might use the tables, search, query, form, and report functions, plus you'll find out why you might want to join two tables.

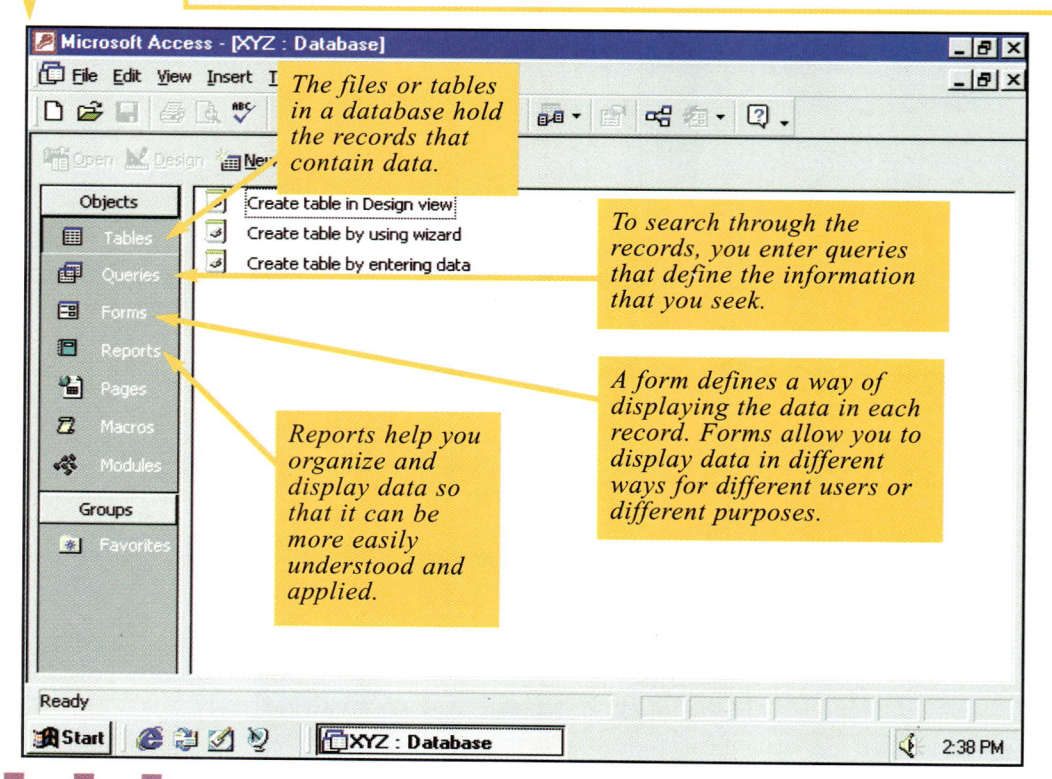

The files or tables in a database hold the records that contain data.

To search through the records, you enter queries that define the information that you seek.

A form defines a way of displaying the data in each record. Forms allow you to display data in different ways for different users or different purposes.

Reports help you organize and display data so that it can be more easily understood and applied.

Chapter 12: Accessing Databases 137

■FAQ How would I create my own database?

Creating a database consists of two tasks; creating a file structure to hold the data and adding the data for each record. The specific procedure you'll use depends on the database software that you've selected, so you will want to refer to your software documentation for exact instructions.

Grab It!
Access Database Templates

Suppose that you want to create a household inventory in case you need it for an insurance claim. First, you will use your database software to create the **file structure**—a specification for the database fields and their characteristics. You'll need to assign a name to each field, such as Category, Item, Description, Purchase Date, Value, and Photo. Some database software might require you to specify the maximum length of each field and the type of data that it will hold—text, numbers, date, or graphic.

Once you have created the file structure, your database software will display it as a blank form that you can use to fill in the data for each household item. You will be able to reliably locate data in your database only if you enter data accurately and consistently. Keep these tips in mind when you enter data:

- As you enter each record, compare the on-screen data to your original documents to verify its accuracy.
- Be consistent with the entries for fields that might be used to group your data. Suppose that you plan to group your household inventory by categories such as jewelry, furniture, appliances, and electronics. You must then enter "jewelry"—not "jewels"—in the Category field for your diamond ring.
- Use consistent capitalization. Most database software is case-sensitive. Be aware that if you enter "Microwave oven," case-sensitive database software will not find anything when you later search for "microwave oven."
- Make sure your spelling is correct. If you misspell an item, such as "portable jacuzi," when you add it to the database, you won't be able to find it if you later search for "portable jacuzzi."
- Use abbreviations consistently. To your database software, TV and T.V. are completely different.
- Be careful about symbols. The telephone number (906)227-1000 is not the same as 906.227.1000.

Play It!

Figure 12-3: *Click the PlayIt! button to learn how to create a database using Microsoft Access. You'll find out how to define the database structure, specify field names, and select data types.*

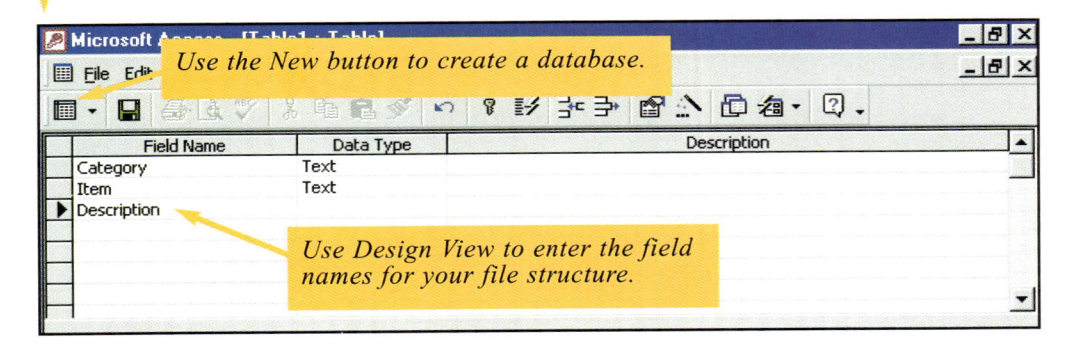

Use the New button to create a database.

Field Name	Data Type	Description
Category	Text	
Item	Text	
Description		

Use Design View to enter the field names for your file structure.

Chapter 12: Accessing Databases

■FAQ Can I really create databases with spreadsheet software?

You can use most spreadsheet software to create and maintain files of information. You cannot, however, use it to join files together and create a relational database. Spreadsheet software typically has special data-handling features that allow you to manipulate the rows and columns of a worksheet as if they were records and fields in a database. You can sort your data, search for data that meets specific criteria, and create reports. As a rule of thumb, spreadsheet software can handle any data that you could put on a set of cards in a card file.

When managing data with spreadsheet software, the Form View displays each row of the worksheet as a "card" containing a series of fields, as shown in Figure 12-4. If you already know how to use spreadsheet software and your data lends itself to the card-file approach to data management, you'll find it easy to use the Form View for basic operations such as entering, modifying, searching, and sorting data.

A process called **filtering** or "extracting" data is a bit more complicated, but useful for creating reports that show only selected data. Suppose, for example, that you have 100 rows in a worksheet that you're using as a database. Each row contains information on doctor visits for members of your family. If you want the worksheet to display only those records for your oldest daughter, you'll need to filter the data using her name. You could then print the filtered version of the worksheet to produce a hard-copy report of her medical history.

Figure 12-4: Click the PlayIt! button for a demonstration of how to use spreadsheet software to manage data.

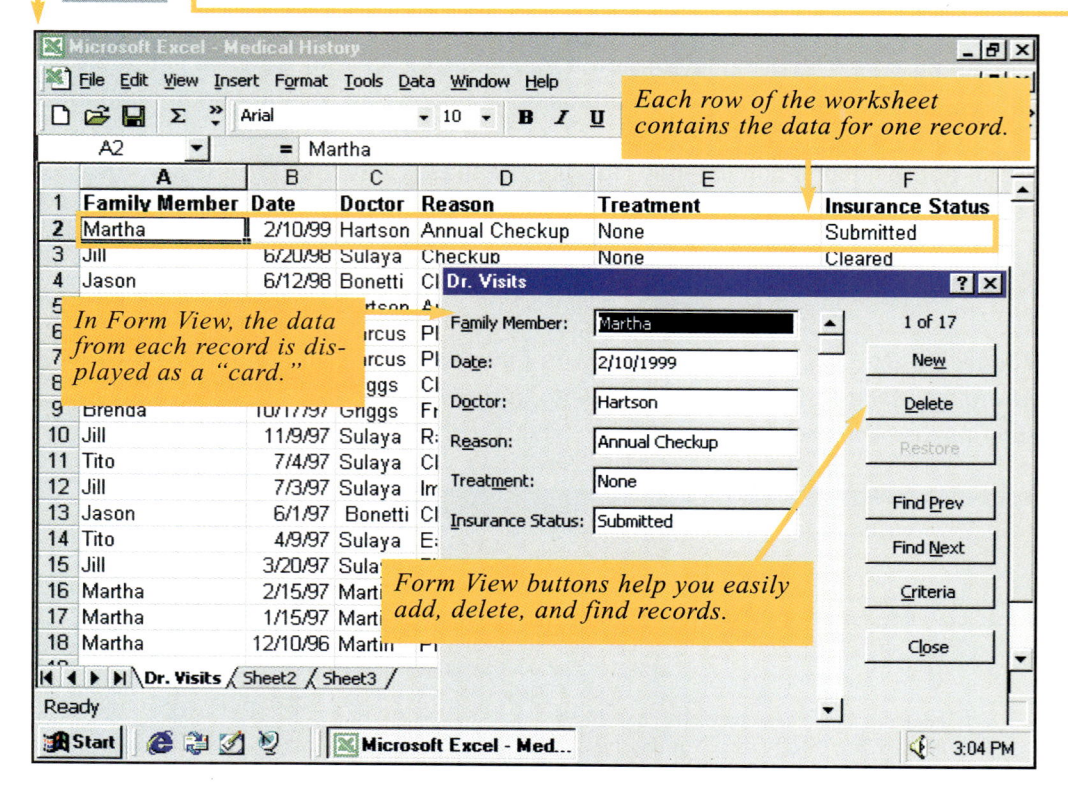

Chapter 12: Accessing Databases   139

■FAQ   What about databases on the Web and CDs?

You'll find many databases on the Web and CDs that are prepopulated with all sorts of information. For example, you can look for your old roommate in a phone-book-style database that covers the entire country; find a low-cost airfare to Beijing in a database that contains flight schedules for the major airlines; look for the author of *Trout Madness* in the U.S. Library of Congress database; check the value of a 1964 Ford Mustang in a digital "Blue Book" database; find a definition of the term "CD-R" in a database of technical terms; or look up the December 1965 feature article in a database of back issues of *National Geographic* magazine.

There is a great deal of overlap between Web and CD databases. As you might expect, the Web is optimal for data that's constantly changing—air fares, for example. CDs provide a low-cost distribution method for less changeable data, which is why CD encyclopedias and medical references are so popular. CDs have an added advantage because the specific data that you access is not tracked by a cookie or Web site and therefore remains private.

On the Web, you'll also encounter databases that actively collect information. To access a Web site you might be required to register and complete a questionnaire about your income level, interests, computer ownership, and so on. The information that you supply is added to a database. You might assume that your registration information would not be made public, but businesses frequently sell their customer databases to research and marketing firms.

Play It!   **Figure 12-5:** Click the PlayIt! button to see some samples of Web and CD databases.

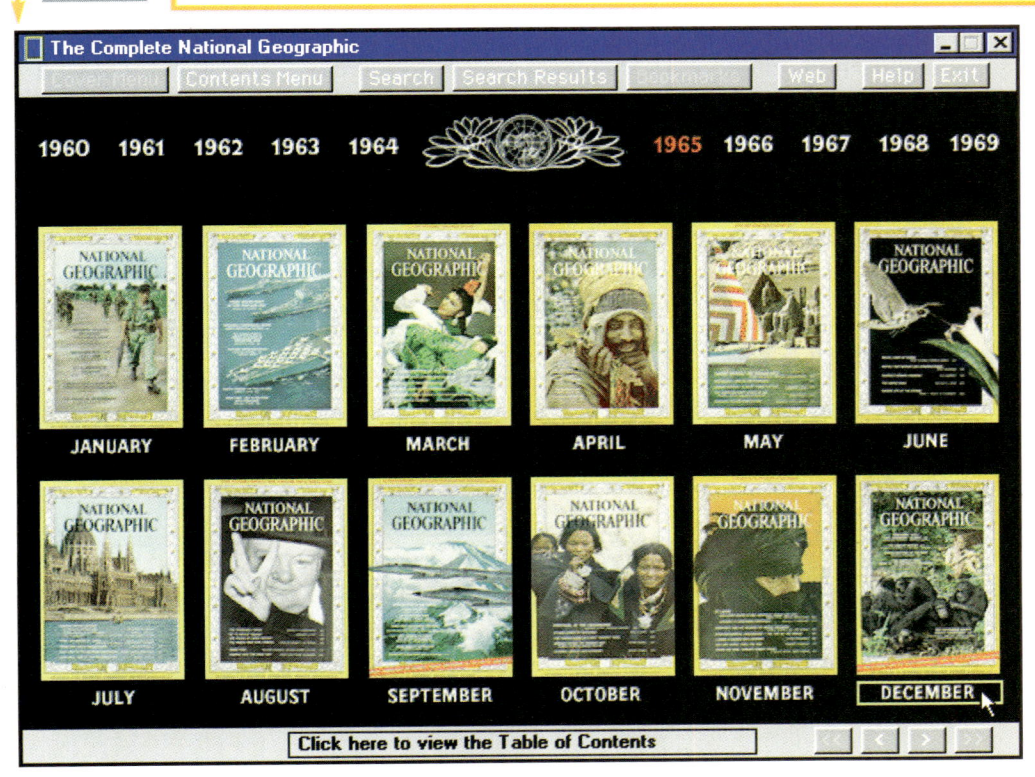

■Hardware
CDs and DVDs

Those silver disks that you nonchalantly slide into your boom box or computer are commonly called "CDs." Technically, several types of these disks exist, and each has unique characteristics and uses. The term CD or "audio CD" originally referred to only those disks that contained music or other audio data. These CDs were designed to replace LP records and cassette tapes. They comfortably held the songs from a typical music album. Why not use a similar technology to store computer data? This brilliant idea produced computer CDs with a typical storage capacity of 650 MB. Computer CDs are sometimes called "CD-ROMs" to distinguish them from audio CDs. The term **CD-ROM** is an abbreviation of "compact disc read-only memory," a reference to the fact that CD-ROM drives only read from disks preloaded with data, but cannot record or store data on them.

Standard CD-ROM drives only read data from premastered CD-ROM disks. However, variations of this technology allow you to store data as well as read it. **CD-R** (CD-recordable) technology allows you to create your own CDs using a CD-R drive and special CD-R disks. The disks you create will also work in standard CD-ROM drives. If you're shopping for a CD-R drive, you'll find one priced between U.S.$350 and $600. A blank CD-R disk typically costs less than U.S.$2. Another variation of CD technology, **CD-RW** (CD-rewritable), allows you to record CDs and then change the data that they contain. CD-RW drives are about the same price as a CD-R drive, but blank CD-RW disks can cost as much as U.S.$20 each. The disadvantage of CD-RW is that the disks it produces can be read only by CD-ROM drives with new "MultiRead" technology developed for this purpose.

Many desktop and notebook PCs include a CD-ROM drive. If one is not included, you can add this device for less than U.S.$50. The price of a CD-ROM drive is linked to the speed at which it can access data. A faster access rate provides you with smoother video playback and speedier database searches.

Figure 12-6: CD-ROM drive speed is indicated as a multiple of the original single-speed drive. Today's 32X drives can access up to 4.8 megabytes of data in one second—a considerable speed improvement on the original drives, which accessed only 150 kilobytes of data per second.

Speed Specification	Data Transfer Rate (per second)
Single-speed	150 KB
2X	300 KB
4X	600 KB
8X	1.2 MB
16X	2.4 MB
24X	3.6 MB
32X	4.8 MB

■Hardware continued

DVD (Digital Video Disc) is a new type of storage and distribution media, designed to replace VHS video tape. DVD has more than enough storage capacity for an entire feature-length film—up to 9 hours of video or 30 hours of CD-quality audio. DVDs can also store computer data. Although it is the same size as a CD-ROM disk, a DVD platter can hold far more data. Data can be stored on a DVD platter using one of four formats, as shown in Figure 12-7.

Figure 12-7: DVD storage capacity depends on whether data is stored on one or two sides of the disk, and how many layers of data each side contains.

Number of Sides	Number of Layers	Storage Capacity
1	1	4.7 GB
1	2	8.5 GB
2	1	9.4 GB
2	2	17.0 GB

DVD access rates of between 600 KB per second and 1.3 MB per second are slower than the latest generation of CD-ROM drives, but technological innovations allow them to provide similar video playback and database search speed. DVD technology does not currently provide any way to record data from your PC.

DVD players can access data from both CDs and CD-ROMs. The newest DVD players, called **DVD-2 drives**, can also access data from CD-R and CD-RW disks. Some PC manufacturers now include DVD drives as standard equipment, but software in DVD format remains somewhat limited. You might consider DVD when you purchase a new computer, but it is not necessary to replace the CD-ROM drive on your current PC with a DVD player.

Figure 12-8: DVD technology looks and works much like CD technology. Click the PlayIt! button for a closer look at DVD.

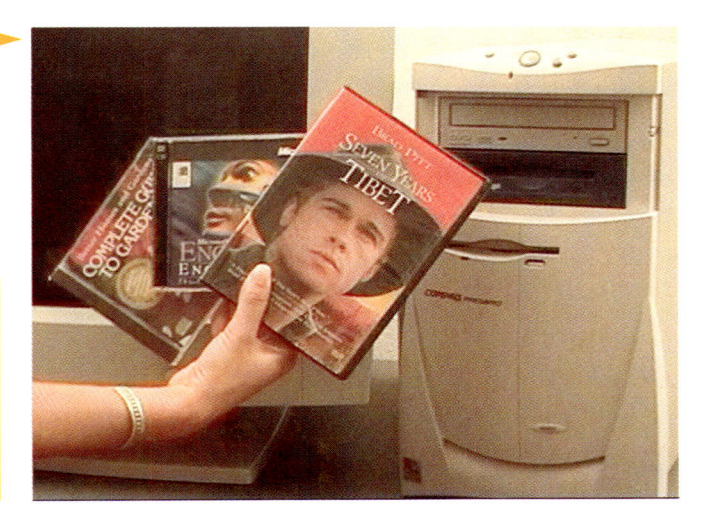

■Hardware
continued

CDs and DVDs are examples of **optical storage technology**, which records data as a trail of tiny pits in the disk surface. The data that these pits represent can then be "read" with a beam of laser light. To manufacture a commercial CD or DVD platter, a special glass master disk stamps an imprint on reflective aluminum foil. The stamping process creates a series of microscopic pits in the foil that represent data. The foil is then bonded to the plastic disk that you insert into the player.

Optical storage media are very durable. Unlike magnetic media, such as floppy and hard disks, CD and DVD platters are not susceptible to humidity, dust, fingerprints, or magnets. If you spill Coke on a CD, simply rinse it off and your platter will be as good as new. CDs are not indestructible, however. You should be careful not to scratch the disk surface or expose the disk to high temperatures.

The data on CDs and DVDs is permanent—an advantage for archival storage, when you intend to keep the data for many years. It is also a disadvantage because, with the exception of CD-RW technology, optical technology does not provide the flexibility of magnetic media for changing data once it has been stored. Magnetic media, such as hard, floppy, and Zip disks, allow you to easily and quickly modify stored data. Therefore, your PC's hard disk is the storage medium of choice for files that will be updated frequently—your documents, spreadsheets, and databases. Optical media are the choice for storing and distributing large data files that will remain relatively stable—a multimedia encyclopedia, a clip art collection, or last year's accounting data.

Figure 12-9: Optical media store data as a series of pits. The size and spacing of the pits determine the storage capacity of the disk.

The purple image is a magnification of the size and spacing of pits on the surface of a CD-ROM. The blue image illustrates the relative size and spacing of pits on a DVD-ROM.

With smaller pits and tighter spacing, a DVD-ROM stores a considerable amount more data than a CD-ROM.

A micron is one millionth of a meter.

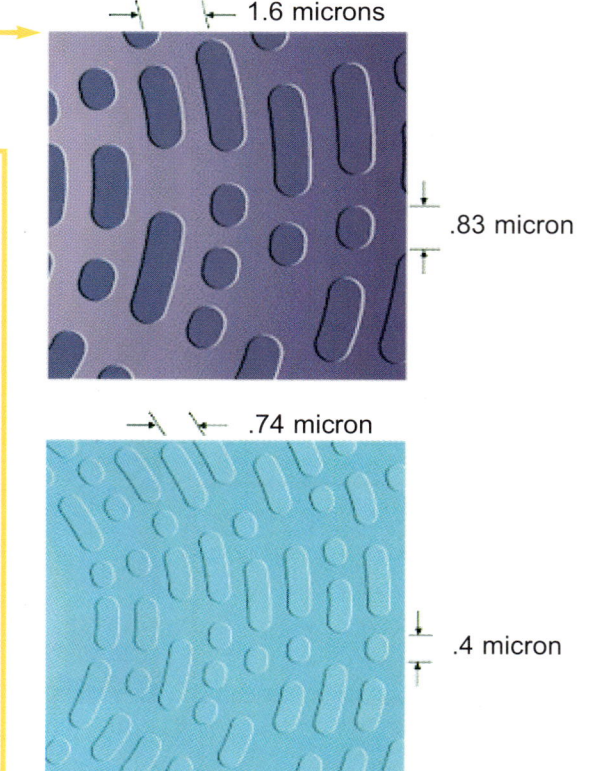

Chapter 12: Accessing Databases

■Tutorial
How to make your own CDs

For professional software developers, small businesses, presenters, multimedia designers, desktop publishers, and home recording artists, CD-R and CD-RW technologies offer inexpensive, durable storage and distribution media. Using these media, however, differs from using a hard disk. Storing data on a CD is slower than storing files on a hard disk because the CD drive actually melts or burns the surface of the CD. The process of "burning" a CD can take up to an hour.

Most CD-R and CD-RW drives ship with special **premastering software** that helps you to select what will go on the disk and how it will be allocated into files and folders within the directory structure. This software also helps you to create an **image file** for better performance when burning CDs. In this tutorial, you'll use a simulated CD-R drive and premastering software to create your own CD.

When you have completed the tutorial, you should be able to:
- Prepare your files.
- Use premastering software to create an image.
- Write the image to the CD.

Figure 12-10: Click the PlayIt! button to begin the tutorial and learn how to create your own CDs. Estimated time: 10–15 minutes. Tracking Disk points: 10.

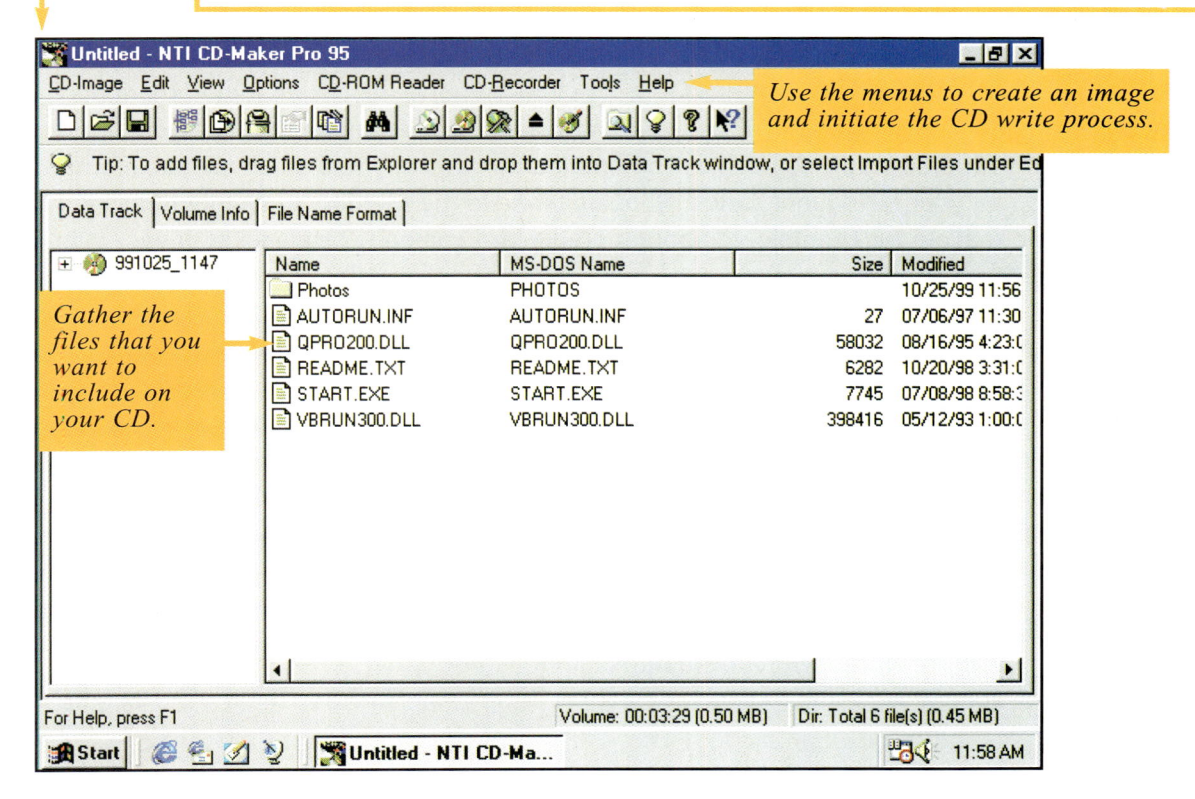

Gather the files that you want to include on your CD.

Use the menus to create an image and initiate the CD write process.

143

■ Issue

Who owns information about me?

There is an astounding amount of information stored about you in computer databases. Your bank has information on your financial status, credit history, and the people, organizations, and businesses to which you write checks. School records indicate something about your ability to learn and the subjects that interest you. Medical records indicate the state of your health. Credit card company records track the merchants with whom you deal and what you purchase in person, by mail, or over the Internet. Your phone company stores your phone number, your address, and a list of the phone numbers you dial. The driver's license bureau has your physical description. Your Internet cookies track many of the Web sites that you frequent. Using this data it would be possible to guess some very private things about you, such as your political views or even your sexual orientation.

When records were manually stored on index cards and in file folders, locating and distributing data was a laborious process that required hand transcriptions or photocopies of sheaves of papers. Today, this data appears in electronic format and is easy to access, copy, sell, ship, consolidate, and alter. Privacy advocates point out the potential for misusing data that has been collected and stored in computer databases. They are encouraging lawmakers to restrict the sale and distribution of information about individuals. One proposal would require your permission before information about you could be distributed.

The wisdom of such a proposal has been questioned, however, and not just by corporate interests. Information about you is not necessarily "yours." Although you might "reveal" information about yourself on an application form, other information about you is collected without your direct input. For example, suppose you default on your credit card payments. The credit card company has accumulated information on your delinquent status. Shouldn't it have the freedom to distribute this information, for example, to another credit card company? Balancing privacy with freedom of speech is a tricky issue for the Information Age.

What do you think?

1. Can you identify an actual incident when you discovered that data about you had been distributed without your approval?   ⦿ Yes ⦾ No ⦾ Not sure

2. Do you accurately fill out all the questionnaires that you encounter on the Web?   ⦾ Yes ⦾ No ⦾ Not sure

3. Do you think that you have a right to be consulted before anyone distributes information about you?   ⦾ Yes ⦾ No ⦾ Not sure

Save It!

Chapter 12: Accessing Databases   145

QuickCheck A

1. A(n) _____ database is able to link the records from two or more files and treat them as a single unit.

2. True or false? To access databases on the Web and CDs, you'll have to purchase database software. _____

3. To create your own databases, you must first design the file _____ by specifying the names for each data field.

4. You can record and change data on _____ disks, but you can read them only by using MultiRead CD-ROM drives.

5. CDs and DVDs are classified as _____ storage technology because data is stored as a series of pits and read with a beam of laser light.

Check It!

QuickCheck B

Carefully examine the entries in the database. Give each record indicated by an arrow an **A** if it meets the criteria described on page 137 for accurate and consistent data. Otherwise, give it an **F**.

1. ☐
2. ☐
3. ☐
4. ☐
5. ☐

Microsoft Access - [Equipment : Table]

Category	Company	Toll-Free Phone	Purchase Date
Computer	Dell	467-1255	9/1/98
Printer	Epson	377-0620	9/1/98
Softare	Microsoft	642-7050	9/1/98
Printer	Hewlett-Packard	439-5387	11/16/97
Computer	IBM	426-4260	3/27/98
Printer	I.B.M.	426-4260	8/12/96
Computer	IBM	426-4260	6/28/97
Computer	dell	467-1255	8/30/99
Software	Adobe	230-2320	6/2/99
Printers	Epson	377-0620	9/30/99
Computer	IBM	426-4260	7/12/91
Software	Microsoft	642-7050	6/30/95
Software	Netscape	675-2388	5/5/97

(Arrows point to records 1, 2, 3, 4, 5)

Check It!

Get It?

While using the Book-on-CD, click the Get It? button to see if you can answer ten randomly selected questions from Chapter 12.

Get It?

Chapter 13

Working with Graphics

What's Inside?

You live in a world filled with strong visual images—kaleidoscopic MTV videos, photo-rich magazines, and lavishly illustrated Web sites. It is more important than ever to learn how to incorporate graphical images in the documents, presentations, and Web sites that you create. Chapter 13 will get you started.

- FAQs:

What kinds of graphics can I work with on my PC?	147
When should I use bitmap graphics?	148
How do I prepare graphics for Web pages?	149
When should I use vector graphics?	150
How do I create 3-D graphics?	151

- Hardware: Digitizing devices	152
- Tutorial: How to edit a digital photo	155
- Issue: Shoes, UFOs, and Forrest Gump	156
- QuickChecks	157

What's on the CD?

Chapter 13 videos and screen tours show you how to become a PC artist.

- Browse through a gallery of computer graphics	147
- Tour the graphics software that's free with Windows	148
- Learn how to make graphics for your Web pages	149
- Check out vector graphics software	150
- Build a 3-D object	151
- Find out how to scan a photograph or newspaper clipping	153
- Learn how to use a digital camera	154
- Take a step-by-step tutorial on digital photo editing	155

Chapter 13: Working with Graphics 147

■FAQ What kinds of graphics can I work with on my PC?

The pictures that you can create, modify, store, download, and transmit using your PC are referred to as **graphics** or **images**. Graphics add visual interest to documents, worksheets, presentations, and Web pages.

Grab It!
Clip Art

If you have any "artistic genes" you'll probably enjoy creating artwork and illustrations using your PC. You don't, however, have to be an artist to spice up your projects with graphics. You can obtain ready-made images from a variety of sources. You'll find clip art collections containing thousands of professionally designed images on CDs and on the Web. You can use a scanning device to convert pictures from books and magazines into image files that you can manipulate on your PC. Even photos from your own collection can be converted into a computer-compatible format. You can also use a digital camera to take photos that don't require any conversion for use on your PC. When using images that you have not created, always make sure that you credit the source and adhere to any applicable copyright laws or licensing restrictions.

You'll typically work with two types of graphics on your PC: bitmap graphics and vector graphics. Understanding the difference between the two allows you to select the type of graphic that is best suited for a project. The rest of the FAQs in this chapter provide the basic information that you need to work with bitmap and vector graphics.

Play It!

Figure 13-1: A bitmap graphics image (upper left) has a distinctly different appearance than a vector graphics image (lower right). Click the PlayIt! button to view a gallery of bitmap and vector graphics.

148 Chapter 13: Working with Graphics

■FAQ When should I use bitmap graphics?

Bitmap graphics, sometimes called "raster graphics," represent an image as a grid of colored dots. Because bitmap graphics produce photograph-like images, you would use them for photos, the images you add to Web pages, and pictures that you convert from paper to computer format. Bitmap graphics can be stored in a variety of file formats, including BMP, TIFF, GIF, and JPEG, and are easily converted from one format to another. To create and manipulate bitmap graphics, you would typically use **paint software**, such as Adobe Photoshop, Micrografx Picture Publisher, and Microsoft Paint.

Grab It! Paint Software

The quality of an image depends on its resolution and color depth. The resolution of an image is expressed as the width and height of the grid that holds the dots. For example, an image with 1024 X 768 resolution is formed from a grid 1,024 dots wide and 768 dots high. High-resolution images exhibit details clearly. Each dot in an image is assigned a code number for its color. The number of bits required to store the color number is referred to as **color depth** and determines the number of colors that the image contains. A 1-bit color depth produces an image containing only two colors: black and white. An 8-bit color depth produces 256 colors. A 24-bit color depth produces 16.7 million colors, sometimes referred to as **true color**. The more colors an image contains, the more realistic it appears. However, an image with lots of colors requires lots of storage space. A true color image takes three times the amount of storage space as a 256-color image.

Play It!

Figure 13-2: *Windows includes a basic bitmap graphics software program called Paint that you can access from the Accessories menu. Click the PlayIt! button to find out how to use Paint to create and modify graphics.*

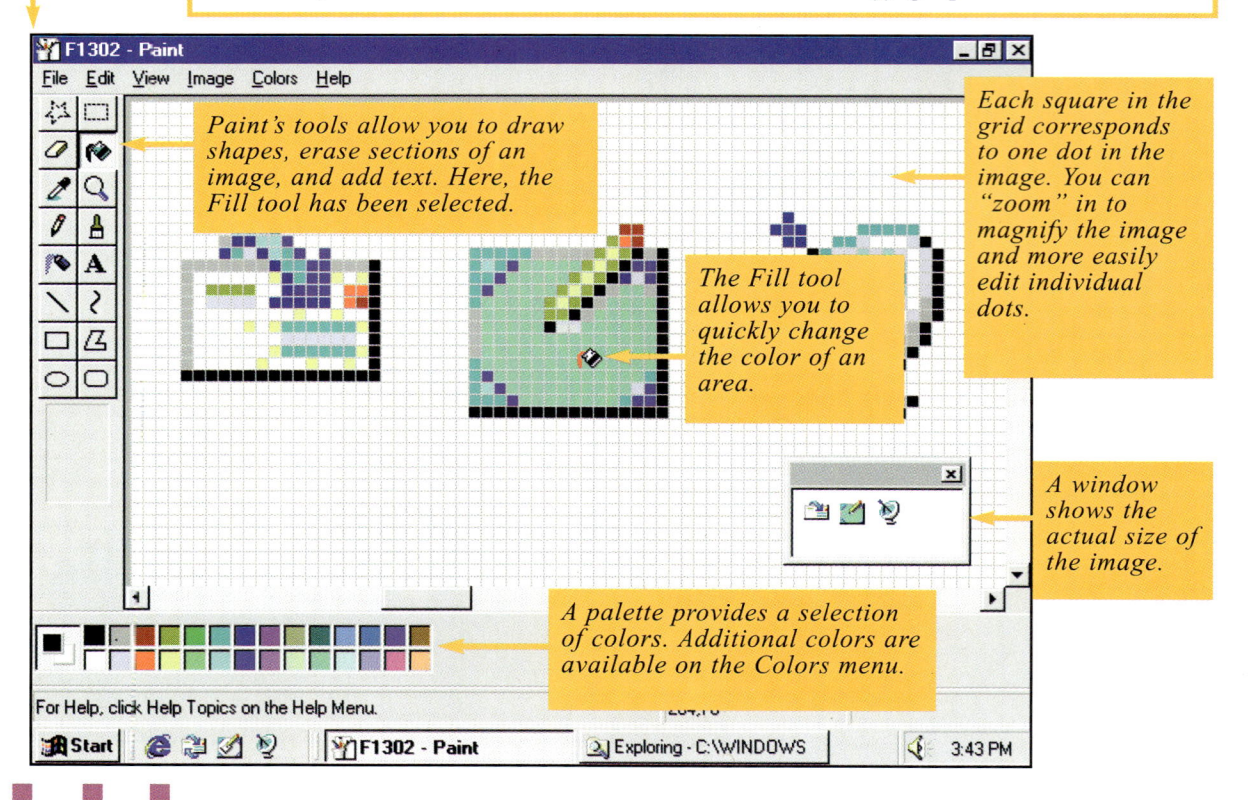

Paint's tools allow you to draw shapes, erase sections of an image, and add text. Here, the Fill tool has been selected.

The Fill tool allows you to quickly change the color of an area.

Each square in the grid corresponds to one dot in the image. You can "zoom" in to magnify the image and more easily edit individual dots.

A window shows the actual size of the image.

A palette provides a selection of colors. Additional colors are available on the Colors menu.

Chapter 13: Working with Graphics   149

▪FAQ   How do I prepare graphics for Web pages?

Your goal is to keep Web graphics small so that they can be rapidly transmitted over the Internet and appear on screen as quickly as possible. "Small" refers to the size of the image file in bytes. Ideally, Web graphics files should be smaller than 20 KB. You can decrease file size by shrinking the physical dimensions of an image, saving it in a compressed file format, or reducing its color depth.

Shrinking the physical dimensions of an image allows you to reduce its file size. A 2" X 2" image can be stored in a file that is one-fourth the size of the same image at 4" X 4". Most graphics software provides the capability to "resize" or "scale" an image. If you're concerned that shrinking an image might eliminate important detail, consider using a thumbnail. A **thumbnail** is a miniature representation of an image that would typically link to a larger version of the image when clicked.

You can also use compression techniques to decrease the image file size. Some file formats provide built-in compression that reduces file size simply by using a more effective storage technique. For example, when stored in BMP or TIFF format, the image in Figure 13-3 requires about 950 KB of storage space. Stored in GIF format, the same image requires only 251 KB of storage space. Using JPEG format, the file size can be reduced to a mere 13 KB. When creating graphics for the Web, you should store them in GIF or JPEG format. If you want to work with graphics that have been stored in other file formats, you can use your graphics software to convert them to GIF or JPEG format.

A true color graphic requires 24 bits for each dot of color in an image, whereas a 16-color graphic requires only 4 bits. Therefore, by reducing the color depth from true color to 16-color, the image file shrinks to one-sixth of its original size. Unfortunately, reducing an image to only 16 colors can have alarming effects, as shown in the right-hand panel of Figure 13-3. A process called **dithering** can create the illusion of more colors by using dot patterns. For example, a pattern of red, yellow, and gray dots can create the illusion of skin color. As a rule of thumb, when preparing graphics for the Web, avoid true color. If the quality of a 16-color dithered graphic is acceptable, use it. Otherwise, convert the image to 256 colors.

> Play It!
>
> **Figure 13-3:** The difference between a 256-color image (left), a dithered 16-color image (center), and a non-dithered 16-color image (right) can be remarkable. Click PlayIt! to learn more about preparing graphics for the Web.

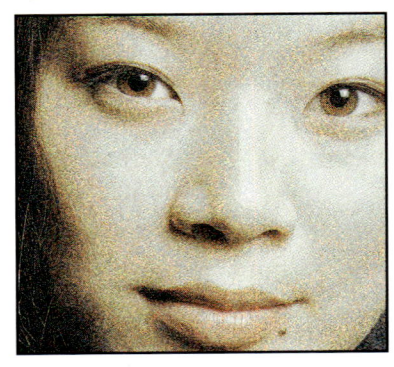

Chapter 13: Working with Graphics

■FAQ When should I use vector graphics?

Vector graphics consist of a set of points, lines, arcs, and other geometrical shapes. Each shape is defined as a series of line segments called **vectors** and attributes, such as line width and fill color. A list of these vectors and attributes becomes essentially a set of instructions for redrawing the image. Vector graphics are ideal for diagrams, line drawings, and **computer-aided design** (CAD), the process of creating technical drawings and blueprints on a PC.

Vector graphics tend not to look like bitmap images. Two-dimensional vector graphics typically have large flat areas of color and more closely resemble line drawings than photographs. Vector graphics have three advantages. First, their files tend to be small because the vectors and attributes describing a shape can be stored very efficiently. Second, vector graphics can shrink or expand with no loss of quality. Third, the shapes in a vector graphic exist as individual objects that you can modify independently without affecting other parts of the image. You'll find many vector graphics files stored in Encapsulated PostScript (EPS) format and Windows Metafile (WMF) format. Popular CAD formats include DXF and DS4.

Grab It!
Drawing Software

Drawing software provides you with tools to create and manipulate vector graphics. Popular packages include Adobe Illustrator, CorelDRAW, and Micrografx Designer. **CAD software** includes Autodesk AutoCAD, IMSI TurboCAD, and Diehl Graphsoft MiniCAD.

Play It!

Figure 13-4: Vector graphics are designed to work with layers of shapes. For example, each circle for the sun in this image is defined by its shape, position, color, and layer. Click PlayIt! to discover how to work with vector graphics.

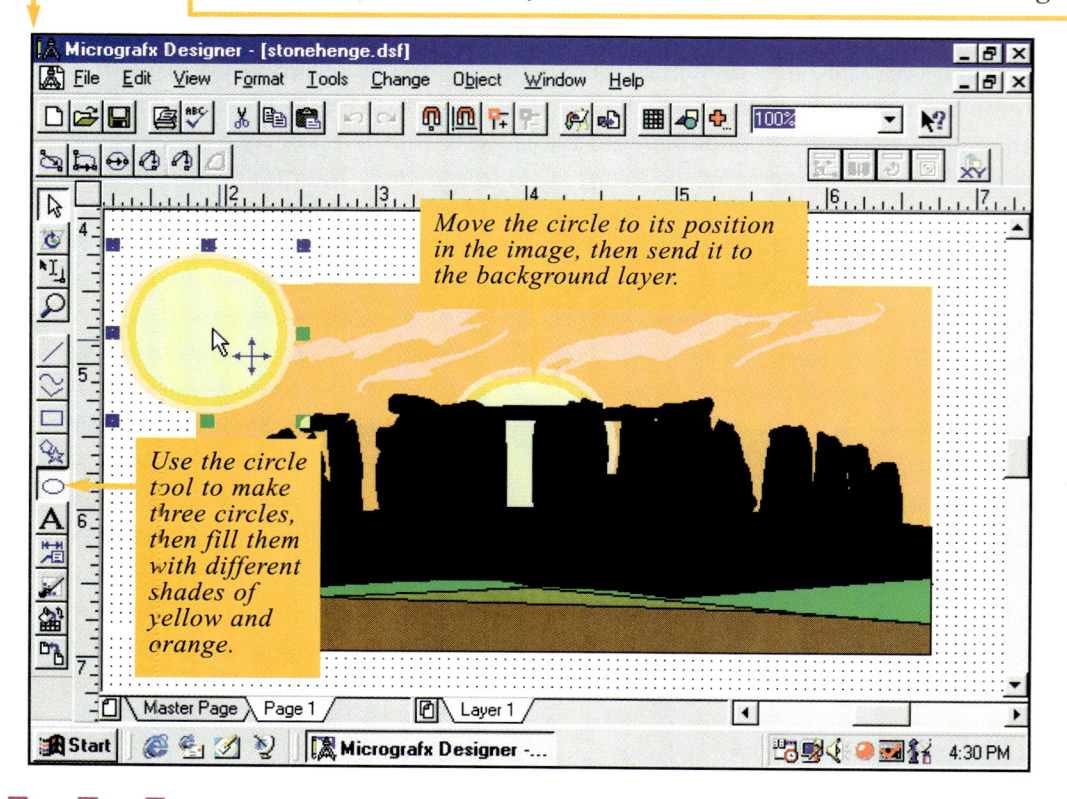

Move the circle to its position in the image, then send it to the background layer.

Use the circle tool to make three circles, then fill them with different shades of yellow and orange.

Chapter 13: Working with Graphics 151

■FAQ How do I create 3-D graphics?

The **3-D graphics** you create on your PC contain one or more objects that appear three-dimensional. A **3-D object** not only looks three-dimensional, but also includes the data necessary to display and view it from any angle, viewpoint, or perspective. Composed of vectors, 3-D objects are typically created using the same drawing and CAD software as two-dimensional vector graphics.

To create a 3-D object, you first produce a line drawing called a **wireframe** by outlining every surface on the front, back, and inside of the object. Once the wireframe is complete, you can define the texture, transparency, and color for each of its surfaces. The process of applying surfaces to a wireframe, called **rendering**, is similar to draping a nylon tent covering over its frame. As part of the rendering process, you can specify a light source and your PC will automatically determine where to put highlights and shadows. This part of the rendering process is called **ray tracing** because your PC essentially traces the rays of light from the light source to the object.

Rendering is a complex activity that requires your PC to carry out extensive calculations. It can take minutes or hours, depending on the complexity of the objects, the speed of your PC, and the resolution of the completed image. Rendered 3-D graphics have a new-car-brochure look that's sometimes referred to as "super-realistic." Objects within the image are perfectly shaped and highly defined. Surfaces appear unflawed and brilliantly highlighted.

Figure 13-5: Click the PlayIt! button to learn how to construct a wireframe, render a 3-D object, and apply ray tracing.

The rendering process creates textured surfaces—for this object, a smooth and highly reflective metal.

A 3-D wireframe is the foundation for the object.

The light source is located at the lower-right corner of the screen. Ray tracing creates highlights where the light rays contact the surface.

■Hardware
Digitizing devices

Before you can work with images on your PC, they must exist in digital format. **Digitizing** is the process of converting an image into a series of 1s and 0s that your PC can store, transmit, and display. **Digitizing devices**, such as graphics tablets, scanners, and digital cameras, allow you to convert real objects, such as sketches and photos, into digital format. These fun-to-use devices can help you produce impressive results, even if you're not a professional artist.

A **graphics tablet** works like an electronic canvas. You use a pen-shaped **stylus** to "paint," and the movement of the stylus is picked up by the electronics in the pad, converted into a bitmap format, and displayed on the screen. The pad is sensitive not only to where you move, but also to the degree of pressure that you apply. When you press hard, you draw a thick, dark line. Lighter pressure produces a thinner, lighter line.

Some graphics software does not fully support the use of a graphics tablet. For example, although you can use the stylus to select tools and draw shapes in Microsoft Paint, this software does not recognize different pressures. If you are serious about using a graphics tablet, you will want to choose graphics software that specifically supports its features—select bitmap painting software rather than vector drawing software, and read the box to make sure it works with a graphics tablet or pressure-sensitive pen. Adobe Photoshop, Kai Art Dabbler, Jasc Paint Shop Pro, and Micrografx Picture Publisher are good companion software packages for graphics tablets.

A graphics tablet typically connects to the serial port of your PC and requires the installation of special device driver software to establish communications with Windows. The price of a basic graphics tablet and stylus starts at U.S.$99. Prices go up from there and can exceed U.S.$600, depending on the size of the pad and the pen accessories that you select. Currently, the best sellers include CalComp's Creation Station and Wacom's Intuos Graphics Tablet System.

Figure 13-6: A graphics tablet is a fun addition to your PC for doodling, and an essential tool for serious artists. You can use the stylus to "paint" pictures. It also substitutes for a mouse to control the menus and tools of your graphics software.

■Hardware
continued

A **scanner** is a digitizing device that "reads" text, images, and bar codes. It is typically used to digitize flat objects, such as photos, newspaper clippings, and documents. These digitized images can be stored on your PC, modified, e-mailed to friends, or posted on the Web.

Among the many types of scanners, **flatbed scanners** that resemble small photocopiers are the most popular with PC owners. To use one, place the item you want to digitize face down on the scanner glass. Next, fire up your scanning software and select the resolution for the scan. Remember that higher resolutions produce sharper images, but can require a tremendous amount of storage space on your PC. For Web graphics, a scan at 300 dpi is usually sufficient. For images that you plan to print, you should set the scan resolution to match that of your printer—either 300 or 600 dpi. Once the actual scan begins, the digitizing process typically takes several minutes to complete. If you're satisfied with the results displayed on your PC's screen, you can save the image as a file, which you can then manipulate with any paint software.

Scanners are surprisingly inexpensive. You can purchase a serviceable basic unit for about U.S.$100. A scanner connects to one of your PC's built-in ports or includes a circuit board that you must install in your PC's system unit. Before you purchase a scanner, read the package to make sure the type of connector it provides will work with your PC.

Scanners are typically bundled with several types of software. The scanner's device driver software, which establishes communication between the scanner and Windows, must be installed when you connect the scanner. **Scanning software** allows you to preview a scan, select a resolution, and initiate the scan from your PC. **OCR (optical character recognition) software** allows you to convert a scanned image, such as a newspaper clipping, into a text file that you can edit with a word processor. The accuracy of today's OCR software is fairly high, but not perfect. Therefore, it is a good idea to use a spelling checker and proofread documents produced by OCR software.

Figure 13-7: When preparing to scan an image, use your software's preview feature to ensure that your photo or document is squarely aligned on the scanner. Specify the part of the image that you want to scan, then select a resolution that produces a sharp image, but a manageable file size.

Chapter 13: Working with Graphics

■Hardware
continued

A **digital camera** takes photos and stores them as bitmap images, instead of on film. When paired with a color ink jet printer and your PC, a digital camera puts you in control of the entire picture taking process—from snapping the picture to printing the final image or posting it on the Web. A digital camera resembles its film-based counterparts, and taking pictures is just as easy. Basically, you point and shoot.

After finishing your photo shoot, you must transfer the photos to your PC. If your camera stores images on a PCMCIA-compatible memory card, you'll remove the card from your camera and insert it into the PCMCIA slot of your PC. If your camera stores images on a floppy disk, remove the disk and insert it into your PC's floppy disk drive. Some cameras store images in special "flash memory," which—contrary to what you might expect—has nothing to do with "flash bulbs." **Flash memory** is a type of memory chip that holds data without a constant supply of power. If your camera stores images in flash memory, you'll need to transfer data over a cable to a port at the back of your PC's system unit. After connecting the cable, use the software supplied with your camera to transfer the images to your PC's hard disk. The process of transferring images from your camera to your PC can take several minutes, depending on the number of photos you've taken. As the images are transferred, they're stored as files on your PC. You can open these image files using most paint or photo editing software.

Manufacturers of digital cameras include familiar names, such as Canon, Fuji Film, Nikon, Olympus, Eastman Kodak, and Minolta. Prices depend on the camera's resolution. Basic digital cameras, priced under U.S.$500, feature resolutions between 640 X 480 and 1280 X 1024. These cameras are suitable for capturing images for use on the Web and for printouts no larger than 3" X 5". Mid-range digital cameras, priced at U.S.$500 to U.S.$1,000, provide resolutions in the neighborhood of 1600 X 1200 and are the preferred choice of dedicated amateur photographers. High-end digital cameras with resolutions that surpass 3000 X 3000 and prices that exceed U.S.$10,000 provide adequate quality for professional portraiture and photo essays.

Figure 13-8: Click the PlayIt! button to learn how to produce your own digital photos. This video takes you through the entire process. You'll find out how to take the photo, transfer it from your camera to your PC, save it, and print it.

Digital camera.

Flash memory.

Chapter 13: Working with Graphics

■Tutorial
How to edit a digital photo

Grab It!
Photo Editing Software

Photo editing software is a specialized type of paint software that provides a set of tools for manipulating and retouching digital photographs. It can rescue pictures that are washed out, too dark, too bright, and out of focus. It even eliminates those poltergeist-like red eyes caused by your camera's flash mechanism.

You can use photo editing software to have some fun with your photographs. For example, you can turn current photos into old-fashioned tin-types. Or you can go for a "Pleasantville look" by hand-coloring parts of black-and-white photos. You can delete unwanted objects from a photo or create an entirely new reality by superimposing objects on backgrounds—like pasting your dog on a lunar landscape. For this tutorial you'll use Microsoft PhotoDraw to learn about photo editing.

When you have completed the tutorial, you should be able to:
- ■ Erase "red eye," adjust lighting, and sharpen a photo image.
- ■ Add or remove objects from a photo.
- ■ Change the size and orientation of a photo.
- ■ Apply special effects to change the appearance of a photo.

Play It!

Figure 13-9: Can this photo be rescued? Click the PlayIt! button to begin the tutorial and learn how to use photo editing software. Estimated time: 10–15 minutes. Tracking Disk points: 10.

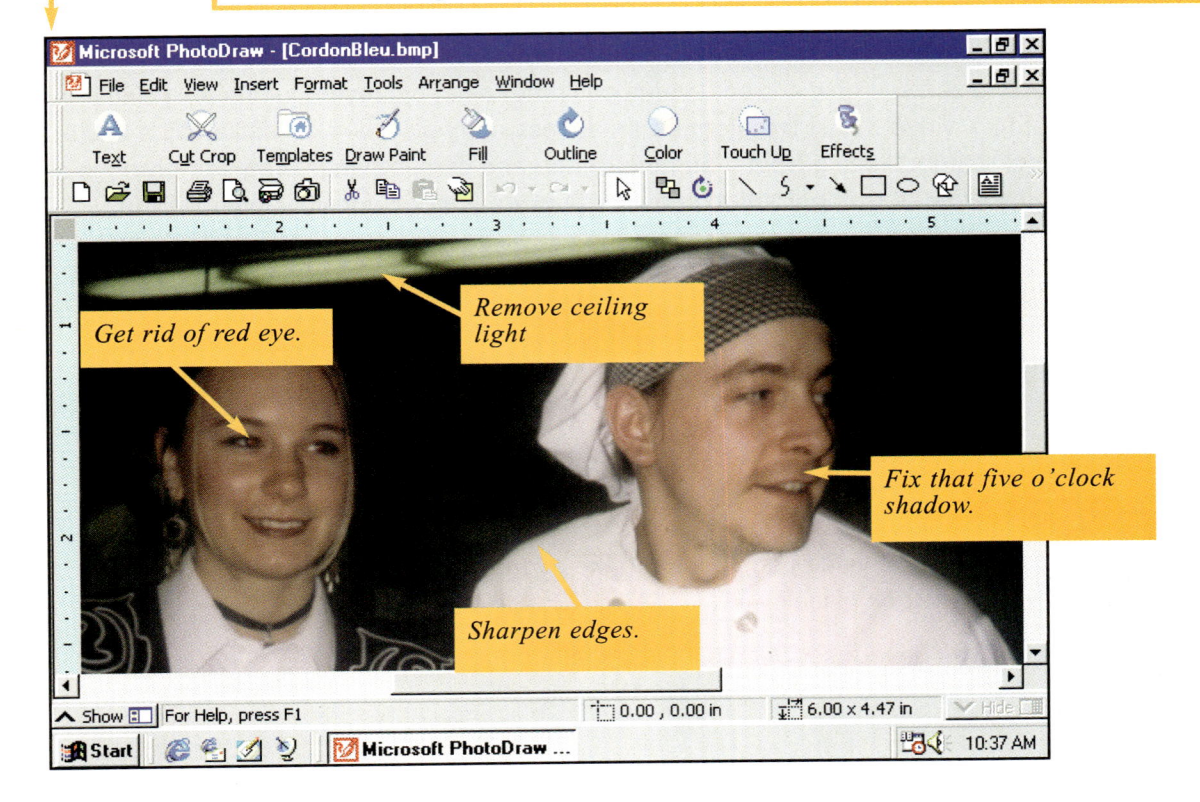

■Issue

Shoes, UFOs, and Forrest Gump

The highly publicized O. J. Simpson murder trial was followed by an equally high-profile wrongful-death suit. Introduced into evidence were a bloody footprint from the crime scene made by a size 12 designer shoe, and a photo of Mr. Simpson wearing such a shoe. Conclusive evidence of guilt? Not according to the defense attorney, who raised doubts about the photo's authenticity.

Faked photos are not a product of the digital age. Long before the first digital cameras, tabloid newspapers in supermarket checkout lanes carried blurry photos allegedly depicting UFOs, the Loch Ness monster, and so on. In those days, most people had confidence that experts could detect photos doctored by amateurs or even by professionals—the deception discovered by a missing shadow, an obvious trace of cut and paste, or inconsistencies in coloration. In today's digital world, however, it is possible to alter the individual dots in a photo. When done carefully, these alterations can be difficult or even impossible to detect. Sure, it can be innocent fun, like when you digitally paste your roommate's head onto a picture of the Three Stooges. Unfortunately, it also introduces a note of uncertainty into the evidence we rely on to form opinions of everyday events and life-and-death situations, such as a murder trial or war crimes investigation.

Even videotapes, once virtually impossible to alter, can today be digitized and doctored. In the film *Forrest Gump*, digital editing techniques were used to paste the star, Tom Hanks, into authentic newsreels of past events—Forrest Gump meets with President Kennedy and history appears to be changed. The film *Wag the Dog* showed how current events could be faked by unscrupulous politicians. In that film, video magic transformed an actress carrying a bag of tortilla chips into a pitiful refugee fleeing from a burning village and carrying an injured cat. Living in a digital world, it is important to consider how you can responsibly evaluate the images that you see in newspapers, on television, and at the movies.

What do you think?

1. In your opinion, should photos and videotapes be allowed as evidence in civil and criminal trials?   ◯ Yes ◯ No ◯ Not sure

2. Do you think that it would be possible for someone to use doctored photos and videotapes to convince people that a fake event actually took place?   ◯ Yes ◯ No ◯ Not sure

3. Do you have a set of criteria for judging the authenticity of newspaper and TV images?   ◯ Yes ◯ No ◯ Not sure

Save It!

Chapter 13: Working with Graphics

QuickCheck A

1. An image with 8-bit _____ can contain up to 256 colors.

2. True or false? To prepare an image for Web use, you should store it in true color BMP format. _____

3. _____ graphics are stored as a set of instructions for recreating the shapes and attributes of an image.

4. To create 3-D graphics, you can use drawing software or _____ software.

5. The part of the rendering process that creates highlights and shadows for a 3-D object is called _____. (Tip: The answer contains two words.)

Check It!

QuickCheck B

There is only one way to correctly match the five objects pictured at right to the five descriptions below. Indicate the correct letter for each description.

1. A wireframe _____
2. A vector graphic _____
3. A bitmap graphic _____
4. A dithered image _____
5. A rendered image _____

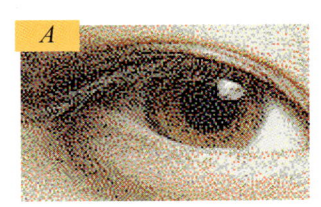

Check It!

Get It?

While using the Book-on-CD, click the Get It? button to see if you can answer ten randomly selected questions from Chapter 13.

Chapter 14

Recording and Editing Sound

What's Inside?

Sounds, such as music and speech, are important features of your environment, so it seems natural for PCs to use sound to provide feedback, entertainment, and education. In Chapter 14 you'll learn how your PC generates sound and how to incorporate sound in your own projects.

- FAQs:

How does sound capability enhance my PC?	159
How does my PC record, store, and play digital sound?	160
How does speech synthesis work?	161
What should I know about MIDI?	162
How do I add sound clips to presentations and Web pages?	163

- Hardware: Sound devices — 164
- Tutorial: How to work with digitized sound — 167
- Issue: RIAA vs. Rio — 168
- QuickChecks — 169

What's on the CD?

Because sound is the topic of Chapter 14, you'll get the most benefit from these screen tours and videos if your PC is equipped with a sound card and speakers (or headphones).

- Take a journey through a PC soundscape — 159
- Compare the quality of different digital sampling rates — 160
- Visit a Web site for a demonstration of speech synthesis — 161
- Find out how to compose MIDI music — 162
- Learn how to add sound to your Web pages — 163
- Take a tutorial on recording and editing digital sound — 167

Chapter 14: Recording and Editing Sound

■FAQ How does sound capability enhance my PC?

Your computer generates sound using a hardware device called a **sound card**, which then routes the sound to headphones or speakers. Sound cards are standard equipment on most of today's PCs. Sound adds a new dimension to your computing experience. Beeps and other sound effects can provide you with feedback as you use your PC. For example, when you click a button that isn't available, a beep might inform you that the action cannot be performed. Music lovers can connect to their favorite music store on the Web and listen to sample tracks. Sound effects can enliven once-dull business presentations. Children can listen while their PCs read stories. Computer game enthusiasts can hear a riot of sound effects as monsters attack, grenades explode, and tanks rumble past. Individuals with visual disabilities can also gain access to computers through technology that reads aloud the content of a PC screen.

Computers work with two general categories of sound: digitized sound and synthesized sound. **Digitized sound** is a recording of real music, vocals, sound effects, or speech that has been converted into electronic signals, which a computer can then store, manipulate, and transmit. **Synthesized sound** has not been recorded from a live source, but instead has been generated by a machine such as a computer. Each category of sound has its unique characteristics and applications. With a little background information on digitized and synthesized sound, you can select the one that is most suitable for your projects.

> [Play It!] *Figure 14-1:* Click the PlayIt! button to take a journey through a PC soundscape. Note: To get the most out of this tour, your computer should be equipped with a sound card and speakers (or headphones).

Chapter 14: Recording and Editing Sound

■FAQ How does my PC record, store, and play digital sound?

To digitally capture sound, you need a microphone, a sound card, and sound software. After you start the software, simply point the microphone at the sound source, and click the software's record button. You can save your digital recording in sound formats such as WAVE (.wav), AUDIO (.au), RealAudio (.ra), VOICE (.voc), and MP3 (.mp3).

You probably know that a sound consists of energy waves, which your ears and brain convert into the voices, music, and assorted sound effects that you hear. A sound wave provides information about a sound. The height of a wave indicates volume, technically called sound **amplitude**. The time between wave peaks indicates the sound's **frequency**—that is, whether it is a high note or a low note.

To digitally store a sound wave, your PC periodically records a **sample** of the wave and stores code numbers for its amplitude. The sequence of samples is then stored as a sound file. The more times your PC samples the wave per second, the more accurately it can reproduce that wave. Sampling rates are measured in KHz (kilohertz), where 1 KHz is 1,000 samples per second. An 11 KHz sampling rate produces fairly realistic digitized human speech. Music, however, requires sampling rates of 22 KHz or 44 KHz for good fidelity. Each sample uses two bytes of storage space, so noncompressed digital sound files are BIG! One second of digitally recorded music requires more than 88 KB of storage space.

Figure 14-2: At higher sampling rates, digital sound samples (shown in green) more closely follow the shape of the sound wave (shown in purple). Click the PlayIt! buttons to compare the sound quality at each sampling rate.

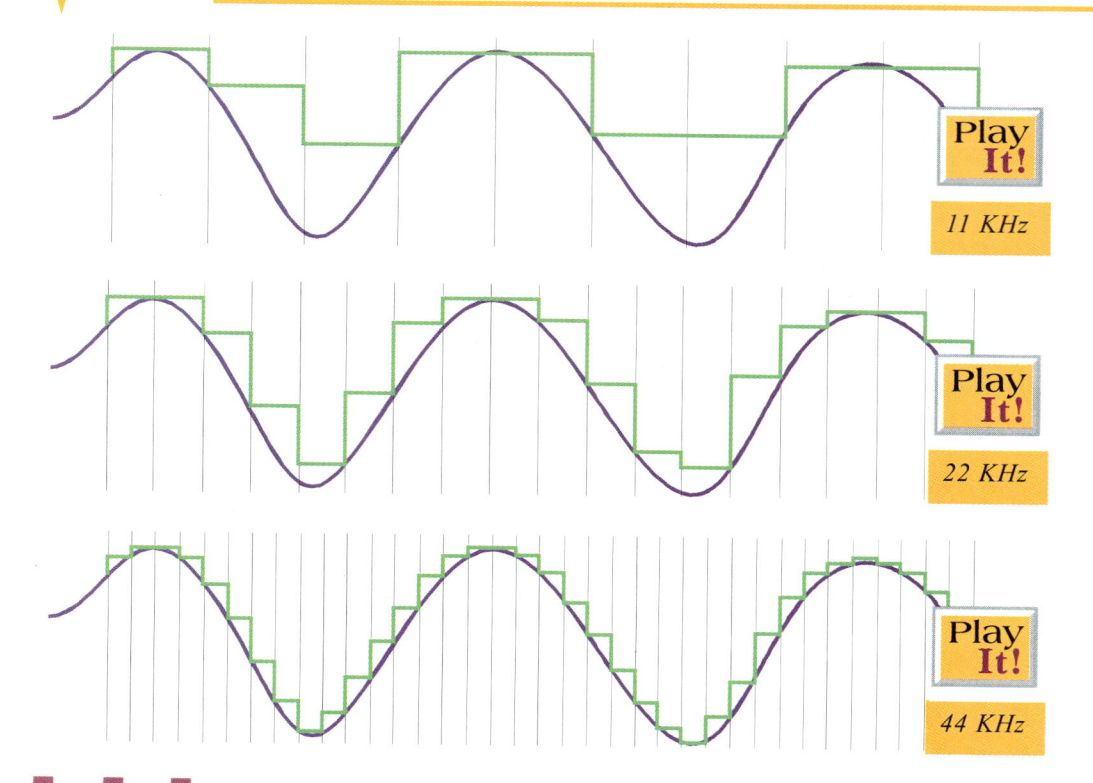

11 KHz

22 KHz

44 KHz

Chapter 14: Recording and Editing Sound 161

■FAQ How does speech synthesis work?

Speech synthesis is the process by which machines, such as computers, produce sound that resembles spoken words. Most speech synthesizers string together basic sound units called **phonemes**. For example, the phonemes "reh" and "gay" would produce the word "reggae."

A speech synthesis system typically includes text-to-speech software and synthesizing hardware. **Text-to-speech software** examines the text stored in a file, displayed on the screen, or entered from the keyboard, then breaks it down into a series of sounds that can be output. **Synthesizing hardware** consists of a sound card or other device that can generate speech or musical sounds.

Unlike digitized speech, synthesized speech can theoretically produce any words or phrases—not just those that you have recorded. Though not a mainstream PC technology, synthesized speech is ideal for applications that require a computer to generate spoken responses to typed or voice input. It provides the underlying technology for voice-response systems, such as telephone directory assistance. It may be instrumental in integrating voice and e-mail, so that you can phone your voice mail system and hear not only your voice mail messages, but also your computer e-mail. Perhaps most important, a speech synthesizer's ability to read a computer screen aloud is the key that unlocks access to PCs and to the Internet for individuals with visual disabilities.

Grab It!
Screen Readers

Play It!

Figure 14-3: Using speech synthesis software, your PC can generate speech using a standard sound card. Click PlayIt! to tour a Web site that demonstrates the quality of synthesized speech.

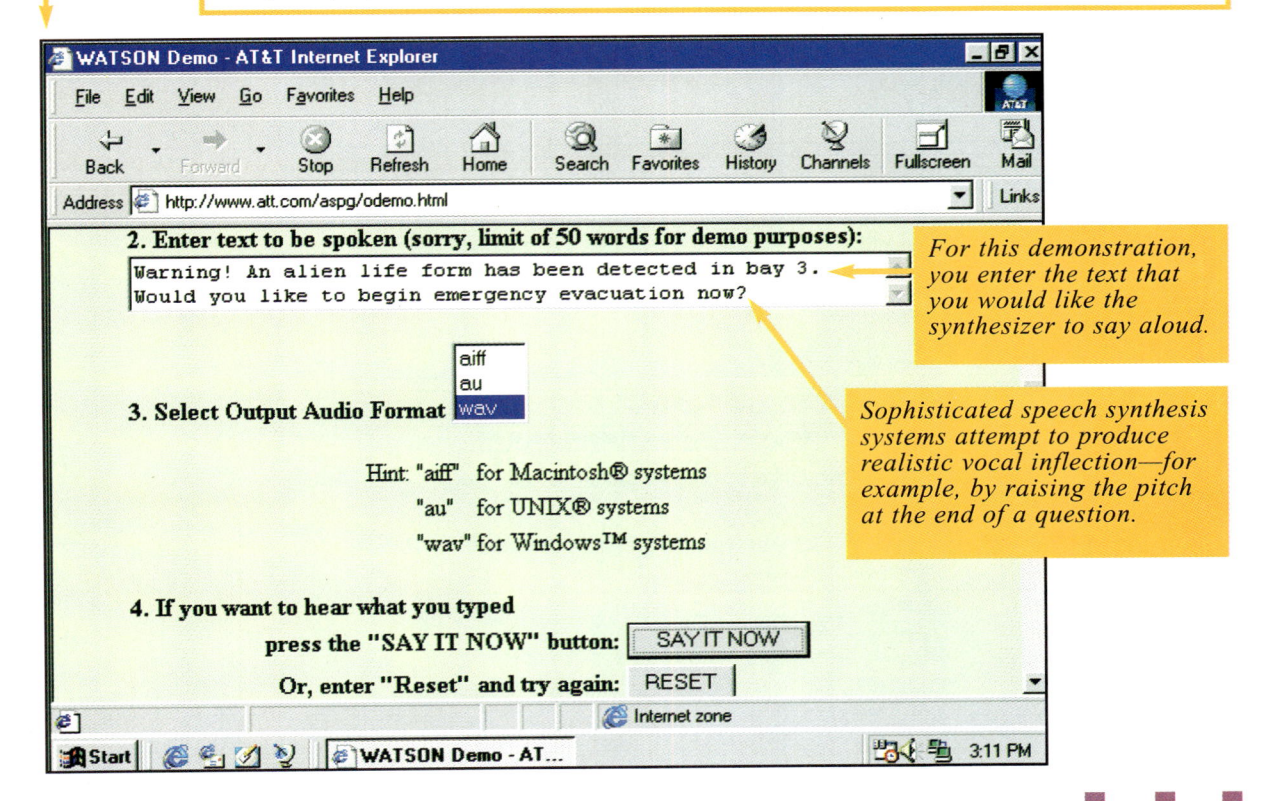

For this demonstration, you enter the text that you would like the synthesizer to say aloud.

Sophisticated speech synthesis systems attempt to produce realistic vocal inflection—for example, by raising the pitch at the end of a question.

162 Chapter 14: Recording and Editing Sound

■FAQ What should I know about MIDI?

MIDI (musical instrument digital interface) specifies a standard way to store music data for synthesizers, electronic MIDI instruments, and computers. Unlike digital sound files, which contain digitized recordings of real sounds, MIDI files contain a set of instructions, called **MIDI messages**, for synthesizing music based on the pitch, volume, and duration of each note made by each instrument. Digital sound is analogous to a tape recording, whereas MIDI music is like a player piano roll that produces notes based on the position of punched holes. MIDI is suitable for instrumental music, but not for vocals because of the complexity of synthesizing the human voice singing lyrics. Its advantage lies in its ability to store lengthy musical sequences in a small file. Three minutes of MIDI music might require only 10 KB of disk space, compared to 1,500 KB for three minutes of digitized music.

Most sound cards allow you to capture music from a MIDI instrument, as well as generate music from MIDI files. However, making MIDI music is not as simple as pointing a microphone at a musician. To create MIDI music, you must assume the role of composer. Special MIDI software helps you enter the notes for your composition on a musical staff or capture the musical themes you play on any MIDI instrument. You can then edit your composition by assigning the notes to different instruments, adding harmony, and inserting a percussion track. Basic MIDI software is often bundled with your sound card. Professional musicians typically prefer to use full-featured MIDI software, such as Cakewalk Pro Audio or Coda Finale.

Figure 14-4: To find out what it's like to compose MIDI music, click the PlayIt! button. Note: To get the most out of this tour, your computer should be equipped with a sound card and speakers (or headphones).

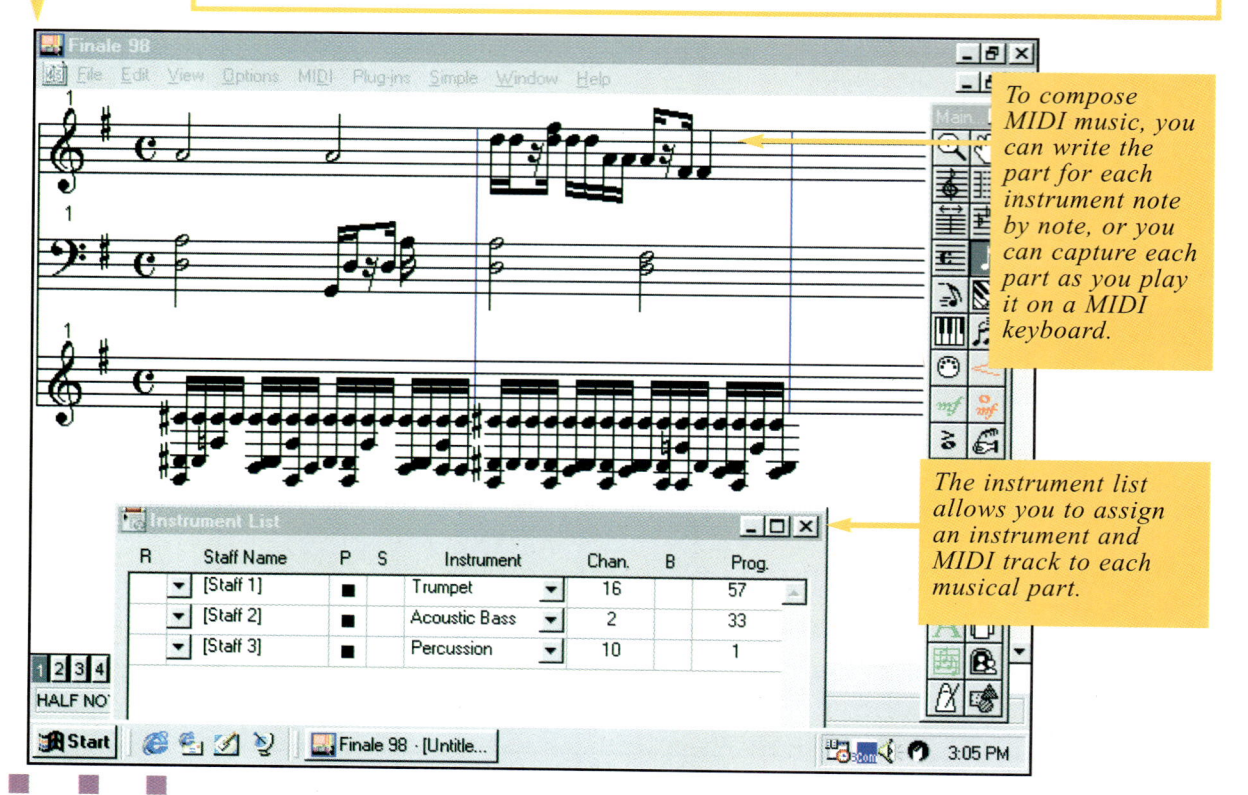

To compose MIDI music, you can write the part for each instrument note by note, or you can capture each part as you play it on a MIDI keyboard.

The instrument list allows you to assign an instrument and MIDI track to each musical part.

Chapter 14: Recording and Editing Sound

■FAQ How do I add sound clips to presentations and Web pages?

Before you can use a sound clip, it must exist as a digitized sound file or as a MIDI file. You can, of course, create your own compositions by recording voices, music, and sound effects or by composing MIDI music. You can also find collections of sound files on the Web and CDs. Before using a sound file that you have not composed yourself, make sure that you have permission to use it. Most sound clip collections clearly specify your rights for using the sound clips they contain. When in doubt, request permission via e-mail or written letter.

To incorporate sound in presentations, check your presentation software documentation for a list of acceptable file formats. Unlike graphics, which are easily converted from one file format to another, it can be difficult to convert sound files. For example, MIDI files don't easily convert to WAVE files. You should capture or create sound files in a format that works with your presentation software.

For the Web, WAVE and MIDI are standard file formats. Remember that the people who receive your Web pages must have software on their PCs to play your sound files. You can typically expect them to have basic WAVE and MIDI capability. If you use other file formats, their Web browsers might need a special software module called a **plug-in** to play your sound files. They can typically obtain the necessary plug-in from the Web site hosted by the publisher that created the file format. For example, the RA plug-in can be obtained at the RealAudio site.

Figure 14-5: Click the PlayIt! button to learn how to play sound from Web pages and add sound to your own Web pages.

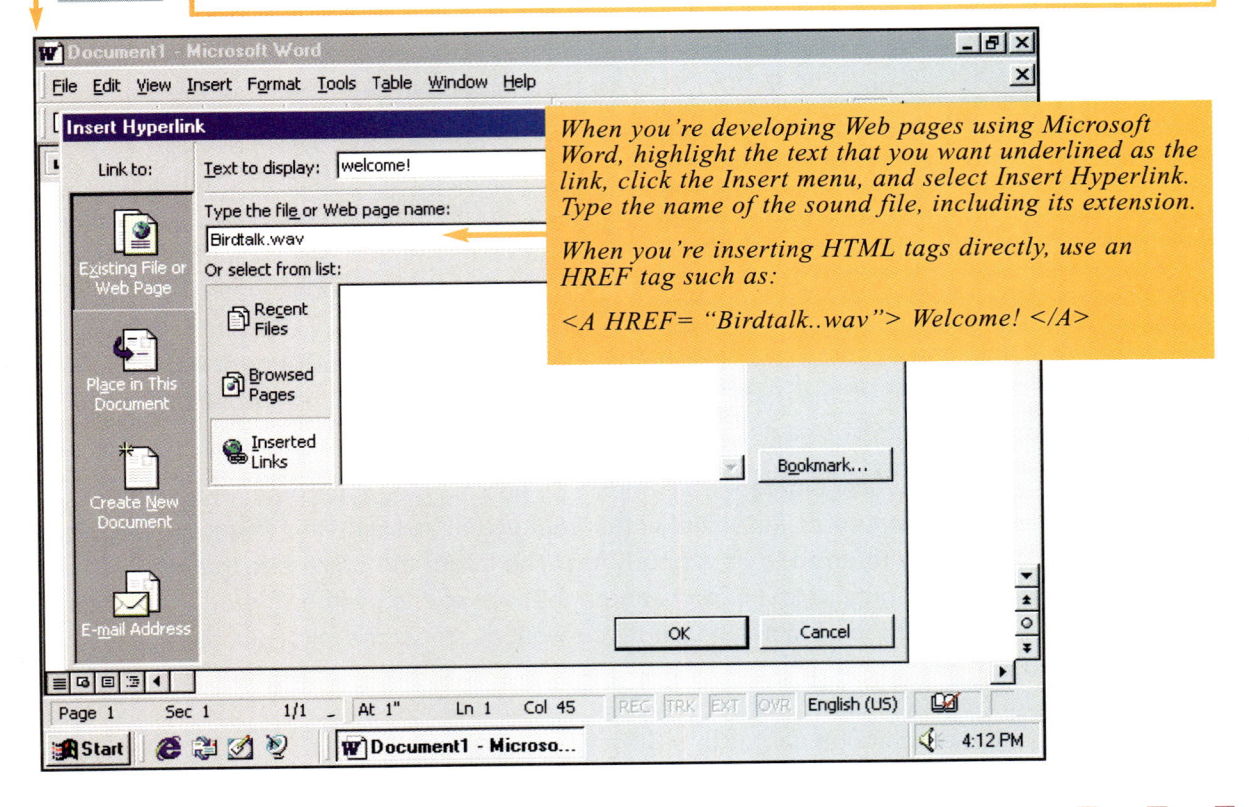

When you're developing Web pages using Microsoft Word, highlight the text that you want underlined as the link, click the Insert menu, and select Insert Hyperlink. Type the name of the sound file, including its extension.

When you're inserting HTML tags directly, use an HREF tag such as:

<A HREF= "Birdtalk..wav"> Welcome! </A>

Hardware
Sound devices

Most PCs today include a basic **sound system** with a sound card, speakers, and possibly a microphone. If you're not satisfied with the quality of sound produced by your PC, consider replacing one or more components of your sound system.

A sound card is a circuit board that typically plugs into an expansion slot on the motherboard of your PC. It provides connectors for a microphone and speakers (or headphones) so that you can record and play back sound. It also provides a joystick port that doubles as a port for MIDI instruments. Most sound cards support both digitized sound and MIDI music. Manufacturers of popular sound cards include Creative Labs, Diamond Multimedia Systems, and Turtle Beach Systems. Prices range from U.S.$40 to U.S.$200, depending on features.

Because a sound card generates the sound that your PC's speakers output, its performance affects the quality of the sound you hear. For playing games, using most business software, and browsing the Web, just about any basic sound card will produce adequate fidelity. However, if you're really serious about sound or you intend to record sound for professional use, a basic card might not meet your needs. You can shop around and find comparative reviews of sound cards in computer magazines or on the Web.

To produce digitized sound, your sound card simply reproduces the digital samples stored in the sound file. The quality of digitized sound that a sound card can generate is affected by several factors. Most basic, perhaps, is its **frequency response**—the range of frequencies or notes that it can reproduce. A frequency response range of 20 to 20,000 Hz is common and includes most of the sounds audible to the human ear.

To produce MIDI music, your sound card receives messages from a MIDI file, listing notes and the type of musical instrument that plays each note. To translate these MIDI messages into music, sound cards use one of two techniques: FM synthesis or wavetable synthesis. **FM synthesis** creates sound waves, essentially from scratch, that imitate as closely as possible the sound of different musical instruments. According to a recent article on the popular MIDI Farm Web site, "FM is Dead!" Indeed, most sound card manufacturers seem to have abandoned FM synthesis in favor of a newer, more realistic-sounding technology.

Wavetable synthesis generates music by patching together a set of sounds that were pre-recorded as individual notes from actual instruments. This set of sounds is sometimes referred to as a **patch set**. The larger the patch set, the more realistic the sound. Most experts agree that wavetable synthesis produces better-quality sound than FM synthesis. If you want the most realistic-sounding MIDI music, look for a sound card that features wavetable synthesis with many "voices" in its wavetable. For example, a 256-voice wavetable produces better-quality MIDI sound than a sound card with a 64-voice wavetable.

Hardware
continued

A sound card outputs sound to speakers or headphones. The speaker-headphone port is built into the edge of the sound card that peeks out of an opening at the back of your PC's system unit. Usually, this port is labeled "line out" or "speakers." If the ports on your sound card are not labeled, refer to the documentation to find out which one to use. Note also that your PC's CD-ROM drive might contain a headphone port designed for listening to audio CDs. On most PCs, however, the CD headphone port will not produce sounds from computer CDs. To hear the sound from CD encyclopedias, for example, you must typically use the speaker-headphone port at the back of the PC system unit.

You're probably familiar with the Bose ads in which a guy listening to speakers is literally being blown away by the sound. Reality seems to be approaching this audio nirvana as speaker and sound card manufacturers introduce new technologies such as surround sound, 3-D sound, and environmental sound. You can check your favorite computer magazine or audio Web site for information on the newest speaker technology.

Although speakers can't improve the quality of sound that your sound card generates, cheap speakers can degrade it. As a rule of thumb, you should purchase a speaker system to match the quality of your sound card. If you're using a basic U.S.$40 sound card, basic U.S.$20 speakers should suffice. With a U.S.$100 mid-range sound card, use speakers that cost about the same. If you have a high-end U.S.$200 sound card, you're probably serious about your sound system and you should look for speakers in the same price range.

Most speaker systems include two speaker units for stereo sound. Many mid-range and high-end systems also include a third unit called a subwoofer that produces enhanced bass sound. Speaker manufacturers include familiar names in the audio business: Altec Lansing, Bose, Philips, and Roland.

Figure 14-6: A sound card is the basic building block of your PC's sound system. It plugs into the system unit of your PC and contains a "mic" port, a "line out" port for speakers or headphones, and a joystick port that doubles as a MIDI port.

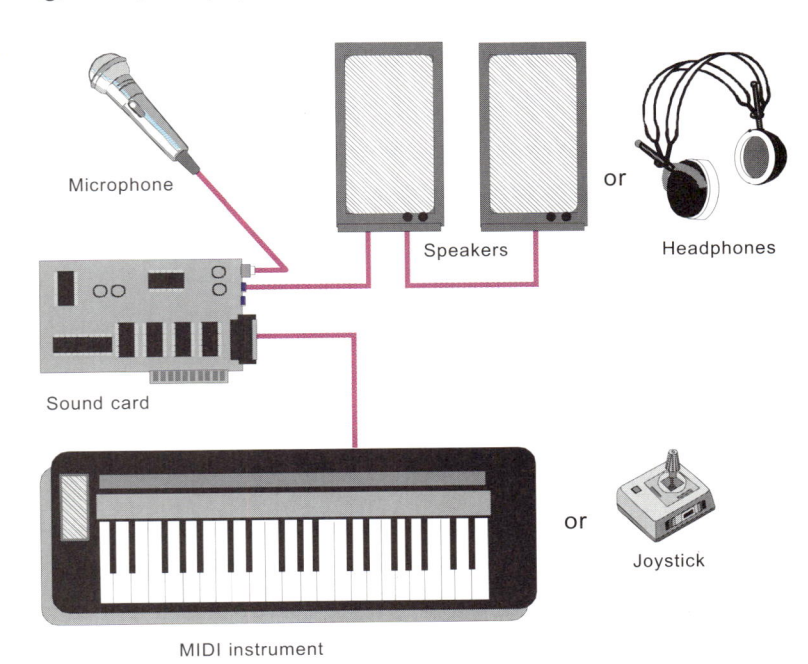

■Hardware
continued

A sound card receives input from a microphone or MIDI instrument. If your PC came bundled with a sound system, an inexpensive microphone was probably part of the package. If you're not picky about sound quality, you'll find the bundled microphone suitable for "radio-quality" voice recording and sound effects destined for Web pages or presentations. For multimedia or professional audio projects—and even for computer karaoke—you'll want to shop for a better-quality "mic." You can connect most standard vocal and instrumental microphones to a computer sound card—you don't need to shop for a special "computer microphone." You must also generally purchase a cable that connects the microphone to the sound card in your PC.

You can also add a MIDI instrument to your PC sound system. A **MIDI instrument** is an electronic device that synthesizes music, usually based on sophisticated wavetables. Before PC sound cards offered high-quality wavetables, the only way to produce decent MIDI sound was to funnel MIDI messages out to a MIDI instrument. Today, musicians continue to use MIDI instruments to supplement a PC sound card and to input notes during the process of composing MIDI music. The most popular MIDI instrument is a piano-like keyboard, called a **MIDI keyboard**. Nowadays, a MIDI keyboard is a standard piece of gear for recording studios, and for the personal computer systems of rock, jazz, and even classical musicians.

MIDI keyboard prices vary from a few hundred dollars to a few thousand dollars. Even if you want only a basic keyboard, most MIDI experts suggest that you shop for one with "full-size" keys (the same size as those on a piano), a four octave range, and velocity-sensitive keys that emulate the feeling of real piano keys. MIDI keyboard manufacturers include Korg, Roland, and Yamaha. A visit to their Web sites can provide lots of information about features and pricing.

Figure 14-7: Just think of "piano lessons" on a MIDI keyboard! You can save your best practice session as a MIDI file and play it back for your piano teacher or while you're playing computer games. Parents, don't forget to watch your children when they claim to be practicing!

Chapter 14: Recording and Editing Sound 167

■Tutorial
How to work with digitized sound

Windows includes a program module called Sound Recorder that lets you record, save, edit, and play digitized sound. It is very basic software for manipulating sound files, but it nicely illustrates how to work with digitized sound on your PC.

To access the Sound Recorder, click the Start button, then point to Programs and then to Accessories. In Windows 95, you'll find the Sound Recorder under the Multimedia menu. In Windows 98, you'll find it under the Entertainment menu.

The user interface is very simple. A series of VCR-like buttons at the bottom of the Sound Recorder window start and stop the playback, fast-forward and rewind a sound segment, and start the record mode. The sound wave that you're recording or playing is displayed in a small window.

When you have completed the tutorial, you should be able to:
- Open a WAVE file and play it.
- Make a digital voice recording at a selected sampling rate.
- Edit a sound file.

Figure 14-8: Click the PlayIt! button to begin the tutorial and learn how to record, save, play, and edit digital sound files. Estimated time: 15–20 minutes. Tracking Disk points: 10.

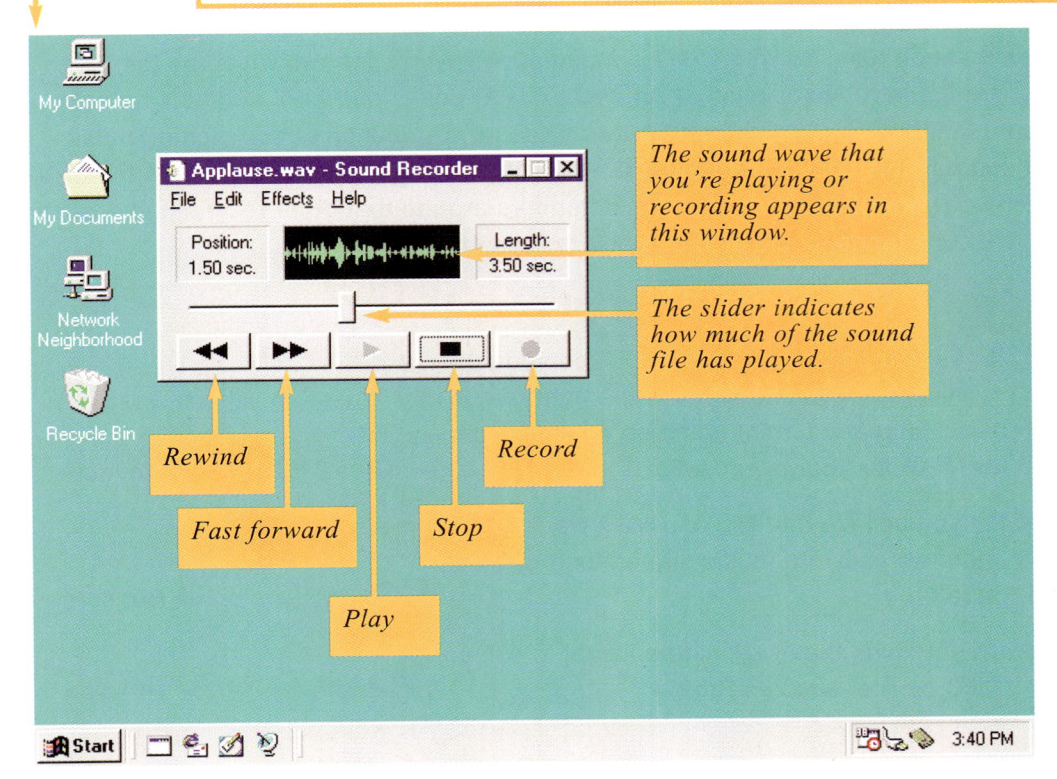

Chapter 14: Recording and Editing Sound

■Issue
RIAA vs. Rio

Grab It!
MP3 Software

The latest craze on the rock, pop, and hip-hop scene is a music compression file format called **MP3**, which stores digitized music files on computer disks in such a way that the sound quality is excellent, but the file size remains relatively small—small enough to easily download from the Web. Famous performing artists and rock-star wannabes can use MP3 files to post sample sound tracks from their albums on Web sites. It is inexpensive marketing. Fans can download a song or two and, if they like the music, they will (theoretically) purchase the entire CD.

MP3 is paving a path for another technology, called a **CD ripper**, that allows you to grab music tracks from an audio CD and store them in MP3 format. You just place any audio CD in your PC's CD-ROM drive, fire up the CD ripper software, and select the tracks you would like. The CD ripper stores the selected tracks in MP3 format on a hard or floppy disk. You can then play the tracks on your PC. If you have a CD-R drive, you can even create your own CD containing a collection of your favorite songs. Pop this CD in a DiscMan and listen to your tunes anywhere. What if you don't have a CD-R drive, and you want to listen to your favorite MP3 files when you're away from your PC? Diamond Multimedia Systems has a solution—a portable, palm-size device called Rio that plays MP3 files. You can use a parallel cable to transfer your MP3 music from your PC to the Rio's special flash memory chips. Unhook the cable and "voila!" Your MP3 music is now portable.

MP3 was designed for use with music from CDs that you have purchased or from files that you have downloaded from authorized Web sites. However, as the Record Industry Association of America (RIAA) points out, MP3 contains no safeguards that prevent illegal duplication, sales, or distribution of copyrighted music. To address this copyright threat, the RIAA filed suit to take the Rio and its bundled MP3 software off the market. Rio's defenders argued that other technologies, such as cassette tapes, could also be used to pirate music.

What do you think?

1. When you purchase a music CD, do you believe that you should have the right to convert it into any format (such as cassette tape or MP3) for your own use? ○ Yes ○ No ○ Not sure

2. Do you believe that Rio and MP3 would be more attractive to music pirates than cassette tape? ○ Yes ○ No ○ Not sure

3. Do you think that it should be illegal to sell an MP3 device, such as Rio? ○ Yes ○ No ○ Not sure

Save It!

Chapter 14: Recording and Editing Sound 169

QuickCheck A

1. For the clearest, most realistic digital recording, you should use a sampling rate of [_____] KHz.

2. Digital sound is analogous to a tape recording, whereas [_____] music is more like a player piano roll.

3. [_____] synthesis generates music by patching together sounds from a set of pre-recorded notes from actual instruments.

4. Windows Sound Recorder software plays, records, and stores digital sound in the popular [_____] file format.

5. True or false? MP3 is a compressed digital sound format. [_____]

Check It!

QuickCheck B

Click the Sound buttons to listen to each sound, then match it with the correct description below:

1. Synthesized voice [__]

2. Digitized voice at 11 KHz sampling rate [__]

3. Digitized voice at 44 KHz sampling rate [__]

4. Digitized music [__]

5. MIDI music [__]

Sound A
Sound B
Sound C
Sound D
Sound E

To use this QuickCheck, your PC must be equipped with a sound card and speakers (or headphones).

Check It!

Get It?

While using the Book-on-CD, click the Get It? button to see if you can answer ten randomly selected questions from Chapter 14.

Get It?

Chapter 15
Creating Desktop Video and Animation

What's Inside?

Today, people are so accustomed to watching moving images on TV that static computer screens somehow seem unsatisfying. Chapter 15 provides information on desktop video and animation that can spark up Web pages, presentations, and even business software.

- **FAQs:**
How do I equip my PC to play video?	171
Can I create my own desktop video?	172
How do I edit a digital video?	173
How does compression affect desktop video quality?	174
How do I create and play an animation?	175

- Hardware: PC display devices — 176
- Tutorial: How to change display settings — 179
- Issue: Idoru — 180
- QuickChecks — 181

What's on the CD?

Wear your director's beret and ascot for Chapter 15. When you've completed the screen tours and videos, you'll be shouting, "Lights! Camera! Action!"

- Find out how to play videos on your PC — 171
- Learn how to digitize footage from your camcorder — 172
- Discover how easy it is to edit a digital video — 173
- Compare different video compression formats — 174
- Learn how to create animated GIFs for Web pages — 175
- Take a step-by-step tutorial on adjusting monitor display settings — 179

Chapter 15: Creating Desktop Video and Animation

■FAQ How do I equip my PC to play video?

The hardware and software necessary to play a video depend on the video source. As you know from Chapter 12, you can watch videos from DVD disks on your computer's screen if your PC is equipped with a DVD drive. Watching broadcast TV, cable TV, or video tape on your PC requires a hardware device called a **TV tuner card** that converts signals designed for a TV into signals useable by your PC's display device. Most TV tuner cards plug into the motherboard of a PC. Accompanying software allows you to change channels and display the TV signal in a resizable area of your PC's screen.

Desktop videos—those accessed from a CD, your PC's hard disk, or a Web page—require no specialized hardware, but do need a software **player** that's designed to work with the file format in which the video is stored. Players for most video file formats are available at no cost on the Web. Popular desktop video file formats include **MPEG** (.mpg), **Video for Windows** (.avi), and **QuickTime** (.mov). Desktop videos that you access from the Web often require lengthy transfer times; depending on the video technology at the Web site, you might have to wait for the entire video to download before you can watch it. To eliminate this wait, many Web sites now use **streaming video** technology that plays the video while it downloads. You don't have to wait for streaming video, but the playback might be somewhat choppy without a fast Internet connection. Streaming video requires a plug-in that tells your Web browser how to transfer and display the video data.

Figure 15-1: Microsoft Windows includes Media Player software for MPEG and Video for Windows. Click the PlayIt! button to find out how to use its start, stop, rewind, and fast-forward controls to view desktop videos.

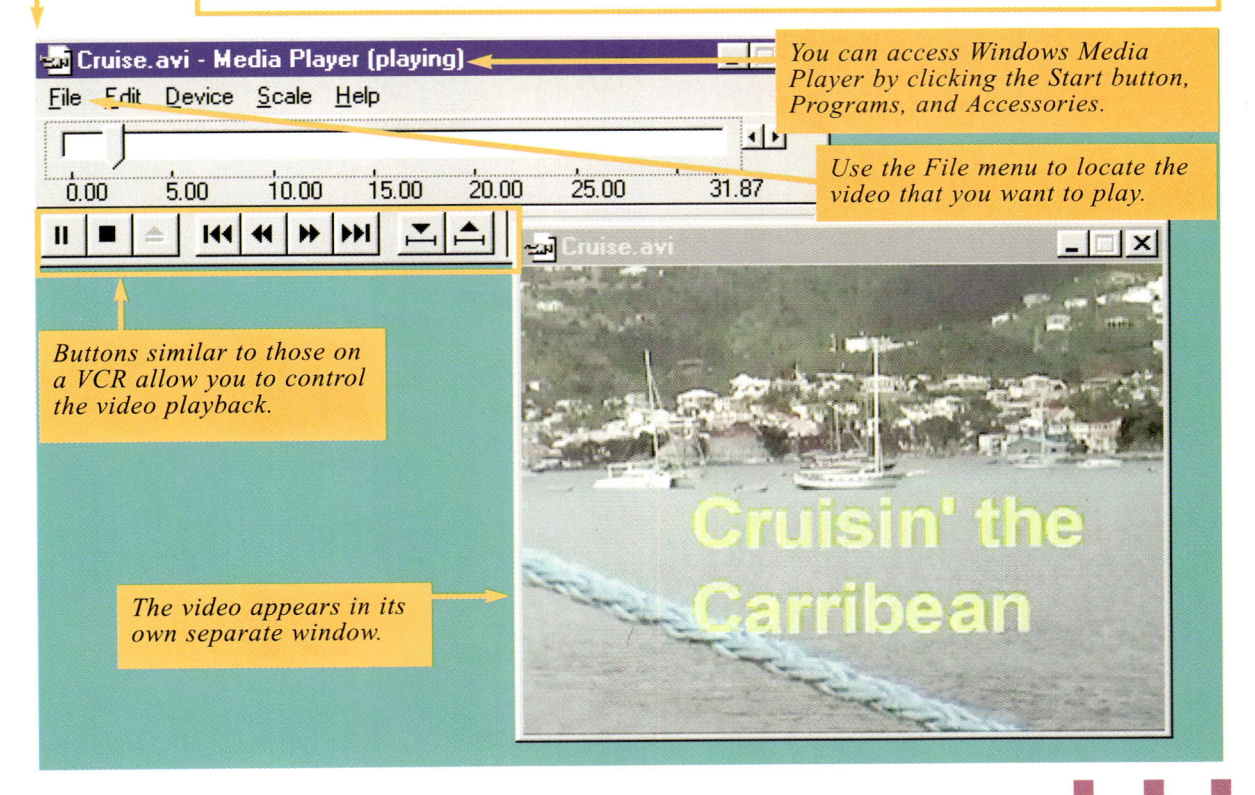

You can access Windows Media Player by clicking the Start button, Programs, and Accessories.

Use the File menu to locate the video that you want to play.

Buttons similar to those on a VCR allow you to control the video playback.

The video appears in its own separate window.

Chapter 15: Creating Desktop Video and Animation

■FAQ Can I create my own desktop video?

You can create your own desktop video, which you then distribute on CDs, video tape, or the Web. Desktop video production is not as difficult as you might think. With very little effort, you can create all kinds of videos for personal and professional use, such as a video scrapbook of your children or grandchildren, a digital wedding album, a desktop sales video, or a video holiday greeting. The equipment needed and the procedures for creating desktop video depend on whether your original footage comes from a nondigital source or a digital source.

Suppose that your video footage originates from a nondigital source, such as a VHS camcorder or a VCR tape. As explained in the previous FAQ, a TV tuner card allows you to watch video tape on your computer screen. However, to "capture" video from a nondigital source in preparation for editing, you'll need a different device. A **video capture device** digitizes video footage by taking periodic "snapshots" from the video, converting each snapshot into a bitmap graphic, and then storing the series of bitmap graphics in a computer file. The documentation for your PC's video card should explain whether it includes video capture capabilities. If it does not, you must purchase a separate video capture device, available either as a card that plugs into your PC's motherboard, or as a small unit that plugs into your PC's parallel port. You control the digitizing process by using **video capture software** supplied with your video capture device. Video capture software allows you to select the display size, frame rate, length, and file format for your digitized segments.

Footage from a digital source, such as a digital video camera or digital video tape, already exists in digital format. You can buy a high-speed **1394 communications link**, popularly known as "FireWire," to transfer this digital video data directly from the video source to your PC.

Whether your footage originates in nondigital or digital format, you'll get the best results by working with a series of short video segments containing only your best footage. As a rule of thumb, each segment should be no longer than one minute to keep file size manageable and to provide good flexibility for editing. You'll later be able to combine these segments and create longer videos.

Figure 15-2: Click the PlayIt! button to take a tour of desktop video production. Learn how to shoot footage, connect your digital camera to a video capture card, and select the footage that you want to digitize.

Chapter 15: Creating Desktop Video and Animation   173

■FAQ   How do I edit a digital video?

The process of capturing and digitizing video segments produces several large files, each containing about a minute of action. **Video editing software** helps you cut out unwanted frames, add special effects to any segment, assemble segments into the sequence of your choice, overlay a soundtrack, and designate transitions from one segment to the next. Popular video editing software includes Adobe Premiere, Ulead Systems MediaStudio, and IMSI Lumiere.

Your completed video will consist of audio tracks containing voices and music, plus video tracks containing video segments and transitions. To begin the editing process, open your video editing software and import the files that contain any video and audio clips you'll need for the final video. Once imported, you'll be able to drag these clips onto a timeline that represents the video stream. Your video editing software also allows you to insert predefined transition effects that control the way one clip blends into another—for example, by fading, flipping, overlaying, or simply cutting to the next scene. To complete your video, you can add titles and other special effects.

Video editing software also allows you to preview your entire video production, complete with sound and transitions. When you're satisfied with your work, you can select a video file format, choose a compression format, then save the video. The next FAQ explains how compression affects the quality of your finished video.

Figure 15-3: Click the PlayIt! button to learn the basic steps of video editing: importing video and sound clips, arranging the clips in sequence, selecting transition effects, and previewing the final masterpiece.

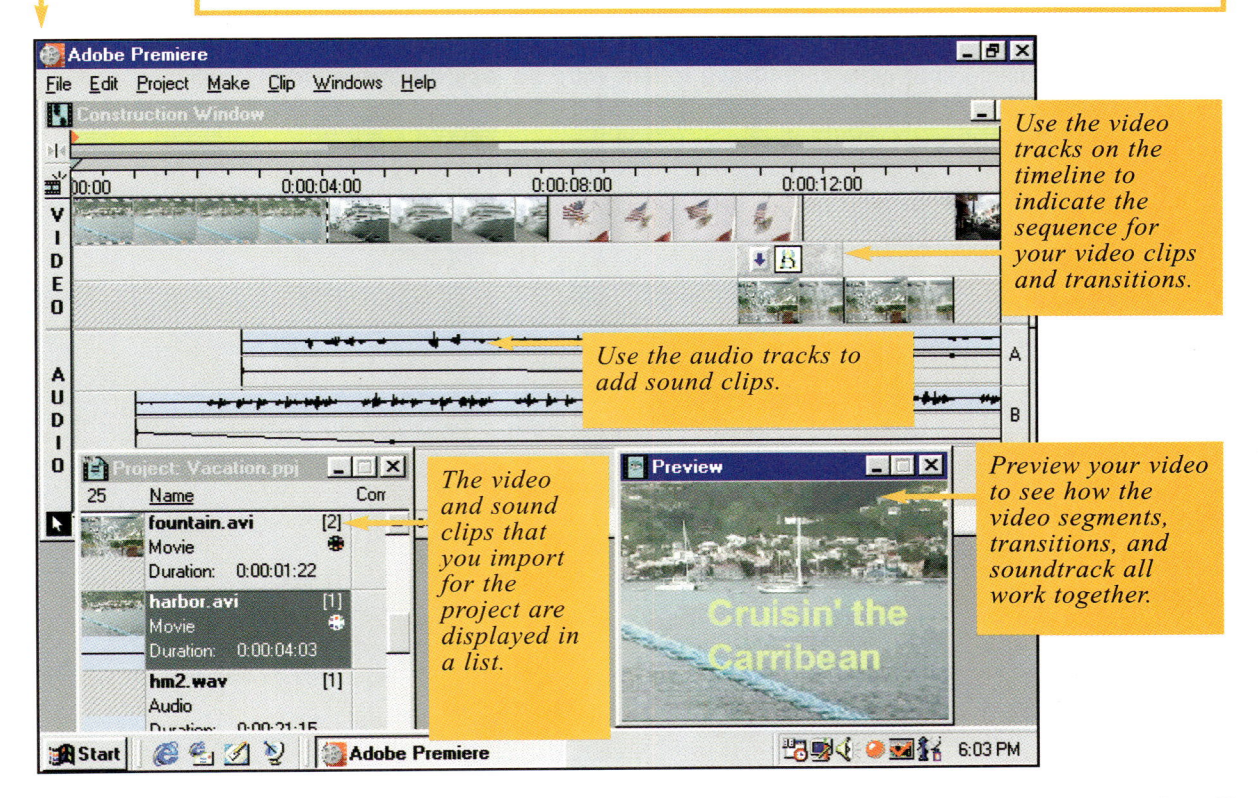

Use the video tracks on the timeline to indicate the sequence for your video clips and transitions.

Use the audio tracks to add sound clips.

The video and sound clips that you import for the project are displayed in a list.

Preview your video to see how the video segments, transitions, and soundtrack all work together.

■FAQ How does compression affect desktop video quality?

Each frame of a digitized video is essentially a full-screen, true color graphic. When stored in an uncompressed format, a single frame would require about 900 KB of storage space. The series of 30 such frames necessary for one second of high-quality video would consume nearly 27 MB of storage space. Therefore, to display this one second of video, your PC would have to read and process 27 MB of data in one second—not practical with today's technology. You can whittle this enormous amount of video data down to a more manageable size by using one or more of the following methods:

- Shrinking the video to one-quarter or one-eighth of the size of your PC screen.
- Reducing the number of frames displayed per second.
- Selecting a **compression technique**, such as MPEG, Indeo, Cinepak, or Video 1, that reduces the amount of data in each frame or stores only the data that has changed from one frame to the next.

With today's PC technology, desktop video production necessitates a tradeoff between quality and file size. Video can be compressed into a small file that downloads from the Web in a reasonable amount of time and occupies a manageable amount of storage space. Unfortunately, a highly compressed video typically looks blurry and has "scratchy" sound. On the other hand, using a different compression technique to create better-quality video often produces a larger file.

When you produce desktop videos, you must balance quality factors against file size as you select a compression technique. For example, you might discover that Indeo compression at 15 frames per second stores a collection of videos in 620 MB. Cinepak compression at the same frame rate produces better-quality video, but requires 850 MB. If you want to store the videos on a single CD with a 650 MB storage limit, you might have to live with the less desirable video quality.

Unfortunately, some older, slower computers cannot keep up with the processing demands of even compressed video, resulting in jerky motion and unsynchronized sound. When you create desktop videos, test your productions on an "average" PC, if possible.

Figure 15-4: Click the PlayIt! buttons to compare video and audio quality produced by different compression settings.

Play It! — Indeo video
Frame rate: 15
Compression: 0
File size: 1,072 KB

Play It! — Indeo video
Frame rate: 5
Compression: 0
File size: 466 KB

Play It! — Indeo video
Frame rate: 15
Compression: 50
File size: 503 KB

Play It! — Video 1
Frame rate: 15
Compression: 0
File size: 6,959 KB

Chapter 15: Creating Desktop Video and Animation

■FAQ How do I create and play an animation?

In elementary school, you probably played with a "flip book" containing drawings of a cartoon character. When you quickly fanned through the pages, the cartoon character appeared to move. Computer animation works on the same principle as a flip book. You create a series of images, each showing a "freeze frame" from a scene in motion. You then compile these scenes into an animation, which you save as a single file in an animation file format such as FLC, known as "Flick." To play the animation, you use the appropriate player software for the animation file format.

Although you can create the individual frames for an animation using almost any bitmap, 3-D, or vector graphics software, you must use animation software to compile the frames into an animated sequence. Consequently, most animators prefer to use an animation software package for the entire process. AutoDesk Animator, NewTek LightWave 3D, and Byte by Byte SoftF/X are popular options.

Grab It!
GIF Animation Software

Web page designers tend to use a unique set of animation tools and formats. The most popular format for Web page animation, called **animated GIF**, is a series of graphics stored in GIF format, then compiled with GIF animator software. The resulting files require relatively few bytes of storage space, so they can be transmitted quickly over the Internet. Each frame for the animation arrives on your computer screen separated by the few seconds required for transmission. Once all frames have arrived, the animation cycles smoothly from one frame to the next.

Play It!

Figure 15-5: Click the PlayIt! button to find out how to create animated GIFs for Web pages.

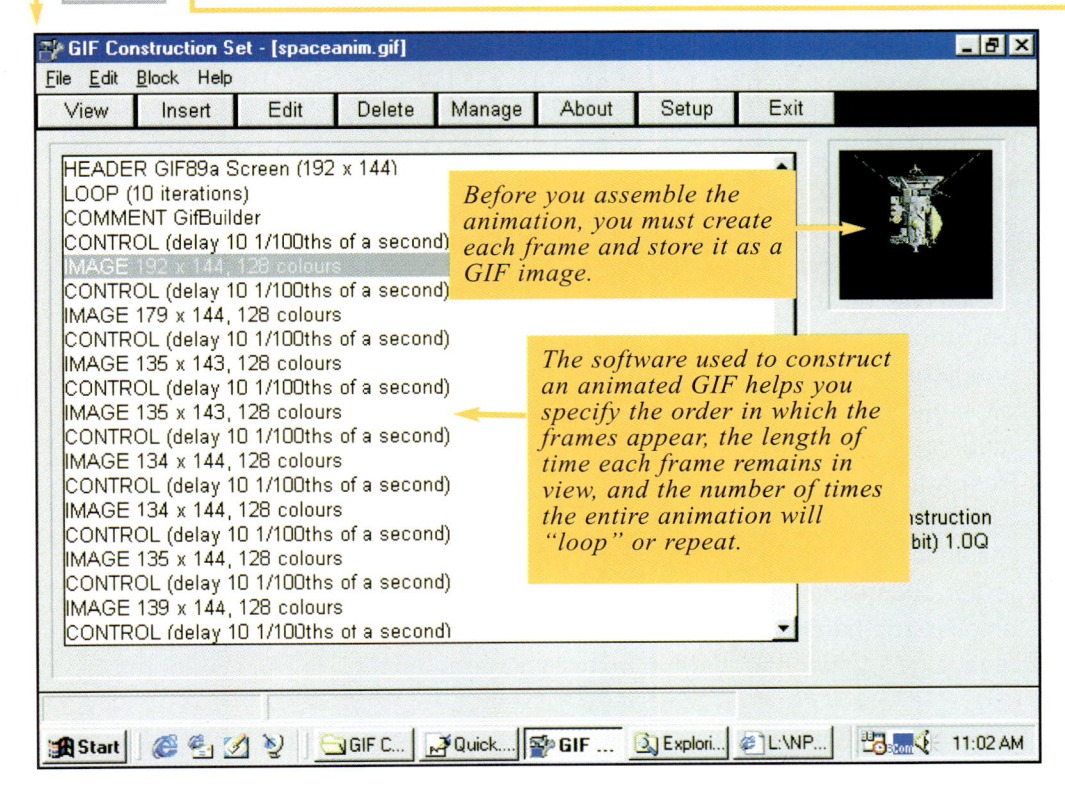

Before you assemble the animation, you must create each frame and store it as a GIF image.

The software used to construct an animated GIF helps you specify the order in which the frames appear, the length of time each frame remains in view, and the number of times the entire animation will "loop" or repeat.

Hardware
PC display devices

A **PC display device**, such as a monitor or LCD display, provides feedback about what's going on as you use your PC. It displays what you've typed. It displays icons to click and menu options to select. It displays windows, dialog boxes, prompts, error messages, graphics, and text. Everything that appears on your PC screen is produced by dots of light called **pixels** (short for "picture elements"). Even vector graphics, which are stored as commands for drawing lines and shapes, must be "rasterized"— that is, converted into dots—before being displayed as points of light on the screen.

The clarity of the image that your PC displays depends on the quality of the source image and the capabilities of the display equipment. Good equipment can't improve a fuzzy bitmap graphic, but a cheap display system can make a high-quality image appear fuzzy and make text difficult to read. Because you will likely spend a good deal of time gazing at your PC screen, it is useful to understand the factors that affect display quality. If you are not satisfied with the quality of your PC display, you can often improve it by purchasing better-quality components.

The most common display device for a desktop PC is a **CRT monitor**, sometimes called simply a "monitor." CRT (cathode ray tube) technology, which is based on rays of electrons that are beamed into a big vacuum tube, is dependable and relatively inexpensive. If you're shopping for a new monitor, experts advise you to buy the one with the biggest viewable area that you can afford. Factors that affect monitor quality and price include the following:

- **Screen size**. A measurement of the glass display screen taken diagonally from corner to corner. Standard sizes are 14", 15", 17", 19", and 21". A 17" monitor typically costs about U.S.$250, whereas a 15" monitor costs only U.S.$150.
- **Viewable image size** (vis). On some monitors, the picture does not stretch to the edges of the glass screen, creating a black border. The viewable image size is a diagonal measurement of the screen area that actually displays the image. For example, a 15" monitor might have only a 13.8" vis. When comparing display devices, use the vis measurement instead of the screen size.
- **Dot pitch**. The distance between the dots of colored light that display the image on screen. The smaller the dot pitch, the crisper the image. A .26 dot pitch means that the dots are 26/100ths of a millimeter apart. Most of today's monitors have a .28, .26, or .24 dot pitch.
- **Resolution**. The size of the pixel grid. The minimum resolution is 640 X 480. The next step up is to 800 X 600, and the next step is 1024 X 768. Higher resolutions open up more screen area for your desktop, enabling you to view larger documents or graphics. At higher resolutions, however, text becomes smaller and harder to read. At 1024 X 768 resolution, you'll probably want at least a 17" monitor so that the text will be large enough to read comfortably.

Hardware continued

Most of today's notebook computers use an **LCD panel**, which produces an image by manipulating light as it passes through a layer of liquid crystal cells and color filters. These panels are compact, lightweight, and have low power consumption requirements. Recent innovations in LCD technology have improved LCD displays so that they produce a clear, bright image that rivals the display quality of many CRT monitors.

LCD technology is now available for your desktop PC. An **LCD monitor** or "flat panel display" incorporates an LCD panel in a free-standing case that you can use instead of a CRT monitor. A 15" LCD monitor costs about U.S.$800. However, a CRT monitor with 15" vis costs only U.S.$150. You should carefully examine whether the advantages of an LCD monitor are worth the additional expense.

LCD monitors do have lower power requirements than CRT monitors. Although this factor is important on a notebook computer that runs on batteries, your desktop PC generally remains anchored to the wall outlet where power is plentiful. Environmentalists, once worried about the amount of power consumed by millions of computer monitors, have been pleased to see new energy-saving features that automatically power down a monitor when it is not in use. Today's CRT monitors don't use much more energy than a light bulb, so switching to an LCD monitor won't significantly reduce your electric bills.

Some health officials have been concerned with the amount of electromagnetic radiation, particularly X-rays, emitted by CRT monitors. It has been suggested that LCD monitors might pose less of a health risk because they do not emit X-rays. Research on the link between CRT radiation and health has been inconclusive, so buyers must weigh the potential risks of each display technology.

An LCD monitor doesn't take up much desk space and is light enough to hang on a wall—you can decide how much that feature is worth to you. The bottom line is that LCD monitors just look "cool" on your desk. If you want cool, though, you'll have to pay a premium price.

Figure 15-6: The image on an LCD display stretches to the edges of the glass, unlike the image on most CRT monitors. When comparing LCD displays and CRT monitors, remember that the specifications for viewable image size provide a more accurate comparison than specifications for screen size.

Chapter 15: Creating Desktop Video and Animation

■Hardware continued

A monitor connects to a socket in the back of your PC called a **video port**, which is part of the display circuitry housed on a circuit board called a graphics card. A **graphics card** converts data from your PC's processor into electronic signals for a display device. It comes as standard equipment with almost every new PC. In ads and product descriptions, you might see graphics cards also referred to as video cards, graphics adapters, or display adapters. The term "video card" might mislead you to expect that it has some special features for desktop video or animation; it does not. A video card is just another name for a graphics card, which handles the display of text, all types of graphics, videos, and animation. A "video capture device," described on page 172, has a similar name, but a different purpose—to digitize data from a camcorder or VCR.

A basic graphics card will suffice for most word processing, Web, and spreadsheet applications. For 2-D graphics, 3-D graphics, video editing, desktop publishing, and computer games, you might want a graphics card with extra memory or graphics acceleration.

Most graphics cards contain memory chips where an image can be constructed before being sent to the display device. These memory chips remove a substantial burden from your PC's main processor and help improve the overall performance of your PC. Because each pixel in an image requires storage space, the amount of memory on your graphics card limits the resolution and color depth available on your PC. A true color 640 X 480 image requires about 1 MB of memory, but a 1024 X 768 image requires more than 2 MB. Your graphics card must supply enough memory for the resolution and color depth that you typically work with.

As a further performance enhancement, some graphics cards also have specially designed accelerator circuitry that speeds up specific 2-D and 3-D graphics operations. These **graphics accelerator cards** are particularly prized by graphics designers and computer game players. You can add a state-of-the-art graphics accelerator card to your PC for about U.S.$200.

Figure 15-7: The amount of memory on your graphics card determines the highest resolution and color depth available on your PC. Use this chart as a guide to the amount of memory that's optimal for your computing activities.

Graphics Card Memory	Application
1 MB	Word processing and spreadsheets
2 MB	Web browsing and presentations
4 MB	2-D graphics, video editing, and desktop publishing
8 MB and above	3-D graphics and computer games

Chapter 15: Creating Desktop Video and Animation

■Tutorial
How to change display settings

You can adjust your PC's display settings to control its color depth, resolution, and power management options. If your display sometimes switches to odd colors, you are seeing an example of **palette flash** caused by the color depth setting. To avoid palette flash, you can switch to a higher color depth.

The resolution setting affects the size of objects that you see on the screen, as well as the number of objects that fit in a window. At lower resolutions, such as 640 X 480, text appears larger, but you might see only a small part of a document in the word processing window.

Your preferred display settings might depend on the software you are using. For example, you might prefer a high resolution when you're working with graphics, but a lower resolution for word processing. Once you know how to adjust display settings, you can experiment to find your preferred settings. When you have completed the tutorial, you should be able to:

- Change the display resolution for your PC screen.
- Change the color depth displayed on your PC screen.
- Adjust energy saving settings for your display device.

Figure 15-8: Click the PlayIt! button to begin the tutorial and learn how to adjust your PC's display settings. Estimated time: 15-20 minutes. Tracking Disk points: 10.

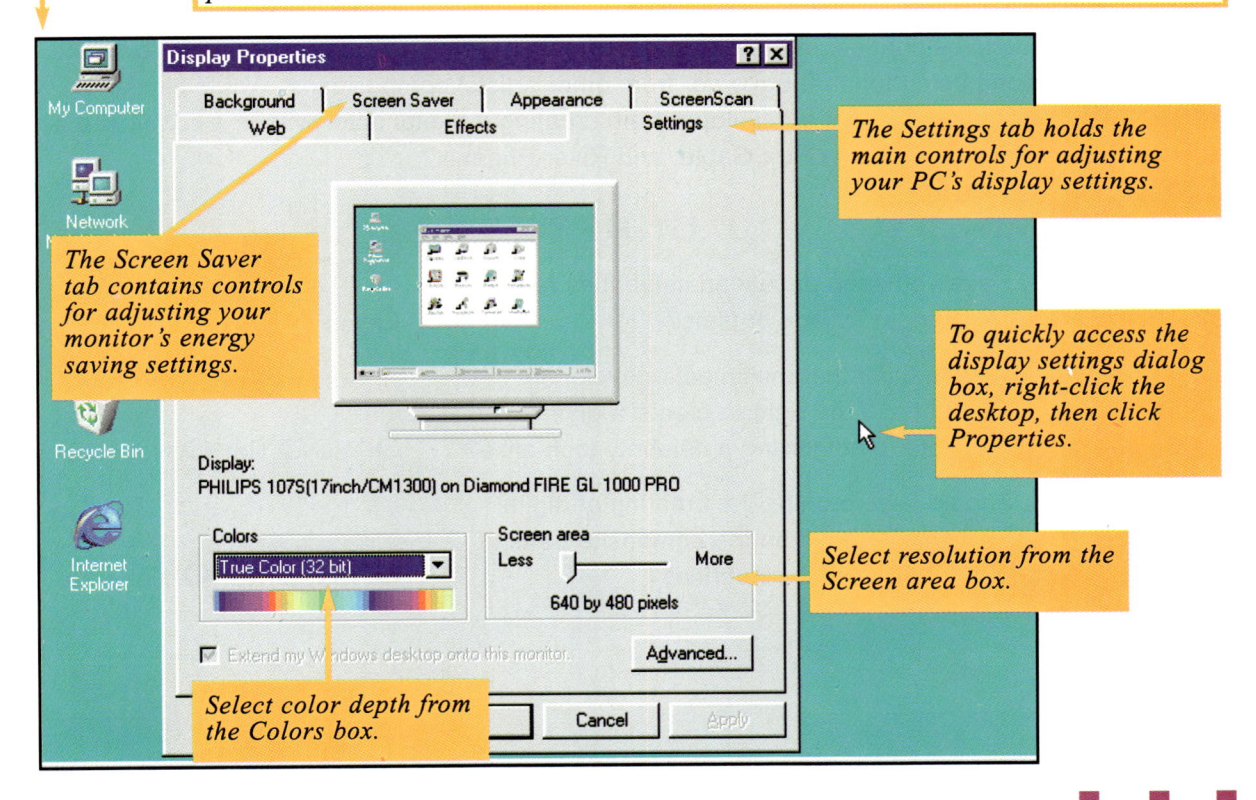

The Settings tab holds the main controls for adjusting your PC's display settings.

The Screen Saver tab contains controls for adjusting your monitor's energy saving settings.

To quickly access the display settings dialog box, right-click the desktop, then click Properties.

Select resolution from the Screen area box.

Select color depth from the Colors box.

Issue
Idoru

In a novel called *Idoru* (the Japanese version of the word "idol"), author William Gibson introduced the concept of a computer-generated celebrity. Unlike a human star, Gibson's idoru could work tirelessly—and for free. In 1995, a team of Japanese multimedia developers embarked on a project to create a "real" idoru named Kyoko Date who could star in movies, appear on talk shows, and sing her way to the top of the pop music charts. Through sophisticated animation techniques based on digitized movements of a real person strapped into a motion-capture suit, a three-dimensional, full-motion model of Kyoko emerged.

Technology that created the fictional Kyoko Date can also reanimate famous dead actors so they can star in new films and endorse new products. But is this application legal? What's to prevent an unscrupulous advertiser from casting a digital image of John Wayne in a Ginsu knife commercial?

In the United States, some states have enacted postmortem "right of publicity" laws that prohibit unlicensed exploitation of deceased celebrities. The application of these laws to digital technology has not yet been fully explored in the courts, however. Outstanding issues include whether a multimedia developer has a right to create a digital image of a deceased celebrity, even if there is no intent to use the image for commercial gain. Further, would the laws that prohibit using the image of a deceased celebrity also prohibit the use of a digital character that was created from the image of a celebrity look-alike? The issue becomes even more cloudy when you consider that a digital character could combine the traits of several celebrities. In the music industry, it is a violation of copyright law to create a song using tunes "borrowed" from other artists' compositions. Would similar restrictions prevent a developer from creating a digital actor who is a composite of Humphrey Bogart, Clark Gable, and River Phoenix?

What do you think?

1. Have you seen deceased celebrities featured in any new TV ads or films?   ○ Yes ○ No ○ Not sure

2. Do you think that multimedia developers should have the right to create a digital character by digitizing a celebrity look-alike?   ○ Yes ○ No ○ Not sure

3. Should laws prohibit the creation of digital characters based on the composite traits of several deceased celebrities?   ○ Yes ○ No ○ Not sure

Save It!

Chapter 15: Creating Desktop Video and Animation — 181

QuickCheck A

1. Popular desktop video file formats include Video for Windows, _____, and QuickTime.

2. If you view a(n) _____ video from the Web without a fast Internet connection, the playback will be rather choppy.

3. The video _____ technique that you select for a desktop video will affect its quality and file size.

4. The most popular format for Web page animation is called animated _____.

5. True or false? If you have a 13" monitor set at 1024 X 768 resolution, the text will appear rather small. _____

Check It!

QuickCheck B

For each task described below, indicate the letter of the appropriate tool.

1. Transfer video footage from a digital video camera to your PC ____
2. Digitize a video from a camcorder or VCR ____
3. Connect a monitor to your PC ____
4. Watch TV or video tapes on your computer screen ____
5. Play desktop video ____

a. Video capture device
b. TV tuner card
c. Graphics card
d. Windows Media Player
e. FireWire

Check It!

Get It?

While using the Book-on-CD, click the Get It? button to see if you can answer ten randomly selected questions from Chapter 15.

Chapter 16
Looking "Under the Hood"

What's Inside?

Suppose that your new desktop PC arrives with a warning, "The microprocessor and graphics card might have been loosened during shipping. Make sure all chips and boards are properly seated before turning on the PC." If you're familiar with the components inside of your PC's system unit, you can deal with messages like this one, perform some basic troubleshooting, and even perform your own upgrades. Chapter 16 gets into the nuts and bolts—more specifically, the chips and circuits—of computers.

- FAQs:

How does a computer work?	183
What does RAM and processing circuitry look like?	184
How does data get into chips?	185
Does a computer use the same code for all types of data?	186
How does software tie into chips, codes, and circuits?	187
- Hardware: Microprocessors — 188
- Tutorial: How to find the technical specifications for your PC — 191
- Issue: Who invented the first electronic digital computer? — 192
- QuickChecks — 193

What's on the CD?

It's impossible to actually see what's happening inside the chips on your PC's motherboard, so Chapter 16 contains animated tours to help you visualize the way computers work.

- Trace the path of input, processing, output, and storage — 183
- Learn about those mysterious black chips on your PC's motherboard — 184
- Take a step-by-step tutorial on finding your PC's system specifications — 191

Chapter 16: Looking "Under the Hood" 183

■FAQ How does a computer work?

A computer works by manipulating data in various ways. **Data** refers to the symbols that describe people, events, things, and ideas. Basically, a computer works with data in four ways: (1) accepting input data, (2) processing data, (3) producing output data, and (4) storing data. **Input** is the data that goes into a computer. A computer gets input from many sources, including the keyboard, modem, and disk drives. What happens to this input? The computer puts it in RAM (random access memory). Recall from Chapter 1, that RAM is a temporary holding area for data. You might think of it as a halfway house for computer data—a place for it to "hang out" until it is processed, stored, or displayed.

How does a computer know what to do with this data that's hanging out in RAM? In addition to data, RAM holds instructions that tell the computer what to do. A computer's processing circuitry "reads" these instructions, then processes the data accordingly. **Processing data** means manipulating it in some way. For example, a computer might process numeric data by performing a calculation. It might process the data in a list by sorting it, or it might process the dots in an image by changing their color. After processing ends, the resulting data is returned to RAM.

Sometimes an instruction indicates that the computer should transfer data from RAM to a device, such as a printer, modem, or display screen. The data sent to these devices is called **output**. Other instructions might direct the computer to transfer data from RAM to a storage device, such as a hard disk drive. This process of **storing data** moves it from the temporary RAM "halfway house" to a more permanent "home."

Figure 16-1: When you think about how a computer works, remember that input data arrives in RAM, then instructions tell the computer how to process, store, or output this data.

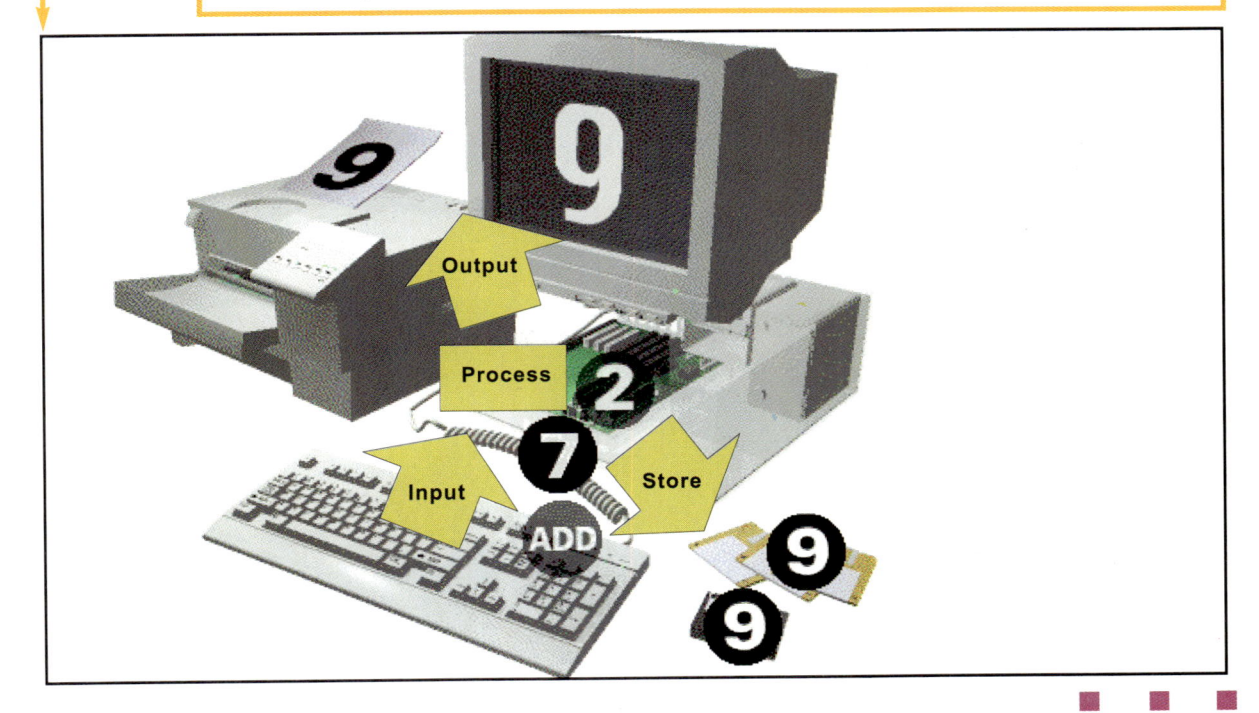

■FAQ What does RAM and processing circuitry look like?

RAM and processing circuitry are contained in "chips" inside your PC's system unit. **Chip** is a nickname for an integrated circuit (sometimes called a microchip or IC). An **integrated circuit** is a thin slice of silicon that has been etched with microscopic circuitry. Different chips are designed to perform different tasks. For example, a **microprocessor chip** carries out most of the processing work that takes place in your PC. **RAM chips** temporarily hold data. One or more **ROM chips** (read-only memory chips) hold the instructions that your PC uses to boot up. Other chips perform support activities to keep the data moving quickly and smoothly from input devices, to output devices, and to storage devices.

A chip is housed in a small, black, rectangular **chip carrier**. Thin wire "feet," which extend from the carrier, can be soldered directly to a circuit board or plugged into a chip socket on a circuit board. A **circuit board** contains electrical pathways that allow data to travel between chips. In a typical PC, a fairly large circuit board, called the **motherboard** or "main board," houses the microprocessor chip, ROM chips, and a variety of support chips. A series of RAM chips are connected to a small circuit board called a **memory module**. Memory modules plug into special slots on the motherboard, allowing data to flow between RAM chips and the microprocessor chip. Other small circuit boards, such as a graphics card, sound card, or modem, also plug into the motherboard, allowing data to travel between RAM and input and output devices.

Figure 16-2: Click the PlayIt! button to learn more about the chips on your PC's motherboard and to see how to reseat loose components.

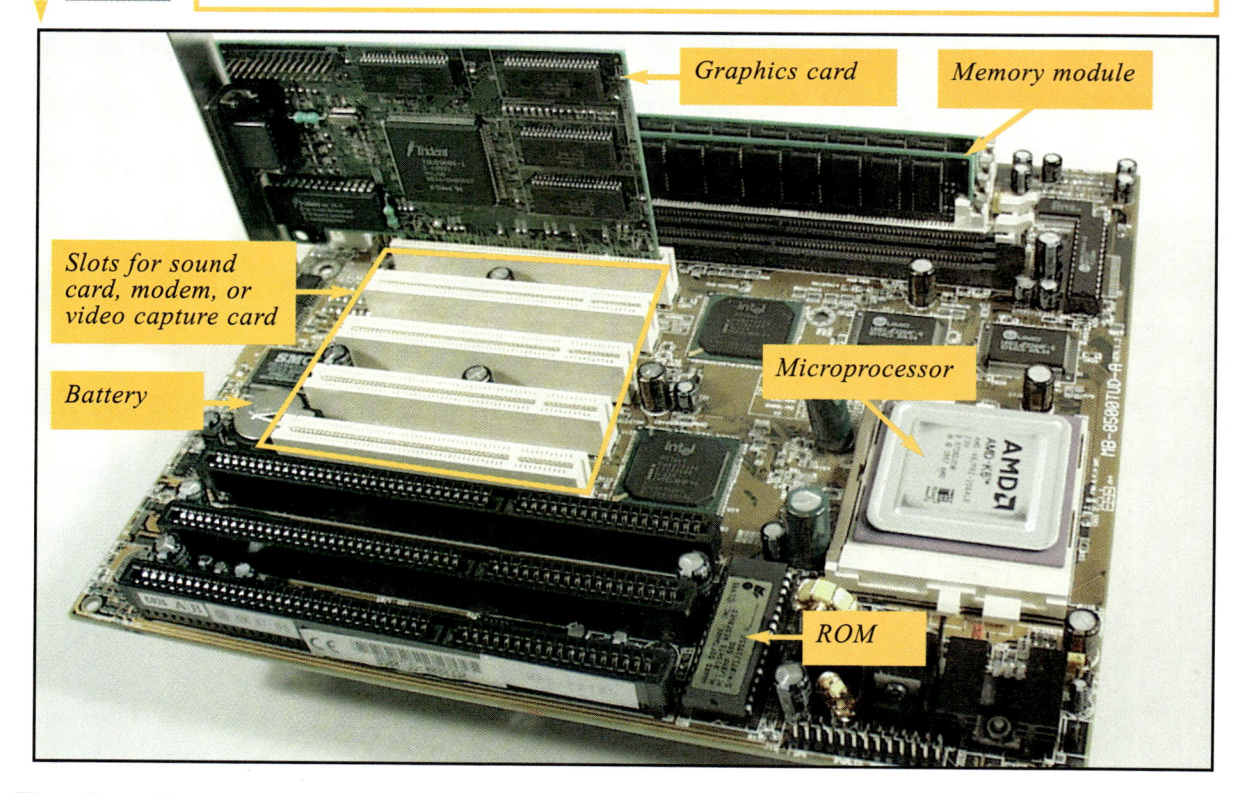

■FAQ How does data get into chips?

Your intuition probably tells you that miniature letters, pictures, and other kinds of data don't somehow squirt through the electronic circuitry inside your PC. Instead, your PC works with data that has been converted into a code and then into electronic signals, which can easily travel through circuits on chips and circuit boards. This treatment of computer data is similar to the way Morse code converts the letters of a message into a series of dots and dashes that can be represented by the flashing of a signal light. Keep in mind, however, that "code" in this context simply means converting data from one form to another and has nothing to do with secret codes, security codes, or encryption.

Computers do not use Morse code, but instead use special computer codes that are based on ones (1s) and zeros (0s). For example, an uppercase "A" might be coded as 01000001. Each 1 or 0 is referred to as a **bit** (short for binary digit). Eight bits form a **byte**, the unit of measurement for data storage.

Once data has been coded, it is a relatively easy task to convert the 1s and 0s into a form that can be stored or transmitted electronically. When data is stored in memory, a 1 is represented by the presence of an electrical charge in a miniature electronic circuit; a 0 is represented by the absence of a charge. On a disk, 1s and 0s are represented by metallic particles with different magnetic polarities. On a CD, 1s and 0s are represented by non-reflective pits and reflective surfaces called "lands." When data is transmitted to print or display devices, the 1s and 0s might be represented by different voltages.

As data is gathered, processed, stored, and transmitted, it is constantly converted from one type of signal to another. Special **controller chips** that convert data are found on the motherboard, graphics card, sound card, and modem of your PC. For example, a controller chip on the motherboard converts each key that you press on the keyboard into the electronic code that corresponds to the letter of the key.

Figure 16-3: In your PC, data has been coded and converted into electronic signals so that it can travel from chip to chip.

The smallest unit of information in a computer is a bit. A bit can be 0 or 1. The electronic circuits in your PC represent a 1 bit as a pulse of electricity.

0 1 1 1 1 1 0 0 1 = y

A series of eight bits is called a byte and typically represents one character.

Chapter 16: Looking "Under the Hood"

■FAQ Does a computer use the same code for all types of data?

Computers use different codes for different types of data. The codes used for text differ from those used for graphics. The coding method for graphics differs from that used for sound.

Computers represent text data (such as letters, numerals, and symbols) by using ASCII, extended ASCII, ANSI, Unicode, or EBCDIC codes. Numbers for calculations are often coded using the binary number system. Computers code bitmap image data by using a binary color code for each dot in the image. Data for recorded sound is coded by using a binary number to represent the height of each wave sample.

Although many methods for coding computer data exist, all of the computer codes that your PC uses share certain characteristics:

- *Digital*. A digit is a single character in a numbering system. To say a code is digital means that it converts data into a finite set of numbers, rather than an infinite set of analog values.
- *Binary*. The binary number system uses only two digits: 0 and 1. Binary coding allows computers to represent all kinds of complex graphical, sound, text, and numeric data using two simple signals, such as "off" and "on."
- *Fixed length*. The length of a computer code is measured by the number of 1s and 0s required to represent each data item. Codes that are fixed length use the same number of bits to represent each data item. For example, if the code represents the letter "A" using a string of eight bits, it represents a "B" and every other letter of the alphabet using the same number of bits.

Figure 16-4: By looking at this table of ASCII codes, you can see that the underlying code is digital, binary, and fixed length. Just for fun, try writing your name in ASCII code.

0	00110000	C	01000011	V	01010110	i	01101001
1	00110001	D	01000100	W	01010111	j	01101010
2	00110010	E	01000101	X	01011000	k	01101011
3	00110011	F	01000110	Y	01011001	l	01101100
4	00110100	G	01000111	Z	01011010	m	01101101
5	00110101	H	01001000	[	01011011	n	01101110
6	00110110	I	01001001	\	01011100	o	01101111
7	00110111	J	01001010	]	01011101	p	01110000
8	00111000	K	01001011	^	01011110	q	01110001
9	00111001	L	01001100	_	01011111	r	01110010
:	00111010	M	01001101	`	01100000	s	01110011
;	00111011	N	01001110	a	01100001	t	01110100
<	00111100	O	01001111	b	01100010	u	01110101
=	00111101	P	01010000	c	01100011	v	01110110
>	00111110	Q	01010001	d	01100100	w	01110111
?	00111111	R	01010010	e	01100101	x	01111000
@	01000000	S	01010011	f	01100110	y	01111001
A	01000001	T	01010100	g	01100111	z	01111010
B	01000010	U	01010101	h	01101000		

Chapter 16: Looking "Under the Hood" 187

■FAQ How does software tie into chips, codes, and circuits?

Think back to the concept that instructions in RAM tell the microprocessor how to manipulate data (page 183). These instructions come from operating system software and application software. Software is simply a collection of one or more computer programs or "program modules" containing a list of instructions designed to help you and your PC accomplish a task. These instructions are written using a computer **programming language**, such as Visual Basic or C++.

Today's programming languages allow programmers to use English-like words and syntax to write the instructions for a program module. However, these English-like instructions must be converted into **machine language** before they can be executed within a microprocessor chip. Machine language instructions are coded in 1s and 0s in a form that can be directly executed by a microprocessor.

The process of converting a programmer's English-like instructions into machine language instructions is called **compiling**. Compiling creates the executable EXE files, which are stored on disk as software applications. When you want to use a software application program, your PC copies the EXE file instructions from disk into memory. Once in memory, these instructions direct the activities that take place in memory and the microprocessor.

Figure 16-5: A programmer writes a computer program using English-like instructions, which must then be compiled into machine language for computer execution.

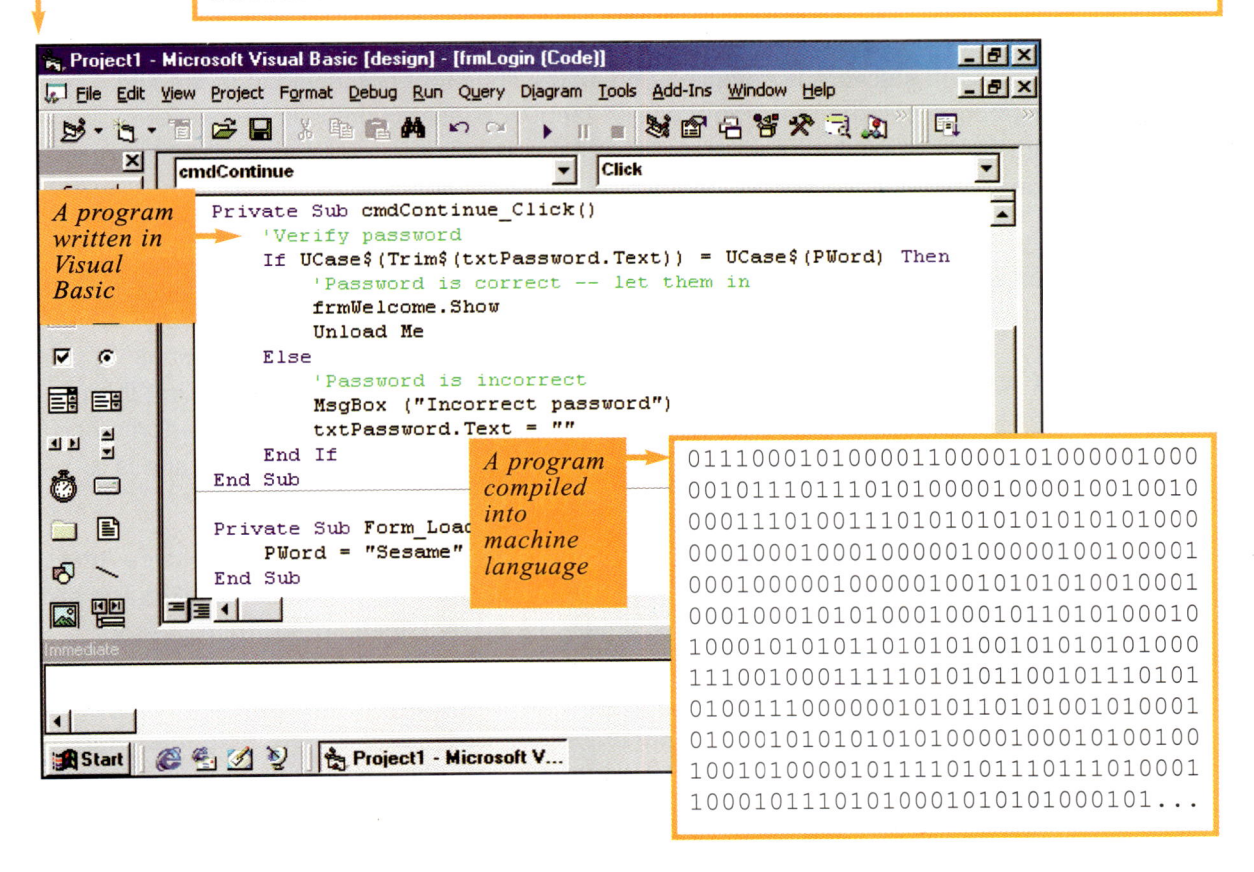

A program written in Visual Basic

```
Private Sub cmdContinue_Click()
    'Verify password
    If UCase$(Trim$(txtPassword.Text)) = UCase$(PWord) Then
        'Password is correct -- let them in
        frmWelcome.Show
        Unload Me
    Else
        'Password is incorrect
        MsgBox ("Incorrect password")
        txtPassword.Text = ""
    End If
End Sub

Private Sub Form_Load
    PWord = "Sesame"
End Sub
```

A program compiled into machine language

```
0111000101000011000010100001000
0010111011101010000100001001001
0001110100111010101010101010100
0001000100010000010000010010001
0010000010000010010101010010001
0001000101000010001011010100010
1000101010110101010010101010100
1110010001111101010110010111010
0100111000000101011010100101000
0100010101010101000010001010010
1001010000101111010101110111010
1000101110101000101010101000101...
```

Chapter 16: Looking "Under the Hood"

■Hardware
Microprocessors

A microprocessor and a microcomputer are not identical. A microprocessor is a single integrated circuit. A microcomputer is a type of computer that uses a microprocessor as its main processing unit. Your PC is a microcomputer that contains a microprocessor. The type of microprocessor that's inside a computer indicates its age, dictates the types of programs it can run, and affects how fast it can perform computing tasks.

Chipmakers have produced many microprocessor models. The microprocessors in microcomputers can be classified into two categories: x86 and PowerPC. x86 processors (also referred to as IBM-compatible or Intel processors) are typically found in PCs that run Windows, whereas PowerPC processors are found in Apple Macintosh computers. Although PowerPC and x86 processors both process data, they differ in terms of their instruction sets. You read on page 187 that software is compiled into a set of instructions that the processor can execute. If software is compiled into instructions that are included in the x86 instruction set, the resulting machine language instructions can be executed directly by an x86 processor. A PowerPC processor cannot execute x86 instructions without using special conversion hardware or software.

Figure 16-6: An Intel Pentium III processor.

The PowerPC is a **RISC** (reduced instruction set computer) chip designed with a streamlined instruction set to simplify its circuitry and increase processing speed. An x86 processor is a **CISC** (complex instruction set computer) chip designed to process complex and specialized instructions. In theory, a RISC chip should be more efficient than a CISC chip. In practice, however, RISC performance is not necessarily superior, though this issue is a source of controversy.

Figure 16-7: An AMD K6 processor.

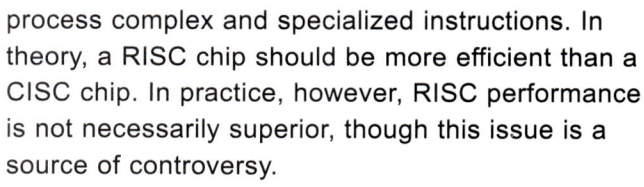

Manufacturers of x86 microprocessors include Intel and AMD. Intel is the original x86 chipmaker and still the largest. Its current lineup of microprocessors includes the Pentium 4, Pentium III, Pentium II, and lower-cost Celeron models. AMD's chip offerings include the K6, Duron, and Athlon. Both Intel and AMD currently offer chips with speeds over 1 GHz or 1,000 MHz.

Hardware continued

Different processors provide your PC with different levels of performance. Computer ads typically hype a processor's clock speed, which is one of several factors that contribute to overall system performance. **Clock speed** is measured in **megahertz** (MHz). One MHz is 1 million cycles per second. The higher the MHz, the faster the clock speed. For example, a 500 MHz clock speed is faster than a 333 MHz clock speed.

Clock speed is analogous to how fast you pedal when you ride a bike. Usually, the faster you pedal, the faster you move. During each clock cycle, the processor executes instructions. The faster the clock speed, the more instructions your microprocessor can carry out in each second. If a 500 MHz processor executes one instruction for each clock cycle, it performs 500 million instructions per second! As a rule of thumb, PCs with faster processors are more expensive than their slower cousins.

Clock speed is not the only factor that affects processor performance. For example, two Intel microprocessors, the Celeron/300 and the Pentium II/300, were both rated at 300 MHz. However, the Celeron/300 delivered only three-fourths the performance of the Pentium II/300. What could account for this difference? Think again about the bike analogy. Your speed depends not just on how fast you pedal, but also on other factors related to the design of your bike, such as gearing and tire size. For example, if your bike allows you to gear down, you can pedal more slowly, but still maintain your speed. Likewise, several factors related to the design of a microprocessor can affect the speed at which it processes instructions:

- *Instructions per clock cycle*. Suppose that during each clock cycle, a processor could perform three instructions, instead of one. It would perform three times as much work in the same amount of time. Processors that execute multiple instructions per clock cycle are referred to as **superscalar**.
- *Cache memory*. Before processing can take place, data and instructions must exist in RAM. RAM chips are several inches away from the processor on the motherboard of your PC. Even traveling at the speed of light, data can require several clock cycles to move from RAM to the processor. **Cache memory** (pronounced "cash") is data-holding circuitry where instructions and data can be accessed faster than from RAM. Typically, cache is measured by its storage capacity in kilobytes (KB) and by the number of cache areas or levels. **Level 1 (L1) cache** is located right on the microprocessor chip. **Level 2 (L2) cache** is on a separate chip from the processor, but sometimes packaged within the same chip carrier.
- *Extended instruction sets*. All x86 processors have a core set of instructions. However, some processors have extended instruction sets that speed up certain types of processing. **MMX** (multimedia extensions) accelerate 2-D graphics, video, and sound. **3DNow!** extensions speed up 3-D graphics—especially handy for the complex screen displays of today's computer games. MMX and 3DNow! facilitate processing only when your PC runs software that has been specially written to include the extended instruction set.

Chapter 16: Looking "Under the Hood"

■Hardware
continued

Grab It!
Benchmark Software

If clock speed doesn't tell you the whole story about processor performance, what does? Rather than relying on clock speed ratings, you can get a better picture of processor performance from the results of benchmark tests. A **benchmark test** is a set of standard processing tasks that measure the performance of computer hardware or software. Microprocessor benchmark tests measure the speed at which a processor performs a set of tasks. Computer manufacturers and independent test labs publish the results of benchmark tests in computer magazines and on Web sites. If you're interested in finding out how your own PC stacks up, you can download benchmark testing software from the Web.

Many benchmark tests are available today, and each measures a slightly different aspect of processor performance. To make sense of the results, it is useful to have some idea of how the test relates to what your computer does in real life. For convenience, you can group benchmark tests into three categories:

- *Multimedia benchmarks* measure processor performance when processing MPEG video, AVI video, digitized sound, and other multimedia data. The Intel Media Benchmark and Norton Multimedia Benchmark are two tests frequently used to measure multimedia processing performance.
- *Integer benchmarks* measure processing efficiency for integer data, which includes the words and numbers that you manipulate when using spreadsheet, word processing, presentation, and database applications. Integer benchmark tests include SPECint95, CPUmark32, and Norton SI32.
- *Floating point benchmarks* measure processor performance for numbers stored in a special "floating point" format that facilitates calculations. Good floating point performance is required for 3-D graphics, computer-aided design, and many of today's computer games. Floating point benchmark tests include SPECfp95, 3D WinBench98, and FPUmark.

Although processor performance is important, it is only one factor that affects overall PC performance. Your PC is only as fast as its slowest component. Just as you can pedal fast on an icy road but not make much headway, a processor can "spin its wheels" while it waits for data to arrive from a slow disk drive.

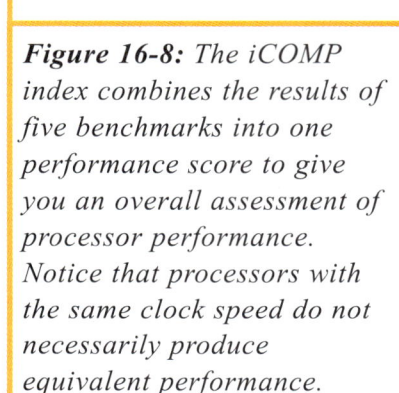

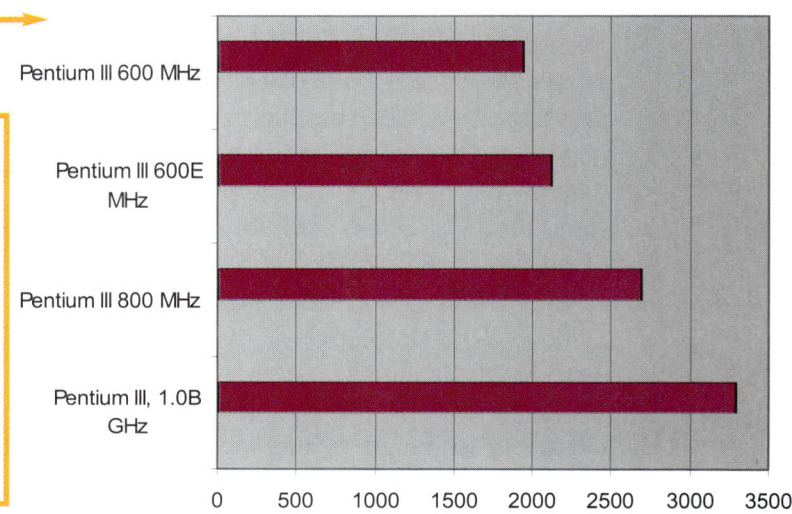

Figure 16-8: The iCOMP index combines the results of five benchmarks into one performance score to give you an overall assessment of processor performance. Notice that processors with the same clock speed do not necessarily produce equivalent performance.

Chapter 16: Looking "Under the Hood"   191

▪Tutorial
How to find the technical specifications for your PC

Which processor is in your PC? How fast is it? How much RAM is installed on your PC's motherboard? What is the capacity of your PC's hard disk drive? The type, capacity, and speed of various components in your PC are called **system specifications**. These specifications are important when you purchase software, upgrade components in your PC, or seek technical support.

You can, of course, find your system specifications by referring to the documentation that was provided with your computer. Sometimes, however, this information is not entirely accurate. You can discover the specifications for your PC using system analyzer software supplied with Windows and with your application software. In addition, you can download shareware to help you with this task. In this tutorial, you'll learn several handy ways to find your PC's system specifications.

Grab It!
System Analyzer Software

When you have completed the tutorial, you should be able to:
- Use the Control Panel to discover basic system configuration information.
- Access Microsoft System Information.
- Find system specifications using shareware.

Play It!

Figure 16-9: Click the PlayIt! button to begin the tutorial and find out how to find the technical specifications for your PC. Estimated time: 15–20 minutes. Tracking Disk points: 10.

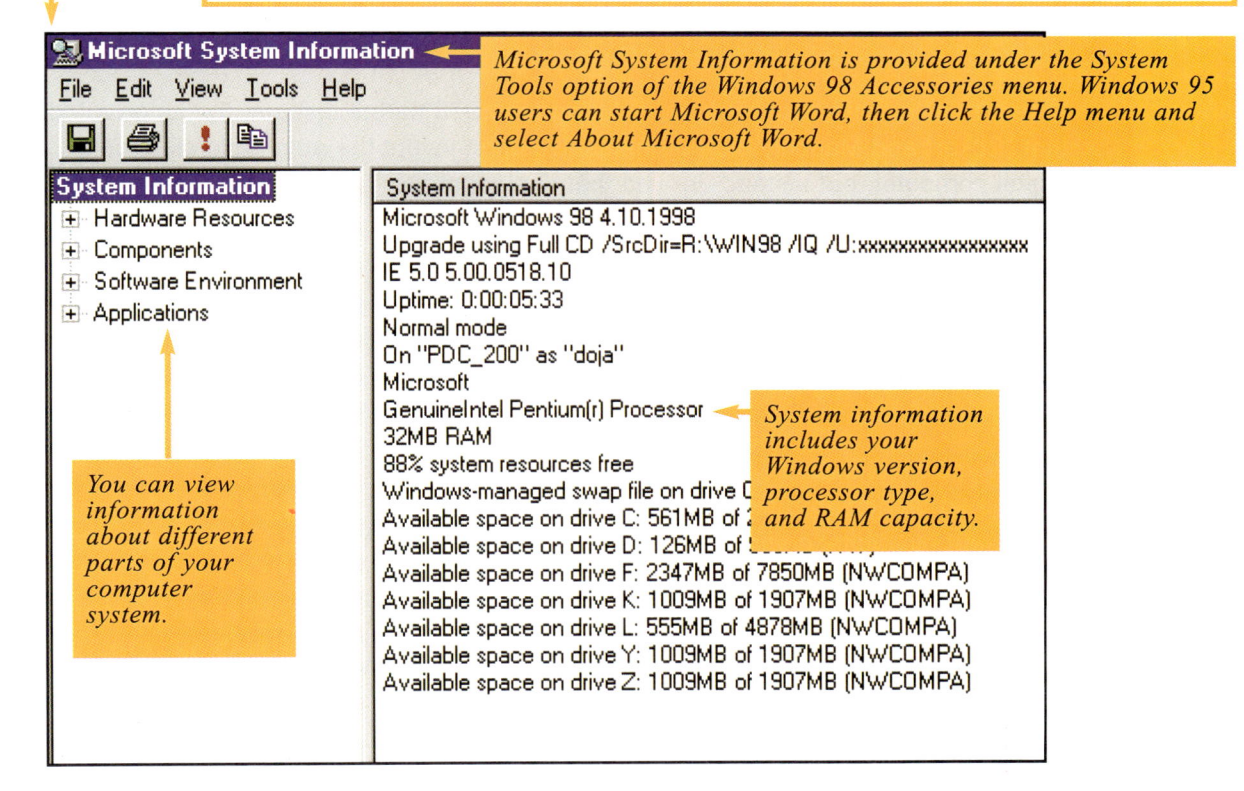

Microsoft System Information is provided under the System Tools option of the Windows 98 Accessories menu. Windows 95 users can start Microsoft Word, then click the Help menu and select About Microsoft Word.

Microsoft System Information
File Edit View Tools Help

System Information:
- Hardware Resources
- Components
- Software Environment
- Applications

You can view information about different parts of your computer system.

System Information:
Microsoft Windows 98 4.10.1998
Upgrade using Full CD /SrcDir=R:\WIN98 /IQ /U:xxxxxxxxxxxxxxxx
IE 5.0 5.00.0518.10
Uptime: 0:00:05:33
Normal mode
On "PDC_200" as "doja"
Microsoft
GenuineIntel Pentium(r) Processor
32MB RAM
88% system resources free
Windows-managed swap file on drive C
Available space on drive C: 561MB of 2
Available space on drive D: 126MB of 5
Available space on drive F: 2347MB of 7850MB (NWCOMPA)
Available space on drive K: 1009MB of 1907MB (NWCOMPA)
Available space on drive L: 555MB of 4878MB (NWCOMPA)
Available space on drive Y: 1009MB of 1907MB (NWCOMPA)
Available space on drive Z: 1009MB of 1907MB (NWCOMPA)

System information includes your Windows version, processor type, and RAM capacity.

Chapter 16: Looking "Under the Hood"

Issue

Who invented the first electronic digital computer?

In a 1973 lawsuit, a computer manufacturing company called Sperry Rand claimed to hold a patent on the technology for electronic digital computers. If the courts upheld this claim, then no company would have been able to manufacture computers without obtaining a license from and paying royalties to Sperry Rand.

Historically, the first inventor to produce a binary digital computer was probably Conrad Zuse, an engineer in Germany who in 1938 completed work on a computer called the Z-1. World War II made collaboration on technology projects difficult, so Zuse's work was not known until after the war. More significantly, Zuse did not file for a U.S. patent. About the same time that Zuse was building the Z-1, John Mauchly and J. Presper Eckert began work in Pennsylvania on a computer called the ENIAC, which became operational in 1946. Mauchly and Eckert obtained a patent for digital computer technology and then formed a computer company. Their company and patent were eventually acquired by Sperry Rand.

At the time of the 1973 lawsuit, Sperry Rand appeared to have a clear claim on digital computer technology. However, a seemingly insignificant meeting dating back to 1941 between Mauchly and a mathematician named John Atanasoff had far-reaching consequences on the Sperry Rand patent claim. In this meeting and in subsequent correspondence, Atanasoff shared his ideas on computer design with Mauchly. Atanasoff had been constructing a computer of his own, but had never filed for a patent. Mauchly and Eckert subsequently incorporated several of Atanasoff's ideas to build the ENIAC computer.

When these events became known during the 1973 patent dispute, the judge ruled that "Eckert and Mauchly did not themselves first invent the automatic electronic digital computer, but instead derived that subject matter from one Dr. John Vincent Atanasoff." The Sperry Rand patent was declared invalid.

What do you think?

1. Does it appear to you that the judge made the right decision, despite the fact that Atanasoff never filed for a patent? ○ Yes ○ No ○ Not sure

2. Do you think that Zuse, instead of Atanasoff, should be declared the inventor of the first electronic digital computer? ○ Yes ○ No ○ Not sure

3. Do you think that the computer industry would be different today if Sperry Rand had won its patent case? ○ Yes ○ No ○ Not sure

Save It!

QuickCheck A

1. A computer accepts input data, produces output data, stores data, and ▭ data.

2. An integrated ▭ is housed inside a chip carrier.

3. True or false? Computer codes are binary because it is a relatively easy task to convert coded 1s and 0s into electronic signals. ▭

4. The process of converting a programmer's English-like instructions into machine language instructions is called ▭.

5. True or false? The Pentium II processor is a RISC chip with MMX. ▭

Check It!

QuickCheck B

Match the letter of the correct motherboard component with each of the following descriptions:

1. A memory module ▭
2. Microprocessor ▭
3. ROM ▭
4. A slot for a modem ▭
5. Battery ▭

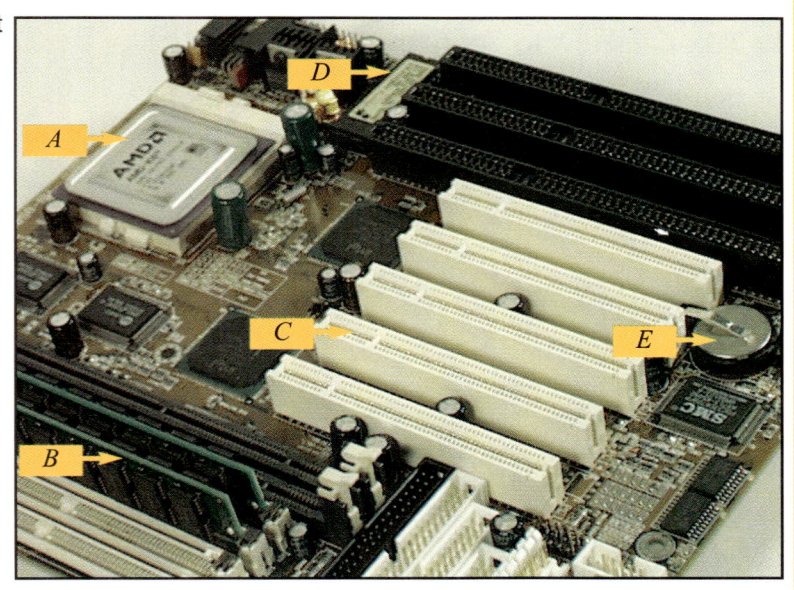

Check It!

Get It? While using the Book-on-CD, click the Get It? button to see if you can answer ten randomly selected questions from Chapter 16.

Get It?

Chapter 17
Upgrading and Expanding Your PC

What's Inside?

When you purchased your PC, it was a top-of-the-line machine. A year later, it might seem a little past its prime. In Chapter 17, you'll find out how to give your "old" PC a makeover by upgrading its components or expanding its capabilities.

- FAQs:
  - Can I upgrade the processor in my PC? 195
  - Will adding RAM improve my PC's performance? 196
  - Can I add more hard disk capacity? 197
  - How do I add or upgrade other devices? 198
  - Can I upgrade my notebook PC? 199
- Hardware: Expansion devices, ports, cards, and slots 200
- Tutorial: How to get technical support 203
- Issue: Upgrade, reuse, recycle, or landfill? 204
- QuickChecks 205

What's on the CD?

Don't be shy about using a screwdriver on your PC. The videos in Chapter 17 show you how to install new chips, cards, and devices. Just remember that the person who disassembles a PC is also the person responsible for restoring it to working order!

- Learn how to install that $800 microprocessor 195
- Discover the secret of SIMM and DIMM slots 196
- Find out how to install a second hard drive 197
- Learn how to insert an expansion card 198
- Tour the ports of a notebook PC 199
- Take a step-by-step tutorial on getting technical support 203

Chapter 17: Expanding and Upgrading Your PC

■FAQ Can I upgrade the processor in my PC?

Expanding your PC usually means adding components that increase functionality. **Upgrading** typically means replacing a component, such as a microprocessor, with one that is newer and that provides enhanced performance. You can upgrade your PC's microprocessor with a faster model. However, before you rush out and purchase the latest, greatest processor, you should find out whether it will fit in your PC's motherboard. You should also consider whether the upgrade will be cost-effective.

Your PC's motherboard provides only one type of connector for a microprocessor. The microprocessor that you select for an upgrade must match that connector. AMD K-6-2 processors use a **Socket 7** connector, while the faster Duron and Athlon processors use a special slot that looks like the slot used with Intel Pentium III processors, but is not compatible with it. Intel Pentium III and Celeron processors use a **Slot 1** connector. Intel Pentium II Xeon processors use a **Slot 2** connector that's just a bit longer than a Slot 1 connector. It's a good idea to check with your PC manufacturer's technical support staff or Web site to find out which processors your PC's motherboard will accept.

Practically speaking, microprocessor upgrades are not always such a good deal. After you've had your PC for a year or so, purchasing a microprocessor upgrade for the next level of speed is relatively inexpensive—about U.S.$300—but it won't dramatically boost the speed at which your PC appears to operate. Upgrading several levels of speed to a state-of-the-art microprocessor will usually produce a noticeable speed increase, but is a much more expensive proposition—costing about U.S.$800.

Installing a state-of-the-art microprocessor in an older PC rarely produces performance equivalent to that of a new computer because processor speed is only one factor that affects computer performance. Other components, such as slow RAM or a slow data path to the slots holding the sound and graphics cards, might create data bottlenecks and impede overall performance. Rather than upgrade your microprocessor, you might be happier with the benefits provided by adding RAM, installing a second hard drive, or upgrading to an accelerated graphics card.

Figure 17-1: A state-of-the-art microprocessor is expensive, so you should install it carefully. Click the PlayIt! button for some tips on how to successfully upgrade a microprocessor that requires Slot 1 (shown at left) or one that requires Socket 7 (shown at right).

Chapter 17: Upgrading and Expanding Your PC

▪FAQ Will adding RAM improve my PC's performance?

Adding RAM to your PC can increase processing efficiency by providing more fast-access storage space for programs and data. Whenever your PC is on, RAM holds parts of the operating system, the software program modules you're currently using, and as much data as possible for the files you have open. With more RAM, larger sections of the programs and data you work with can be held in memory circuits, instead of remaining on disk. The processor works more quickly if it can access program instructions and data without waiting for them to arrive from disk storage. Today's PCs typically have 32 or 64 MB of RAM. Adding RAM is fairly inexpensive, with a 32 MB memory module costing about U.S.$80.

Before you add RAM, find out the current RAM capacity of your PC by using system analyzer software, such as Microsoft System Information (page 191). Next, refer to the documentation for your PC to find the maximum RAM capacity. You can add memory only up to this limit. The documentation should also provide the specifications for the RAM that you'll purchase. RAM specifications include speed, capacity, package, and type:

- *Speed*. Memory access time is measured in nanoseconds (ns). A **nanosecond** is one billionth of a second. Lower access speed means faster data availability. For example, 60 ns RAM is faster than 70 ns RAM.
- *Capacity*. Measured in megabytes (MB), capacity refers to the amount of data that each memory module can hold. Memory modules are typically available in increments of 32, 64, 128, or 256 MB.
- *Package*. RAM chips are packaged onto memory modules such as **SIMMs** (single in-line memory modules) and **DIMMs** (dual in-line memory modules). DIMM is the newer technology and provides a wide data path that allows 64 bits of data to travel simultaneously. SIMMs provide only a 32-bit data path. Your PC's motherboard might provide slots for only one type of package, or both.
- *Type*. The memory modules in today's PCs typically contain **DRAM** (dynamic RAM) chips, which require a constant supply of power to refresh the data that they hold. DRAM comes in several types, including SDRAM (synchronous DRAM), EDO (extended data output), and FPM (fast page mode).

Figure 17-2: *Adding RAM is one of the least expensive and most effective ways to increase the performance of your PC. Your PC's motherboard might contain SIMM slots, longer DIMM slots, or both. Click the PlayIt! button to find out how to install SIMMs and DIMMs.*

Chapter 17: Expanding and Upgrading Your PC   197

■FAQ Can I add more hard disk capacity?

With today's software, it is always a good idea to have at least 100 MB of free space on your hard disk. When you reach this capacity, you can delete files that you no longer need and empty the Recycle Bin to clear some drive space. If these measures help only temporarily, however, it is probably time for a new hard drive. Rather than replace your current hard drive with a larger one, for about U.S.$200 you can usually add a second hard drive using the EIDE connection built into your PC's motherboard.

An **EIDE** (enhanced integrated drive electronics) connection provides a data path between the motherboard and storage devices. Most computers include two EIDE connections. Each connection has channels for two devices. A hard drive and CD-ROM drive usually take up two of your PC's EIDE channels. A ZIP drive or tape drive might use additional channels. If an EIDE channel is available, you can install a second EIDE-compatible hard drive. When purchasing a hard drive—or any storage device—you can find information about the type of connection it requires on the package. Despite their very different names, "Fast IDE," "Ultra ATA," and "Ultra DMA" all refer to EIDE-compatible storage devices.

If you run out of EIDE channels, you can purchase a hard drive that uses a SCSI connection, instead of an EIDE connection. A **SCSI** (small computer system interface) connection provides high-speed data transfer between your PC and devices, such as a hard drive, tape drive, CD-ROM drive, or scanner. If your PC does not have a built-in SCSI connection, you can usually purchase and install one.

Before you purchase a second hard drive, check inside your PC's case for an available drive bay. A **drive bay** is simply a shelf or compartment to which you attach the drive mechanism. Screws hold the drive in place. Most system unit cases provide a number of 3.5" and 5.25" drive bays. Some bays are accessible from outside the case to accommodate removable media such as floppy and Zip disks; bays for hard drives are not accessible from outside the case. If the appropriate type of drive bay is not available, you must purchase an external version of the storage device, which typically will use a parallel or SCSI connection, rather than an EIDE connection.

Figure 17-3: The easiest and most cost-effective way to increase your PC's hard disk storage capacity is to add a second internal hard drive using an existing EIDE connection. Click PlayIt! to find out how to locate the EIDE connection and complete the hard drive installation.

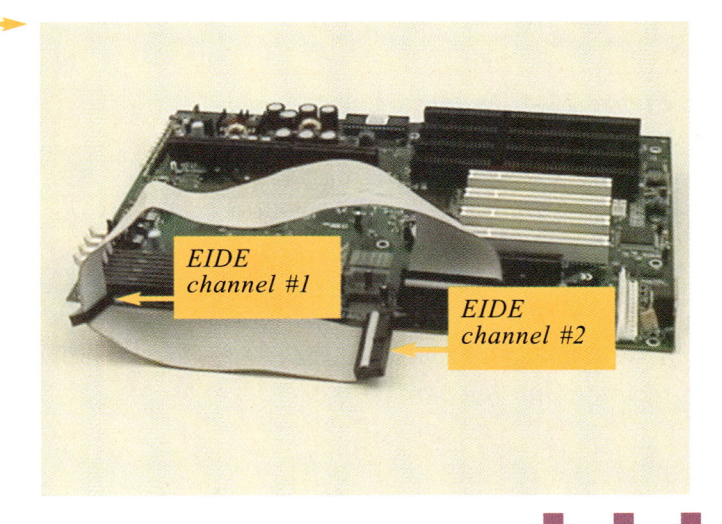

Chapter 17: Upgrading and Expanding Your PC

■FAQ How do I add or upgrade other devices?

So far, you've learned that you upgrade a processor using a Socket 7, Slot 1, or Slot 2 connector; you add RAM using SIMM and DIMM slots; and you typically add storage devices using the EIDE connector. To upgrade or add other hardware devices to your PC, you can either use ports or slots.

Your PC contains a variety of **ports**, which provide external cable connections for various devices, such as a mouse, monitor, and printer. Your PC also has some multipurpose ports, including the parallel, serial, SCSI, joystick/MIDI, and USB ports. Even if the circuitry for a port is built into the motherboard, the connector itself will be accessible from outside of the case. Using a port to add a device is usually as simple as plugging a cable into the port.

The expansion slots on your PC's motherboard provide additional potential for expansion and upgrades. An **expansion slot** (or just "slot") is designed to hold a circuit board called an expansion card. An **expansion card**, such as a modem or a graphics card, contains circuitry and often a cable connector of some sort. To add a modem, you slide its card into an expansion slot. To upgrade a graphics card, you remove the old card from its slot and replace it with a new one. Your PC's motherboard includes several types of slots:

- **AGP** (accelerated graphics port). Primarily used for graphics cards, an AGP slot provides a high-speed data pathway that's particularly handy for 3-D graphics. If your PC's motherboard has an AGP slot and you're upgrading your graphics card, make sure that you purchase an AGP-compatible card.
- **PCI** (peripheral component interconnect). PCI slots offer fast transfer speeds and a 64-bit data path. You would typically use a PCI slot for a graphics card if your PC's motherboard does not include an AGP slot. You might also use PCI slots for a sound card, SCSI card, video capture card, modem, or network card.
- **ISA** (industry standard architecture). ISA slots are an older technology, used today for modems or other relatively slow devices. Many new motherboards have few or no ISA slots.

Figure 17-4: Expansion slots were originally designed to make it possible to easily expand and upgrade a computer. Note that an expansion card can gradually work its way out of its slot if not secured in some way. Click the PlayIt! button to find out how to correctly remove, insert, and secure expansion cards.

Chapter 17: Expanding and Upgrading Your PC

■FAQ Can I upgrade my notebook PC?

Unlike a desktop PC, a notebook computer typically does not provide its owner with access to the motherboard. Many notebook components, such as a sound card and graphics card, are incorporated in the motherboard circuity and are not meant to be upgraded. Although your notebook PC provides few upgrade options, it does provide ports, PCMCIA slots, and a docking station connection for expansion.

Typically, a notebook PC provides ports for a mouse, a printer, speakers, and one serial device such as a scanner or a digital camera. You'll often find two additional ports, one for connecting an external monitor and the other for connecting an external full-size keyboard. Your notebook PC might also include other types of ports, such as an **infrared port** that allows you to "beam" data to a printer without a cable connection. The notebook manufacturer's documentation should contain a list and diagram of the available ports.

Most notebooks include a **PCMCIA slot** for special circuit cards called PCMCIA cards (also called "PC cards"). PCMCIA slots are named for the Personal Computer Memory Card International Association, a nonprofit group that develops expansion standards for notebook PCs. Most of today's notebooks have a Type III PCMCIA slot, which can hold one Type III or two Type II cards. Type III cards, which are thicker than Type II cards, are commonly used to add a second hard disk drive. Type II cards are used to add a modem, CD-ROM drive, digital camera, Zip drive, network interface card, or more memory.

If the built-in ports and PCMCIA slot do not provide enough connectivity, you might consider a docking station. A **docking station** is a device that contains the same selection of ports and expansion slots that you would find in a desktop PC. You can add cards to the slots, just as you would for a desktop PC, then connect your notebook to the docking station. Note, however, that two similar devices cannot be active simultaneously—one in your notebook computer and one in its docking station. For example, because your notebook already has a built-in graphics card, you would not add one to a docking station.

Figure 17-5: Notebook PCs tend not to provide internal expansion slots. Notebook owners have to settle for an external PCMCIA slot and an array of ports. Click the PlayIt! button to take a tour of the connections available for expanding a typical notebook PC.

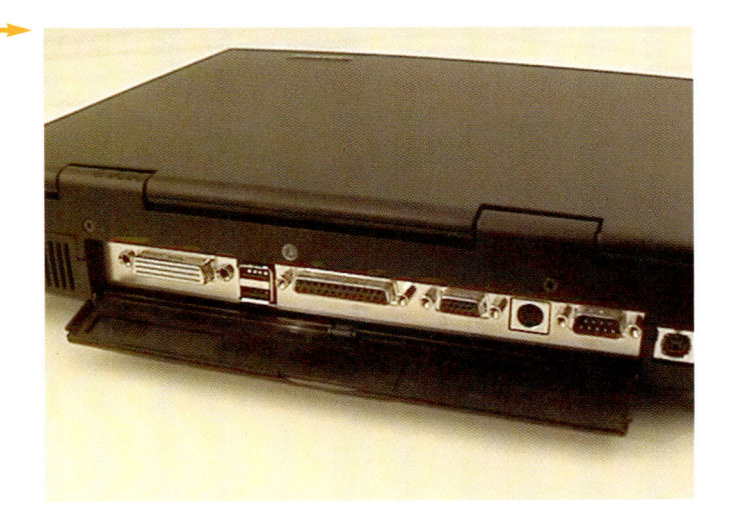

Chapter 17: Upgrading and Expanding Your PC

■Hardware
Expansion devices, ports, cards, and slots

The input, output, and storage devices that you connect to your computer are sometimes referred to as **peripheral devices**. Your PC provides a variety of ways to connect these devices. Internal devices tend to use one set of connections, and external devices tend to use others.

An **internal device**, such as an internal hard drive or modem, is housed inside your PC's system unit and taps into its power supply, if necessary. An **external device**, such as a scanner or printer, is housed in its own case, sits outside of your PC's system unit, and often comes with its own power supply. Some devices, such as printers, scanners, keyboards, monitors, and mice, are available only in external models. However, modems and most storage devices are available in both external and internal models.

Most PC owners prefer internal devices, which are usually less expensive than their external counterparts, require less desk space, and don't contribute to cable clutter. Unfortunately, your PC has room for only a limited number of internal devices. At some point in your expansion plans, you might be glad that an external version of the device is available.

Figure 17-6: Whether you prefer an internal or external device, don't purchase it until you're certain that your PC provides a connection for the device. Today's PCs typically provide the connectors shown in the photo.

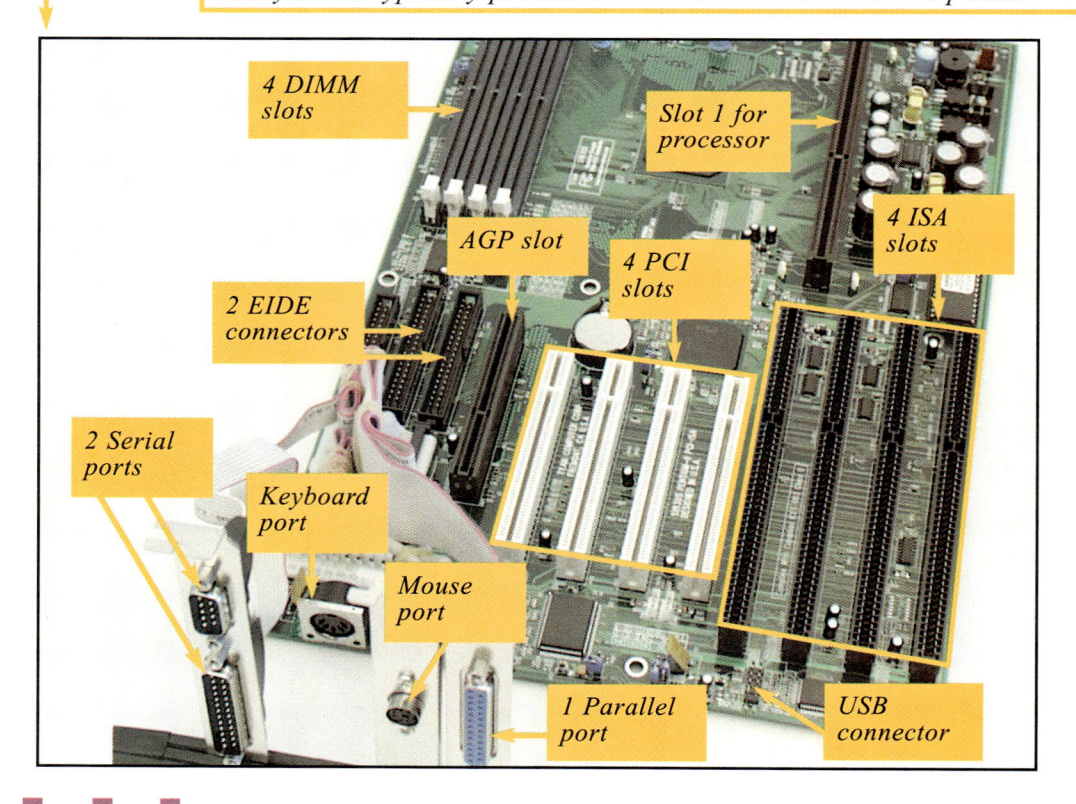

- 4 DIMM slots
- Slot 1 for processor
- 4 ISA slots
- AGP slot
- 4 PCI slots
- 2 EIDE connectors
- 2 Serial ports
- Keyboard port
- Mouse port
- 1 Parallel port
- USB connector

Hardware continued

Which connectors shown in Figure 17-6 would you use for an external device? External devices connect to one of the ports on your PC. As you know, a port is a connection point into which you plug a cable. Your PC comes with a diverse array of ports, most of which appear at the back of the system unit. Some ports, such as the keyboard, mouse, and video ports, are designed for specific devices. Other ports, such as the serial, parallel, USB, SCSI, MIDI, and FireWire (IEEE 1394) ports, can be used as connection points for a variety of input, output, and storage devices. Before you purchase an external device, check the box to find out what type of port it has and make sure that your PC has a corresponding unused port. Technically, some ports can handle multiple devices. For example, a single USB port is designed to accommodate up to 128 devices at the same time. In practice, however, you'll find it simplest to use one port for each peripheral device.

Suppose that you want to add a scanner, which requires a SCSI port. Your PC, however, does not provide a SCSI port. You can purchase an expansion card containing one or more ports, which protrude from the back of the system unit once the card has been installed. You can, for example, add a SCSI port to your PC by purchasing and installing a SCSI expansion card. When purchasing an expansion card, you must make sure that it is the correct type for the slot that you plan to use. Today's PCs typically include AGP, ISA, and PCI slots, which differ in speed and physical size. If, for example, you purchase a SCSI expansion card that is designed for a PCI slot, you cannot use it in the ISA or AGP slots.

External devices connect to ports, but what about internal devices? Your PC's motherboard provides a special set of EIDE connectors for internal storage devices, such as disk, tape, and CD-ROM drives. Adding other internal devices would usually require an expansion card. For example, an internal modem is housed on an ISA or PCI expansion card. Before you purchase an internal device, make sure that your PC is equipped with an unused connector or slot of the appropriate type.

After you've selected a peripheral device, adding it to your PC is usually a straightforward process. First, you connect the device to your PC. The Windows **plug and play** software should then automatically recognize the new device and walk you through the process of installing the software device drivers. If you run into trouble during the installation process, you might need to call the manufacturer for technical support.

Some devices are **hot pluggable**, which means that you can plug them in and unplug them while your computer is turned on. Usually, you can hot plug PCMCIA, USB, and FireWire devices, but never attempt to hot plug a device that requires you to open your PC's system unit case. When in doubt, check the manufacturer's documentation.

Hardware continued

Follow these tips to successfully add a peripheral device:

- Before you purchase a device, make sure that you can connect it to your PC.
- Read the manufacturer's instructions before installing any hardware device.
- Always turn your PC off and unplug it before opening the system unit case to add or replace components.
- Check the manufacturer's documentation before attempting to hot plug PCMCIA, USB, or FireWire devices.
- As you disassemble your PC, sketch quick diagrams to help you remember where each cable and card belongs.
- You might have to reboot your PC before it recognizes a new device.

Figure 17-7: Use this handy chart to find out what kind of devices you can connect to the ports and slots in your PC.

Port, Slot, or Connector	Maximum Speed	Types of Devices	Hot Pluggable
Serial	56 K bits/second	Mouse, keyboard, modem, graphics tablet	N
Parallel	1,200 K bits/second	Printer	N
Enhanced Parallel, "EPP," "IEEE 1284"	12,000 K bits/second	Printer, external Zip drive, external tape drive, external CD-ROM drive, digital camera	N
USB (universal serial bus)	12,000 K bits/second	Scanner, monitor, digital camera, joystick, speakers, modem, keyboard, mouse	Y
IEEE 1394, "FireWire"	400,000 K bits/second	Video camera, DVD player	Y
SCSI (small computer system interface)	80 MB/second (Ultra2 SCSI)	Scanner, hard drive, external Zip drive, external tape drive, external CD-ROM drive	N
AGP (accelerated graphics port)	1 GB/second	Graphics card	N
PCI (peripheral component interconnect)	133 MB/second	Internal tape drive, internal hard drive, internal CD-ROM drive, network card, video capture card	N
ISA (industry standard architecture)	16.6 MB/second	Same as PCI	N
PCMCIA (Personal Computer Memory Card International Association)	132,000 K bits/second	Hard drive, modem, network card, CD-ROM drive, Zip drive, memory, digital camera, SCSI card, video capture card	Y
EIDE (enhanced IDE), "Fast IDE," "Fast ATA," "Ultra ATA"	33 MB/second (Ultra ATA)	Internal tape drive, internal hard drive, internal CD-ROM drive	N

Tutorial
How to get technical support

When plug and play works and a hardware installation goes smoothly, upgrading your PC is the proverbial "piece of cake." Unfortunately, you might encounter problems while attempting to install a new peripheral device. Where can you turn for technical support?

Most hardware manufacturers offer technical support via telephone, fax, or the Web. To get the help you need, however, you'll need to have a clear idea of the problem and be able to explain it intelligently. "It doesn't work" is hardly an explanation that will lead to an effective solution. In this tutorial, you will learn how to deal with technical support resources to solve hardware installation problems.

When you have completed the tutorial, you should be able to:
- Determine whether the source of a problem is hardware or software.
- Gather the information that you need to explain the problem.
- Determine the best way to access technical support.
- Find the solution to the problem.

Figure 17-8: When you've tried to solve a problem, but the solution eludes you, it's time to seek technical support. Click the PlayIt! button to begin the technical support tutorial. Estimated time: 15–20 minutes. Tracking Disk points: 10.

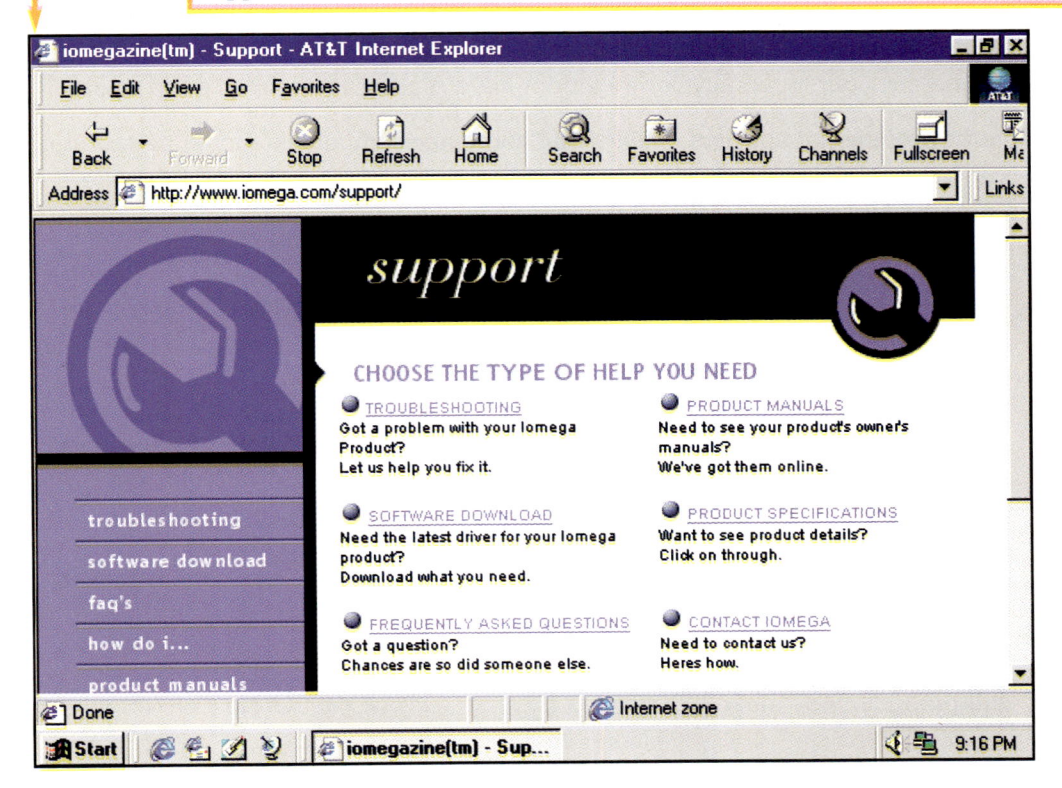

■Issue
Upgrade, reuse, recycle, or landfill?

Worldwide, an estimated 150 million computers will be discarded by the year 2000. In the United States alone, more than 12 million computers are thrown into landfills annually. So far, it is estimated that U.S. landfills contain more than two million tons of computer and electronic parts. Computers contain toxic materials such as lead, phosphorus, and mercury, which can contaminate groundwater if not disposed of properly. Many computers end up in landfills because their owners were unaware of the potential environmental hazards. Unfortunately, even well-meaning PC owners may find that landfill is the only option for their old computer.

When you decide that upgrades are no longer cost-effective, you'd think it would be easy to find a deserving home for your old PC. School administrators constantly lament the scarcity of funds for classroom computers. Also, advocates for economically disadvantaged families continue to publicize the gap between the computer haves and have-nots. However, many schools don't really want old PCs. And although some innovative programs, such as San Francisco's computers-for-guns exchange, have found homes for old computers among the economically disadvantaged, such programs exist in only a small number of communities.

If you can't find anyone to reuse your old PC, you might be able to recycle its components. About 30% of a computer is steel, 50% is plastic, 10% is aluminum, and the remaining 10% is composed of circuit boards and miscellaneous wire. Computers even contain a small amount of gold—a valuable commodity. Unfortunately, your local recycler might not have a program for electronic waste.

Some environmental activists believe that computer companies should be required to promote public awareness about computer reuse and recycling, and provide free recycling for all computers they manufacture. A few computer manufacturers do provide recycling services, but these services are not well publicized.

What do you think?

1. If you did not have a computer, would you accept any free computer as long as it ran some basic software?   ◯ Yes ◯ No ◯ Not sure

2. Do you think that your current school or business would accept a donation of 100 five-year-old computers?   ◯ Yes ◯ No ◯ Not sure

3. Do you believe that computer companies should take more responsibility for recycling the products they make?   ◯ Yes ◯ No ◯ Not sure

Save It!

Chapter 17: Expanding and Upgrading Your PC

QuickCheck A

1. True or false? Upgrading your PC's microprocessor is the most cost-effective way to increase overall performance. ☐

2. Whenever your PC is on, RAM holds parts of the ☐, software program modules, and data for open files.

3. To increase hard drive capacity, should the typical PC owner (a) replace an old hard drive with a larger one or (b) add a second hard drive? ☐

4. AGP, PCI, and ISA refer to ☐ into which you can insert expansion cards.

5. External devices usually connect to a(n) ☐ on the back of your PC.

Check It!

QuickCheck B

Indicate the letter of the component that correctly matches each of the following descriptions:

1. SIMM slot ☐
2. PCI slot ☐
3. ISA slot ☐
4. Port ☐
5. EIDE hard drive connector ☐

Check It!

Get It?

While using the Book-on-CD, click the Get It? button to see if you can answer ten randomly selected questions from Chapter 17.

Get It?

Chapter 18
Buying a PC

What's Inside?

Whether you're purchasing your first computer or buying a replacement, Chapter 18 provides a generous collection of practical tips to help you select a dependable computer from a reliable merchant at a reasonable price. You'll learn a simple, but effective shopping strategy that's tailored to today's computer marketplace.

- FAQs:

So many options—where do I begin?	207
Where can I find prices and specifications?	208
How much computing power do I need?	209
Where can I find the best deal?	210
Is it O.K. to "mail order" a PC?	211

- Hardware: Accessories and add-ons 212
- Tutorial: How to buy a computer online 215
- Issue: The ethics of e-shopping 216
- QuickChecks 217

What's on the CD?

Getting a "good deal" on a computer system requires a little bit of research and comparative shopping. Don't be afraid to ask questions as you shop. The video in Chapter 18 provides tips on how to order a computer by phone. In the tutorial for this chapter, you'll also learn how to navigate the Web to expertly compare prices and place orders.

- Eavesdrop on an experienced shopper ordering a computer by phone 211
- Take a step-by-step tutorial on buying computers online 215
- Quiz yourself with interactive QuickChecks and Get It? questions 217

■FAQ So many options—where do I begin?

The thought of buying a computer might make you a bit apprehensive. A computer costs a lot of money, and you want to make sure that you get a "good deal." However, finding that good deal seems to require a certain level of technical know-how. What if you make a mistake because you don't understand the specifications in a computer ad? Could you be ripped off by a salesperson who convinces you to buy something that you don't really need?

A "good deal" on a computer means that you pay a reasonable price to a reliable merchant for a dependable computer. You don't need to find the absolute lowest price. Spending days to track down a savings of $20 wastes time that you could more profitably spend at your new computer. Follow these steps to replicate the successful shopping strategy of experienced computer buyers:

- ■ Choose a platform.
- ■ Decide whether you want a notebook or desktop computer.
- ■ Browse through computer magazines, computer catalogs, and Web sites to get an idea of current prices and features.
- ■ Make your final selection by comparing prices, features, availability of technical support, and warranty coverage.
- ■ Buy it!

Your first step is to choose a platform. A **computer platform** is simply a category or "family" of computers. Two platforms currently compete for consumer dollars: the PC platform and the Mac platform. The PC platform includes any computers that run Microsoft Windows and contain an x86 microprocessor, such as the Intel Pentium III. More than 95% of computer buyers select the PC platform, the most popular option. The Mac platform includes all of the Macintosh computer models manufactured by Apple Computer. Much of the extensive selection of hardware and software that's designed for the PC platform is not compatible with the Mac platform. As a result, most experts recommend that you choose the PC platform unless Macintosh computers are the standard in your school or workplace.

After selecting a platform, you should decide whether you would like a desktop or notebook computer. Obviously, if you need to carry around a computer, you should select a notebook. But would it be reasonable to purchase a notebook PC even if it was destined to spend most of its life on your desk? The answer to this question is different than it was a few years ago, when notebook PCs had barely readable screens, limited storage capacity, and no CD-ROM drive.

The features of today's notebook PCs essentially match those of a desktop PC. In addition, a notebook PC is housed in a compact case that you can easily tote around—for example, when you move back home at the end of a semester or if you need to temporarily convert your home office into a guest bedroom. You pay a premium for this mobility, however. A notebook PC can be more than twice as expensive as a desktop PC with equivalent specifications. If you're on a tight budget and don't really require computing mobility, then go for a desktop PC.

Chapter 18: Buying a PC

■FAQ Where can I find prices and specifications?

Assuming that you've decided on the PC platform and whether you want a notebook or a desktop computer, your next step is browsing to get an idea of current prices and specifications. Contrary to what you might expect, in this shopping phase, you're not yet looking for the computer you want to purchase. Instead, you are trying to get a handle on the current market by identifying PC specifications in three price ranges: under U.S.$1,000, U.S.$1,000–$2,000, and over U.S.$2,000. Finding these specifications can be quite an interesting project.

As you look at computer ads, pay particular attention to the (1) microprocessor manufacturer and model, (2) microprocessor speed, (3) RAM capacity, (4) hard disk capacity, (5) monitor size, and (6) price. After looking at several ads, a pattern will emerge; specifications in each price range tend to be similar. You can create your own price-range table like the one in Figure 18-1 and fill it in with the results of your research. You should be aware, however, that such a table will remain valid for only a few months, because computer prices and features are constantly changing.

You'll find that the specifications are similar in each price range, regardless of the merchant. Once you recognize these specifications, you can be assured of getting a reasonable deal. Be wary of any computer that doesn't meet the specifications for the price range—it is probably overpriced. Also, be careful of a computer that has far better specifications than you would expect for that price range. A super-low-cost computer might be reconditioned, used, or a floor model—not necessarily a bad deal, if the computer works and can be serviced.

To find information on current prices and specifications, you can look at the ads in computer magazines and in computer catalogs. Many shoppers turn first to *Computer Shopper*. Each monthly issue of this magazine contains hundreds of ads, and reviews of computers and peripheral devices. Popular computer catalogs include those published by MicroWarehouse and PC Connection. Otherwise, you can request a catalog by phone or at the catalog company's Web site. You can also check pricing at Web stores, such as Computer Discount Warehouse (www.cdw.com).

Figure 18-1: As you browse through computer magazines, catalogs, and Web sites, consider creating a table like the one below and filling it in with current information on the average specifications for each price range.

Specification	Under $1,000	$1,000–$2,000	Above $2,000
Processor manufacturer/model	AMD K6-2, AMD Duron, Intel Celeron, Intel Pentium II	AMD Duron, AMD Athlon, Intel Pentium II/III	AMD Athlon, Intel Pentium III
Processor speed	550 MHz	600–850 MHz	600 MHz–1 GHz
RAM capacity	32–64 MB	64–128 MB	64–256 MB
Hard disk capacity	8–18 GB	10–30 GB	20–60 GB
Monitor size	15"	17"	19"

■FAQ How much computing power do I need?

After you have completed your price-range research, it is time to decide how much computer power you need and can afford. Starting at the top, a PC priced higher than U.S.$2,000 is the computer equivalent of a luxury automobile. A computer in this price range contains state-of-the-art components: the latest, greatest Intel microprocessor, the newest, fastest graphics card, the coolest sound system, and the fastest modem on the market. You can also expect a generous amount of RAM and a copious amount of disk storage space. A top-of-the-line PC runs the newest versions of the operating system and application software with ease, and typically works with older versions as well. Because such a computer contains state-of-the-art components, you're not likely to replace it as quickly as a less expensive computer.

Figure 18-2: Once you decide on a price range, you can use this checklist to compare specific brands and models.

| Manufacturer: |
| Model: |
| Price: |
| Processor model: |
| Processor speed: |
| Cache: |
| RAM capacity: |
| RAM type: |
| Hard drive capacity: |
| CD-ROM drive speed: |
| DVD drive included? |
| Zip drive included? |
| Modem speed: |
| Sound card type: |
| Speaker description: |
| Graphics card type: |
| Graphics card RAM: |
| Monitor type (LCD, CRT): |
| Monitor size & dot pitch: |
| Type of pointing device: |
| USB port included? |
| IEEE 1394 port included? |
| Operating system: |
| Bundled software (list): |
| Warranty coverage: |
| Technical support quality: |

Computers that retail for between U.S.$1,000 and U.S.$2,000 might be considered the "four-door sedans" of the computer marketplace, because the majority of buyers select a PC in this price range. These popular PCs lack the flashy specifications of their state-of-the-art cousins, but provide ample computing power to run current versions of the operating system and application software.

In the computer industry, the equivalent of a compact car is a sub-$1,000 PC. The technology in these computers is usually a few years old and you can expect reduced processor speed, memory capacity, and drive capacity. Nevertheless, these budget PCs are equivalent to state-of-the-art PCs with which people were perfectly happy just a few years ago. Barring any drastic change in the operating system or application software, you can expect current software to perform adequately on a sub-$1,000 PC. You might, however, need to replace a budget PC sooner than a more expensive PC.

If you're on a budget, you'd consider buying a used car. Should you also consider a used computer? The answer is yes, if the specifications for the used computer at least match those you've listed for sub-$1,000 PCs in your price-range table. You should be able to negotiate a price that is approximately half of what you would pay for a new computer with similar specifications. You are not likely to get a warranty with a used PC, so make sure that it works before you buy it.

■FAQ Where can I find the best deal?

You can purchase a PC from a computer superstore, mass-market merchant, computer reseller, manufacturer, or computer catalog. By understanding the advantages and disadvantages associated with each of these shopping outlets, you can better evaluate the "deals" that they offer.

When shopping for a computer in a conventional store, you can "kick the tires" by comparing the speed and response of PCs with different microprocessors, trying out keyboards and pointing devices, and examining the image quality of different monitors. Computers are sold in a variety of stores, including huge computer superstores such as CompUSA, where you'll see a staggering array of products at great prices. The sales staff is trained to help you select a computer to meet your needs and budget, but you might have to pay for after-purchase technical support.

If you don't live close to a computer superstore, check your local office superstores, such as Staples and Office Max, as well as mass-market stores, such as Wal-Mart, K-Mart, Circuit City, and Sears. These stores typically provide a smaller selection and have slightly higher prices than a computer superstore. The sales staff might have very little computer background, so you're on your own as far as your selection goes. These stores rarely offer after-purchase technical support, instead directing you to the computer manufacturer's toll-free support line.

Most cities and even small towns have computer stores run by **independent computer resellers** who specialize in selling computers and providing consulting services to individuals and small businesses. When you make a purchase from an independent reseller, you're likely to pay a premium price for a brand-name computer, such as Dell, IBM, Gateway, Hewlett-Packard, or Compaq. You might also have to wait for delivery if the model you've selected is not in stock. Independent resellers also assemble **generic PCs** using standard computer circuit boards, cases, and storage devices—often the same parts as those used by computer manufacturers to build brand-name computers. A generic PC may offer a cost-effective alternative to a brand-name PC.

Some computer manufacturers sell computers directly to customers. With this **manufacturer direct sales** option, you can place your order over the phone or at a Web site. Most manufacturers offer a range of models. You can purchase one of these models in the standard configuration, or you can have it customized with more RAM, a faster processor, a better graphics card, and so on. When you buy direct from a reputable manufacturer, you can expect good pricing and the flexibility of having a computer made to order. One disadvantage of buying direct is that you can't typically try the computer before you buy it. Also, local technical support might not be available. Instead, you must contact the manufacturer's technical support center by phone or access its Web site. Companies that provide direct sales include Dell, Gateway, IBM, Compaq, and Micron.

Computer catalogs, such as MicroWarehouse, PC Connection, and MidWest Micro, offer another shopping option that allows you to place your order by phone or on a Web site. Prices are often competitive with manufacturer direct sales, and you can choose from a variety of brands and models.

■FAQ Is it O.K. to "mail order" a PC?

"Mail order" is one of the most popular ways of buying a computer—you either phone in an order or place it at a Web site. Your new computer arrives "by mail," which usually means by a courier service such as FedEx, UPS, or Airborne Express. The main caution about mail order is to buy from a reputable dealer. When in doubt, check with the Better Business Bureau (www.bbb.org).

If you're ordering a computer by phone, a salesperson will answer your questions about equipment or warranties, take your order, and provide details about current pricing. Make sure that you obtain the following information related to your order: the salesperson's name, order number, expected ship date, total price (including shipping), and who to contact if you have questions or problems with the order.

When ordering on the Web, you'll typically follow prompts on the screen to select a computer, choose custom options, enter your shipping address, and provide your credit-card billing information. You'll receive confirmation of your order by e-mail or regular mail. Review the order confirmation to make sure that it includes all of the items that you ordered, the correct price, and the right shipping address. Hang on to your order confirmation—it contains your order number and information on how to keep track of your order.

Whether you've placed an order by phone or on the Web, your new computer won't fit in your mailbox, so you must make arrangements for someone to be home when your shipment arrives. Otherwise, you can arrange to pick up your packages at the courier's office. Be aware that shipments are occasionally delayed or lost. If your computer does not arrive when promised, immediately contact your vendor to initiate a search for your packages.

No matter where you buy your computer, you should receive a purchase receipt. Keep it handy in case you need it as proof of purchase date for warranty claims. Most computers come with a one-year parts and labor warranty. Read the warranty carefully, so that you understand what it covers and exactly which repair services it provides. Many merchants also offer extended warranties—some lasting as long as five years. Depending on the price and coverage, an extended warranty can be an excellent deal.

Figure 18-3: When you order a computer by phone, make sure that you get the information necessary to track your order. Click the PlayIt! button to eavesdrop on an experienced shopper who is ordering a computer by phone.

Hardware Accessories and add-ons

In some ways, ordering a computer is similar to ordering a hamburger at a fast-food restaurant. You can purchase a standard sandwich, or you can customize it a bit by adding extra pickles or holding the onions. A computer ad or catalog description typically lists the important specifications for standard PC systems. In many cases, these standard systems can be customized with accessories or other add-ons—for a price, of course.

Notebook PC accessories include extra batteries, an A/C adapter for using an electrical wall outlet, a D/C adapter for in-car use, an external battery charger, and a docking station. Because many of these accessories are designed specifically for a particular notebook PC model, you should purchase any accessories you are likely to need at the same time that you buy your notebook PC. After a year or two, as models change, these accessories might no longer be available.

You can often customize your notebook PC with add-ons, such as extra RAM or a larger hard disk. If you include these add-ons when you make your purchase, they will be installed and tested by a trained technician. Usually, the price of an add-on includes installation charges.

Figure 18-4: Many notebook ads include pricing for add-ons and accessories, as well as specifications and pricing for the standard system. If your budget allows, buy all accessories and add-ons at the time of your initial purchase.

For serious work—and serious play!
These powerful notebooks arrive multimedia-ready. You can further enhance your system with additional memory, extra batteries, network adapter, modem, and internal Zip drive.

- Powerful processor
- Brilliant LCD display
- Huge hard disk capacity
- 24X CD-ROM or DVD drive
- Built-in sound card, speakers, and mic
- Built-in v.90 56 Kbps modem
- Windows Millennium
- Manufacturer's one-year warranty

VStar 1800 Series Notebook Computers

Model	Processor	HDD	RAM/MAX	Display	CD-ROM	Price
1801	500MHz Celeron	6GB	32/128	12.1"	24X	$1499
1811	600MHz Pentium III	10GB	64/128	13.3" XGA	DVD	$1999
1821	750MHz Pentium III	20GB	128/256	14.2" XGA	DVD	$2799

Accessories!

Item	Description	Price
OP3217	64 MB SDRAM	$199
OP1487	Lithium-Ion Battery	$129
OP1573	3-Year Extended Warranty	$189
OP1473	Internal Zip Drive	$299
OP1117	56K V.90 PCMCIA Modem	$179
OP2137	10/100 10Base-T PCMCIA NIC	$109
OP2142	10Base-T/V.90 Modem PCMCIA	$299

■Hardware continued

Unlike notebook PC ads, the ads for desktop computers tend not to offer options for accessories. They do, however, provide options for add-ons, such as a faster processor, additional memory, a larger hard disk, a Zip disk drive, a tape drive, network interface card, or a larger monitor. The price of a desktop PC can change dramatically, depending on the options that you select. Before you settle on a system with lots of custom add-ons, check other models in the product line to make sure that an equivalent "standard system" is not offered at a lower price.

Most merchants offer add-ons at very reasonable prices—especially considering that the price includes installation. A trained technician will install any extra equipment that you select, load the required software drivers, and verify that everything works. Even computer experts take advantage of these installation services because they know from experience that some hardware devices are "tricky" to install. For example, some DVD drives don't work with certain sound cards. Your computer merchant should know which devices pose compatibility problems and can save you the headache of trying to install an incompatible device.

Figure 18-5: A desktop computer ad might look daunting, but just think of it as the menu from your favorite burger joint. Select a standard system first, then decide which add-ons you might like.

The Family PC–Z350
$1229

- Intel Pentium III 800 MHz
- 128 MB SDRAM
- 20 GB Ultra ATA-66 Hard Drive
- 3.5" Floppy Disk Drive
- DVD-ROM Drive
- 8 MB 3-D AGP Graphics Card
- .28 Dot Pitch 17" Monitor
- SoundBlaster AudioPCI 64V
- Altec Lansing ACS5 Speakers
- 3Com U.S. Robotics V.90 Modem
- Keyboard and Mouse
- Microsoft Windows ME
- One-year Parts and Labor Warranty with On-site Service*

Call 1.800.555.1212

*Warranty terms and conditions available on request. On-site service is administered by PCTS and is not available outside the continental U.S. All pricing and specification subject to change without notice or obligation.

Add-Ons:
Intel Pentium III 850 MHz $150
Intel Pentium III 933 MHz $300
Iomega Zip Drive $99
Aiwa Travan Tape Drive $219

Ask for pricing on our digital photo and small business add-on packages!

Hardware continued

The merchant that sells you a computer would like to supply you with as much additional gear as you can afford. Obviously, the merchant's primary motivation is maximizing profit, but another reason exists as well—the merchant wants you to be happy with your purchase. Merchants have discovered that customers are happiest with their PCs when they can use them for fun, interesting, educational, and productive projects. Eliminating the hassle of installing hardware add-on devices and software is truly a useful service to customers.

A new trend in add-on marketing is task-related packages. For example, a digital photo package might include a digital camera for taking pictures, photo-editing software for touching up your photos, a color printer for making photo prints, and a CD-RW drive for archiving digital photo files. A deluxe game package might include a super-fast graphics card, a force-feedback joystick, and a selection of popular game software. These add-on packages can be great deals if they include equipment and software for the kinds of computer projects you want to undertake.

What about software? The software that's supplied with your PC is called **bundled software**. PCs typically come with the current version of Microsoft Windows pre-installed. Many merchants also offer a bundle of basic productivity software, including word processing, spreadsheet, money management, desktop publishing, game, and encyclopedia software. Computers with bundled software are inevitably priced a bit higher than those without comparable packages, but the additional cost is far less than what you would pay to purchase each application separately. Unless you already own software that you're planning to legally remove from an old computer, you'll save money if you buy a PC that includes bundled software. Look carefully, however, at the software titles that are included in the bundle to make sure they coincide with the software packages that you would like to use.

Figure 18-6: As a prospective computer buyer, you should be aware that the prices in some desktop computer ads do not include a monitor. The picture in the ad might show a monitor, but the fine print says "monitor not included." If the specifications do not list a monitor, assume that one is not included.

BEST.COM

$999*

This is the computer you've been waiting for!

- AMD Duron 600 MHz
- 64 MB SDRAM
- 12 GB hard drive
- 3.5" floppy disk drive
- Sound card, speakers, mic
- Graphics card w/16 MB RAM
- Keyboard and mouse
- Windows ME
- One-year warranty

Call 24 hours a day 7 days a week 800-555-1212 or visit best.com on the Web

*monitor not included

■Tutorial
How to buy a computer online

You can use the Web to access online versions of computer manufacturers' sales outlets, computer superstores, and mass-market merchants. At these Web sites, you can shop at your leisure and without pressure from a salesperson. You can browse through the descriptions and review the prices for standard PC packages. At some sites, you can create customized computer systems, without committing to a purchase until you submit your credit-card billing information.

The Web provides another shopping option. At "price quote" sites, you can enter the brand and model of the PC you'd like to purchase. After a brief search, you'll see a list comparing prices at different online stores. Just be aware that some price quote sites search only those merchants that have paid to participate.

When you have completed the tutorial, you should be able to:
- Purchase a standard computer package from a manufacturer's Web site.
- Select custom options for a standard computer package.
- Purchase a computer from an online store.
- Use a price quote Web site to compare prices for a computer system.

Figure 18-7: Click the PlayIt! button to begin the tutorial and learn how to shop for a PC online. You'll check manufacturers' sites and visit a price quote site. Estimated time: 15–20 minutes. Tracking Disk points: 10.

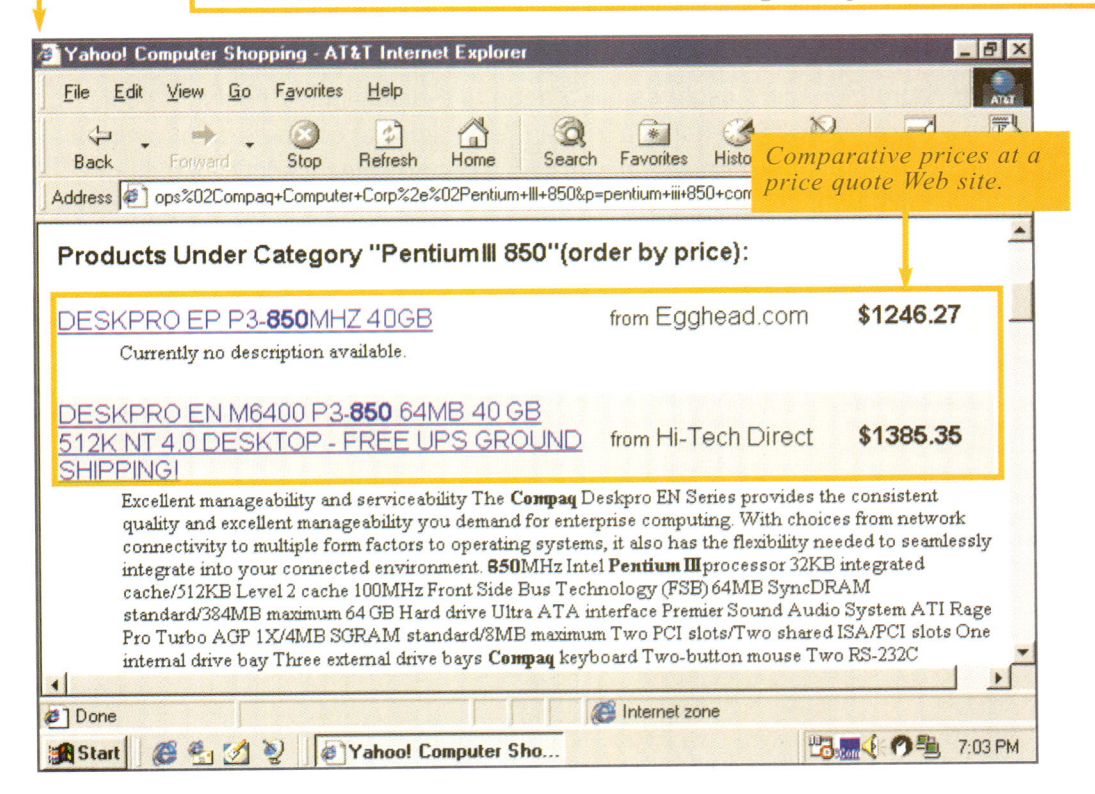

Comparative prices at a price quote Web site.

■Issue
The ethics of e-shopping

The Internet appears to be a catalyst that is changing the way that millions of people shop. **E-commerce** allows you to shop "electronically" from manufacturers' Web sites and Web-based catalogs. In addition to computers, e-commerce sites sell almost everything, including food and clothing. Currently, e-commerce offers advantages to both vendor and customer. A vendor isn't required to pay overhead for a retail store, one Web site serves customers from all over the world, and inventory can be stored in a single location. A customer can go "e-shopping" from home in comfort and privacy, choose from a broad selection of merchandise, and easily compare prices.

The potential of e-commerce is staggering, but some forms of it make many merchants cringe. A hand-held e-commerce device that's currently on the drawing board provides shoppers with remote access to price quote sites. You could easily carry this device with you on a trip to the mall. Suppose that you wander into a bookstore, thumb through a few cookbooks, and discover that you simply can't live without *The Encyclopedia of Tex-Mex Cuisine*, priced at $49.95. Whipping out your handy e-commerce device and connecting instantly to a price quote site, you see that Amazon.com offers the same book for $32.50. In the e-shopping world of the future, you might then march up to the cash register and say, "I can get this book from Amazon.com for $32.50. Are you willing to sell it to me for that price?"

The bookstore manager will probably tell you (and the next 100 people who try the same strategy) to forget it. After enough potential customers walk out the door, however, store managers might sense a need to reassess their pricing models. But can any pricing model enable a walk-in retail store to compete with a "virtual" e-commerce operation that pays no rent and hires no sales clerks? Also, some merchants might question the ethics of shoppers who enter a retail store, browse through its merchandise, then demand the same price offered by a Web merchant that does not provide any retail store at all.

What do you think?

1. Has e-commerce changed your shopping habits? ○ Yes ○ No ○ Not sure

2. Can you think of any types of merchandise that you would not order from an e-commerce site? ○ Yes ○ No ○ Not sure

3. Would you consider it unethical to examine a product in a retail store, if you know that you intend to order it from the Web? ○ Yes ○ No ○ Not sure

Save It!

Chapter 18: Buying a PC   217

QuickCheck A

1. One of the first steps in selecting a computer is to choose between the PC and Mac _____.

2. True or false? To prepare yourself to evaluate the "deals" offered by computer merchants, you can create a table of current specifications in three price ranges. _____

3. True or false? Experts advise you to avoid purchasing a used computer, no matter how good a deal it appears to be. _____

4. A(n) _____ PC, uses standard computer circuit boards, cases, and storage devices, but does not carry a brand name.

5. For warranty service, you'll need a copy of your _____ as proof of purchase date.

[Check It!]

QuickCheck B

Fill in the blanks to complete this computer ad:

- _____ Pentium III 850 MHz Processor
- 128 _____ SDRAM
- 30 GB Ultra-ATA _____
- 3.5" Floppy Disk Drive
- DVD-ROM Drive
- 16 MB 3-D AGP _____ Card
- .28 Dot _____ 15" Monitor (13.9" vis)
- SoundBlaster AudioPCI 64V
- Stereo Speakers
- 3Com U.S. Robotics 56 Kbps Modem
- Keyboard and Mouse
- Microsoft Windows ME
- One-Year Parts and Labor Warranty

New! **Val-U-Point Model P450-64**

Call Today!

[Check It!]

Get It? While using the Book-on-CD, click the Get It? button to see if you can answer ten randomly selected questions from Chapter 18.

[Get It?]

Index

AC adapter, 9
Accelerated graphics card, 195
Access hatch cover, 44
Access time, 56
Accessories and add-ons, 212-214
Accessories menu, 78
Add Printer wizard, 119
Add/Remove Programs icon, 34, 55
Address book for e-mail 107, *107*
Adobe Acrobat Reader, 28, 35
 default file extension of, 41
Adobe Illustrator, 150
Adobe PageMaker, 114
Adobe PhotoDeluxe, 155
Adobe Photoshop, 148, 152
Adobe Premiere, 173
AGP (accelerated graphics port), 198, 201, 202
Airborne Express, 211
Alta Vista, 90
Altec Lansing, 165
Amazon.com, 136
AMD microprocessors, 188, 195
 K6 processor, *188*
America Online (AOL), 75, 77
Americorps*VISTA organization, 12
Amplitude of sound waves, 160
Analog signals, 80
Animated GIF, 175
Animation, creating and playing, 175
ANSI codes, 186
Antivirus software, 66
Apple Macintosh computers, 188, 207
Application program, 16
Application software, 3
Application window, *17*
Archive, 67
Arguments, in spreadsheet software, 125
ASCII codes, 46, 186
 table of, *186*
Atanasoff, John, 192
AT&T Worldnet, 75, 77
Athlon, 188, 190, 195
ATM LAN technology, 104
Attachments, 98-109
Audio CDs, 140, 165
AUDIO sound format, 160
AutoDesk Animator, 175
Autodesk AutoCAD, 150

Backup, frequency of, 70
Backup systems, 67
Bad sector, 64
Bandwidth, definition of, 79
Benchmark test, 190

Bernstein v. *Dept. of State,* 48
Better Business Bureau, 211
Binary coding, 186
Bit, definition of, 81, 185
Bitmap graphics
 compared with vector graphics, 147
 illustration of, 148
 using, 148
BMP format, 101, 102, 148, 149
Bogart, Humphrey, 180
Boot process, definition of, 4
Bose, 165
Browser, 89
Browsing the Web, 86-97
Bugs, 7
Bundled software, 214
Byte, definition of, 45, 185

Cable modems, 92
Cable TV access to the Internet, 93, *93*
Cache memory, 189
CAD software, 151
Cakewalk Pro Audio, 162
CalComp Creation Station, 152
Caligari TrueSpace, 150
Canon, 117, 154
CDs, 140-142
 making, 143
CD-R (CD-recordable) technology, 140-141
CD ripper, 168
CD-ROMs, 140, 199
 drive speeds, chart of, *140*
CD-RW (CD-rewritable) technology, 140-142
Celeron microprocessor, 189, 195
Cell reference, 124
Cells, 123
Cellular phone modems, 92, 94
Censorship, 96
Chart wizard, 127
Check box, *18, 23*
Chip carrier, 184
Chip, definition of, 184
Cinepak compression, 174
Circuit board, 184
Circuit City, 210
CISC (complex instruction set computer) chip, 188
Claris Works, 136
Client computer, 75
Clip art images, 131, 147
Clock speed, 189
Close button, 17, *17*
CMYK color, 117
Coaxial cable, 105
Coca-Cola Company, 88

Coda Finale, 162
Color depth, 148
Color graphics, types of, 149
.com, 88
Commercial software
 definition of, 36
 license agreement of, 36
Communications menu, 78
Communications software, 77, 78
Compaq, 210
Compiling instructions, 187
Compression
 effect of on video quality, 174
 software for, 102
 technique for, 174
CompUSA, 210
Computer Discount Warehouse, 208
Computer Shopper, 208
Computer
 adding devices to, 198
 bugs in, 7
 buying a, 206-216
 buying by mail order, 211
 buying online, 215
 chart of ports and slots on, 202
 display devices for, 176-178
 finding the best deal on, 210
 and "haves" and "have-nots," 12
 improving performance by adding RAM, 196
 karaoke on, 166
 LCD projection panels for, 128
 LCD projector for, 129
 locating prices and specifications for, 208
 options for old models, 204
 options in buying, 207
 platform, 207, 297
 price-range table for, 208
 projection devices for, 128-130
 setting up, 11
 shopping strategy steps, 207
 starting, 4
 technical specifications for, 191
 turning off, 7
 upgrading and expanding, 194-205
 workings of, 182-193
Computer-aided design (CAD), 150
Computing power
 checklist for comparison, 209
 determining amount needed, 209
Connecting to the Internet, 74-85
Control Panel, 82
Controller chips, 185
Cookie, 89, 138, 144
Copy and paste, 54

Copy Disk feature, 54
Copying files to disks, 54
Copyright on the Web, 91
CorelDRAW, 150
Corel Paradox, 136
C++ programming language, 187
CPUmark32 benchmark test, 189
Creative Labs, 164
Credit cards, and the Internet, 84
CRT monitors, 176
  and electromagnetic radiation, 177
Cyrix microprocessors, 188, 195

Data
  coded for chips, 185
  definition of, 183
  files of, 39
  processing, 183
  representation of in CDs, 185
  representation of in circuits, 185
  storing, 183
  types of, 186
Databases
  accessing, 134-145
  on CDs, 139
  creating, 137
  creating with spreadsheet software, 138
  definition of, 135
  freeform, 135
  linking files in, *135*
  need for software, 136
  relational, 135
  structured, 135
  on the Web, 139, *139*
Data/fax modem, 81
Data/voice modem, 81
Date, Kyoko, 180
Default, definition of, 41
Default printer, 119
Defragmentation utility, 58, *58*
Deleted files, 60
Dell Computer Corporation, 210
Demo, definition of, 36
Desktop computer, 8
  desktop style of, 8, *8*
  tower style of, 8, *8*
  typical system, *3*
Desktop publishing (DTP)
  capabilities of software compared with WP software, 115
  definition of, 114
Desktop videos
  creating, 170-181
  compression affects quality, 174
Desktop vs. notebook computers, 207
Dial-up connection, 75
Dialog box, 18
Dialog box tab, *23*
Diamond Multimedia Systems, 164, 168
Diehl Graphsoft MiniCAD, 150
Digital video, editing, 173
Digital camera, 147, 154, *154*, 199
Digital cash, 84
Digital coding, 186
Digital photo, editing, 155
Digital signals, 80
Digitized sound, 159, 164
  recording, storing, and playing on PCs, 160
  working with, 167
Digitizing devices, 152-154
  digital camera, 154
  graphics tablet, 152
  scanner, 153
Dilbert, 76
DIMMs (dual in-line memory modules), 196, 198
Direct satellite service (DSS) to the Internet, 92, 93, *93*
Disaster recovery plan, 67
DiscMan, 168
Disconnect button, 78
Disk crash, 84
"Disk Full" message, 55
Disk space, running out of, 55
Display devices, 176-178
Display settings, changing, 179
Distribution CD, 32, 33, 39
Dithering, 149
DOC format, 101, 102
Docking station, 199
Document option, 39, *39*
Documentation, 31
Documents
  formatting with WP software, 112
  standard styles available in WP software, 113
  writing and printing, 110-121
Dot matrix printers, 116
  print heads of, *116*
Downloading, 35
  time for, 79
Dpi, 116
DRAM (dynamic RAM) chips, 196
Drawing software, 150
Drive bay, 197
DS4 CAD format, 150
DSL, 92
Duron, 188, 190, 195
DVD-2 drives, 141
DVDs (Digital Video Disk), 141-142, 171
DXF CAD format, 150

E-commerce activities, 84
E-mail, 76, 77, 78, 79, 99, 123
  and attachments, 98-109
  client software for, 99
  definition of attachment, 101
  junk mail, 103
  message, 99
  privacy of, 106
  sending and receiving messages, 100
  server for, 99, *99*, 104
  server software for, 99
  size limits for messages and attachments, 102
  smileys in, 103
  and spams, 103
  tips for using netiquette, 103
  using address book, 107, *107*
Eastman Kodak, 154
EBCDIC codes, 186
Eckert, J. Presper, 192
EDO (extended data output) chips, 196
.edu, 88
EIDE (enhanced integrated drive electronics), 197, 201, 202
Electromagnetic radiation and CRT monitors, 177
Electronic digital computer, inventor of, 192
Electronic Frontier Foundation, 48
Emoticons, 103
Encapsulated PostScript (EPS) format 150
Encryption software, 48
ENIAC computer, 192
Environmental sound, 165
Epson, 117
Error message, 31
Ethernet LAN technology, 104
Eudora, 99
Excite, 90
EXE file instructions, 187
EXE format, 101
.exe extension, 101
Executable file, 39
Expansion card, 198
Expansion devices, ports, cards, and slots, 200-202
Expansion slots, 198, *198*
Export routines, 42
Extended ASCII codes, 186
Extended instruction sets, 189
Extensions, Hide option of, 52
External device, 200
External modems, 80, *80*
External tape drive, *68*

Fax machines, 81
FDDI LAN technology, 104
FedEx, 211
Feedback device, 21
Field, in database, 135
File extension, definition of, 41
File formats, table of, 41
FileMaker Pro, 136
File menu, 17, 18
File server, 104
Files

changing names of, 52
converting format of, 42
copying to other disks, 54
creating and saving, 47
in database, 135
definition of, 39
finding, 59
finding a list of, 51
and folders, organizing, 50-61
length of name, 40
lost, 63
moving with cut and paste, 53
naming and saving, 38-49
organizing, 53
protecting, 62-73
saving frequently, 63
storing, 43
structure of, 137
Filtering software, 96
Filtering to extract data, 138
Find option, 29
Find program, 59, *59*
FireWire devices, 172, 202
FireWire (EEE 1394), 201, 202
Fixed disk, 57
Fixed length coding, 186
Flame wars, 103
Flash memory, 10, 154
Flatbed scanners, 153
FLC ("Flick") animation format, 175
Floating point benchmarks, 190
Floppy disk drive, definition of, 45
Floppy disks, 43, *44, 45,* 55
 access hatch cover of, 44
 as backup medium, 67
 definition of, 44
 and floppy disk drives, 43, 44-46
 storage capacity of, 45
 write-protect window of, 44
FM synthesis, 164
Folder Options, 52
Folders, 43, 53
Font, definition of, 112
Force-feedback joystick, 21, *21*
Formatting, of disks, 46
Formulas
 determining, 125
 in a worksheet, 124
Forrest Gump, 156
FPM (fast page mode) chips, 196
FPUmark benchmark test, 189
Fragmented disk, 58
Fragmented file, 58
Frames, 114
Freeform database, 135
Freeware, definition of, 36
Freeze up, overcoming, 7
Frequency of sound waves, 160
Frequency response, 164
Fuji, 69, 154
Full backup of files, 70

Functions in spreadsheet software, 125

Gates, Bill, 12
Gateway 2000 Inc., 210
Generic PCs, 210
Getting started, 2-13
Gibson, William, 180
GIF format, 102, 148, 149
Gigabytes (GB), definition of, 45
.gov, 88
Grab It! button, 35, *35*
Graffiti alphabet, 20
Grammar checker, 111
Graphical user interface, 20
Graphics
 kinds of, 147
 preparing for Web pages, 149
 saving, 91
 working with, 146-157
Graphics accelerator cards, 178
Graphics cards, 178, 198
 and memory requirements, *178*
Graphics links, 87
Graphics tablet, 152, *152*
Graphs
 creating, 127
 types of, 127

Handwriting-recognition software, 20
Hanks, Tom, 156
Hard disk, 68
 bad sector in, 64
 definition of, 56
 increasing capacity of, 197
Hard disk drives, 56-58, *56*
 ceasing working, 64
 definition of, 4
Hardware
 accessories and add-ons, 212-214
 alternative input devices, 20-22
 CDs and DVDs, 140-142
 computer projection devices, 128-130
 definition of, 3
 desktops, notebooks and PDAs, 8-10
 digitizing devices, 152-154
 expansion devices, ports, cards, and slots, 200-202
 floppy disks and floppy disk drives, 44-46
 hard disk drives, 56-58
 high-speed and wireless Internet-access equipment, 92-94
 installing and uninstalling software, 32-34
 local area networks (LANs), 104-106
 microprocessors, 188-190
 modems, 80-82

PC display devices, 176-178
 printers, 116-118
 sound devices, 164-166
 tape backup devices, 68-70
Head crash, 63, *63,* 64
Help Contents, 29
Help Index, 29
Help pointer, 29
Hewlett-Packard, 117, 210
"Hide the extensions" option, 52
High-speed Internet access, 92-94
Home page, 87
Home PC, connecting to the Internet, *75*
HTML (Hypertext Markup Language), 88
 documents in, 95
 tags in, 88, 89
HTTP (Hypertext Transfer Protocol), 88
Hub, 104
Hypertext links, 87
Hypertext Markup Language (HTML), 88
Hypertext Transfer Protocol (HTTP), 88

IBM, 75, 210
iCOMP index, *190*
Icons, definition of, 15
Idoru, 180
Image file, 143
Images, 147
Impact printers, 116
Import routines, 42
Improving writing with word processing software, 111
IMSI Lumiere, 173
IMSI TurboCAD, 150
Inbox, 100
Incremental backup, of files, 70
Indeo compression technique, 174
Independent computer resellers, 210
Information, false and misleading, 120
Infrared port, 199
Ink jet printers, 117
 ink cartridges in, *117*
Input, definition of, 183
Input devices, 6
 alternative, 20-22
Input method, 20
Installation guide, 27
Installing software, definition of, 32
Instruction manual, 27
Integer benchmarks, 190
Integrated circuit, 184
Intel Media Benchmark, 190
Intel microprocessors, 188
Intel Pentium II/III/4 processor, *188,* 189, 195, 207, 209

Intellectual property rights, 91
Internal device, 200
Internal modems, 80, *80, 81*
Internal tape drive, *68*
Internet, 31, 39, 48, 66, 78
  access to, 12
  connecting to, 74-85
  cookies on, 89, 138, 144
  definition of, 75
  downloading software from, 35
  filtering controversy on, 96
  high-speed and wireless access to, 92-94
  items required for connection to, 77
  reasons for connecting to, 76
  rumors from chat group on, 120
  setting up connection to, 83
  surfing the, 5, 24
  table of symptoms and solutions for delays on, 79
Internet Explorer, 24
Internet server, definition of, 75
Iomega Jaz drive, 57, *57*
ISA (industry standard architecture) expansion card, 201
ISA slot, 198, 201, 202
ISDN service, 92
ISP (Internet service provider), 79, 82, 83
  connecting to, 78
  definition of, 75
  questions to ask, 77
Issues
  are deleted files legally garbage?, 60
  computer "haves" and "have-nots," 12
  do we need anonymous digital cash?, 84
  filtering controversy, 96
  how private is e-mail?, 108
  Idoru, 180
  is it legal to install this software?, 36
  is it the medium or the message?, 132
  monopoly is not just a game, 24
  RIAA vs. Rio, 168
  shoes, UFOs and Forest Gump, 156
  should governments regulate encryption?, 48
  upgrade, reuse, recycle, or landfill?, 204
  what about a "good" virus?, 72
  what's truth got to do with it?, 120
  who invented the first electronic digital computer, 192
  who owns information about me?, 144

Jasc Paint Shop Pro, 152
Jaz disks, 57, *57*
Jordan, Michael, 40
JPEG format, 102, 148, 149
Junger v. *Christopher*, 48
Junk e-mail, 103
Justification, definition of, 112

Kai Art Dabbler, 152
Kennedy, President, 156
Keyboard, *6*
Keystoning, 129
Kilobytes (KB), definition of, 45
Kirk, Captain, 22
K-Mart, 210
Korg MIDI keyboards, 166

LAN. *See* Local area networks
Laptop computer, 9
Laser printers, 118
LCD (liquid crystal display) screens, 9, 20
LCD monitor, 177, *177*
LCD projection panel, *128*
LCD projector, 129, *129*
Lexmark, 117
List box, *18*
Local area networks (LANs), 104-106
  Internet access through, 104
Local ISP, 83
Loch Ness monster, 156
Login script, 106
Logoff procedure, 106
Long filenames, 40
Lotus Approach, 136
Lotus 1-2-3, 123
Lotus Word Pro, 111
LS-120 drive, 45, *45*
Lycos, 90

Mac platform, 207
Machine language, 187
Macintosh computers, 34, 207
Mackenzie, John, 132
Magnetic tape, 68
Manufacturer direct sales, 210
Mauchly, John, 192
Maximize button, 17, *17*
Maxwell, 69
MCI, 75
McLuhan, Marshall, 132
Medium or message question, 132
Megabytes (MB), definition of, 45
Memory module, 184
Menu bar, 17, *17*
Menu option ellipsis, *23*
Menu option triangle, *23*
Michelangelo virus, 65
Microcomputer, 188
Micrografx Designer, 150
Micrografx Picture Publisher, 148, 152

Micron, 210
Microprocessor chip, 184
Microprocessors, 188-190
  definition of, 3
  factors affecting speed of, 189
Microsoft Access, 136, *137*
Microsoft Corporation, 12, 23
Microsoft Excel, 123
  default file extension of, 41
Microsoft FrontPage, 95
Microsoft Internet Explorer, 89
Microsoft Network (MSN), 77
Microsoft Outlook Express, 99
Microsoft Paint, 148, 152
  default file extension of, 41
Microsoft Publisher, 114
Microsoft System information, 191, 196
Microsoft Windows, 207, 214. *See also* Windows
Microsoft Windows 3.1, 19
Microsoft Windows 95, 19, 40, 78, 167
Microsoft Windows 98, 19, 40, 78, 99, 167
Microsoft Word, 42, 95, 111
  default file extension of, 41
  software for, 101
Microsoft Word 97, 101
Microsoft Works, 42, 136
MicroWarehouse, 208, 210
MIDI (musical instrument digital interface), 162
MIDI file, 163, 167
MIDI instrument, 166
MIDI keyboard, 166, *166*
MIDI messages, 162
MIDI music, 164
MIDI port, 201
MidWest Micro, 210
Minimize button, 17, *17*
Minolta, 154
Mirror systems, 67
Misinformation, 120
MMX extension, 189
Mobile Internet access, 94
Modems, 78, 80-82, 198
  definition of, 77
  speeds of, 81
  three configurations of, 80
  troubleshooting tips for problems with, 82
Monitors, factors affecting quality and price, 176
Monopoly-Microsoft issue, 24
Motherboard, 184, 196, 197, 198, 199, 201
  connectors on, *200*
Motorola, 94
Mouse, *6*
MP3 music compression files, 168
MP3 sound format, 160

MPEG format, 171, 174
Multimedia benchmarks, 190
Multimedia encyclopedias, 33
My Computer window, *46*
My Documents, 53

Naming a file, 40
   rules for, 40
Nanosecond, definition of, 196
National Computer Security Association, 65
National Geographic magazine, 139, *139*
National ISP, 83
NEC, 117
Netiquette, 103
Netscape Composer, 95
Netscape Mail, 99
Netscape Navigator, 24, 89, 99
Network, definition of, 5
Network interface card (NIC), 105, *105*
Network Neighborhood icon, 106, *106*
Network server, 104
Network specialists, 105
New option, 47, *47*
NewTek LightWave 3D, 175
Nikon, 154
Nokia, 94
"Non-system disk" message, 4
Norton Multimedia Benchmark, 190
Norton S132 benchmark test, 189
Notebook computers, 9, *9*, 20
   accessories for, 212
   upgrading, 199
NSP (network service provider), 75

OCR (optical character recognition) software, 153
Office Assistant, 30, *30*
   used to access online Help, 30
Office Max, 210
Okidata, 117
Olympus, 154
1394 communications link, 172
Online Help, *29*, 31
   how to use, 29
Open, *47*
Open dialog box, *42*, 51, 60
Open option, 39
Operating system software, definition of, 3
Optical storage technology, 142, *142*
Option button, *23*, 18
.org, 88
Organizing files and folders, 50-61
Outbox, 100
Outpost.com, 208
Output, definition of, 183
Output method, 20

Packard-Bell, 210
Page format options, 112
Page Setup option, 91
Paint software, 148
   bitmap graphics illustration, *148*
Palette flash, 179
PalmPilot PDA, 20
Paper clip icon, 101
Paper clip cartoon. *See* Office Assistant
Paragraph format options, 112
Password
   creating, 5
   definition of, 5
Patch set of sounds, 164
Payload, of a virus, 65
PC cards, 9
PC Connection, 208, 210
PCs
   adding devices to, 198
   bugs in, 7
   buying a, 206-216
   buying by mail order, 211
   buying online, 215
   chart of ports and slots on, 202
   display devices for, 176-178
   finding the best deal on, 210
   and "haves" and "have-nots," 12
   improving performance by adding RAM, 196
   karaoke on, 166
   LCD projection panels for, 128
   LCD projector for, 129
   locating prices and specifications for, 208
   options for old models, 204
   options in buying, 207
   platform, 207, 297
   price-range table for, 208
   projection devices for, 128-130
   setting up, 11
   shopping strategy steps, 207
   starting, 4
   technical specifications for, 191
   turning off, 7
   upgrading and expanding, 194-205
   workings of, 182-193
PCI (peripheral component interconnect) expansion card, 201
PCI slot, 198, 201, 202
PCMCIA (Personal Computer Memory Card International Association) cards, 9, 129, 154, 199, 201, 202
PCMCIA modems, 80, *80*
PCMCIA slots, 105, 129, 154, 199, *199*, 202
PDA (personal digital assistant), 10, *10*, 20
PDF (portable document format file), definition of, 28
Pentium II Xeon processors, 195

Pepsi, 129
Peripheral devices, 200
Personal digital assistant (PDA), 10, *10*, 20
Personal information and privacy, 144
Philips, 165
Phoenix, River, 180
Phonemes, 161
Photo editing software, 155
Pirated software, definition of, 36
Pixels, 176
Platters, hard disk, 56
Player for videos, 171
Plug and play software, 201
Plug-in module, 163
Ports, *11*, 198, 201
PostScript language, 118
PowerPC processors, 188
Power switch, 3
Premastering software, 143
Presentations
   adding sound clips to, 163, 166
   making slides for, 131
   preparation for, 130
   software for, 131
"Price quote" Web sites, 215
Print dialog box, 18, *18*
Print server, 104
Printer Control Language (PCL), 118
Printer driver, 119
Printers, 116-118, 200
   dot matrix, 116
   duty cycle of, 118
   ink jet, 117
   installing and selecting, 119
   laser, 118
Privacy and personal information, 144
Processing circuitry, 184, *184*
Processor, upgrading, 195
Program modules, 33
Programming language, 187
Programs menu, 33, 39, 51
Programs option, 16
Protecting your files, 62-73
PSINet, 75
Pull-down menu, *23*

Qualcomm, 94
QuarkXPress, 114
Quattro Pro, 123
Question mark (?) button, 29
QuickTime format, 171

RA plug-in, 183
RAM (random access memory), 183, 184, 195
   adding to improving PC performance, 196
   definition of, 3

222

RAM chips, 184
Random-access storage medium, 68
Range, as series of cells, 127
Raster graphics, 148
Ray tracing, 151
Read/write head, 46
Readme file, 27, *27*
RealAudio sound format, 160
RealAudio Web site, 163
Record, in database, 135
Record Industry Association of America (RIAA), 168
Recording and editing sound, 158-169
Recycle Bin, 55, 60
Reference manual, 27
Registration card, 32
Registry, 33, 34
Relational database, 135
Removable hard disk, 57
  as backup medium, 67
Renaming a file, 52, *52*
Rendering, 151
Resolution, 116
RIAA (Record Industry Association of America) vs. Rio, 168
Right-clicking, definition of, 51
Rio's flash memory chips, 168
RISC (reduced instruction set computer) chip, 188
Roland MIDI keyboards, 165, l66
ROM chips, 184
"Running" applications, 16

Sampling rates of sound waves, 160
Save As option, 47, *47*
Save command, 17
Save dialog box, *42*, 51
Save option, 47, *47*
Saving a file, 40
ScanDisk, 64
Scanner, 153, *153*, 200
Scanning device, 147
Scanning software, 153
Schwarzenegger, Arnold, 72
Scroll bar, 17, *17*
SCSI (small computer system interface) connection, 197
SCSI port, 201, 202
SDRAM (synchronous DRAM), 196
Search engine, using, 90
Search option, 29
Sears, 210
Sectors, on disks, 46
Sending e-mail and attachments, 98-109
Sequential-access storage medium, 68
Setting up your computer tutorial, 11
Setup program, 33, 34

Shareware, definition of, 36
Shut Down command, 7
SIMMs (single in-line memory modules), 196, 198
Simpson, O.J., 156
Sleep mode, 7
Slide templates, 131
Slides, 128
Slot 1 connector, 195
Slot 2 connector, 195
Smileys, 103, *103*
Socket 7 connector, 195
Software
  definition of, 3
  determining legality of installing, 36
  downloading from the Internet, 35
  installing and learning, 26-37
  installing and uninstalling, 32-34
  tutorial on, 27
  tying into chips, codes, and circuits, 187
  upgrading, 32
Software company, Web site of, 31
Software documentation, 27
Software Publishers Association, 36
Software publishers' toll-free support lines, 31
Sony, 69
Sound
  amplitude and frequency of, 160
  capability of and PCs, 159
  recording and editing, 158-169
Sound card, 159, 164, 198
Sound devices, 164-166
Sound Recorder, using, 167
Sound system, 164
Spams, 103
SparQ cartridges, 57
SPECint95 benchmark test, 189
SPECtp95 benchmark test, 189
Speech recognition software, 22
Speech synthesis, 161
Spelling checker, 111
Sperry Rand, 192
Spin box, *18*
Spreadsheet software
  creating databases with, 138
Form View in, 138
Spreadsheets
  and presentations, 122-133
  definition of, 123
  software for, 123, 138
Staples, 210
Star Trek, 22
Star Wars, 135
Start button, definition of, 15, *15*,16
Start menu, 15, 16, *16*
Storage devices, 3
Store-and-forward technology, 99
Streaming video technology, 171

Strong encryption, 48
Style, definition of, 113
Style list, 113
Style sheet, 113
Stylus, 152
  definition of, 20
Subfolders, 53
Subwoofer, 165
SuperDisks, 45, *45*, 55, 56, 57
  as backup medium, 67
Superscalar processing, 189
Surround sound, 165
Synthesized sound, 159
Synthesized speech, 161
Synthesizing hardware, 161
SyQuest drive, 57
System disk, definition of, 4
System requirements, checking before purchasing, 32
System specifications, 191
System unit, 3

T-1 service, 92
Tags, 88, 89
Tape backup
  devices for, 67, 68-70
  software for, 70
  strategy for, 70
Tape cartridges, 69, *69*
Taskbar, definition of, 15, *15*
TDX, 69
Technical support
  getting, 203
  steps to do before calling for, 31
Technology glitches, preparing for, 130
Template wizards, 113
10Base-T cable, 105
Terminator virus, 72
Text and graphics, saving, 91
Text links, 87
Text-to-speech software, 161
Thesaurus, 111
3-D graphics, 198
  creating, 151
3-D sound, 165
3DNow! extension, 189
Three Stooges, 156
3m, 69
Thumbnail, 149
TIFF format, 102, 148, 149
Time magazine, 135
Title bar, 17, *17*
Token Ring LAN technology, 104
Toolbar button, 17
Toolbars, 17, *17*
ToolTip, *23*, 29
Top-level domain, 88
Touch-sensitive LCD, 20-21
Toyota, 125
Tracks, on disks, 46

Transition effects, 131
Trout Madness, 139
True color, 148
Turtle Beach Systems, 164
Tutorials
 how to buy a computer online, 215
 how to change display settings, 179
 how to create and save files, 47
 how to create your own Web pages, 95
 how to download and install software from the Internet, 35
 how to edit a digital photo, 155
 how to find files, 59
 how to find the technical specifications for your PC, 191
 how to get technical support, 203
 how to install and select printers, 119
 how to make slides for an effective presentation, 131
 how to make your own CDs, 143
 how to set up your computer, 11
 how to set up your Internet connection, 83
 how to use Windows Backup, 71
 how to use Windows controls, 23
 how to use your e-mail address book like a pro, 107
 how to work with digitized sound, 167
TV tuner card, 171
TXT format, 102

UFOs, 156
Ulead Systems MediaStudio, 173
Unicode, 186
Uninstalling software, 55
 definition of, 32
UPS (uninterruptible power supply), 63
UPS (United Parcel Service), 211
URL (uniform resource locator), 88, 90
USB devices, 202
USB port, 201, 202
U.S. Census Bureau, 12, 28
Used computers, 209
User ID, definition of, 5
User interface, definition of, 20
U.S. Library of Congress, 79, 139
UUnet, 75

Vector graphics, 176
 compared with bitmap graphics, 147
 illustration of, *150*
 using, 150
Vectors, 150
Verbatim, 69

VHS video tape, to be replaced, 141
Video 1 compression technique, 174
Video capture card, 198
Video capture device, 172
Video capture software, 172
Video editing software, 173
Video for Windows format, 171
Video port, 178
Video, equipping PC to play, 171
Virus infection, 65
Virus signature, definition of, 66
Viruses, 67, 101
 definition of, 65
 "good," 72
 Michelangelo, 65
 protecting your files from, 66
 Terminator, 72
 watchdogs, 72
Visual Basic language, 187
v.90 modem, 81
VOICE sound format, 160
Voice-data cellular phones, 94, *94*
Voice-response systems, 161

Wacom Graphics Tablet, 152
Wag the Dog, 156
Wal-Mart, 210
Warranties, 211
WAV format, 101
WAVE files, 163
WAVE sound format, 160
Wavetable synthesis, 164
Wayne, John, 180
Web, 75, 79, 123, 132, 147, 148, 164, 168, 174, 190
 browsing and searching, 86-97
 copyright on, 91
 "price quote" sites on, 215
 regarded as freeform database, 135
 saving text and graphics from, 91
Web browser. *See* Browser
Web graphics
 scan resolution for, 153
 size of file, 149
Web page animation, 175
Web pages, 39, 87
 adding sound clips to, 163, 166
 addresses of, 88
 creating your own, 95
 preparing graphics for, 149
Web servers, 87
Web sites, 87, 136, 139, 171
Webmaster, 87
"What-if" scenarios, 123
WinBench98 benchmark test, 189
Window, definition of, 17
Windows
 looking at, 14-25
 versions of, 19

See also Microsoft Windows
Windows Backup program, using, 71
Windows CE operating system, 10
Windows Clipboard, definition of, 53
Windows Control Panel, *34*
Windows controls, *18, 23*
 using, 23
Windows desktop, *4,* 15, *15*
Windows Dial-Up Networking, 78
Windows Explorer, 51-53, 55, 56, 59, 60, 104
 Folder, Options of, 52
 guided tour of, 51
Windows Internet Connection Wizard, 83
Windows Metafile (WMF), 150
Windows NT, 19, 40
Windows operating system, 3, 24, 33, 106
Windows Start menu, *7*
Wireframe, 151
 constructing, *151*
Wireless access to the Internet, 92-94
WordPerfect, 111
Word processing (WP) software
 capabilities of compared with DTP software, 115
 formatting a document with, 112
 improving writing with, 111
 standard document styles, 113
Word wrap, 112
Worksheets, 123
 accuracy of results in, 126
 creating, 124
Workstation, 104
"World Wide Wait," 79
World Wide Web. *See* Web
Write-protect window, 44
Writing
 and printing documents, 110-121
 improving with word processing software, 111

x86 processors, 188, 207

Yahoo!, 90
Yamaha MIDI keyboards, 166

Zip disk, 45, *45,* 55, 56, 57
 as backup medium, 67
Zip drive, 45, *45,* 199
Zips, 102
Z-1 computer, 192
Zuse, Conrad, 192